GUNSMOKE

An American Institution

GUNSMOKE

An American Institution

Celebrating 50 Years
of Television's Best Western

by Ben Costello

FIVE STAR PUBLICATIONS
INCORPORATED
Chandler, AZ USA

Linda F. Radke, President
FIVE STAR PUBLICATIONS, INC.
P.O. Box 6698
Chandler, Arizona 85246-6698
480-940-8182

www.50YearsofGunsmoke.com

Library of Congress Cataloging-in-Publication Data

Costello, Ben.
  Gunsmoke: an American institution celebrating 50 years of television's best western / Ben Costello.
      p. cm.
   Includes index.
ISBN-13: 978-1-58985-222-8
ISBN: 978-1-58985-166-5 (CD-ROM Edition)
eISBN: 978-1-58985-029-3
  1. Gunsmoke (Television program) I. Title.
  PN1992.77.G86C67 2005
  791.45'72–dc22
                                                    2005014522

05 06 07 08 09 10 9 8 7 6 5 4 3 2

Electronic edition provided by

 eStarPublish.com

the eDivision of Five Star Publicaitons, Inc.

Printed in USA

Editor: Sue DeFabis
Cover design: Jeff Church
Interior design: Janet Bergin

ACCOLADES FOR GUNSMOKE

"This marvelous tome helps me re-live my work with the superb *Gunsmoke* cast."
— Actor Morgan Woodward

"Thanks for all the memories!"
— Actress Mariette Hartley

"Ben - If it's as good as it is heavy - you're a hit!"
— Actor Robert Donner

"Ben - I am so honored to be a part of your beautiful book."
— Actress Laurie Prange

"A wonderful book on a wonderful show!"
— Actor John Saxon

"Ben - A wonderful book - thank you for doing it! Much love..."
— Actress Beverly Garland

"Thank you for this great book."
— Actor Robert Pine

"This book is wonderful!"
— Actress Dawn Lyn

"I THOUGHT THAT GUNSMOKE WAS A TERRIFIC SHOW TO BE ON, AND I DIDN'T KNOW IT THEN, BUT SOME OF THE HAPPIEST YEARS OF MY LIFE WERE ON THAT SHOW."

– BURT REYNOLDS

"Your *Gunsmoke* book is amazing and you are a delight."
— Actress Lane Bradbury

"Many congratulations on your fine book."
— Actor William Smith

"Congratulations! You must be very proud of your wonderful book. I really enjoyed reading it and seeing all the wonderful pictures you gathered. It was a great trip down memory lane that brought back some memories of the good ole days...you deserve huge kudos."
— *Gunsmoke* Casting Director, Pam Polifroni

"THE REASON FOR THE RECORD-BREAKING LONGEVITY OF GUNSMOKE IS SIMPLE: QUALITY."
— ACTOR & AUTHOR ALEX CORD

"Your book is one of the VERY BEST BOOKS on *Gunsmoke*, and I'm proud to have it in my collection."
— Robert Kagan, Founding Member, The Autry Museum

"This book is a gift for the series' fans. Costello's respect and admiration for television's longest-running Western shine through in his impressive retrospect *Gunsmoke: An American Institution*...with hundreds of photographs, a memorabilia chapter, and even a few favorite cast recipes, this book offers an ideal way to head back to the Long Branch Saloon. And it would make a great stocking stuffer for any fan of TV Westerns - though given the size and heft of the book, you'll need a pretty big stocking."
— David Hofstede, *Cowboys and Indians Magazine*

"Although there have been other books about the legendary Western series, nothing published before has ever come close to Ben Costello's amazing accomplishment. Costello's 600 plus page chronicle is a lively and thoroughly researched work that does honor to its subject."
— C. Courtney Joyner, *Wild Westerns Magazine*

"With over 600 pages liberally laced with hundreds of episode and behind-the-scenes photographs, biographies of lead performers, updates on surviving cast members, a complete episode log and interviews with the show's luminaries, this book could get you out of the saddle and under a reading light until the wee hours of the morning...this meticulously researched book is a memorable tribute to a lasting legacy."

— *Deadwood Magazine*

"...sure to satisfy the appetite of even the most devout fan of this popular television series."

— *New Mexico Magazine*, March 2006

"*Gunsmoke: An American Institution* by Ben Costello is the ultimate, be-all, end-all, definitive work on this television classic. Ben was my guest on "Topeka Talks" today and I was disappointed that the book had not arrived in time for the interview. Lo and behold, in this season of miracles, the promised goodies arrived DURING the interview and I excitely ripped into the box on the air. It's a hefty volume—5 pounds and not an ounce of fat. Every page is a treasure. There is a synopsis of each episode along with the cast of guests for that show, as well as interviews, narrative, quotes, and hundreds of photos. There are endless hours of pleasure in this volume."

— Deb, *Topeka Talks*

"Ben Costello's *Gunsmoke: An American Institution* (Five Star Publications, Inc.) is an exhaustive appraisal and episode guide to the longest-running network show in history."

— Scott Eyman, *Palm Beach Post*, Sunday, March 12, 2006

"Let's just say the book contains everything you'd wish to know about the show, and more!"

— Allan Pierleoni, *Sacramento Bee*

"In *Gunsmoke: An American Institution*, author Ben Costello has provided the legions of fans for America's most popular and long-running television Western series with an exhaustive compendium showcasing and celebrating all twenty seasons (comprising a total of 635 episodes) of Matt Dillon and his many friends and foes. Profusely illustrated with literally hundreds of photos about what went on both in front and in back of the cameras, *Gunsmoke* covers the major cast members, as well as the producers, writers and directors, and features especially insightful interviews with Dennis Weaver, Buck Taylor, and Burt Reynolds. There are even sections featuring *Dean Martin Celebrity Roast* highlights; reminisces of distinctive guest stars; *Gunsmoke* memorabilia, the post-television series *Gunsmoke* films, and so very much more. A certain to be popular addition to any community library American Popular Culture collection, *Gunsmoke: An American Institution* is a 'must read' for anyone who grew up with Matt Dillon, Miss Kitty, Doc, Chester, Festus, and all the other denizens of Dodge City and the Old West."

— The Midwest Book Review, *MBR BOOKWATCH*, April 2007

"Every form of popular culture has its icons, and when you consider television's place in American society, to be a TV icon is no small thing which is why it's so much fun to peruse *Gunsmoke: An American Institution* by Ben Costello...It is definitely a must-have for the Western buff on your shopping list, and a great gift for anyone who remembers when prime-time network TV offered something better and more enduring."

— David Chesanow, *The News Tribune*, WA

"On the landscape of American television, *Gunsmoke* was a giant. It had a giant star in 6-foot-7-inch James Arness as Marshal Matt Dillon… a new book, like the show, is a giant. *Gunsmoke: An American Institution* weighs about 5 pounds and has 600 plus pages and a barrel full of photos."

— Ken Beck, Staff Writer, *The Tennessean*, Tuesday, September 13, 2005

"The book features more than 500 photos, 60 interviews with cast and crew members, and complete credits for all 635 episodes."

— Lucinda Dyer, *Show Daily BEA*, Friday, June 3, 2005

"Fans of the show are in for a special treat with the release of *Gunsmoke: An American Institution - Celebrating 50 Years of Television's Best Western*. This is a comprehensive book that contains just about everything you've ever wanted to know about *Gunsmoke* and the characters that made the show so popular..."

— Wayne Price, Editor's Page, *Rural Electric Nebraskan*, November 2005

"Author hits bulls-eye with book on *Gunsmoke*."

— Mark Wheeler, *Hi-Desert Star*, Tuesday June 14, 2005

"*Gunsmoke* was part of my childhood, so when I saw this on the list of Five Star Publications, Inc., I had to have it...This would make a very special gift for someone who also enjoyed the series. It's still playing on TV Land...Give them their own little piece of history that they can pick up again and again and remember 'the good ole days.'"

— Jo Ann Hakola, bookfaerie.com and proud member of Independent Online Booksellers Association

"WHAT A BOOK, WHAT A SHOW, WHAT A CAST, CREW AND PLEASURE IT WAS TO BE PART OF IT."

— ACTOR LANCE LEGAULT

"The lines on my show lit up with Ben Costello talking about his book *Gunsmoke: An American Institution* — with a promise to my listeners of having Ben back. My dad loved *Gunsmoke* and for this reason Ben's book brought back so many fond memories for me. One hour was not enough time to talk with Ben. What a great guy! Great book! I wish we had two hours to talk!"

— Jack Evans, *The Jack Evans Show*, WMBS-CBS. Uniontown, PA

"*Gunsmoke: An American Institution* by Ben Costello is a dream come true for a big fan like me. Ben spent five years of his life putting this great work together. I promise you will learn things about the TV show you haven't heard before and you will really enjoy stories about the cast as well. Mr. Costello was on my radio show January 24th and it was a wonderful experience. Just hearing him talk about the book took me right to the middle of the action in Dodge City. I only wish I could have spent the entire day talking to him."

— Dugg Collins, Journal Broadcast Group,
Morning Drive AM 1070 THE RANCH/KFTI, Wichita, KS

"I APPEARED IN A LOT OF WESTERNS IN THOSE DAYS, AND GUNSMOKE WAS THE KING OF THEM ALL."
— ACTRESS ANGIE DICKINSON

"I never realized how important of a show *Gunsmoke* was until I spoke with Ben Costello. He was able to paint a picture about this icon of American television heritage that I hadn't expected…one of a more thought provoking well-thought out show, rather than a shoot 'em up cowboy series than I had always envisioned it to be. Ben was able to 'spur' our listeners into action by providing a great trivia question to call in and win a copy of his beautiful book. By the way, that listener drove 30 miles that day just to pick up the book which he was absolutely thrilled with! Ben Costello, is a friendly, warm, informative interview that will round up all your listeners to find out more about *Gunsmoke*."

— Jane Meyer, KLTF, Little Falls, MN

"…I think it's terrific. I'm loving all the 'inside stuff' about the show, especially the struggles and politics of the early production and transition from radio to TV. Great photos. So valuable in the library of a TV buff. Invaluable in the library of a *Gunsmoke* fan."

— Joe Oleksiewicz, KCHO/KFPR Northstate Public Radio. Cal State University Chico

"Your beautiful *Gunsmoke* book is something I will treasure always...You have written an incredible book that you can be extremely proud of (I know I am!)"
— Brooklyn Barbara D'Andrea, *Gunsmoke* Fan

"We knew there were a lot of *Gunsmoke* fans in Montana but when we gave away Ben's book after his interview the phone started ringing and hasn't stopped! Ben makes you want to grab your pillow, plop down in front of the T.V. and stay there forever!"
— Bell Braaten, Producer for KBUL Radio, Billings, MT

"*Gunsmoke: An American Institution* is an exceptional tribute to TV's longest-running drama, which recently celebrated its 50th anniversary on TV...I'll admit to feeling a little cocky, believing I had seen all the photos and heard all the stories about my favorite TV show. But *Gunsmoke: An American Institution* is full of pleasant surprises. I was delighted by the dozens of candid pictures and interviews that were new and fresh. And I also enjoyed the Foreword by *Gunsmoke* scripter Jim Byrnes and the Preface by Jon Voight. Like the series it honors, Costello's book will entertain and delight fans for many years to come. I know it tops my holiday gift list this year."
— Sandy Henry, Author, *A Child's Bedtime Companion* and
Something Borrowed, Something Blue

"The title says it all. 'An American Institution.' That's what *Gunsmoke* was and became. That's why it has run nonstop for 51 years now, and will for many more years. Author Ben Costello, in his Five Star Publications, Inc. book, celebrates all things *Gunsmoke* in the best possible way. The 500-plus page book is almost canonical in its approach to the show. Interviews with the late Dennis Weaver, Burt Reynolds, and Buck Taylor, profiles of the cast, producers, writers, and directors, memorabilia and a COMPLETE 635 episode guide pack this book with *Gunsmoke* lore beyond all."
— Tim Lasiuta, Co-Author, *The Misadventures of a Roving Cartooonist*

"What a wonderful tribute to a beloved landmark Western series. Like most everyone of that era, I was an unabashed fan of the timeless stories told through marvelous actors and presented with great craftsmanship."

— Cheryl Rogers-Barnett, Author, *Cowboy Princess: Life with My Parents Roy Rogers and Dale Evans*

"THE GUNSMOKE BOOK IS ONE OF THE BEST BOOKS EVER." - WILLIAM A. SMITH, GUNSMOKE FAN, INDIANA, APRIL 2006

"…Best Books 2006 winner for Ben Costello's book…a well-deserved award…I am not surprised at all because you all deserve the recognition you receive plus more! Please know as we have mentioned before you have made a family very grateful by giving our mom such pleasure referencing Ben's book. She is a faithful *Gunsmoke* viewer and keeps her memory sharp by using the book to verify her knowledge of each episode. We wish you all continued success and satisfaction knowing how much joy you are bringing to many people's lives."

— Pat Ward, *Gunsmoke* Fan, Las Vegas, NV

"I just received Ben Costello's *Gunsmoke: An American Institution* and I am thrilled to bits with it! It's size and magnitude alone express it's stature as a stunning tribute and a loving memorial."

— Sydney Kent, *Gunsmoke* Fan

"The best book written on a television show - ever!"

— Film Historian Bob Burns, Republic Pictures 75th Anniversary Celebration, Sept. 25, 2010

CONTENTS

Costello family photo—2000

This book is lovingly dedicated to my father
Ed Costello and my son Eddie Costello—inspirations both.

"Two Ed's are better than one."

ACKNOWLEDGEMENTS

Where to begin...perhaps best at the beginning. Thanks to my parents, of course, for everything, including a loving household and for allowing *Gunsmoke* into our living room when I was a child growing up in the sixties and seventies. To my father—my critic and proofreader—thanks for everything, always. Your strength is indeed a blessing. Thanks to my brother Chuck for his sense of humor and prompting my interest in old movie stars such as Laurel and Hardy and John Wayne, and for regaling me with tales of his youth spent watching his Western matinee heroes. Thanks to my sister Judy and her husband Ken Tyree, for their love, laughter, encouragement and help during, prior to and after this project. To my nieces and nephews, particularly Dana, Joe and Jake, my love and gratitude forever, with thanks for the enrichment you have added to my life.

To my late grandparents, particularly my grandmothers Kathryn and Jane for their pride and gentle words. To aunts and uncles Millie, Fran, Joe and Jim—to cousins, particularly Chuck and Tina, thanks for the positive influence in my life.

To my son Eddie, thanks for being the best child a man can ask for—you are my source of pride, happiness and inspiration. I love ya, kid! With you in my life I can accomplish anything and there isn't a day that goes by where I don't thank the Good Lord for blessing me with you.

To my friend Bob Anderson, who years ago said, "Hey, why don't you write a book on *Gunsmoke*?" Your technical advice and friendship is much appreciated—as is your warped sense of humor.

Thanks to my super-agent Janette Anderson for so much—the connections, advice, knowledge and last but not least, the friendship. You're my rock and I truly appreciate all that you have done—this would not have been possible without your expert guidance.

To Linda Radke and Five Star Publications, Inc., thanks for your trust and faith in this project as well as your guiding hand. Thanks also to Janet Bergin, Sue DeFabis and Patty Lavelle. As for the wonderful website you developed for the book— www.50YearsofGunsmoke.com— truly appreciated! Sue and Janet, your round-the-clock dedication did not go unnoticed—I'm forever grateful for your professionalism, patience and kindness. Many thanks!

Thanks to all who shared their time, talent, thoughts and memorabilia—some even personal—on this book: Paul and Laurie Savage, Vincent McEveety, Morgan Woodward, Pam Polifroni, John and Angela Mantley, Carol Vogel, Bernard McEveety, Paul Picerni, Anthony Caruso, James Gregory, William Schallert, Laurie Prange, Cliff Osmond, William Smith, Andrew V. McLaglen, Harry Carey, Jr., Ben Cooper, Jacqueline Scott, Lane Bradbury, Lou Antonio, Steve Stevens, Anthony James, Dennis Weaver, Mark Rydell, Susan Gordon, Peter Mark Richman, Suzanne Lloyd, William Windom, Wright King, Robert Donner, Charles Gray, Karen Sharpe Kramer, Bo Hopkins, France Nuyen.

Barbara Luna, Jack McBride, Chris Alcaide, Martin Kove, Dawn Lyn, Miriam Colon, Robert Pine, Gwynne Gilford, Tom Reese, Michael Forest, Paul Carr, Stuart Whitman, Alex Cord, Harry Harris, Jr., Richard Meinardus, Angie Dickinson, Butch Patrick, Kim Darby, Beverly Garland, Harry Stradling, Jr., Will Hutchins, Jimmy Don Cox, Dean Smith, Buck and Goldie Taylor, Ron Honthaner, Ken Chase, Warren Vanders, Earl Holliman, Katharine Ross, Lance LeGault, Burt Reynolds, Donna Johnson, Gary Lockwood, Jonathan Goldsmith Lippe, and last, but not least, Jon Voight. Again, my profound thanks for your time, talent and kind consideration towards this project.

To Jim Byrnes, a very special thank you for so much—your contributions to this endeavor are immeasurable—for all you've done, I'm honored and grateful. My appreciation to your lovely wife Toni, also. Here's to friendship!

To fellow fans everywhere for the assistance, advice and kind words—especially from Mary Jo Barlow, Eldon McKelvie, Michael Blake, Barbara D'Andrea, Sydney Kent, Rebecca di Clemente, Robert Kagen, Jim Newman and Sandy Henry. A special nod to Debbie Flaugher and the Del Phi Gang—great *Gunsmoke* talk at forums.delphiforums.com/gunsmokeforum.

To my former teachers and counselors, including Bob Miner, Honore Mallett, Bob Hettig, Marilyn Steely and Dave Maldewin, for your positive influence during school and years afterward—my deepest appreciation.

To my friends—past and present—for the great times and laughter; for the help and understanding through the bad times. To Kay Meads, Mona Brehm, Monica Budd, Marguerite and Jess Kirkpatrick, Mike Mason, Denise Morrow, Marc Malanson, Wayne Feltges—always kind words.

To Cindy Costello, Warren and Diane Lavender, Ron and Renee De Maio, Joe Dimmick, Raynolds and Lois Johnson, Ron and Candy Vreeken, Bob and Lori Pattillo, Lance and Nancy Gent, Bob and Carolyn Burke, John and Elizabeth Huff, Fred and Mary Shepherd, Joe, Ilma and Jody Lukatich—your encouragement and friendship through the years has meant so much.

Marvin and Robin Schmelling—great times, great laughs. Marv, this book would have never been possible without your expertise and dedication above and beyond...thanks also for teaching me how to survive "technical tirades." Robin, I'm honored to be husband #2. To Fran Dimmick—my admiration always for pushing gently and believing—your friendship is treasured.

To Jeff Drozd for defining courage to me and for making me appreciate everything just a little more these days—you and Kerry are the best. John and Patti Babrowski, Darryl and Glenda Whitley, Don Whitley— thanks for the smiles, laughs and guidance—much needed. To Teresa Graham, C.E. "Dusty" Dilley and Richard Shook—thanks for the lessons taught.

Tom and Vicki Crochetiere—the best friends one could ask for...Tom—as this book goes to press—thirty-one years as friends! Here's to many more "tightwad Tuesdays!"

To Mardee Poist and the ladies at Valley Independent Printing—thanks for all the help. A special thanks to laser setter Jeff Church for help with the cover design.

So many people have touched my life—I'm truly grateful. Alex and Staci Conti—you and your beautiful children mean so much to me—I thank God for your friendship. And for that special friend who remains permanently in my heart and soul—KC—you have enhanced my life more than words can express.

Unless otherwise noted, the photos included in the book are from my personal collection. Thanks to everyone credited inside the book for the use of material from their private collections.

To the many memorabilia stores and outlets—eBay, The Hollywood Collectors Show, Milton T. Moore, Movie Star News, Jerry Ohlingers Movie Material Store, Inc., Cinema Collectors in Las Vegas (thanks Marilyn and Buddy), 'Just Claire' at Eddie Brandt's Saturday Matinee, Mark Willoughby at Collectors Book Store, Hollywood Book & Poster Company, Hollywood Movie Posters, Dan Schwartz at Movie Collectables Etc., and Larry Edmund's Book Store, for help with stills, memorabilia and materials.

To CBS for producing and presenting *Gunsmoke*, with thanks to James Arness, Amanda Blake, Ken Curtis, Roger Ewing, Burt Reynolds, Milburn Stone, Glenn Strange, Buck Taylor and Dennis Weaver for their brilliant characterizations and to the producers, writers and directors of *Gunsmoke* whose combined talents and visions made the show the classic it is.

If I have forgotten anyone, please forgive me—so many contributed so much to this project.

And last, though never least, I offer a tip of the Stetson to the good Lord above—through which everything is ultimately possible.

WRITER JIM BYRNES

FOREWORD

This year we celebrate the 50th anniversary of *Gunsmoke*. A new book chronicling the twenty years of the legendary series has now come our way. Four years ago I received a phone call from a fellow named Ben Costello. He revealed he was writing a book on the history of *Gunsmoke* and would like to meet for an interview. After spending an entire afternoon together I realized how true the saying is, "You don't know how great it was until it's over."

I also learned Ben and I had a great deal in common. Not only our shared affection for *Gunsmoke*, but also the same brand of tenacity. He was as determined to get this book published as I was to become a writer many years ago. By God, through Ben's dauntless perseverance and pure grit he achieved what he set out to do and got it done. It was a long haul, but he never quit.

All of us who worked on the show owe Ben a great deal. He is keeping the legend alive through his extensive research and interviews and most of all his love for the series and its participants.

My meeting with Ben triggered a flood of nostalgic memories. In 1968, two most significant turning points in my life took place. First, I married the girl I had been pursuing for three years. Upon returning from our honeymoon I received a call from my agent. The producers on the hit series *Gunsmoke* had read a screenplay of mine and decided to take a gamble on a fledgling writer. They offered me an episode! Now mind you, right up to that time I was driving a truck, which after three years I unaffectionately dubbed "The Iron Lung." So it was that first episode, my first real job in the entertainment business, that freed me from the cab of that truck and I became a full-time professional writer.

That particular episode, *Lobo*, led to an assistant story consultant job on the very show I had never missed growing up. There were long hours and new adventures for this kid from Ames, Iowa, but the people were so great and the money wasn't bad either.

I worked under Paul Savage who became a terrific and generous colleague. However, I owe that first break, not to mention my career, to the Executive Producer, John Mantley. I learned more working with John and Paul than I did in the years of all the workshops and extension courses put together. Those first two years proved to be my university. My relationship with *Gunsmoke* continued an additional five years and I worked with the best. Writers such as Ron Bishop, Bill Kelley, Jack Miller, Calvin Clements and many more. Directors such as Vince McEveety, Bernie McEveety, Robert Totten and Gunnar Hellstrom were such professionals and so on target in their portrayals of the West.

Our lead cast members such as Jim, Amanda, Milburn, Ken and Buck were always good at recounting their stories of years spent together. However, the countless other actors who went on to successful careers such as Morgan Woodward, Victor French, Earl Holliman, Steve Forrest, Strother Martin, Slim Pickens, Ben Johnson, Richard Dreyfuss, Jon Voight and many others, made the experience even more gratifying. The producers beside John Mantley such as Joe Dackow and Leonard Katzman became good friends that I knew for many years. Some of these folks have passed on, others have gone on and thrived.

In 1975, after twenty years, *Gunsmoke* was cancelled but we all believed we could have gone another twenty. It was the best of all times and I was privileged to have written thirty-seven episodes.

During those years I worked on *Gunsmoke*, Executive Producer John Mantley referred to us as a tightly knit "family." Next to my wife and two sons, it was the best damn family I ever had. I am incredibly honored to be asked to write the foreword for my friend Ben's book entitled, *"Gunsmoke: An American Institution."*

Jim Byrnes
April, 2005

ACTOR JON VOIGHT

PREFACE

I was a young actor out of New York. I traveled to the coast to do a season of Shakespeare in San Diego, and then I went up to Los Angeles to see if I could get some work there. What I got was my first episode of *Gunsmoke*. It was the part of a young Swedish boy, and it was a big deal for me because I needed a role that was large enough that I could show myself off. It was a big deal to get my first *Gunsmoke*.

Being on *Gunsmoke* was a childhood dream for me, as it probably was for many actors. Many young boys want to be a cowboy hero: You want to be in a cowboy movie. I grew up in Yonkers, New York, and I used to play cowboys and stuff in the neighborhood.

Then I got the opportunity as an actor to work in a show that was depicting those days. Meeting Jim Arness and "playing cowboys" with Jim Arness and the cast of *Gunsmoke* was a big deal for me, and it was a lot of fun— a little bit of a dream come true that I could be a part of.

The experience also had a little bit of adventure to it. I showed that episode of *Gunsmoke* to Jerry Hellman, who was going to do *Midnight Cowboy*. At the time, he said I was wrong for the part.

But when they actually began production several years later, I met with Jerry again and said, "I'm right for this part."

It was because of *Gunsmoke*—that energy that I had, is what got the attention of director John Schlesinger. I remember it vividly.

It was an important credit—to say that you did a *Gunsmoke*, and you were a guest star on it—that was a big deal for a young actor. It was a mainstay. The show was tremendously popular.

Pam Polifroni was the one who was the casting director. I've always felt great affection and gratitude for Pam. She was a wonderful person—very smart and very nice.

It was a pleasant journey. There was a lot of humor on the *Gunsmoke* set. No one took him—or herself too seriously, and I think a lot of that had to do with James Arness. He set the tone. He was a guy who was quiet in many ways, but he was a father figure in a certain sense. He had wonderful qualities, and everybody followed suit. He had a wonderful sense of humor, and there was a lot of chuckling on the set. Everybody got along very well. Once you were in that family, even if you were a young actor who didn't know the ropes too well and was intimidated to some degree and wanted to make an impression, you were immediately welcomed in a very nice way. You were expected to do your work and therefore you felt comfortable. You were a part of the family, and the cast surrounded you in a nice way. They were a very warm family, very embracing, very generous to the new ones. They took care of you. *Gunsmoke* helped other people, too. Burt Reynolds played the blacksmith on the show for a bit. I had met Burt briefly when my wife at the time, Lauri Peters, did a show with him. He was brought into the *Gunsmoke* family, too. Later on, when John Boorman suggested him for *Deliverance*, I knew who Burt was. He was an actor who didn't have a whole lot of visibility before *Deliverance*, but of course, the movie made him a star.

On the last episode I did, *The Prisoner*, I got a chance to work with Kitty. It was nice to work with each member of the family. I was especially impressed with Kenny Curtis. In my heart, I am a character actor and, this guy just seemed to be something out of the pages of a book about the time. He seemed very authentic. The craziness of his outfit, his hat, even his accent was so extraordinary. Kenny is a refined and a very intelligent guy, and he played this crazy rube—just a delightful character. I always tried to see the Kenny Curtis scenes because I knew he'd come up with something in each scene. I wanted to see how he'd play it. I'd read what was on the page and then go see what Kenny would do with it. Terrific!

Milburn would come in, and he knew exactly what he was going to do. He had this kind of wry character and it would play so well off Kenny's energy. It was great to watch those guys do it. For me, I was drawn to the character actors and that particular character of Festus is a special one. When I did the movie *Holes*, you'll see there's a relative to Festus there.

I like to see things authentic. I like to see details in the work. Kenny's portrait of this man was so full of detail. He had these big jangling spurs—what the soundman must have thought when this guy got his outfit and walked on the set!

He inhabited that character so well, you figured that this guy must have fallen off a truck or something, he was so authentic. You couldn't believe he was anything other than Festus.

They had such a nice balance: *Gunsmoke* was one of the great teams. When you're an actor growing up in New York studying all the stuff, falling in love with that legacy from Stanislavski and all that, you don't consider that Westerns are in the same category. You tend to think the genre is something less—but it is not true. The acting of the *Gunsmoke* team was quite sophisticated. I had a lot to learn from that—from the relaxation, the poise and the professionalism of it. It was something that stayed with me, and it was very good for me to be a part of that family.

God Bless.
Jon Voight
March 29, 2005

INTRODUCTION

Monday night. 7:30. The family has already had dinner and the table is cleared, the dishes cleaned. We assemble in the family room. Dad is in his chair, Mom is in hers. My older sister is curled up on the couch, and me, I'm on the floor with a pillow. We face the front of that twenty-inch screen surrounded by a maple chest that Dad brings to life with a loud clunk from the three-buttoned brick in his hand called a remote.

CBS.

There he is—the good guy facing the bad guy in the dusty streets of Dodge City. They draw...

Close to thirty years later, the screen is now somewhat larger, fifty-one inches to be exact. I'm now a Dad sitting in my chair holding a billfold-sized remote with a hundred or so buttons on it. My lovely wife is sitting in her chair and our three-year-old son is standing on the floor—his cowboy hat in place, his hog leg strapped on.

TVLAND.

There he is—the good guy facing the bad guy in the dusty streets of Dodge City. They draw—the bad guy is quicker—shoots first. The towering good guy fires a quick second, accurately. My son fires third, fourth, fifth, backing up our favorite cowboy hero, Marshal Matt Dillon.

Enduring images. The White House. Mount Rushmore. The Hollywood sign. Joshua Tree National Park. The Alamo. Americana—enduring images.

The tall lawman. The Stetson. Leather vest. Long-sleeved salmon colored shirt. Tan pants. Boots. A badge. A stag-handled .45 around his waist. Matt Dillon. Marshal.

Dodge City.

The beautiful flame-haired saloon owner. The craggy-faced bartender. The cantankerous M.D. The good-hearted deputy with the limp. The scruffy deputy offering homespun opinions. Miss Kitty. Sam. Doc Adams. Chester. Festus. Don't forget Newly, Thad, Quint, Burke, Louie, etc. *Gunsmoke.*

Americana—enduring images.

It came into this world as a radio show on CBS. Dillon was voiced by William Conrad, later of television's

Cannon and *Jake and the Fatman*. Writers Norman Macdonnell and John Meston pitched an adult Western to CBS execs entitled *Jeff Spain* with an outline stating no characters would be caricatures. No gimmicks. No faithful horse and no stuttering, lisping second-banana. In short, no bullshit.

CBS didn't think much of the less than commercial pitch and initially passed on *Jeff Spain*. Then in 1952 an unexpected hole in their broadcast schedule forced the studio to take on the series, but not before wisely changing the title from the forgettable to the simplistic, yet everlasting, (if they only knew), *Gunsmoke*.

A modest hit, *Gunsmoke* arrived in the waning days of radio. Television, no longer in its infancy but still in a toddler stage, seemed the perfect home for the oater and the colorful inhabitants of Dodge.

But who to star? Conrad sounds the part perfectly, but visually? All wrong. Dillon has to be tall. Tough. Fearless. A symbol of the American West. Pull no punches—again, no BS.

On the big screen, we have Gary Cooper, Randolph Scott, Joel McCrea, Audie Murphy. John—hey not bad. The Duke. What about John Wayne? The legend passes, but not before making a casting suggestion...

Ben Costello
February 15, 2001

OPENING SHOT

In his Beverly Hills office, a six-time Academy Award winning writer-director was asked why he never directed for television. His reply..."Television is crap, all television is crap. Except for sports...and *Gunsmoke*."

Billy Wilder, July 3, 2000.

Was Billy Wilder serious or was this just another example of the sharp, biting wit of this true cinematic genius? Frequent Wilder player, as well as five-time *Gunsmoke* guest star, Cliff Osmond offered, "Those two things are mutually exclusive. One of the reasons his wit was so trenchant and holds up so well is that it was based on the truth. From my estimate of Billy, that was both a sign of his wit and what he meant. He's right. It's one of the great moral shows. It was the best of its kind."

What began as a "radio seed" germinated three years later into television's best loved and longest running Western. The radio version, starring robust actor William Conrad, debuted on April 26, 1952, and ran until June 18, 1961, racking up 413 episodes. Many radio shows made the transition from audio only to audio/visual when The Eye, The Alphabet and The Bird—networks, CBS, ABC and NBC, respectively, gambled on that funny piece of furniture that began gaining national attention in 1948.

Established comedies and comedians made the transition easily—witness the successes of Milton Berle, George Burns & Gracie Allen, Jack Benny, Red Skelton and Bob Hope, to name but a few. Children and the child in us all could now see our cowboy heroes—Gene Autry, The Lone Ranger and Roy Rogers—right in our own living rooms!

After World War II, motion picture Westerns, for the most part, became grittier with less silly fluff than witnessed before. Stars Randolph Scott, James Stewart, Gary Cooper, Henry Fonda, Glenn Ford and Alan Ladd, all made their marks in the genres new direction.

Television's first "adult" oater, *The Life and Legend of Wyatt Earp* debuted on September 6, 1955. Four days later—motion picture heavyweight, Western superstar and later American icon, John Wayne, introduced Marshal Matt Dillon and company into homes nationwide. This intro lasted an impressive 20 years, producing 635 episodes—first-run episodes—an astounding record that holds today.

Much has been made of late regarding Kelsey Grammer's Dr. Frasier Crane tying James Arness' Matt Dillon in the record books—Grammer has played the same character on television for twenty years, as did Arness. While Grammer's accomplishment is noteworthy, a little clarification is certainly in order. Consider this, Arness played the Marshal from 1955 to 1975, and then again from 1987 to 1993 in several television reunion movies. In the series first season alone, he saddled up in 39 installments—a far cry from today's 22 to 26 episode seasons. It has been said that Arness may well be the most filmed celebrity of the twentieth century.

Stars Arness, Milburn Stone and Amanda Blake, like the show, have never left the little screen since the 1955 debut. Established stars and future superstars such as Bette Davis, Jon Voight, Jean Arthur, Nick Nolte, Forrest Tucker, Carroll O'Connor, Cicely Tyson and Harrison Ford ambled onto the Dodge City soundstages. Performers who made their marks as villains included Steve Forrest, Morgan Woodward, Victor French and Harry Morgan. Western reliables, icons really, that made the trek down Front Street were led by Leo Gordon, Jack Elam, Harry Carey, Jr., Slim Pickens, Marie Windsor, Strother Martin, Robert Wilke and Jeanette Nolan.

Behind the scenes reads like a Hollywood *Who's Who*. Andrew V. McLaglen directed an amazing ninety-five episodes during the show's first decade. Mark Rydell cut his directorial teeth on the show. Screenwriter-turned-director Sam Peckinpah filled pages for the citizens of Dodge. Television super-producer Aaron Spelling even flexed his acting chops on an early, memorable episode.

Beginning with radio stories by John Meston, the show always employed the very best writers the industry had to offer. Talented scribes included Kathleen Hite, Paul Savage, Ron Bishop and Jim Byrnes, to name but a few.

The keen eye of the casting director began with Lynn Stalmaster and ended with the businesses best, Pam Polifroni.

From the first episode produced by Charles Marquis Warren to the last by John Mantley, *Gunsmoke* always employed the best of the best. Amanda Blake recalled, "We really were a family, we were close and it showed in the final product. Oh, there were squabbles and some strong disagreements. When people left, well, take Dennis Weaver, it felt like that divorce all families go through. Family members left, but the love remained."

Television allows the viewer to become a member of a bigger family...we allow these folks into our homes week after week, day after day. Marshal Dillon, James Arness. Miss Kitty, Amanda Blake. Doc Adams, Milburn Stone. Chester, Festus, Quint, Newly, Sam. Dennis Weaver, Ken Curtis, Burt Reynolds, Buck Taylor, Glenn Strange.

It is *Gunsmoke* and it has become an American institution. Let us celebrate 50 years and may the family reunions continue for many a day to come.

"Good evening, my name's Wayne. Some of you may have seen me before, I hope so, I've been kicking around Hollywood a long time. I've made a lot of pictures out here—all kinds, and some of them have been Westerns. And that's what I'm here to tell you about tonight, a Western. A new television show called Gunsmoke. No, I'm not in it—I wish I were though, because I think it's the best thing of it's kind that's come along, and I hope you'll agree with me. It's honest, it's adult, it's realistic. Now when I first heard about the show Gunsmoke, I knew there was only one man to play in it—James Arness. He's a young fella and may be new to some of you, but I've worked with him and I predict he'll be a big star. So you might as well get used to him, like you've had to get used to me. And now I'm proud to present my friend Jim Arness in Gunsmoke."

—John Wayne, September 10, 1955

RADIO CAST William Conrad as Matt Dillon, Georgia Ellis as Kitty, Howard McNear as Doc and Parley Baer as Chester Proudfoot. The show debuted in 1952.

THE FORMATIVE YEARS

April 26, 1952. Marshal Matt Dillon, portrayed by actor William Conrad, spoke his first words. Radio corralled many a western show in its day, with *Gunsmoke* being among the first of the genre labeled 'adult.' The CBS radio network program originated in Hollywood, California, broadcasting from station KNX.

Western entertainment was immensely popular following World War II and into the early fifties. Stage versions of *Annie Get Your Gun* and *Oklahoma!* were presented both on the legitimate stages in New York City and on the boards of community theatres nationwide. Radio listeners were offered heroes such as Tom Mix, the Lone Ranger and Tonto and the Cisco Kid. At the local cinema, kids of all ages thrilled to the adventures promised in the B-western programmers starring Allan "Rocky" Lane, Lash LaRue, Sunset Carson and Hopalong Cassidy, to name but a few.

Top box-office draws included singing cowboys Gene Autry and Roy Rogers, both bucking studio orders and embracing television early on. The television networks immediately immortalized Clayton Moore as the Lone

TV COUNTERPARTS Dennis Weaver as Chester Goode, James Arness as Matt Dillon and Milburn Stone as Doc Adams.

ORIGINAL VISION Charles Marquis Warren, center, in Kanab, Utah with actor Charles Gray, left, and actor Dick Gilden, work on a pilot for an unsold Western. (photo courtesy of Charles Gray)

Ranger and Duncan Renaldo as the Cisco Kid. In a shrewd business decision, William Boyd revitalized his sagging film career and brought 'Hoppy' into the nation's living rooms.

Annie Oakley, The Adventures of Wild Bill Hickok and *The Range Rider* soon followed. Even Walt Disney entered the foray with *Davy Crockett, Indian Fighter,* a program so successful it nearly wiped out the nations raccoon population. Kids everywhere had to have a Fess Parker coonskin cap.

In a decade that offered cultural frenzies ranging from bomb shelters to television and atomic monsters to rock and roll, John Meston and Norman Macdonnell created *Gunsmoke* for radio, insisting upon authenticity.

The program premiered on the airwaves as the popularity of radio was beginning to wane. The audio medium was never a threat to the motion picture industry, in fact, it enhanced it. Studio stars would headline or guest on numerous radio programs, touting or sending up their latest project. However, with the advent of television, both films and radio were threatened.

Amazingly, *Gunsmoke* held its own during these drastically changing days of American entertainment, with the ratings for the radio version an almost immediate success. In addition to William Conrad as Matt Dillon, the show offered a core of colorful actors and characters, notably, Georgia Ellis as Kitty Russell, Howard McNear as Doc Adams and Chester Proudfoot voiced by Parley Baer. The aural *Gunsmoke* had a respectable nine year run on radio and was the medium's last great dramatic series. The final episode was heard on June 18, 1961.

TEAMWORK—MESTON AND MACDONNELL

Whenever a motion picture or television program runs, hit or miss, people tend to place all plaudits or pundits on the star or stars of the project. For every Spielberg there are dozens of directors whose names draw blanks when mentioned…"who?" is asked more times than Lou Costello ever questioned Bud Abbott. The recognition is slightly worse when referring to writers. Unsung heroes. John Meston and Norman Macdonnell fit the bill perfectly, and that is unfortunate.

John Meston, the youngest of three children, grew up in Pueblo, Colorado. An early infatuation with horses grew into bronc riding and rodeo performances. Education was a first priority in the Meston household, with their youngest studying from Exeter to Dartmouth to Harvard, and across the ocean to Paris at the Sorbonne.

After a stint in the Army, Meston was hired by CBS and became a censor. Writing came naturally to this "cowboy literate" and his style evoked his upbringing and love for all things Western…a style both subtle, like a Kansas prairie, and colorful, like a stand of Aspen trees in Colorado. Meston was the authenticity injected into first the *Gunsmoke* radio scripts, and later, the stories for television. He penned almost half of the stories and scripts for the radio version, and almost a third of the televised presentations, setting the Western style and tone that *Gunsmoke* will forever be remembered for.

If Meston was the visionary for the show, Norman Macdonnell was the mixmaster. Born in 1916, a native of Pasadena, California, Macdonnell began his life in show business as a guide for CBS Radio in Hollywood at the age of twenty-two. He left this post to answer the call from Uncle Sam for World War II duty…ending up in Normandy and taking part in D-Day.

Stateside, Macdonnell returned to CBS and became an assistant director for their radio division, rising to producer-director in 1947. Macdonnell had a knack for knowing the best writers, actors and directors suited to various programs and could combine the necessary

TEAM PLAYERS Writer John Meston and producer Norman Macdonnell on the set with series star James Arness.

elements to conceive and produce future projects. *Gunsmoke* was one such project...Macdonnell's fingerprints were everywhere during nine years of radio broad-

IF MESTON WAS THE VISIONARY FOR THE SHOW, NORMAN MACDONNELL WAS THE MIXMASTER.

casts and, after season one, another nine years on the little screen.

Together, Meston and Macdonnell would make entertainment history. They coined the phrase "adult Western" and created a stampede, for lack of a better word, of television Westerns popping up as a result of the success of their fables in and around Dodge City, Kansas. Regarding *Gunsmoke*, writer Paul Savage attested, "The baby was Norm's, and never do I see proper homage paid to that man for what has evolved and what has come to be an icon of American entertainment. He got that baby on its feet, patted it on its ass and sent it on its way...Norman Macdonnell deserves more recognition than I think he's ever been paid. Not in any books, any of the trades, or publicity. It started with Norman."

What magic director-writer-producer Billy Wilder and writer-producer I.A.L. Diamond conjured on the big screen, Macdonnell and Meston matched on our home screens, and originally, via radio. Much like their movie counterparts, they were able to assemble the best in the business to work with, especially performers. Their stable of "reliables" included John Dehner, Virginia Gregg, Jack Kruschen, Jeanette Nolan, James Nusser and Vic Perrin, to name a few. These performers, under the guiding hands of Meston and Macdonnell, left their marks on both versions of the show.

Neither man sought fame or the attention that an attachment to a hit show often brings. At best, their attitudes could be described as self-effacing. Understandably proud of their efforts, Meston and Macdonnell only wanted the best in a finished product, a feat they achieved more often than not.

ON TO TELEVISION

Motion picture studio heads despised the home invasion that TV represented, originally disallowing contract stars to participate on television projects. It took close to a decade for television and movies to mesh and fully complement each other, resulting in the late night love fests we have today where stars of every magnitude can hawk their latest film, cosmetics line or fashion offerings.

Entertainment genres have long evolved from one form to another, offering stars and shows a promotion. For example, in the late twenties, many burlesque and vaudeville comedians appeared in short, two-reel sound comedies and/or radio shows based on their stage personas. In the fifties, many established radio shows made the transition to television, with Jack Benny, *The Lone Ranger* and Burns and Allen among the most successful transplants. The trend continued right into the new century with stand-up comedians good and bad being offered sitcoms tailored for their comic stylings. *Gunsmoke,* with solid ratings and fan approval for the radio version, was a natural candidate for CBS to transform into a program for the newest medium labeled "furniture" by the movie studio bigwigs.

With an obvious "job well done" for Meston and Macdonnell bringing *Gunsmoke* to life, one would assume that they would head the transition from radio to television. This was not to be. CBS wisely recognized the vast differences of the mediums and realizing the fact that Meston and Macdonnell had little or no experience in television, decided to bring in a third party to helm the new show. The job was first offered to producer-director Don Siegel, famous for his later collaborations with Clint Eastwood, *Coogan's Bluff* and *Dirty Harry,* among them, and for John Wayne's last film, also one of his best, *The Shootist.* Siegel simply wasn't interested in the job offer and without hesitation, turned CBS down. Charles Marquis Warren, a veteran of motion picture writing and directing, fit the bill, and after many personal misgivings about television, took the job and changed the face of television westerns forever.

Comedian Jack Benny resisted bringing his success-

CHESTERFIELD AD Arness and Blake pose for the program sponsor in 1958. (photo courtesy of Sydney Kent)

ful radio program to TV for many years, fearing that visually, the show had a lot of hurdles to clear. For years his faithful listeners had clear pictures in their minds of what the frugal comic's car, his Maxwell, "looked like" and they had a clear vision of his legendary bank vault, complete with moat and alligators. Great care would be taken to bring these symbols to life on television, careful not to disappoint his radio audience. Bringing the fictionalized version of Dodge City to "life" would present the same problems and concerns. Brilliantly, Warren took the radio show and gave it a visual stamp that would last for twenty years. Warren approved the designs for the Long Branch and the Marshals office. He okayed the look for every character, from boots to hats, and both hair colors and styles. His most important contribution? His choices for casting the four lead roles.

A native of Baltimore, Maryland, Warren was forty-three years old when CBS offered him *Gunsmoke*. He was already successful in motion pictures, and, like most in the industry, looked upon television with distaste. Put off twice, CBS finally offered Warren seven-thousand dollars a week and the director knew he would be hard pressed to find a better deal on any project in the industry. With the announcement of his signing and participation, the radio cast and crew began to fear the worst. Meston and Macdonnell felt they would head up the new production and that their cast would step into the television roles. CBS never seriously considered the radio actors for employment beyond their current obligation, but they would accept stories from Meston, many already aired on radio, and would make Macdonnell associate producer.

Warren and Macdonnell did not get along from the beginning, and Meston resented the newbie interfering with his stories. For the most part, the characters remained the same, save for a little tweaking here and there. For television, both Kitty and Doc cleaned up their acts a bit, Dillon was a little less heroic and Chester left the family tree of Proudfoot for Goode.

CBS and Warren bowed to pressure and tested the radio stars in their respective roles, however, Warren had some definite casting ideas of his own. Many tested for the parts, before Warren and the network decided on James Arness, Dennis Weaver, Amanda Blake and Milburn Stone for the roles of Matt Dillon, Chester Goode, Kitty Russell and Doc Adams.

Stone was personally called by Warren to read for Doc. Both men held contempt for each other from a prior working relationship, but Warren knew that Stone was the only actor to portray the gruff, cantankerous Doc. Stone wanted the role, but wanted nothing to do with Warren. The actor signed on and season one under Warren, was a rough one. In an interview with Ronald L. Davis for *Kansas History*, the actor confided, "In all fairness I must say that I don't know anybody in the world I dislike with the same fervor that I do Charles Marquis Warren." Feelings aside, Stone won the role that would provide him a steady paycheck for twenty years, unheard of in the entertainment world.

Warren had worked with Dennis Weaver on the film *Seven Angry Men* and the two of them got along very well. As reported in a 1963 *TV Guide* article, Warren recalled

MISS KITTY Amanda Blake fought for and won the role of Ms. Russell.

hiring Weaver to play Chester, "because he is such a fine actor. In *Seven Angry Men* he had to go insane, and he did it so well that I knew he could do anything."

Amanda Blake had a harder time reading for the role of Kitty Russell. For some unknown reason, the network didn't want to test Blake. She was adamant, sitting outside the casting office until someone would give her a chance. At an Actors And Others For Animals benefit in the eighties, Blake shared, "Everybody in town wanted to play Kitty, the original 'whore with a heart of gold,'" breaking into her famous, infectious laugh. "I think every actress in Hollywood, even a few drag queens in the right age range, tested for the part," her laughter continued.

Once tested, Blake impressed the powers that be, and Warren ordered a second round of tests with two actors, John Pickard and Denver Pyle, who were seriously being considered for the pivotal role of Marshal Dillon. After the tests were filmed and screened, Pickard was no longer considered for casting, failing to generate the proper chemistry with Blake. On a Friday afternoon, Pyle and Blake were told they had won the roles of Matt and Kitty, however, by the following Monday morning, things would change a bit.

After testing scores of men for the role of Matt Dillon, including Royal Dano, Raymond Burr and Peter Graves, little brother in real life to James Arness, Warren felt Pyle would be perfect for the part. Motion picture star John Wayne was originally courted for the role, but the network couldn't afford him and the Duke didn't want to be tied down with series work. He did, however, agree to film the introduction for the series premiere, due in large part to his friendship with Warren and the actor eventually cast as Dillon.

Television has always worked best when creating its own stars as opposed to borrowing them from movies or theatre. Casting John Wayne in *Gunsmoke*, however inspired, probably would not have worked beyond the first season and it is almost certain Duke wouldn't have portrayed Dillon for twenty of them. His historic introduction of episode one was perfect—a gesture that signaled the quality and lasting value the series would ultimately deliver.

Wayne suggested an actor to Warren and executive Harry Ackerman for testing; hesitant and at the last minute, they agreed to interview James Arness. At first sight, both Warren and the network executives knew they had found their man. Pyle was released and Arness was hired, although the 6' 7" actor was beginning to have second thoughts about this new job offer. With tremendous misgivings, Arness turned to Wayne for advice. After a drink or ten, Wayne convinced his buddy, who was under contract to him at the time, to "Give this show all you've got and you'll be a big star." Wayne sold Arness' contract to the studio and recalled in a 1970 cover story in *TV Guide*, "Know what he said to me when I sold his contract to CBS? 'Duke, you ruined my career!' Haw!"

With cast in place, work began on the pilot episode, *Hack Prine*, written by John Meston. The four leads became quick friends, for the most part, having worked together before on various motion picture projects. Stone, already tense around Warren, didn't care for the professionalism, or lack thereof, of star Arness. Almost immediately, the seasoned veteran wanted off the show.

As reported in the June, 1965 issue of *TV Guide*, Stone explained, "I spent the first three years hating Jim Arness. I couldn't stand him professionally—or his attitude. He'd be late or wouldn't show up—never apologize. And once he was there he'd clown around." They would not become friends for at least three seasons, at which time the diminutive Stone put the gigantic Arness in his place.

With several episodes in the can, Warren and the network decided to delay airing the pilot *Hack Prine* and in a stroke of genius, picked a later episode for the program's debut. On September 10, 1955, the television Western landscape changed forever, when *Gunsmoke* entered the CBS corral. Fans of the radio show were more or less ready for what would unfold that evening. Those not familiar with the fictional folks of Dodge City, were in for a shock. This new Western broke all the rules set up to this date. No hero in the white hat effortlessly gunning down the bad guys in black. The hero in this version, would be gunned down himself in the opening minutes of the episode, near death. *Matt Gets It* was the apt title of the first episode, and the viewers were hooked almost immediately.

Not an immediate success, the show soon bested competitor George Gobel and eventually knocked *I Love Lucy* out of the number one Nielsen rating spot. Soon, every network added Westerns to their lineups. Children everywhere had to dress up like their favorite heroes, and memorabilia flew off store shelves. By 1959, close to thirty Westerns were on the network schedules, with

THIS NEW WESTERN BROKE ALL THE RULES SET UP TO THIS DATE.

Gunsmoke remaining on top.

With a very successful first season under his belt, Warren was not happy working on the show. He felt success went to the heads of his players, especially Arness. He grew tired of the constant confrontations he endured with Stone and Macdonnell. He grew restless and bored, beginning to hate the program. Warren left the show shortly after the beginning of season two. He later began work on *Rawhide*, preferring this series over *Gunsmoke*. In fact, it took close to twenty years for Warren to look back and appreciate his time in Dodge City. He died on August 11, 1990, in West Hills, California.

With Warren out, CBS logically promoted Macdonnell to producer. The cast welcomed him with open arms, and during his nine year tenure, *Gunsmoke* enjoyed its highest ratings and public popularity.

AMERICA'S FAVORITE Striking portrait of Arness as Dillon.

THE CAST

JAMES ARNESS

Matt Dillon 1955-1975, 1987-1994
Born: James Aurness, May 26, 1923, Minneapolis,
Minnesota

A YOUNG ACTOR An early head shot of Arness.

Before becoming an entertainment icon, thanks to his portrayal of Marshal Matt Dillon, the Minnesota native, along with his younger brother Peter, led a life comparable to fiction's Huck Finn and Tom Sawyer. Born in 1923, Arness enjoyed swimming, fishing and exploring. Taller than most of his school classmates, he felt awkward and shy, causing a lifetime aversion to crowds and social gatherings.

"I was a drifter when I was a kid. At 18 I was gone from our home outside of Minneapolis. My brother Peter was an independent guy, too. Maybe it's our Norwegian heritage," recalled Arness in a 1971 *Ladies' Home Journal* interview. A free spirit, he enjoyed life riding freight trains into the Dakotas for field work and to Idaho for logging jobs.

With the advent of World War II, the 6' 7" adventurer yearned to serve his country, with his induction into the Army becoming a realization in early 1943. Buck private

Arness soon found himself in Monte Cassino, Italy—landing at Anzio in 1944. He was severely wounded on February 1st of that year, suffering gunshot wounds to his right leg, causing a year of recovery, the loss of one inch to his injured limb, and several surgeries throughout the years.

After the war, Arness returned home and attended the University of Minnesota to study Radio and Announcing. By the beginning of 1946 however, the drifting bug bit again, and he and a friend made the trek to Los Angeles, California. In rapid succession, Arness joined a theatre group, which led to a series of screen tests for the likes of David O. Selznick, Warner Brothers and eventually, Dore Schary at RKO Studios.

In true Hollywood style, Arness was cast in his first film, *The Farmer's Daughter* starring Loretta Young, in her Oscar winning performance. While looking for other film roles, Arness returned to the stage in a performance of *Candida* at the famed Pasadena Playhouse. He fell in love with his co-star Virginia Chapman and the two were married on February 12, 1948. Around this time, brother Peter Aurness (James had dropped the "u" in their last name) had arrived on the West Coast to try his hand at acting—success followed him also when he became Peter Graves.

Arness knocked around at all of the studios, working steadily at 20th Century-Fox, MGM, Universal and Republic Studios—quite often cast in Westerns. He played the silent, deadly carrot-like creature in the classic Sci-Fi

THE THING James Arness as the alien creature found at a lonely Arctic outpost in producer Howard Hawks sci-fi classic, 1951.

film *The Thing*, a character that is now considered an icon. Not many performers can boast icon status on their resumes—Arness however, can claim two.

In 1952, he caught the eye of motion picture heavyweight John Wayne, who cast him in *Big Jim McClain*.

SUNDAY BEST Arness as Marshal Dillon attends a wedding in the episode MAVIS MCCLOUD in 1957.

The Duke liked the work Arness yielded and offered him a contract with Wayne-Fellows Productions, resulting in many more films, including the Western classic, *Hondo*. Wayne loaned his star out to Warner Brothers for yet another shot at Sci-Fi immortality—1954's paean to giant ants wreaking havoc on Los Angeles—*Them!*

IN 1952, HE CAUGHT THE EYE OF MOTION PICTURE HEAVYWEIGHT JOHN WAYNE...

It was around this time that CBS had decided to take their radio show *Gunsmoke* and add it to their television schedule. Writer-producer-director Charles Marquis Warren remembered Arness from an earlier appearance in his film *Hellgate*, and was urged to have him audition for the role of Marshal Matt Dillon. Reluctant to attach himself to a television series, Arness had serious misgivings about the audition—giving in only after heeding the stern advice of John Wayne. The rest is, as they say, history.

In 1963, Arness and wife Virginia divorced. A California court awarded him custody of their three children—Craig, Jennie Lee and Rolf—a decision uncommon even by today's standards. In his professional life through his portrayals, James Arness has always given his audience full access. However, when it comes to his private life, Arness steadfastly remains a private man. To this day, he refuses to discuss any aspect of his first marriage and

1958 EMMY AWARDS BANQUET
James and his first wife, Virginia,
enjoy the festivities at Hollywood's
Cocoanut Grove. Dennis Weaver is
seen in the far right background.

HOLD IT
MARSHAL Little
Evelyn Rudie gets
the drop on
Arness at the
1958 Emmy
Awards
celebration.

LOVELY DAUGHTER James' daughter
Jenny Lee Aurness, at age 14, appeared
in the GUNSMOKE episode AUNT
THEDE in 1964.

MANY RIVERS TO
CROSS Arness in a
publicity photo from
the 1955 MGM
Western that starred
Robert Taylor.

ETHEL MEETS MARSHAL
DILLON Even stars became
starstruck when meeting Arness.
Here Vivian Vance of I LOVE LUCY
fame greets a fellow CBS employee.

CIRCA 1974 Arness on the GUNSMOKE set.

ARNESS AS ZEB Always ready for action, Arness traded his GUNSMOKE badge for buckskins, first in THE MACAHANS and again in the series HOW THE WEST WAS WON for ABC-TV.

DETECTIVE TEAM Arness starred in his third television series, MCCLAIN'S LAW, shown here with Marshall Colt for NBC-TV in 1981.

FUNSMOKE Arness clowns with Red Skelton, left, and on the set of ALIAS JESSE JAMES 1959 with Bob Hope.

TV VETERANS Arness and Brian Keith star as Jim Bowie and Davy Crockett, respectively, in THE ALAMO: 13 DAYS TO GLORY for NBC-TV in 1987.

subsequent dissolution.

His guarded private life took an unexpected turn for the better when the towering TV star met Janet Surtees in 1974. Set up by his longtime makeup man Glen Alden and his wife June, Arness and Janet soon became inseparable, resulting in marriage on December 16, 1978.

CBS gave *Gunsmoke* it's walking papers in 1975 after an astonishing 20 year run. Arness was looking forward to more time devoted to his passions—surfing, skiing, sailing and flying—but was coaxed by the ABC Network to star in a mini-series called *The Macahans*. His portrayal of Jeb Macahan was the complete opposite of Dillon, rewarding the actor with critical success and a broadening fan base.

Tragedy struck the Arness family in 1975 when daughter Jennie Lee died May 16th of that year from a prescription drug overdose. Arness gives full credit to Janet for helping him survive this horrible event. In 1977 with a bizarre twist of fate, his ex-wife Virginia was found dead due to an accidental overdose of sleeping pills and other medications.

With *The Macahans* a resounding hit, the mini-series evolved into *How the West Was Won*, becoming a popular favorite with fans until it left the air in 1979. He was again having trouble with his right leg and more surgery was needed. Arness was off work for two years when NBC offered him the starring role in *McClain's Law* in 1981. As a change of pace, Arness wore a badge in modern day, nary a horse in sight. A good show, it never clicked and lasted only one season. After starring in three series, one for each major network, the actor semi-retired.

It took six years to lure the private one to appear

RED RIVER *Gregory Harrison, Arness and Bruce Boxleitner star in the 1988 television remake of the 1948 John Wayne/Howard Hawks classic film. (CBS-TV)*

Matt Dillon in *Gunsmoke: Return to Dodge,* to air in 1987. The reunion movie rated respectably, and CBS would go on to make four more installments starring Arness through 1994. For almost forty years James Arness and Matt Dillon were one—nobody in the history of television broadcasting has portrayed the same character so successfully, for so long.

Today, the star is still happily married to Janet and living in the Brentwood area of Los Angeles, California. With author/historian James E. Wise, Jr., he penned his memoirs, *James Arness—An Autobiography* in 2001. Published by McFarland & Company, Inc. and featuring a foreword by his former *Gunsmoke* co-star Burt Reynolds, the work covers many areas of the actor's life, with the World War II section a highlight.

before cameras again—he was back in the saddle and would remain in one for the rest of his career. Long associated with mentor John Wayne, Arness appeared in two TV movie remakes associated with the Duke – *The Alamo: 13 Days to Glory* and *Red River,* 1987 and 1988, respectively.

But the big news was the announcement that James Arness would once again portray the legendary lawman

Tragedy again struck the Arness family on December 14, 2004, when eldest son Craig Aurness died of lung and anemia complications. Craig was an accomplished photographer for *National Geographic* and a stock photo agent.

Arness is a doting grandfather and enjoys his time with his family. He and Janet are tireless crusaders for

ONE MORE TIME Arness posed on the set of GUNSMOKE: ONE MAN'S JUSTICE, in his final outing as Matt Dillon, 1994.

RARE PUBLIC APPEARANCE Arness autographs his new book for one of the multitude of fans that attended the signing at the Autry Museum of Western Heritage in Los Angeles, November 3, 2001. (photo by Mary Jo Barlow)

countless charities, chief among them, The United Cerebral Palsy Organization. Many non-profit outlets thank him for his generosity. Millions of fans thank him for his honest performances and generous spirit. Arness truly loves to hear from his admirers—drop him a line at www.jamesarness.com, his authorized website.

AMANDA BLAKE

Kitty Russell 1955-1974, 1987
Born: Beverly Louise Neill, February 20, 1929, Buffalo, New York
Died: August 16, 1989 Sacramento, California

er portrait hangs in the National Cowboy Hall of Fame in Oklahoma City, Oklahoma. The painting, Miss Kitty, is an oil by acclaimed artist Bettina Steinke, measuring 30$^{1}/_{4}$" x 34$^{1}/_{4}$." It is a striking piece of work, as is the subject matter.

Prior to becoming the most famous saloon proprietress in the history of—well, in history—flame haired Amanda Blake entered this world as Beverly Louise Neill. Her parents Jesse and Louise raised their daughter in Buffalo, New York, her birthplace.

The desire to perform began before she was ten years old, making her stage debut in 1939 in a school pageant, which led to studies at The Studio Club in Buffalo. As a young adult, she moved to Claremont, California, furthering her education there and at nearby Pomona College, before finishing her studies in Gainesville, Georgia as a member of the Brenau University Academy Class of 1947.

Determined to succeed as an actress, Blake began summer stock work in the New England states. "I played in everything, and got to be pretty good with a brush painting scenery and lots of backdrops," recalled the

STARLET DAYS Early publicity shot of the beautiful Beverly Louise Neill, aka Amanda Blake.

actress. Talent notwithstanding, luck always plays a major role in any Hollywood career and luck entered Blake's professional life in 1950. MGM boasted that they had "More stars than there are in heaven" and Blake became the latest "shining light" for the studio.

She was promptly cast opposite Joel McCrea and Ellen Drew in *Stars in my Crown*, which featured another up-and-coming actor by the name of James Arness. Featured roles followed as the actress honed her craft in movies and television. Blake particularly enjoyed "live" TV.

In 1955, Blake was convinced she was the only woman to play the role of Kitty in the upcoming "adult Western" for CBS television—*Gunsmoke*. Her persistence paid off, and, after testing dozens of other women, she was awarded the role that would make her name a household word the world over.

Blake brought the character of Miss Kitty to life with a skillful amount of underplaying and a touch of humor thrown in for good measure. It would have been easy to caricature the role with a louder, sassier take, but wisely, Blake never took the lazy route. The character and performer fit each other like a glove; both were tough and independent, reliable and understanding. She gave the role many layers all the while making her performances look effortless.

Her love for animals began as a child and blossomed after joining the gang of *Gunsmoke*. When first cast, Blake had a fear of horses, particularly after suffering a fall from one of them. As explained in a December 1960 *TV Guide* cover story…"It began with the directions in a script: 'Kitty comes down the street riding a horse sidesaddle.' Norman Macdonnell recalled, 'She roared into my office, waving

AMANDA BLAKE as Kitty Russell

the script, screaming that she's afraid of horses. It was pure redheaded terror. When I finally calmed her down she said, "Tell me Norman, do you know a good riding instructor?' She's been on horses ever since.'"

Known for her bawdy sense of humor and raucous laugh, Blake enjoyed going to work so much that she often appeared on the set on many scheduled days off. Unlucky in love, married and divorced five times, the actress told *TV Guide* in January 1964, "*Gunsmoke* is great for me emotionally. It's steady, secure—like a home away from home." In June of the same year, Blake reiterated to *TV Guide*, "I feel just as much at home in that saloon as I do here—more so, because I spend more time there! When the show ends, I'll have 'em pack up that set and move it out here. I don't know what I'd do without it—and besides, the bar is practical."

She made many friends in Hollywood, even earning the respect of Bette Davis after her 1966 appearance on the show. The legendary actress stated, "Amanda Blake is one of the best," and admired her for her work ethic. Casting director Pam Polifroni remembered, "Amanda didn't want to do the show, she was so terrified...but, of course, she and Bette fell in love and became hugging buddies."

With another marriage in 1967, Blake relocated to Phoenix, Arizona, sometimes flying back and forth to Los Angeles as much as three times a week. A hectic schedule she kept for several years, this was one of many factors considered when the twentieth season of *Gunsmoke*

IT'S A GIFT Blake washes the gift she gave herself to celebrate her casting on GUNSMOKE—a new car.

started without the proprietress of the Long Branch saloon, Miss Kitty. After nineteen years, Blake was gone.

She continued her professional career with sporadic appearances on television, including guest shots on *The*

FOUR EARLY POSES Blake as everybody's favorite saloon proprietress, Miss Kitty.

COFFEE BREAK *Blake and co-star James Arness enjoy some brew between scenes.*

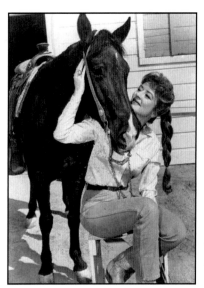

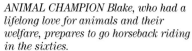

STRONG WOMAN *Blake was determined to win her role on GUNSMOKE—happily her persistence paid off.*

ANIMAL CHAMPION *Blake, who had a lifelong love for animals and their welfare, prepares to go horseback riding in the sixties.*

LONG BRANCH PALS *Blake and co-star Ken Curtis as Festus pose on the set of the episode DOUBLE ENTRY, which aired in 1965.*

THREE TV ICONS *Blake, Don Knotts and Red Skelton appear in a sketch on Skelton's TV show.*

SCREEN LEGEND Bette Davis takes aim in THE JAILER. Blake was intimidated by the movie icon.

STRYKER Blake and Andy Devine pose on the set in 1969.

A KISS FOR THE WINNER Blake offers a congratulatory buss to Jack Albertson who won the Best Supporting Actor Oscar the night before reporting to CBS for his guest stint on GUNSMOKE.

TELEVISION LEGEND Blake fires back in THE JAILER. Davis gained great respect for her small screen co-star. (photo courtesy of Sydney Kent)

STILL RAVISHING Blake in a mid-seventies portrait proves to be just as stunning as when she first appeared as Kitty in 1955.

STILL ACTIVE Blake courageously continued her craft after many devastating setbacks.

Quest, Hart to Hart and the daytime soap opera, *The Edge of Night.*

A heavy smoker, two packs a day in fact, Blake was diagnosed with cancer in 1977 and underwent oral surgery for the removal of a tongue malignancy. Recovered, she became a tireless spokesperson and advocate for the American Cancer Society, winning their Courage Award in 1984, an honor bestowed upon her by then President Ronald Reagan at the White House.

Performing less, she devoted more and more time to her beloved animals, raising funds and awareness with such organizations as Actors And Others For Animals and for the Performing Animals Welfare Society, better known as PAWS. She served on the board of the Humane Society of the United States, was a trustee of the Arizona-Sonora Desert Museum in Tucson, Arizona and became a hard-working member of the Phoenix Zoo Women's Auxiliary.

Her last marriage in 1984 to real estate consultant/developer Mark Spaeth moved the actress to Austin, Texas. This union would prove to be another disaster for the actress, ending in divorce less than a year later in 1985. Blake moved back to Los Angeles and Spaeth would die later that same year of AIDS.

Devastated, Blake eventually moved near longtime friend Pat Derby, who ran the PAWS wildlife ranch in Galt, California, near Sacramento. Always happy around her beloved animals, Blake also received the joyous news that she was offered her old role of Kitty Russell in the upcoming television movie, *Gunsmoke: Return to Dodge,* released in 1987. With her speech at times thick and slightly slurred from her cancer ordeal, Blake again turned in a great performance in a role that had earned her three Golden Globe nominations when the series *Gunsmoke* originally aired.

With a solid performance behind her and in what can only be described as a cruel twist of fate, Hollywood seemed to turn its back on the veteran star. Writer Jim Byrnes recalled a sad event. "We were at one of those Golden Boot Award ceremonies, and my wife Toni and I were mixing with everyone at the bar in the banquet room. I went off and my wife saw Amanda just standing

PRESIDENTIAL HONOR Blake receives the American Cancer Society Courage Award from President Ronald Reagan on March 29, 1984. (photo courtesy of the Ronald Reagan Presidential Library)

there, alone. So she went over to her and introduced herself as my wife, and I came back and found them so we took her with us, bought some drinks and talked to her. Nobody was paying attention to her, she was alone. What a shame, she was a nice lady."

In 1988, Blake's worst nightmare became a startling reality—she had AIDS. In 1989 she turned sixty and within six months, the actress once referred to as "a shining light," died, truly a horrible end for such a wonderful person. As reported November 20, 1989 in *People* magazine, "...Blake didn't die of oral cancer as originally reported. Instead she has become the first Hollywood actress of note to die of AIDS. 'There was no recurrence of cancer,' her physician, Dr. Lou Nishimura, says now. 'Technically she died of liver failure brought on by viral hepatitis, which was AIDS-related.'"

Blake left her entire estate estimated at four-hundred-thousand dollars to her beloved PAWS. Per her wishes, she was cremated and her ashes were spread over the animal reserve she helped establish.

In 1991, Blake was honored with two blocks on the AIDS quilt. 1997 saw the opening of the Amanda Blake Memorial Wildlife Refuge at Rancho Seco Park in Herald, California, near Galt. She was inducted into the Brenau University Hall of Fame in 2000. In November of 2001, PAWS dedicated the Amanda Blake Museum and Visitor Center, again, near Galt. Tours may be scheduled by calling PAWS at (209) 745-2606. Donations in memory of Blake are both welcomed and needed.

For reasons beyond her time on *Gunsmoke*, Blake may be gone but she will never be forgotten.

RETURN TO DODGE Blake portrayed Miss Kitty for the last time in 1987.

DENNIS WEAVER

Chester Goode 1955-1964
Born: June 4, 1924 Joplin, Missouri

With an acting career spanning over fifty years, Dennis Weaver has consistently turned in first-rate performances—his television track record is virtually second to none.

A native of Joplin, Missouri, Weaver was born on June 4, 1924. A natural athlete, he excelled both in academics and sports. School was interrupted by service in the Navy during World War II, where Weaver trained as a pilot.

In 1945 he married his Junior College sweetheart Gerry Stowell. Never one to buckle to show-biz stereotypes, the Weavers' marriage has been a strong and happy union entering a sixth decade...practically unheard of in Tinseltown. They are the proud parents of three boys, Rick, Robby and Rusty.

After the war, Weaver attended the University of Oklahoma. There he became one of the Midwest's top track and field stars. Courting Olympic possibilities, he took sixth place at the National tryouts for the Games in the decathlon in 1948.

The acting bug bit Weaver around the same time, so dreams of sporting a gold medal gave way to career aspirations as an entertainer...aspirations that would lead to another type of gold medal win. Soon the Midwesterner

EARLY PORTRAIT Weaver at his home circa 1963.

headed to New York City, (shades of *McCloud* to come), and began training at the Big Apple's famed Actors Studio.

Within no time, Weaver made his Broadway debut, eventually touring in *Come Back Little Sheba* with Shirley Booth. Many productions followed, including *A Streetcar Named Desire* and *The Glass Menagerie*—vehicles that gave Dennis the occasion to be spotted by Hollywood

FAN FAVORITE This shot was sent to many GUNSMOKE fans during Weaver's time on the show—he still autographs this photo today—fifty years later!

DENNIS WEAVER as Chester Goode

Horizons West, starring Robert Ryan and Rock Hudson. He found a friend on the picture in co-star James Arness— a friendship and rapport that would reach tremendous heights in just a few short years. The studio liked his work in the routine oater, so much so that Weaver would appear in ten additional Western films in a row.

Prior to being cast on *Gunsmoke* in 1955, Weaver worked on many projects. Even after his casting on the television show, he was the only *Gunsmoke* performer who worked steadily in front of a camera when the show went on hiatus.

The role of Chester Goode fit Weaver like a glove and he brought to life perhaps the most endearing and celebrated sidekick in television history. Chester was such a popular character that Weaver was often overwhelmed with fan mail. People constantly wondered if he was in pain due to his "limp" so believable on the little screen.

When fans would meet Milburn Stone in person, they would inevitably ask Doc how Chester was feeling. In 1959, press releases were sent out showing Weaver leaping in the air—assuring folks that he was fine and that his handicap was nothing more than good acting.

Not only a fan favorite, Weaver was a hit with critics too. Nominated twice for an Emmy, Weaver struck gold in 1959 and won for Best Supporting Actor In A Drama Series.

It was during this stint that the actor was given the opportunity to direct on television as well, at the helm on several memorable *Gunsmoke* installments. Fame

producers and agents.

Fellow Actors Studio classmate and Universal Studios contractee Shelley Winters led some talent scouts his way and in 1952 the studio saw potential in Weaver and signed him up immediately.

Out west in Hollywood, Weaver made his motion picture debut for director Budd Boetticher in the Western

CHESTER AND MATT Weaver and James Arness ride into action.

GOODBYE CHESTER Weaver left GUNSMOKE in 1964 for the short-lived series KENTUCKY JONES.

I'LL PROTECT YOU LITTLE BUDDY No, it's not an ad for a new vaudeville act, just a cartoon from 1963 featuring Matt and Chester.

HUMANITARIAN Weaver has been involved in countless charities throughout the years, including Love Is Feeding Everyone, with co-founder Valerie Harper.

WHITTLING TIME Weaver and Milburn Stone take care of the business at hand on a typical day in Dodge City.

notwithstanding, Weaver would grow tired of the character and often talked of leaving *Gunsmoke* while he was still on top of his game. After nine seasons and two previous attempts to vacate Dodge, or at least the CBS Studios facsimile thereof, Weaver moved on to other work.

When his departure became official, feelings from his castmates ranged from sadness to anger, however, Weaver was nonetheless encouraged by all of them in his future endeavors. Even though roles on the big screen followed, Weaver continued to find his niche on television. *Kentucky Jones, Gentle Ben, Emerald Point N.A.S.* and, of course, *McCloud,* are just some of the series he left his indelible mark on.

Television movies are a memorable part of the Weaver oeuvre also, including some of the best the medium has to offer. *Bluffing It, Cocaine: One Man's Seduction* and *Amber Waves* are but a few of the projects that showcased his versatility. And let's not forget a little dandy entitled *Duel,* marking an early directing effort by a

IT'S LIKE THIS *Doc and Kitty (Milburn Stone and Amanda Blake) react as Chester (Weaver) tells another story.*

young filmmaker named Spielberg.

Not one to rest on his laurels, Weaver also cut many entertaining Country and Western music albums...recordings still popular today. After John Wayne's death in 1979, Weaver took over as pitchman for Great Western Savings in a series of memorable television spots.

In 1976, Weaver was a "roastee" on *The Dean Martin*

33

TV IMMORTALITY Thanks to his role in GUNSMOKE for CBS and later in MCCLOUD for ABC, shown here, Weaver is one of the medium's true superstars.

Celebrity Roast, reuniting him briefly with his *Gunsmoke* co-stars Milburn Stone and Amanda Blake. Many celebrities joined in the fracas, including radio's Matt Dillon, William Conrad, and Peter Graves, to name but a few. After the taping, Weaver, Blake and Stone reminisced about the good times they had as a trio performing live all over the United States in countless state fairs, rodeos and industry functions.

Weaver successfully served as President of the Screen Actors Guild from 1973 to 1975. A true humanitarian, Weaver has many interests, from Actors and Others For Animals to Love Is Feeding Everyone, the latter being an organization dedicated to helping hungry people that he co-founded with actress Valerie Harper. Providing meals for four hundred people a week in the beginning, L.I.F.E. now helps over one hundred and fifty thousand people a week in Los Angeles County. The success of this group has paved the way for other groups throughout the United States, helping to end hunger in our country.

Weaver now lives in an environmentally friendly solar powered home in Colorado, made mostly from recycled cans and used automobile tires. The fruition of this project, as well as a love for the environment and ecology, has led Weaver to found the Institute of Ecolonomics, a non-profit organization dedicated to the realization that both our ecology and economy must be sustainable.

Still in great demand as an actor, Weaver recently appeared in a classic Western remake, *The Virginian*, on TNT. He played a real heavy opposite Bill Pullman and Diane Lane, scoring positively again with both fans and critics, for his uncharacteristic and against-type portrayal. Weaver has been a spokesman and host for the Westerns Channel for several years now and continues his witty, insightful and educational program introductions today.

Hampton Roads Publishing, Inc., released the actor's autobiography in 2001, entitled *All the World's a Stage*.

RECENT STUDY Weaver still stays busy with charitable projects, personal appearances and as the frequent host for the Starz Encore Westerns Channel.

Weaver penned a thoroughly entertaining tome filled with anecdotes regarding his life as a performer, a respected family man and spokesperson for our planet Earth.

Retire? Doubtful. Slow down? Not likely. Weaver is a true rarity among men—one who gives his all, always. His contributions to *Gunsmoke* and the television medium are unequalled; his contributions to the world and ecology are immeasurable.

For more information on the Institute of Ecolonomics, contact:
P.O. Box 257, Ridgway, CO 81432
(970) 626-3820
www.ecolonomics.org
weaver@dennisweaver.com

Author's note: Sadly, Dennis Weaver passed away on February 24, 2006 due to complications from cancer. Weaver was 81 and is survived by his wife, three sons and three grandchildren.

Upon hearing of his death, friend and Gunsmoke costar Burt Reynolds stated: "He was a wonderful man and a fine actor, and we will all miss him." I'll echo Reynolds' sentiments by adding that Weaver never disappointed—whether on screen or off—and I will forever treasure our meetings and phone conversations together. As of January 2007, plans are under way to dedicate the Dennis Weaver Memorial Park—a 60-acre public park and nature preserve along the Uncompahgre River in Ridgway, Colorado. I can't think of a more fitting tribute to a wonderful humanitarian.

MILBURN STONE

Doc Adams 1955-1975
Born: Milburn Stone, July 5, 1904 Burrton, Kansas
Died: June 12, 1980 La Jolla, California

ilburn Stone's portrayal of Doc Adams showcases what happens when material and actor are destined for each other. When said material is an ensemble show, such as *Gunsmoke*, this feat is all the more impressive.

One of three children, Stone was born eighty miles from the real Dodge City in Burrton, Kansas in 1904. By the time he was two, Stone's family relocated to Fort Larned, Kansas. Now thirty miles out of Dodge, his father owned and operated a country store.

Because of his outstanding scholastic record and a close family tie, Stone received a Congressional appointment to the U.S. Naval Academy at Annapolis. Although the appointment was a great honor, Stone turned it down, much to the disappointment of his mother, basing his decision on three things. One, he had appeared in four plays during his senior high school year. Two, his cousin, "Uncle" Fred, was Stone of Stone and Montgomery, of vaudeville fame. Finally, at the time of graduation, a tent show came to town and with a promise of "life upon the wicked stage" and fifty dollars a week, the young Stone joined the troupe when they left town.

The leader of the company, Arthur Names impressed upon Stone a work ethic that would stay with the actor

MILBURN STONE as Doctor Galen Adams

UNIVERSAL STUDIOS PLAYER *Basil Rathbone, Stone and Dennis Hoey in SHERLOCK HOLMES FACES DEATH, 1943.*

EARLY STUDY *Great photo of Stone as Doc from 1955.*

throughout his entire career, telling him, "Milburn, acting is not the most noble profession in the world, but it can be very gratifying and quite remunerative if you never let anybody catch you at it." For six years, they toured Kansas and northern Oklahoma in a series of two-night stands.

In 1924, Stone joined the Harold English Players. Nellie Morrison played the ingénue in the group and would become Stone's leading lady, onstage and off. They married that same year and by 1926 Nellie gave birth to their daughter, Shirley.

Stone made his first attempt at legitimate theatre, heading to New York in 1929. Upon arrival, the stock market crashed, as did his hopes for a Broadway debut. It would be five more years on the road before Stone's Broadway dream would become a reality. He played a Confederate soldier opposite "Uncle" Fred Stone in the play *Jayhawker*, which opened in 1934 at the Cort Theatre.

Hollywood beckoned, and Stone made his motion picture debut in 1936 opposite Marie Wilson in *Ladies Crave Excitement,* leading to appearances in over one hundred and fifty films. Stone would work with some of the best directors Tinseltown offered, including legends John Ford in *Young Mr. Lincoln* and Cecil B. DeMille in *Reap the Wild Wind.*

Tragedy would strike the Stone family in 1937 with Nellie's sudden illness and subsequent death. Making matters worse, Nellie was in the early stages of pregnancy with their second child. This double loss "was very traumatic for dad," recalled Stone's daughter Shirley.

Film roles continued with Stone working at various studios, including those on poverty row such as Monogram, with serial work. In 1940, Stone married Jane Garrison, an executive with the Ralph Edwards Production Company; this union would last forty years.

Universal Studios signed Stone to a long-term contract

PASSING TIME James Arness, Amanda Blake and Stone enjoy a quick game between setups.

in 1942, resulting in over forty feature film appearances in four years. Whether supporting Abbott and Costello or Basil Rathbone's Sherlock Holmes, Stone was a reliable member of the studio's stock company.

In the early fifties, Stone listened to several episodes

C.S.I. DODGE *Sometimes Doc examined much more than patients, as shown here with series star James Arness.*

TAKE MY ADVICE *Stone was so convincing in his portrayal of Doc—strangers often asked him for medical advice.*

COMING TO A TOWN NEAR YOU *Chester, Kitty and Doc, (Dennis Weaver, Amanda Blake and Stone) were among the top attractions at rodeos and fairs around the U.S.*

CLOSE FRIENDS *On screen, Kitty seeks the advice of Doc. Off screen, Amanda Blake and Stone were very close friends.*

ON THE TOWN *Stone and his second wife Jane enjoy a night out in Hollywood.*

PROUD DISPLAY Stone was an
accomplished carpenter and made
many fine pieces of furniture, such
as this one, for family, friends and
castmates.

UNDER THE GUN Stone takes aim at
bandits in the 1966 GUNSMOKE episode
STAGE STOP.

GONE FISHIN' Ken Curtis joined Stone and
guide Gil Hamm on a fishing trip in
Minnesota where they caught muskie. Their
journey aired on THE AMERICAN SPORTS-
MAN January 10, 1971 on ABC-TV.

COMING HOME Buck Taylor, Glenn
Strange, James Arness and Ken Curtis
celebrate Stone's release from the hospital
with his wife Jane.

DOC ADAMS Charles Marquis
Warren cast Stone in the role knowing no one else could play him with
such authority and talent.

THE GOLDEN YEARS One of the last portraits of Milburn Stone, circa 1979, the year before his death at the age of 75.

MATT AND DOC After a rocky start, James Arness and Stone became close friends and respected each other's talent.

of a popular radio western and particularly enjoyed the role of the town doctor, musing to himself about the fun he could have playing the role. In 1953, Stone was cast by director Charles Marquis Warren in the film *Arrowhead*. Aside from working with one of his best friends, Charlton Heston, Stone did not enjoy the experience, especially the constant tension and ill feelings between himself and Warren.

When CBS began casting for the televised version of *Gunsmoke* with Warren in charge, Stone was asked to read for the role of Doc Adams. Though both Stone and Warren detested each other, the actor was cast in the role that would make him a famous, wealthy man. However, like his earlier Annapolis appointment, Stone did his best to turn down this latest "golden opportunity." During the first season, Stone didn't enjoy working with Warren or the star of the show, James Arness, threatening to quit on several occasions.

Warren left the show after one season and Stone and Arness would soon patch up their differences and become friends. He began touring the country in live appearances with co-stars Amanda Blake and Dennis Weaver, setting attendance records at most venues. In 1960, with the show and live appearances number one in ratings and ticket sales, Stone was made an honorary member of the Kansas Medical Society. In 1961, the Society bestowed their Outstanding Service Award to the actor, an accolade normally reserved for actual medical professionals.

For his performance in the 1967 episode *Baker's Dozen*, Stone won an Emmy award for Best Supporting Actor. The fact that the episode was written by his brother Joseph, proved icing on the cake for the proud actor. In his ever decreasing spare time, Stone enjoyed two hobbies that he approached with the same fervor he displayed as an actor, furniture making and fishing.

His furniture pieces were made as gifts to family and friends, with co-stars Dennis Weaver, Amanda Blake and Ken Curtis adorning their homes with these handmade treasures. When time permitted, Stone would be found at Lake Mead, Nevada, on first a twenty-eight foot cabin cruiser, and later a forty-one footer that towed a seventeen foot fishing boat. Co-star Ken Curtis and his wife Torrie, writer Paul Savage and his wife Laurie, all had fond memories of joining "Doc" and Janie on these fishing jaunts. Lake Mead also furnished many memorable occasions for Stone and his four grandchildren.

Both Stone and Arness appeared on *Gunsmoke* during all twenty seasons, earning them both places in the record books. However, in 1971 during the seventeenth season, Stone missed a handful of episodes due to open-heart surgery. Recovered, Stone made a triumphant return to *Gunsmoke* the same season with the program's only three-part episode, *Gold Train: The Bullet*, written by Jim Byrnes.

With the cancellation of *Gunsmoke* in 1975, Stone more or less retired, save for two notable exceptions. In 1976, Stone, along with former co-star Amanda Blake, appeared on *The Dean Martin Celebrity Roast*: Dennis Weaver, trading insults with his old pal Chester. Then in 1979, Stone reunited with Ken Curtis and, as Doc and Festus, appeared on the star-studded variety show, *When the West was Fun: A Western Reunion*. Hosted by Glenn Ford and featuring over thirty Western television stars from the fifties and sixties, this would be Stone's final appearance as Doc, as well as his final performance.

After a series of heart attacks, Stone was again hospitalized in June of 1980. Ken Curtis came to visit his good friend with a fishing pole in hand, just as he had done

A TEAR IS SHED This poignant cartoon appeared around the country when Stone passed away. So simple, yet it says so much. (courtesy of Bob Anderson)

so when Stone had open-heart surgery nine years prior. When Curtis arrived, Stone was napping. Not wanting to disturb Stone, he left the pole with the charge nurse, telling her, "Ol' Doc'll know what to do with this and who it's from." Festus gave Doc a playful wink and left. Stone never woke up.

The actor was laid to rest at El Camino Memorial Park in La Jolla, California. At the time of his death, Stone was working on his autobiography. His wife Jane donated his papers, photos and interviews to the Cowboy Hall of Fame in Oklahoma City, which is now known as the National Cowboy & Western Heritage Museum.

During his lifetime and long career, the actor received many honors and awards, including an honorary doctorate from St. Mary of the Plains College, in Dodge City, Kansas. Distinguished Professor Emeritus of Theatre at Kansas State University, Dr. Norman Fedder, wrote an original one-man play about Stone and his role on *Gunsmoke*. The play debuted in 1989 at Saint Mary of the Plains College and was revived at Hutchinson Community College, also in Kansas, in 1995. The title of the show? *Never Let 'Em Catch You At It: An Evening with Milburn Stone.*

KEN CURTIS

Festus Haggen 1962, 1964-1975
Born: Curtis Wain Gates, July 2, 1916, Lamar, Colorado
Died: April 28, 1991 Clovis, California

Born in Lamar, Colorado to Dan and Millie Gates in 1916, Curtis was raised in nearby Las Animas where his father was a homesteader. When Curtis was a young boy, his dad was elected County Sheriff. The Gates family lived on the ground floor of the County Sheriff's building, while the jail cells and office equipment were located upstairs. His mother cooked meals for their "visitors" and Curtis helped with daily chores both down and upstairs.

Curtis had a love for music that began in his childhood, culminating by playing the saxophone in his high school band.

After high school, Curtis entered Colorado College in Colorado Springs. Majoring in medicine, he soon tired of his medicinal studies and focused more on his love of music and newfound skills as a songwriter.

In 1939, Curtis headed west to Hollywood, where he found steady work as a staff singer for NBC radio, doing guest spots here and there. Big Band singer Jo Stafford heard him and arranged a meeting between the young singer and her boss, bandleader Tommy Dorsey. Dorsey liked the style of Curtis Gates but detested his name, suggesting a change to the better sounding Ken Curtis.

He also sang with bandleader Shep Fields before Uncle Sam came calling and Curtis answered by joining the Army in 1942.

At the end of World War II, Curtis returned to Hollywood and resumed his singing career. Columbia Studios soon became home for the singer, making him the nation's newest singing cowboy in his film debut, *Rhythm Roundup*. As the forties came to a close, so did his Columbia contract.

He soon joined the world famous singing group, The Sons Of The Pioneers, catching the ear, and eventually the eye, of director John Ford. The group can be heard on the soundtrack to Ford's *Wagon Master* and appeared singing in *Rio Grande*. He landed a role in Ford's classic *The*

RIO GRANDE Ken Curtis sings with members of The Sons of the Pioneers in a scene from the John Ford classic in 1950.

KEN CURTIS as Festus Haggen

Quiet Man and landed a bride in real life when he married the famed director's daughter Barbara, both in 1952.

Curtis left the "Sons" in 1953, but rejoined them at RCA Studios for recording work two years later. Also around this time, his father-in-law hired him for a small role in his latest John Wayne Western, *The Searchers*, released in 1956. Goofing around on the set between takes, Curtis began speaking with a "dry-land" dialect. Ford, nicknamed Pappy, heard this and insisted that Curtis use it in his characterization of Charlie McCorry. The seeds for what was to become Festus were planted that day.

Curtis next took advantage of the current Sci-Fi nuclear craze that swept the country by producing two low-budget films, *The Giant Gila Monster* and *The Killer Shrews*, both released in 1959 with Curtis only appearing in the latter. 1959 also saw the actor appearing on television, with his first of many appearances on *Gunsmoke*, however, not as Festus Haggen.

From 1959 through 1961 he appeared in many of the Westerns that ruled the airwaves then, including *Wagon Train*, *Rawhide* and *Have Gun—Will Travel*. In 1961 Curtis co-starred with Larry Pennell in the syndicated series *Ripcord*, a half hour adventure show about skydivers. The show lasted for 76 episodes before cancellation.

Director Andrew V. McLaglen fondly remembered working with Curtis in an episode of *Have Gun—Will Travel* where Curtis again played a variation of his Charlie

CLASSIC FILM *Curtis as Dolan shares a moment with Henry Fonda in* MISTER ROBERTS, *Warner Brothers, 1955.*

McCorry character. With Dennis Weaver again announcing his desire to leave *Gunsmoke*, McLaglen and producer Norman MacDonnell threw around ideas for replacing the seemingly irreplaceable character Chester. In 1962 writer Les Crutchfield turned in a script called *Us Haggens* and Curtis was cast as Festus Haggen. The episode proved to be popular and CBS, McLaglen and MacDonnell kept Curtis and his character in mind when and if Weaver left the show for good.

Late in 1963 it was decided that Curtis would reprise his role of Festus and join the cast of *Gunsmoke* as Dennis Weaver and Chester slowly left the series. Beginning in January 1964 Curtis and Haggen joined the

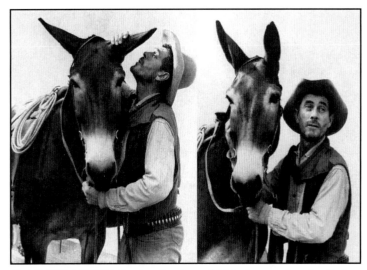

MAN'S BEST FRIEND Curtis talks shop with his flop eared co-star, Ruth.

THE SEARCHERS John Ford directed Vera Miles and his then son-in-law Curtis as Charlie McCorry—a characterization that figured prominently when the actor joined the cast of GUNSMOKE.

FOOL'S GOLD In his own inimitable style Festus (Curtis) explains things to Matthew (James Arness) at the end of THE REWARD from season eleven.

DON'T YA SEE? Milburn Stone and Curtis, better known as Doc and Festus, were one of television's great teams.

TENDER SIDE *Jacqueline Scott as Abelia and Curtis made a great pair, shown here in 1968. (photo courtesy of Jacqueline Scott)*

ISLAND IN THE DESERT *Curtis with guest star Strother Martin in the great two-parter from 1974, penned by Jim Byrnes.*

A COUPLE OF MUGS *Guest star Benny Rubin reacts to a little chewin' from Festus in DOCTOR HERMAN SCHULTZ, MD, 1970.*

WELCOME TO DODGE *Curtis was often the first cast member to welcome guests to the GUNSMOKE set. Here he greets Lee J. Cobb and his daughter Julie during the filming of THE COLONEL in 1974.*

PROUD GUESTS *Curtis and his wife Torrie, chat before the GUNSMOKE cast won the Western Heritage Award from The Cowboy Hall Of Fame on April 25, 1981, in Oklahoma City, Oklahoma. (photo courtesy of Paul Savage)*

show and remained for 11 years.

At first the camps were set—those who loved and missed Chester and those who accepted change and allowed Festus into their homes as part of the *Gunsmoke* family. This division did not last long as fan mail for Curtis increased and he began touring the country in rodeos and live appearances as the scruffy, likeable Festus. He absolutely loved his *Gunsmoke* character and continued playing the role long after the program was cancelled in 1975.

When the actor first learned of the program's demise, he immediately approached the prop department and asked to purchase the roll top that adorned the set for Doc's office. For the next sixteen years the desk was a permanent fixture in his bedroom. Curtis tended to his fan mail and would often eat his meals while enjoying television at the desk.

In 1964 he and Barbara divorced. During his live appearances, Curtis met and later, in 1966, married rodeo secretary Torrie Connelly.

With solid bookings for live appearances, Curtis still found time for film and television work, including an appearance on *How the West was Won* with pal James Arness. In the 1983-84 television season, Curtis landed his last regular role in a network show playing Hoyt in *The Yellow Rose*. After this, Curtis more or less retired—he made a few public appearances, enjoyed reading and answering his substantial fan mail, and sporadically appeared on TV, appearing opposite Willie Nelson in *Once*

LAST SERIES ROLE *Curtis portrayed a cowboy named Hoyt on* THE YELLOW ROSE *for NBC-TV during the 1983-84 season.*

Upon a Texas Train.

Mr. and Mrs. Curtis bought a ranch in Clovis, California, quickly becoming hometown favorites. UPS driver Eldon McKelvie shared, "I delivered to Ken's home and was lucky enough to become good friends with him and his wife Torrie. It was exciting to get to know Ken as

FITTING TRIBUTE This statue of Festus stands in the town of Clovis, California, where Curtis and his wife lived for many years.

If there are to be prayers said for me, let them be said in the hearts of my friends and those whose lives I may have touched during my life time — by all means let there be no saddness or grief — I want my family and friends to remember only the happy times we were together, my attributes (if any) and try to overlook all of my faults — (That should keep you busy until the time we all meet up again!!)

Ken Curtis

Courtesy of Eldon McKelvie.

I'm an over-the-top TV and movie buff, and like you, a big *Gunsmoke* fan. Whenever I could engage him in conversation about his career, I was thrilled, to say the least."

His last television film reunited Curtis with his *Yellow Rose* co-star Sam Elliott—*Conagher*, shot in 1990 and released in 1991—proved to be a fitting exit for the beloved actor.

Ill during much of the *Conagher* shoot, he never complained. Curtis always thought of his family, including two sons and eight grandchildren, as well as friends and fans first—with this in mind, he penned the following note..."If there are to be prayers said for me, let them be in the hearts of friends and those whose lives I may have touched during my lifetime—by all means let there be no sadness or grief—I want my family and friends to remember only the happy times we were together, my attributes (if any) and try to overlook all of my faults. (That should keep you busy until the time we all meet up again!!)"—Ken Curtis.

In late April, 1991, Curtis had enjoyed another personal appearance as Festus, riding in a nearby parade and greeting his many fans. Once home, he retreated to his room and again sat at Doc's desk and enjoyed television and supper. Nodding off, he woke up a short time later and settled into his easy chair located next to the rolltop, drifting off to sleep.

for a breakfast break. As I was taking my young son Eddie out of his car seat, I lifted him up to my shoulder and he began yelling, "Daddy, Fettus! There's Fettus! Fettus daddy!" I looked around and there, across the street, was a life-sized statue of Ken Curtis as Festus! At that point in time, I had never heard of Clovis or the connection to one of my favorite television stars. If not for the keen eye of my little *Gunsmoke* fan, I probably would've missed seeing this wonderful memorial.

Sculptor Sam Hutchings donated the stunning piece of work to the Town of Clovis in 1992, quickly becoming a local and tourist favorite. It originally stood outside the Clovis Big Dry Creek Historical Museum—due to remodeling, it has been moved temporarily in front of a local bank.

FESTUS SPEAK
by Sandy Henry

Down there in Dodge City, a Haggen resides
In a shanty northwest of the creek.
His first name is Festus (the mule's name is Ruth).
And he's got this particular "speak."

When talking to Dillon, the marshal of Dodge,
It's usually "Matthew" or "Matt."
And when he's a problem to "study" and solve,
He turns to Miss Kitty to chat.

On April 28, 1991, Curtis died in his sleep of an apparent heart attack. Per his wishes, his body was cremated and his ashes were scattered in Colorado, near his birthplace.

On a personal note, while driving from our home in Southern California to Sisters, Oregon on vacation in 2000, my family and I stopped in a small California town

Of course he respects her—she's "thoughty" and kind.
And "looksome" she is, don'tcha see?
He "swallers" a beer at the Long Branch Saloon,
Though often he has two or three.

His friend the Comanche's the blacksmith in town,
And "fullers" 'round Dodge know they're friends.
With April the "ninny" he tries to be tough,
Though she knows that he only pretends.

His best friend in town is a "quackety quack,"
Galen Adams, known fondly as Doc.
"Golly bill," that "old scudder" can insult and taunt.
Though he never would hurtfully mock.

Haggen though has a temper, it shows now and then,
Like a "red tailed ole' badger" he'll growl.
But mostly he's ornery, shifty, carefree.
He's a crooner, and boy can he howl.

You "stay in the buggy" he's said once or twice,
When danger was lurking about.
And when he encounters a "blabberty mouth,"
He tells 'im to just "cut it out."

In spite of the whiskers and hat full of dust
(and always a scarf at his nape),
He cleans up real perty, and dare you say not,
He's on you "like ugly on a ape."

A "pearl buttoned bangled" old billy he'd be
If he had a new suit in his poke.
A visit to Jonas for fancy new duds
would make Festus the stud of Gunsmoke!

Poet Sandy Henry is also a novelist. Her book, *Something Borrowed, Something Blue,* is published by Llumina Press. She is also working on a book of *Gunsmoke* stories, tentatively titled *Legends of the Long Branch.* You can visit her website at www.sandyhenry.com.

BURT REYNOLDS

Quint Asper 1962-1965

Born: Burton Leon Reynolds, February 11, 1936, Waycross, Georgia

Football hero. Stunt man. Television star. Superstar. Icon. Survivor.

Burt Reynolds has done it all. From humble beginnings, born to Burton and Fern Reynolds, he was raised with his siblings in Riviera Beach, Florida. His father was a cowboy turned chief of police and his mother, a nurse.

An average student, Reynolds became a hero on the gridiron for both Palm Beach High School and Florida State University. By 1955 he had attracted the scouting attention of several pro teams, including the Detroit Lions and the Baltimore Colts. A near fatal car accident on Christmas Eve that same year dashed all hopes of a pro ball career. Recuperating, he continued his education at Palm Beach Junior College, enrolling in a life-changing course, English Literature.

Reynolds soon made his college acting debut in *Outward Bound*, which led him to hit the boards in New York, landing a small role in *Mr. Roberts* starring Charlton Heston. Soon the athletic actor made his live television debut—he was hurled through a glass window on a Sunday morning religious program.

By 1959, Reynolds moved up to supporting roles on several television shows, including *M Squad* and *Playhouse 90*. Stunting less and acting more, he would soon be cast in his first regular role in a network series.

He portrayed Ben Fraser on *Riverboat*, starring opposite Darren McGavin for NBC. Reynolds and McGavin never quite got along. Wanting out of his contract, he was released after tossing an assistant director overboard from the riverboat set and into a studio lake.

Predicting the worst, Reynolds felt his Hollywood career was over. However, by 1961 he made his big screen debut in *Angel Baby* for Allied Artists.

Alternating from film to stage work, Reynolds was again courted by television, winning a recurring role on *Gunsmoke*. His casting as Quint Asper was the first time his parents were proud of his chosen profession, acting.

Whatever distaste he had for television quickly vanished as the newcomer to Dodge was impressed by the professionalism of castmates James Arness, Amanda Blake, Milburn Stone and, later, Ken Curtis.

While traveling and doing publicity for *Gunsmoke*, Reynolds met his first wife, comedienne Judy Carne. He was a popular addition to the show and soon generated the most fan mail among his fellow actors. Happy with the public reaction, he was unhappy with the way his portrayal of the half-breed blacksmith was developing.

Going nowhere, and with a recent regime change in the production staff, he left behind a role in a popular show, as well as a steady, generous paycheck.

A divorce from Carne coincided with many

BURT REYNOLDS as Quint Asper

JOINS THE CAST Reynolds, shown here with his fellow castmates, Amanda Blake, James Arness and Milburn Stone, joined GUNSMOKE in 1962.

mediocre projects, including the short-lived series, *Hawk*, in 1966.

Film roles continued into the early seventies, with 1972 seeing the release of the classic, *Deliverance*. Reynolds has compared that shoot to the professional, ego-free atmosphere he enjoyed on *Gunsmoke* a decade earlier.

Hollywood touted Reynolds an "overnight success." Director Andrew V. McLaglen recalled working with Reynolds on *Gunsmoke*: "Burt was fine. He enjoyed doing the blacksmith. If somebody wanted to make a bet with you that he'd be the number one movie star in the world, you could've got a ten-thousand to one bet. But, that's what he became."

With success came notoriety. Films such as *The Longest Yard, Gator* and *Smokey and the Bandit,* as well as his highly publicized liaisons with Dinah Shore, Chris Evert and Sally Field, lifted Reynolds to the number-one box-office position.

In the early eighties, during a string of big screen disappointments, Reynolds began a paparazzi, gossip magazine-pleasing relationship with actress Loni Anderson. 1984 found Reynolds filming *City Heat* with longtime friend Clint Eastwood, and on the first day of production, he was seriously hurt shooting a fight scene. Hit in the jaw, Reynolds suffered a fractured temporomandibular joint, or TMJ.

With both his career and health in a downward spiral, Reynolds struggled just to stay alive and keep above the malicious gossip said and printed worldwide.

After nursing him through the hard times, Anderson and Reynolds married in 1988. That same year the newlyweds adopted a baby boy, whom Reynolds named Quinton, a decision made in part by his fondness for his role as Quint on *Gunsmoke*.

Reynolds signed with ABC for the series

FESTUS AND QUINT Ken Curtis and Reynolds shared many a good time off screen and a lot of dustups on screen

FRIENDS FOR LIFE When James Arness published his autobiography in 2001, Reynolds supplied the foreword.

BEEFCAKE Reynolds received record amounts of fan mail during his tenure in Dodge City.

DELIVERANCE The 1972 film made Reynolds a huge star.

B.L. Stryker, a private-eye programmer that lasted only two seasons. His next foray into episodic television, however, was much more successful. For his role on *Evening Shade*, Reynolds won an Emmy for Best Actor.

Things were not as successful on the home front. Enough has been written about the breakup of his marriage to Anderson and the subsequent legal wranglings. Through it all, Reynolds has maintained his dignity, and most importantly, a close and loving relationship with his son.

Professionally, 2004 saw Reynolds at the Cineplex in at least six projects. Reynolds is again bankable, busy and working as much as he pleases, his future again looking bright. In 2005, he shows no signs of slowing down, with his appearance in the remake of his own classic *The Longest Yard*, being no exception.

After an Oscar nomination for his supporting turn in the 1997 movie *Boogie Nights*, the years of blockbuster successes, the Emmy win and comeback after comeback, Reynolds still considers his time spent in Dodge as one of his favorites.

SMOKEY AND THE BANDIT Iconic role from 1977.

BUCK TAYLOR as Newly O'Brien

BUCK TAYLOR

Newly O'Brien 1967-1975, 1987

Born: Walter Clarence Taylor III, May 13, 1938, Hollywood, California

hen you look up the word multitalent in the dictionary, right next to the definition should be a photo of actor, artist, horseman, stuntman, hunter and, most importantly, family man, Buck Taylor.

Touring the country exhibiting his artwork on an average of ten months a year, Taylor has had the pleasure of meeting thousands of *Gunsmoke* fans.

The son of veteran character actor Dub "Cannonball" Taylor, he grew up in Southern California. Born a true Hollywood cowboy, Taylor was literally raised in show business with both the influence of his family and neighbors such as Yakima Canutt, Russ Hayden, Chill Wills and Tex Ritter.

During his high school years, Taylor developed his prowess with a paintbrush, earning him a scholarship to the Chouinard Art Institute in Los Angeles, California.

A gifted athlete, Taylor became a world-class competitor on the horizontal bars and rings, trying out for the U.S. Olympic gymnastics team. After barely missing a position on the team, Taylor concentrated on his education, attending the University of Southern California. With the intention of becoming a professional artist, Taylor

A LIGHTER MOMENT Taylor shares a laugh with James Arness during the filming of A MAN CALLED SMITH, 1969.

studied art, cinema and theatre arts.

After a year of college, Taylor was activated with his Naval Reserve Unit, beginning a two year stint in Japan as a U.S. Navy firefighter. Upon discharge, he turned his attention to a career as a stuntman and actor.

A natural for the then popular television Western genre, he appeared in *The Rebel, Death Valley Days* and *Have Gun–Will Travel*, eventually landing a recurring role on *The Monroes* opposite Ben Johnson.

In 1967, Taylor was cast as a heavy in a two-part episode of *Gunsmoke* entitled *Vengeance!* He made a strong impression on both those in front of and behind the camera, holding his own against guest stars John Ireland and James Stacy.

DEPUTY AND MARSHAL Searching for Miss Kitty, Newly and Matt find her battered coach in a scene from THE LOST, 1971.

Taylor was immediately asked to test for the role of Newly, the latest addition to Dodge City. He would portray the gunsmith and occasional deputy until the show went off the air in 1975. Promoted to Marshal, Taylor would reprise his role in *Gunsmoke: Return to Dodge*, airing in 1987.

A proud father of four, Taylor and his first wife, Judy Nugent, raised daughter Tiffany and sons Adam, Matthew and Cooper Glenn in Montana. With obvious pride for his work on *Gunsmoke*, he named one son after a certain Marshal and another after his good friend and co-star, Glenn Strange.

Divorced, Taylor returned to his artwork in the eighties to great acclaim, balancing his life on film and on canvas. His sons followed in the family bootsteps; Adam behind the camera as first assistant director on *Tombstone*, Cooper with acting and stunts and Matthew, a top stuntman on many projects, including *24* with Kiefer Sutherland.

Taylor has appeared in over forty films for both the big and little screen, including *Gettysburg, The Sacketts, Wild, Wild West* and most memorably, *Tombstone*. He was briefly reunited with his *Gunsmoke* co-stars Ken Curtis

MEN FROM DODGE *Taylor with castmates James Arness, Milburn Stone and Ken Curtis, on the set of THE GUNS OF CIBOLA BLANCA, 1974.*

READY FOR ACTION *Taylor as Newly in the episode THE BULLET from 1971.*

TOMBSTONE *Taylor had a featured role in the popular oater, sharing the big screen with Val Kilmer, Kurt Russell, Michael Rooker and Peter Sherayko. (photo by John Bramley; Cinergi Productions, Inc. and Cinergi Productions N.V.)*

SAM AND NEWLY *Glenn Strange and Taylor were a popular duo on the rodeo circuit. Strange regaled Taylor with stories from his cowboy beginnings.*

and James Arness in *Pony Express Rider* and *Alamo: 13 Days to Glory*, respectively.

Shortly after completing *Tombstone*, Taylor lost his son Adam to a tragic motorcycle accident in 1994. A short time later in the same year, his father Dub passed away. Taylor produced a striking watercolor tribute, *Dad and Me*, featuring himself and his father that inspired Michael Wayne to commission the artist to render a similar tribute to Michael and his father, John Wayne.

Living in Texas and Louisiana, Taylor met his second wife Goldie, a rodeo star, (barrel racer), at one of his popular art exhibits in 1995. Married after a courtship of just three months, he gives Goldie credit for her positive influence on his life citing, "This is the best time of my life."

His artwork ensures that our Western heritage will be remembered forever, prompting favorable comparisons to Russell and Remington.

Taylor's painting often reflects his acting career and has become highly sought after. A series of prints from Tombstone proved extremely popular amongst his fellow cast members and public alike.

His subjects have included the aforementioned John Wayne, as well as Sam Elliott and a few self-portraits. In 2003, Taylor unveiled the print *He Kept the Lid on Dodge*, featuring James Arness as Marshal Dillon, with the release date honoring Arness' eightieth birthday.

Nothing pleases Taylor more than his time spent on *Gunsmoke* and meeting his multitude of fans at various rodeos, fairs and gallery exhibits. His professional

1987 REPRISAL Taylor returned to the role of Newly in the television movie RETURN TO DODGE.

demeanor at these shows began with his upbringing and was further nurtured when he toured the country promoting *Gunsmoke*. "It all stems from the lessons I was taught by Doc and Festus, and my dad too, he was a professional entertainer and a good one. They reconfirmed the fact that you go out and you accommodate everybody. You always have time for everyone. You want an autograph, you got it. You want a photo? Come on, let's take a picture," stated Taylor.

Make it a point to attend one of his appearances and say hello. You'll be treated to a memorable meeting with one of the nicest cowboys around. If that's not possible, be sure to check out Taylor's website at www.bucktaylor.com, you'll be impressed.

GLENN STRANGE

Sam Noonan 1961-1973
Born: George Glenn Strange, August 16, 1899, Carlsbad, New Mexico
Died: September 20, 1973 Burbank, California

Rodeo performer. Boxer. Stunt man. Wrestler. Bit player. Character actor. Butch Cavendish—the villain who made a certain Ranger "Lone." The Frankenstein monster. Six-foot-four Glenn Strange, nicknamed "Peewee" by those closest to him, was all that and much more during a kaleidoscope career that culminated in his favorite role, that of bartender Sam Noonan. His portrayal was the most famous drink pourer until another Sam came along—Ted Danson on *Cheers*.

Born in Carlsbad, New Mexico, he was a true cowboy. While bronc busting in the Texas rodeo circuit, Strange impressed cowboy star Hoot Gibson, who hired "Peewee" to join him in Hollywood and his personal rodeo shows.

Prior to his discovery, Strange began performing at age 12, playing fiddle at several square dances. His deep western drawl led him to radio in 1928, with several cattle drives and heavyweight boxing matches in between.

Gibson ushered Strange into the cinematic world in 1929 as a stunt man. His natural acting flair and rugged looks elevated Strange to supporting player; a heavy that

GLENN STRANGE as Sam Noonan

HEAVY Strange as Butch Cavendish, the outlaw leader of a gang that ambushes a company of Texas Rangers, save for one "lone" survivor in ENTER THE LONE RANGER from THE LONE RANGER TV pilot from 1949.

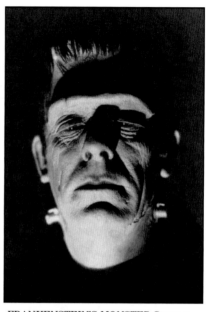

FRANKENSTEIN'S MONSTER Strange played the hapless creature three times for Universal Studios, beginning with HOUSE OF FRANKENSTEIN in 1944.

FRANKENSTEIN MEETS FRANKENSTEIN Strange left the Long Branch long enough to catch up with his monster mentor, Boris Karloff, who was filming an episode of WILD, WILD WEST in 1966.

B-A-A-A-A-D BOYS Strange had a tough time acting monstrous around comedian Lou Costello during the filming of the Universal Studios classic, ABBOTT & COSTELLO MEET FRANKENSTEIN, 1948.

FAMILY PORTRAIT Strange loved his time on GUNSMOKE, stating shortly before his death: "The Lord's been good to me. I've been lucky to have worked with so many grand people in this business."

menaced the likes of Hopalong Cassidy, Gene Autry, Roy Rogers, Tex Ritter, John Wayne and even his mentor, Hoot Gibson.

In 1932 he tested for *Tarzan the Ape Man* losing the title role to Olympian Johnny Weissmuller. Though stardom eluded him, he kept busy well into the forties.

While at Universal Studios in 1944, Strange traded his cowboy boots for a different style of bootwear—those belonging to the Frankenstein monster! He was the fourth actor to breathe life into the studio's popular creature, following Boris Karloff, Lon Chaney, Jr. and Bela Lugosi. Strange portrayed the monster in three films—*House of Frankenstein, House of Dracula* and most memorably in the classic, *Abbott and Costello Meet Frankenstein.*

Even though Glenn had worked once before with comics Bud and Lou in 1947's *The Wistful Widow of Wagon Gap*, nothing prepared him for the wild times ahead while shooting his final *Frankenstein* outing in 1948. One scene has the monster seated in a throne-like chair as Lou Costello's "Wilbur" sits on his lap, unbeknownst he is there. Every time Costello would begin his hilarious "scare-take," Strange would break character time and again. Out-takes exist showing the scary monster laughing like a school kid over and over again.

When television arrived, Strange worked at a breakneck pace, chalking up close to five-hundred performances. On *The Lone Ranger* he played a human monster—the sinister Butch Cavendish, who, with his cutthroat gang, ambush a group of Texas Rangers, killing all with the exception of one survivor, the Lone Ranger.

On March 18, 1961, he first played Sam the bartender on *Gunsmoke* in the episode *Old Faces*. Urged to join the cast on a weekly basis by star/producer James Arness, Strange became a regular when the series kicked into a seventh season in 1962.

During his tenure behind the bar, Strange made many personal appearances around the United States at both rodeos and state fairs—first with Milburn Stone and Ken Curtis, and later with Buck Taylor, playing fiddle as he did at age 12.

Gunsmoke was a personal highlight in the actors crowded resume and he stayed with the show until his death from lung cancer in 1973. He passed away on September 20th at St. Joseph's Hospital in Burbank, California. *Gunsmoke* producer John Mantley delivered the eulogy on September 24th at Strange's funeral at Forest Lawn in Hollywood Hills.

Sorely missed by his Dodge City co-stars and friends, Strange left behind his wife Min and daughter Janine.

IN TOON This comical caricature hung in Strange's home for many years.

CREATORS Producer Norman Macdonnell stands behind his writer and friend John Meston.

THE PRODUCERS

After the abrupt exit of Charles Marquis Warren during the beginning of season two, Norman Macdonnell took over the job that he figured should have been his from the start. At first the stars were uncertain with the regime change, with the exception of Milburn Stone.

Stone did not enjoy the first season working with Warren. He considered quitting almost every day that he was around Warren, and during the first hiatus, Stone did his best to get out of his contract and not have to show up when shooting resumed. Thankfully, the gifted character actor did report for the sophomore season, not knowing that Warren wanted out just as badly as he did. Warren left and Stone was ecstatic.

With Macdonnell in place and John Meston by his side, the show would now begin to hit its stride with the entire cast, the critics and the viewers. As both the ratings and the popularity of the show began to soar, competition seemed to surround the denizens of Dodge City. By 1959 there were close to thirty primetime Westerns on the air. Every week, every night, viewers could pick what location or what hero would deliver their favored brand of Western

UP THROUGH THE RANKS From story consultant to executive producer, John Mantley joined GUNSMOKE in 1964.

entertainment. Choices included Steve McQueen as Josh Randall in *Wanted: Dead or Alive*; Gene Barry as and in *Bat Masterson*; John Russell as Dan Troop in *Lawman*; *Richard Boone* as Paladin in *Have Gun—Will Travel*; even screen veteran Henry Fonda threw his hat into the crowded ring as Simon Fry in *The Deputy*.

Against staggering competition, *Gunsmoke* held its own. Shortly after Macdonnell took over, *Gunsmoke* would reach number eight in the ratings. By 1957 the show hit number one and would remain in that coveted position for the next four seasons, regardless of the programs stacked against it. However, 1959 saw the debut of another Western, one that would become the strongest contender for the *Gunsmoke* crown, *Bonanza* on NBC. People usually cite *Bonanza* or *Gunsmoke* as their favorite Western, rarely liking both with fan camps clearly divided. Writer Paul Savage observed, "You know, speaking of that, I'm astounded when conversation comes around, that *Gunsmoke* and *Bonanza* are synonymous. (laughs) There was never a speck of dirt on anyone on *Bonanza*—they were Technicolor beautiful."

"The stories?" continued Savage, "Three grown men saying 'Yes pa.' A thirty-five year old saying, 'Yes pa, I shouldn't have done that, you were right.' (laughs) And they called it a Western."

By the 1961-62 season, *Bonanza* managed to climb to number two in the ratings, with *Gunsmoke* trailing close behind at number three. By the next season, *Gunsmoke* fell to number 10, then to number 20 by season nine.

When the ratings were number one, the network treated Macdonnell as a golden child, but when they started to slip, like most businesses—especially Hollywood, Macdonnell became the network whipping boy. Ultimately, Macdonnell was fired and never saw it coming. Many theories as to why CBS unceremoniously dumped the producer abound, however, Macdonnell rarely spoke of the situation, therefore shedding no new light on the subject. In a widely circulated story, studio executives felt the show needed a recurring bad guy added to the cast. Actor Jack Palance was the suggested heavy; Macdonnell wanted no part of the suggestion or Palance and he made his opinion loud and clear.

Director Harry Harris was just one of the many *Gunsmoke* personnel infuriated by the network action. Because of the ratings, "The show was about to come to an end," explained Harris, "it was almost cancelled many times. Every year or two they'd say, 'This is the last year,' and then at the last second, they'd get a reprise."

According to Harris, James Arness was unhappy about the periodic cancellation threat, and was eventually approached by the network with an offer. Arness was asked, "Would you like to keep the show on for a couple more years?" Harris added, "I know this for a fact because Jim told me this..."

Arness replied, "Well, yeah."

"Well, they want to put new blood in here."

"What do you mean?"

"Well, we've got Phil Leacock and John Mantley, a

LEONARD KATZMAN He began producing GUNSMOKE in 1970, and went on to produce many other series, including top-rated DALLAS.

story editor. We think if you let us bring these two guys in we can keep the show on for a couple more years."

"What about Norman?"

"Well, that means Norman's got to go."

Harris continued, "...and Jim gnashed his teeth and said, 'Okay.' That's how much he thought about it after all those years. And when that happened I just said, 'Oh Jesus, that's really rotten.' Norm Macdonnell's whole life was that show from day one—radio—all through the half hours, all through the hours. They bounce him out of there for no reason at all. I had to help him carry his things out to his car; they wouldn't let him on the lot."

Director Andrew V. McLaglen stated, "After eight years of *Gunsmoke* being on top, Hunt Stromberg, who was an executive at CBS, decided to relieve Norman of his job—after eight fantastic years! Perhaps Stromberg thought that he was making his own little empire with *Gunsmoke* and he wanted to break it up. He brought in Philip Leacock. Leacock was nice enough as a director but why they made him the producer of *Gunsmoke*— nobody will ever figure that one out."

Macdonnell moved on to other projects, most notably *The Virginian* at Universal, "...which he hated," recalled Harris. "He and his wife split up...he moved into a little one-room apartment and died. That was a tragedy. This was probably one of the most polished gentlemen I've ever met in my life. I have such great respect for him." Harris, who left *Gunsmoke* shortly after this debacle, added, "But, that's the way the business is, what're you

WELCOME John and Angela Mantley in their California home, March 27, 2001. At this point in his life, Mantley looked remarkably similar to a certain Dodge City doctor.

going to do?" McLaglen added, "Norman was the right producer for that show. He was a terrific guy, a terrific producer. John Meston died before he did—when Meston died, that was enough for Norman. I think Norman died of a broken heart in 1979."

With Macdonnell gone, John Meston and writer Kathleen Hite soon followed, of their own accord. Directors McLaglen and Harris joined the exodus a short time thereafter. Phillip Leacock had his hands full when he became producer. He faced resentment from most of the crew, on and off-camera. In a June 1965 *TV Guide* cover story, Stone admitted, "I wouldn't presume to know how to run a network, or be the producer of a show, but I do know the flavor of *Gunsmoke*. You can detect the changes." As for Macdonnell's dismissal, Stone stated, "We were all stunned." As angry as Stone was, Amanda Blake was even angrier—truly hurt by the networks seemingly rash decision.

Writer Paul Savage reflected, "Philip Leacock became the producer. He never said it to me but I do know he was reported to have said, in effect, to someone, "Tell me dear chap, was there truly a town called Dodge City?" This story has been confirmed by many others, including Andrew V. McLaglen and Kathleen Hite.

Savage continued, "I went in with a kind of hesitancy because there's no friggin' way this English director is going to be able to do the character-rich people-driven stories we do on *Gunsmoke*. Well, I got to know Philip as a person—he was a fabulous man." Two films by Leacock made an impression on Savage—*Little Kidnappers* and *Hand in Hand*. When I realized that he could do that with characters, I was happy to sit at the feet of Buddha. Working together...he acceded a lot to me, I felt. He listened when I said, 'You know *Gunsmoke* da da da.' We did a lot of good shows together."

Born in London, England in 1917, Leacock began working with documentary filmmakers straight out of high school. After joining the British Army in 1938, Leacock continued his fascination with celluloid by making training films for the service. Upon discharge, he became a director of mainstream films, eventually relocating to America and working for Columbia Studios in Hollywood. During his tenure on *Gunsmoke*, Leacock welcomed big-name guest stars and instructed the writers to fashion shows around secondary characters instead of constantly focusing on the leads.

Leacock wouldn't be around long enough to implement many changes to the established *Gunsmoke* formula. During his producing tenure, the show dropped out of the top twenty in the ratings altogether. With the premature cancellation in 1967, Leacock became the producer for the new ambitious CBS Western *Cimarron Strip* starring Stuart Whitman. Whitman enjoyed working with Leacock. "He had a great story sense," stated Whitman. "Easy to work with." *Cimarron Strip* was an excellent Western but unfortunately it only lasted one season. Leacock would return to Dodge City occasionally though not as a producer, but as a director.

When *Gunsmoke* rose from the cancellation ashes, Mantley was immediately promoted to producer. His meteoric rise in the ranks began when he joined the show in 1964 as a story consultant, was named associate producer in 1965 and was promoted to producer the following year in 1966. In 1967, Mantley became executive producer, taking the reins from Leacock. Born in Toronto, Canada, in 1920, he grew up in a show business family. Both parents were theatre performers and Mantley was a second cousin to legendary silent film actress Mary Pickford, known as "America's Sweetheart." In fact it was Mantley who delivered the eulogy when Pickford died in 1981.

Mantley graduated from high school in St. Catharine's, Ontario and earned a bachelor's degree at Victoria College of the University of Toronto in 1942. During World War II, he served as a fighter with the Canadian Air Force. After the war, Mantley moved to the States and earned a master's degree in theater arts from the Pasadena Playhouse in 1947. Mantley began his entertainment career as an actor, touring the country in stage productions such as *Summer and Smoke* with Dorothy McGuire and *Elizabeth, the Queen* with Jane Cowl. His last performance was as Cyrano in *Cyrano de Bergerac* at, appropriately enough, the Kansas City Theatre. Actor/director Lou Antonio recalled, "Mantley was a smart, frustrated actor. He had a picture of himself in his office when he played Cyrano—big nose and everything." As a producer, Antonio simply offered, "He was real good at his job."

Frustrated with acting, Mantley turned to directing in 1951, working live television in New York City. He relocated to Rome in 1952, and for the next four years directed television and movies abroad. Returning to the States in 1956, Mantley turned to writing when he was unable to secure employment as a director. During this period of his life, Mantley wrote television scripts for *The Outer Limits*, *The Untouchables* and *Rawhide*, as well as two best-selling novels, *The 27th Day* and *The Snow Birch*. As a producer, he worked on *The Wild, Wild West,* and with Leacock, co-produced the motion picture Western *Firecreek,* which starred James Stewart and Henry Fonda.

Mantley really had an uphill battle taking on *Gunsmoke* in 1967. Practically written off by CBS at this point, Mantley didn't receive much support or encouragement from the network. However, with the time-slot switch from Saturday to Monday night, *Gunsmoke* began to find a younger audience. This, combined with Mantley's edict to emphasize stories with even more guest stars than before, put *Gunsmoke* back in the top ten highest rated programs for the next six seasons. It remained in the top twenty, ranking fifteenth, during season nineteen. After the cancellation in 1975, Mantley would again team up with Arness on *How the West Was Won* for ABC-TV, which began as the miniseries *The Macahans.*

"John Mantley, he really worked that show," recalled actress Beverly Garland. "He was a part of that show, he wasn't an absentee producer at all. It was important to him." Casting director Pam Polifroni offered, "John was a great producer—really excellent producer. Mantley was a real perfectionist, and that was good. He was a story man, first and foremost...always realized that all the great fences and scenery in the world won't sell a show if you don't have a good story and good people. So that, I think, is one of the reasons *Gunsmoke* worked so well all those years." Director Bernard McEveety stated simply, "He was a hell of a producer." Though Mantley and writer Paul Savage did not have the best working relationship, Savage

STAR AND PRODUCER James Arness and John Mantley go over a detail in the current script. The two men remained close friends until Mantley's death in 2003.

admitted, "John did a wonderful job, he deserves a lot of credit for keeping that show on the air for so many years."

Mantley certainly made his share of unpopular decisions while on *Gunsmoke*. Amanda Blake and Mantley did not have the best working relationship; a relationship that worsened with each progressing season. Ken Curtis and Mantley wound up at odds with each other and after a fight over the telephone in the eighties, never spoke to one another again. Actor James Nusser who superbly played the town soak Louie, had asked Mantley for a "pay or play" contract—much like the contracts that Glenn Strange, Milburn Stone and others had—Mantley refused and immediately fired Nusser. Dennis Weaver, who had played Chester for so many years, expressed an interest to do a guest shot on the show, reprising his beloved character. Mantley refused the offer. On the other hand, at his urging, Milburn Stone sought medical help when he first suffered minor chest pains. "I sent him to get his heart fixed—there was some resistance—but it saved his life," stated a teary-eyed Mantley. "He thanked me."

Mantley died at the age of 82 on January 14, 2003, at his home in Sherman Oaks, California. He had suffered from Alzheimer's disease for many years. Series star James Arness, interviewed by *Los Angeles Times* Staff Writer Dennis McLellan at the time of Mantley's death, stated, "The ratings were sliding a bit, and they wanted to get some new blood on the show. They luckily were able to get John, and he came and just completely revived the show." Arness continued, "John ran that show and made it work better than it ever had before. He was a guy who was just completely dedicated to doing the best possible job that could be done on the show...he lived for the show, and he had the desire for excellence."

What Meston and Macdonnell created, Warren, Leacock and Mantley embellished, becoming a transgenerational phenomenon. *Gunsmoke* has secured a permanent space in the pop culture psyche worldwide. "The audience, they vicariously lived the best part of themselves through the series," offered actress Laurie Prange. "It was an era of our history that people yearn for a little bit now. There's not a lot of nobility, and that series showed nobility, honor, character and integrity. It reflected the best in ourselves. In these crazy, crazy times, there is such a fondness for *Gunsmoke*—the best of America."

WRITER-TURNED-DIRECTOR *The legendary Sam Peckinpah, on the movie set for his classic* THE WILD BUNCH, *began his career as a writer, most notably for* GUNSMOKE.

THE WRITERS

An idea for a show can come to anyone. Bringing it to life however, takes just a little more talent. Sustaining that life, takes a miracle. Those who put pen to paper, strike the correct keys or process the right words are the true miracle workers of the entertainment world.

From inception, *Gunsmoke* corralled the best writers the business had to offer. John Meston and Norman Macdonnell attracted many powerful scribes to *Gunsmoke*, even before the series debuted on television in 1955.

In a 2001 interview in *Trail Dust* magazine, James Arness stated, "All of our early TV episodes were lifted from John Meston's radio scripts and they were really great, unique character studies. As far as I know no other TV Western series at that time had an equivalent to that. We certainly were in a special category. John's radio stories were all so good they just picked out the best ones for the first few seasons we were on television."

During season one, many of the radio scripts penned by Meston were fine tuned by director-producer Charles Marquis Warren, much to the displeasure of both Meston and Macdonnell. With Warren's abrupt and unexpected

WRITER'S DIGEST *Kathleen Hite and James Arness made the cover in 1963.*

SET VISIT Writer Paul Savage visits on location with James Arness. (photo courtesy of Paul Savage)

been buried in a respectable cemetery. My name's Dillon, I'm a lawman, United States Marshal out of Dodge City—over there. It's a town that has more than it's share of riff-raff. But there are plenty of good citizens too. Yet I keep remembering, on any given day something can happen that turns good men bad, for that one day. That's when I'm called in—that's when it's tough."

Arness was always fond of the cemetery set-ups, recalling, "What a great opener they were, depicting what a tough, unpleasant job the Marshal had. And these openings were taken from the radio program. Then they decided not to use the Boot Hill footage anymore, which I thought was a mistake." Radio and film icon Orson Welles was a huge (no pun intended) *Gunsmoke* fan, citing the writing style of Meston for both mediums, radio and television, as excellent. In the first couple of seasons, very few scripts were challenged by production members or the cast, with Arness explaining, "...because we had those great stories from John Meston. There really wasn't much to dispute about those scripts."

Many radio writers made the transition to television, Kathleen Hite being no exception. Hite was a true pioneer for television writers in many areas. She was one of TV's first successful female writers and, along with Margaret Armen, made a lasting mark on Westerns, Hite on *Gunsmoke* and Armen on *The Rifleman*. In the fifties, television and especially Western writing, was a predominantly male-oriented profession.

First employed at CBS, though not as a writer, Hite,

exit, Meston and Macdonnell took over the reins of producing and writing shortly after season two began.

Many episodes from the first few seasons opened with Marshal Dillon wandering around Boot Hill, pondering, staring at the many graves scattered about—graves that may or may not have found occupants due to the towering lawman. A good example of the opening monologue occurred in the episode *Hot Spell*, which first aired on September 17, 1955:

MATT: Sometimes I wonder if there's some good men planted here on Boot Hill. On a given day, any man can be a bad man—with enough anger inside of him, he can be a killer. Take that one day out of his life and he'd

in a February 1963 interview in *Writer's Digest*, reminisced, "CBS had a rule—no women staff writers. I got a job as a secretary, so I could be on the inside. Finally, when there was an opening in the writing department, I managed to break their rule and get the job." As a staff writer, Hite worked with Meston and John Dunkel, another *Gunsmoke* contributor, and wrote everything from audience participation bits to station break cues. Again from 1963, Hite continued, "This present association with *Gunsmoke* is one I like very much."

Hite wrote an average of twelve scripts a year during her tenure in Dodge. "One a month is enough," offered Hite. "I find it takes the better part of a month from the idea through the story line to the finished screenplay." She worked with Meston and Macdonnell on the radio show and remarked, "I have great respect and affection for them. I don't know any show which puts so much stress on characterization—which is, after all, the most important thing. There are no gimmicks in *Gunsmoke*; the stories aren't plotty or contrived."

A vivid storyteller, Hite would supply the show with memorable, defining dialogue. A wonderful example occurs in the 1963 episode, *The Cousin*, when the character Moran describes Dodge City and a certain resident:

BAKER'S DOZEN *Charles Joseph Stone, brother of Milburn, visits the set in 1967. Amanda Blake, James Arness and Ken Curtis join in the fun.*

MORAN: "It's about, uh, five saloons and a livery stable—surrounded by the biggest Marshal you ever saw."

Hite stayed with the show for seven years, leaving only after Meston and Macdonnell's controversial departure. After a long illness, Hite died on February 18, 1989.

Legendary writer-director and, because of the way he cut scenes together, choreographer, Sam Peckinpah, honed his writing skills on *Gunsmoke* and later on *The Rifleman*. Before directing such classics as *Ride the High*

Country, The Wild Bunch and *The Getaway*, to name a few, Peckinpah penned some fascinating, shady character studies for *Gunsmoke*. He provided actresses Cloris Leachman and June Lockhart memorable, quirky roles in the episodes *Legal Revenge* and *Dirt*, respectively, and did the same for actors Keye Luke in *The Queue* and Strother Martin in *Cooter*. His writing on *The Guitar* stands up today as one of the best half hour segments ever written for television, providing super-producer then struggling-actor Aaron Spelling a superb role in a gem of a story with a dark, twisted ending. All of his scripts for *Gunsmoke* began as radio tales by John Meston, with Peckinpah putting his personal stamp on the stories and characters.

Peckinpah was paid nine-hundred dollars per script, and over the first three seasons, turned in ten episodes. He disliked the task of writing and never typed, scribbling on pads of lined paper or the backs of discarded letters. He would then employ various typists to decipher his jots before turning in his work to the producers.

Originally, Peckinpah would spend day after agonizing day working on the stories, at times taking two weeks to three months to complete a first draft. After his fifth or sixth assignment, his writing style streamlined.

In the 1994 biography *If They Move...Kill 'Em!* by David Weddle, Peckinpah remembered his time on *Gunsmoke*, "It was hell, because I hate writing. I suffer the tortures of the damned. I can't sleep and it feels like I'm going to die any minute. Eventually, I lock myself away somewhere out of reach of a gun and get it on in one big

HAPPY COUPLE Paul Savage and his wife Laurie in 2001.

push...I'd never realized what a lot of goddamn anguish is involved. By the end I was able to knock one out in about eight hours. Eight hours, that is, after twenty straight hours of lying awake getting my ideas together." Peckinpah's self-destructing ways began early, and he also faced the first of many battles with censors that became commonplace during his directorial days. Nicknamed "Bloody Sam," Peckinpah decided on a directing career while working those three seasons on *Gunsmoke*.

Many TV series receive harsh criticism for storylines that slant to viewer dictates and fan preferences, with said segments rarely making sense, and more often than not, resulting in the slow demise of the program itself.

Main characters often receive the silly storybook ending; that "happy wrap up" that real life rarely deals. Some fans would have loved to see Matt and Kitty marry, for example, a situation that almost all involved protested, especially the writers. They were able to convey a union that the viewer never really witnessed physically, or did they?

Clever hints were everywhere, and combining the talented writing, directing and acting the show offered, viewers were kept guessing, without an answer, to this day. Writer Paul Savage offered, "They never, ever, ever, played it, except in those oblique moments...Matt would

WRITER'S DREAM Ken Curtis and Milburn Stone in one of their classic verbal spats that enhanced many GUNSMOKE segments.

come into the saloon and Kitty would say, 'I've got a nice bottle of brandy upstairs in my room, cowboy.' Matt would reply, 'That sounds interesting." Perhaps this is a big reason the show went on for twenty seasons...it was never presented in an "in your face—nothing left to the imagination" style.

A few of the writers were also hired as story consultants, including Paul Savage, Calvin Clements, Jim Byrnes and Jack Miller. Many of the final shooting scripts were partially, sometimes completely, rewritten by the consultants, with the credit staying with the original writer. A perfect example is a story submitted by Charles Joseph Stone, brother to Milburn. The script, *Baker's Dozen*, was originally written for Dennis Weaver/Chester, and bounced around the production offices for many years, much to the dismay of the Stone brothers. Producer John Mantley finally gave the script to Savage with the edict to "make it work." With a little retooling, Savage turned in a final product that was shot quickly in five days and became highly successful, winning Milburn an Emmy for his performance in this segment. "That to me is a memorable episode...that's just one out of twenty years," recalled Savage. "You stand in awe when you think of the numbers of the ones that were that good."

Savage began his career on the radio version of *Gunsmoke*, not as a writer but as an actor. Macdonnell took a liking to the young man, and when Savage gave up acting for a career in writing, some of the first scripts he sold were to Macdonnell.

2001 REUNION Writer Jim Byrnes, right, with series stars Buck Taylor and James Arness in a rare public gathering. (photo courtesy of Mary Jo Barlow)

The work could be tough, but most always, rewarding and never formulaic. "*The Moonstone* all but wrote itself," remembered Savage of his 1966 episode. "It was atypical when you think of it. Atypical meaning not your usual *Gunsmoke*; it wasn't just the *Gunsmoke* people who were involved. That's the wonderful thing of that kind of show...you could do stories where our regular cast was peripheral. They were involved and that was the difficult thing to do, make their involvement legitimate and honest and involving for the audience."

Another classic Savage script is *The Long Night* starring Bruce Dern from 1969. It features a wonderful scene and performance by James Nusser as drunken Louie. "I've got to tell you, that moment came from the old Edward G.

Robinson movie with Claire Trevor...*Key Largo*," confessed Savage. Gangster Robinson forces Trevor to sing for a drink; outlaw Bruce Dern tries to force Nusser into begging for a drink..."We milked the hell out of it," remarked Savage of this memorable moment. Guest star Lou Antonio recalled the performance by Nusser, "Wasn't he heartbreaking?" Indeed, a standout performance in a standout episode. "That's a bottle show, do you know what a bottle show is?" asked Savage.

"In the beginning of a season you spend a lot of money on production values and as the season went on, more and more was spent," explained Savage. He continued, "Toward the end of the season the bucks were a little shorter so Mantley would say, 'We need a bottle show.' That's where it is contained; *The Long Night* was all in the Long Branch waiting for Matt to return. That's wonderful for camera and the rest of it, because the crew knew that set so well they could almost do it blindfolded. That's the genesis of *The Long Night*—give us a show we can do in five days or shorter."

Both Savage and his wife Laurie cite *Owney Tupper Had a Daughter* as their personal favorite *Gunsmoke* episode. Laurie persuaded her husband to submit his script to the Writer's Guild for their annual awards show. Much to their surprise and delight, Savage received a nomination for best script...sharing the spotlight with two other projects from a field of hundreds of scripts that were submitted that year.

As written, Marshal Dillon was a hero, but not one of heroic proportions. At times he would risk everything he had, including his life, to protect both friends and strangers alike. However, he was not a squeaky clean badge, as witnessed in the 1957 episode *Never Pester Chester* and in *Hostage!* airing in 1972, for example. Dillon upheld the law, though not always to the letter, and did his job to the best of his quick-thinking abilities. His responsibility, both to a town and a code of honor, were put to the test at moments of great stress, and viewers watched week after week to see how the marshal would react to these tense situations. This hook began with the written word and remains a testament to the talent that the *Gunsmoke* writers possessed.

Writing for stars with established characters can be a nightmare; some long established favorites have been known to count the amount of words they had in each script or would count the number of pages before their first entrance. This was never the case on *Gunsmoke*. Through the years as the cast roster changed, attitudes did not. Each performer knew their characters inside and out and with this knowledge came the instinct of what dialogue would or would not fit their characters. Arness would give away some of his dialogue to Festus or Newly; Stone would often say, "Doc would never say this to Kitty." Savage reinforced, "And by God he was right! Kenny would say, 'This is a Doc scene, Doc should have that line, not Festus.' It was never on a personal level, it was always concern for the character." Concern for the character that made the final product better, and ultimately, the entire twenty seasons.

Curtis and Stone would often see a section in a script, a "germ of an idea" as the writers referred to them, that would offer a hint of their characters latest verbal spat. The actors would confer and work out the scene together, developing these argumentative classics as Festus and Doc, rivaling the best verbal routines of the Marx Brothers and Abbott and Costello. A superb example happened in a script and "germ" by Ron Bishop, blending Curtis' flair for comedy and Stone's vaudeville and burlesque training; from 1973...

FESTUS: Whew, she's hotter than a jug full of red ants, ain't she?

DOC: No.

FESTUS: No?

DOC: No, I won't buy you a beer.

FESTUS: Well if that ain't the downrightest, orneriest thing I've ever...I didn't ask you -

DOC: I...no, I knew you were going to though, I knew exactly—

FESTUS: I wasn't gonna do no such thing—fact is, I was fixin' to offer to buy you a beer...

DOC: Oh certainly you were, of course you were, your pockets are always just bulging with money.

FESTUS: All right Mister Smart Aleck, what's that look like to you right there? (holds up silver dollar)

DOC: Now where'd you get that?

FESTUS: I been a' workin'.

DOC: Well now I asked you a simple question, there's no need for you to lie to me Festus!

FESTUS: I ain't storyin' to you now! I went to work and put new shoes on six of ol' man Scroggins horses and he gave me that dollar.

DOC: And now you're just gonna run out and squander it on something foolish! Why don't you take that money and invest it in something...why don't you do that?

FESTUS: Invest it in what?

DOC: There's wonderful land values outside of Dodge, now why don't you go out there, someplace, look around, and buy yourself a lot?

FESTUS: A lot of what?

DOC: A lot! A lot of land!

FESTUS: Well fiddle, I can't afford to buy a lot of land— you probably could the way you been a bilkin' and gougin' folks here in Dodge with—

DOC: Oh hush up! I'm trying to help you for heaven's sakes! It don't cost a whole lot to buy a little lot.

FESTUS: What do you mean it don't cost a whole lot to buy a little or a whole lot to buy a lot, what do you mean?

DOC: Well, I mean, a little lot of land!

FESTUS: But there ain't no such a thing— a little's a little and a lot's a lot—there ain't no little lot or lot a little, don't ya see? Now, you want that beer or don't ya?

DOC: No, I-I'm all worn out! (he leaves)

FESTUS: If you change your mind, me and Newly'll be over at the Long Branch having a whole lot of little beers—phew—I'm buyin'!

No, that was not from *Abbott and Costello Meet Gunsmoke*; it occurred in the opening moments of the episode *Whelan's Men*. "Those are wonderful moments they used to have, those two guys going at each other. Fun to watch," offered Jim Byrnes.

Byrnes joined the show in 1968 and is perhaps the most successful Western screenwriter working today. While in writing class, Byrnes wrote a spec script for *Gunsmoke*, a show he had enjoyed watching for years. Through an agent, his spec made it to the desk of then story consultant, Paul Savage. "John Mantley took a couple of scripts and Paul told me that about an hour later, John walked into his office, tossed my script on his desk

A BYRNES SCRIPT Miriam Colon and Arness in a scene from CHARLIE NOON. (photo courtesy of Jim Byrnes)

<u>TEASER</u>

FADE IN:

1. EXT. DESERT - DAY   1.

    ANGLE ON the skull and sunbleached bones of a steer.
    HOLD, then PAN UP to reveal MATT and his prisoner,
    CHARLIE NOON. They study the remains, then the long,
    dry stretch ahead of them. Evidenced by their looks,
    they've ridden a long way...unshaven, dusty. Their
    hats are pulled down tight, faces pinched against the
    glare of sun. Noon is about 40, dispassionate, calm...
    but dangerous. We see manacles around his wrists as
    he lifts his hat slightly and squints up at the sun.

                    NOON
            Long way between here and
            Dodge City, Kansas...
                (pointed)
            Canteens're dryer'n that
            critter's bones.
                (indicates)
            Take a good look, lawman...
            'cause you'll be joinin' him.

    Matt ignores the outlaw as his eyes trace the
    desolate terrain.

                    MATT
            You aren't thirsty, huh?

                    NOON
            Yeah...but just for tequila.
            I'll be drinking it back in
            Mexico while the buzzards're
            pickin' you clean.

    However, Noon's remarks fail to dent Matt as he
    motions the outlaw to move out, and they do.

2. NEW ANGLE   2

    FOLLOW as they ride toward a rocky ridge, then Matt
    abruptly reins to a halt. He listens, ears
    straining. In the distance we can barely hear the
    movement of horses. Noon quickly picks it up. Matt
    pulls off his hat and holds it up to block out the
    sun. Noon follows his gaze.

CHARLIE NOON A page from the script by Jim Byrnes, 1969.

and said, 'Now there's a writer.' So they called me and asked me if I wanted to do a *Gunsmoke*," Byrnes recalled.

Jumping at their offer, Byrnes pitched several ideas to Mantley and Savage, striking out initially. This would continue until Byrnes came up with a storyline he was certain had never played on *Gunsmoke* before. Not wanting to face his rejectors again, he snuck his outline into Mantley's office. "I waited until they all went to lunch. The guard knew me, the loser walking in and out," Byrnes laughed. "I dropped the outline on Mantley's desk...three hours later he calls me, 'Got your story, love it, we'd like you to write it.' The original title was *Renegade Wolf*—when it came out it was called *Lobo*," Byrnes stated. Morgan Woodward starred in the episode and it remains one of his favorite episodes, "*Lobo*—I remember that very well, that was a good show," stated the actor.

By the time Jack Miller was story consultant, Byrnes was writing every other episode, earning the reputation of "trek" writer. "Mantley used to call me the best trek writer he'd ever met. 'Anytime we need a trek story, get Byrnes.' So I wrote shows where people were out in the middle of nowhere, starving to death or dying of thirst," laughed Byrnes. Every so often, the production went on location for shooting...Grants Pass, Oregon; Kanab, Utah; Lancaster, California, etc. Some fans objected to this, but the fact of the matter remains that had the show stayed in Dodge only, the storylines would have certainly become monotonous and repetitive. The "trek" stories that Byrnes supplied were some of the best episodes aired.

A two-parter that starred Strother Martin, was filmed near Lake Powell, Arizona. Byrnes remembered, "When I was writing *Island in the Desert*, they flew me to Lake Powell and said they were going to expand the episode to two hours. So I finished the script there on location. It was hot, one-hundred and thirty degrees. I felt sorry for the actors—I'd visit the set and get to the shade as quick as I could!" UCLA held a seminar in the late seventies honoring Westerns, including appearances by many actors, Strother Martin among them. "They asked the actors what their best Westerns were, etc. When it came to Strother everyone thought he'd say *The Wild Bunch*...he said *Island in the Desert* was the best he'd ever done," recalled a proud Byrnes.

Classic Byrnes episodes include *Charlie Noon*, *The Busters*, *Gold Train: The Bullet* and *Thirty a Month and Found*. Mantley felt that *Thirty a Month and Found* was the "best *Gunsmoke* ever." Byrnes and the episode won many awards, including a Writer's Guild Award. "We were nominated before, but never won. This was the only time *Gunsmoke* ever won a Writer's Guild Award," stated Byrnes. "It won a bunch of stuff." The writing, look and feel of the episode seems a precursor of the style that *Lonesome Dove* would achieve many years later. Highlights of Byrnes' post-*Gunsmoke* work include *The Sacketts* and *How the West Was Won*. He also penned the first reunion film, *Gunsmoke: Return to Dodge* and was the supervising producer on the third installment, *Gunsmoke: To the Last Man*.

MAKING A POINT As for the success of GUNSMOKE, series star James Arness stated: "It began with quality material, stories and characters that the writers created."

With all his success, Byrnes fondly credits his time on *Gunsmoke* as, "The best learning process I ever had. I learned more than any writing class just spending six weeks as story editor. I learned so much—that's where I became a writer. I learned so much from Mantley...an experience that will never be matched. I don't think anything I'll write will match that experience again."

"The situation that show was in when I joined it—independent, no interference, we did what we wanted to do. When you wanted to get a show approved you'd call John, he'd say okay and that was it. It will never happen again...a great, great experience and it's too bad it will never be duplicated," Byrnes concluded.

Beginning in 1970, the Western Writers of America awarded *Gunsmoke* their coveted Spur Award every year until the show went off the air in 1975. The winners were...

1970 – *Chato* by Paul Edwards

1971 – *Lynott* by Ron Bishop

1972 – *Bohannon* by William Kelley

1973 – *The Deadly Innocent* by Calvin Clements

1974 – *Thirty a Month and Found* by Jim Byrnes

1975 – *The Busters* by Jim Byrnes

"All of the writers were exceptional," stated producer John Mantley. "Jack Miller—terrific writer. Jim Byrnes, of course—he has a real knowledge and love of the West. Ron Bishop—he was really a powerful person. He was such a wonderful writer—an enormous appetite for life. Probably the best writer we had."

Ron Bishop contributed some of the best character studies *Gunsmoke* had to offer. He joined the show in 1967 and brought to life some of the most memorable roles the series was famous for. His bad guys weren't just the textbook variety appearing on television at the time, they were loathsome, psychotic scumbags...deadly, yet at times charismatic. Actor Victor French benefited several times from the pages that came out of Bishop's mind, most notably in *Waco*, *Trafton* and *Matt's Love Story*.

As the ruthless Trafton, French portrays a sick, twisted murderer in Bishop's gripping narrative of good versus evil. *Matt's Love Story* is a good example of how Bishop would give every character and every line unimprovable detail. Arness and guest star Michael Learned have wonderful scenes between them, but it is the rambling weaving of French's character, Lester "Favorite" Dean, that binds the story together. For example, after trying to kill Dillon, Favorite winds up staying at the ranch where the marshal, suffering from amnesia, is recuperating, and says to himself..."Never thought I'd be taking bait under a roof tonight. No sir, not after that pass up yonder with the wind howling like lost souls hunting for graves..." A sequel to this episode became the basis for the second reunion movie, *Gunsmoke: The Last Apache*; Mantley dedicated the film to, among others, "Writer Emeritus" Ron Bishop.

One character created by Bishop ranks as the number-one villain ever to walk the wooden floor of the Long Branch—Will Mannon, superbly portrayed by Steve

Forrest. As written, Mannon is the personification of evil, dressed in black fittingly, though never caricatured. When Mannon makes his intention of killing Marshal Dillon clear, he states, "I'm gonna walk across Matt Dillon like you walk across short grass." Brief, to the point, yet it conjures quite a vivid image.

Another writer who doubled as story consultant, Paul F. Edwards, truly enjoyed his employment on *Gunsmoke* and felt the experience to be a quality one, never to be equaled on another project. Borrowing elements from the 1969 Gregory Peck film *The Stalking Moon*, he provided guest star Ricardo Montalban a wonderful role in and as *Chato*. A taut hunter/hunted chase story, it stands as a tribute to Native Americans...message delivered, never demeaning. His best *Gunsmoke* hour has to be *Hostage!* in 1972. His treatment centers around the villainous Bonner brothers and at the same time provided strong roles for Festus, Matt, Doc, Newly and, most notably, Kitty. One of the most brutal, heart-wrenching episodes television audiences have ever witnessed, *Hostage!* also provided actor William Smith with a career-defining role—Jude Bonner.

Prior to his work on *Gunsmoke*, Edwards was a photographer and journalist covering the war in Vietnam. When he returned to the States, he decided to try his hand at screenwriting.

As for the continued success and appeal of the show, Arness, as reported in *Trail Dust* magazine, offered, "*Gunsmoke* was a one-of-a-kind series. It began with quality material, stories and characters that the writers created. That's hard to do. Most Westerns at that time were action stories. *Gunsmoke* delivered much more into the characters. Then the public became absorbed in the stories we were telling. Matt Dillon's character and the stories represented qualities that are now harder to find." For the most part, CBS and the producers relied on a core group of scribes for the oater. "...they didn't change over to new writers all the time and I think that had a lot to do with the quality of the show," stated Arness.

With various backgrounds, upbringing and education, the writers on *Gunsmoke* were a mixed bunch, offering different styles and approaches via their storytelling. This eclectic mix guaranteed a show that refused to be marginalized as a mere Western. The writers the show employed invented and re-invented characters that allowed *Gunsmoke* to bestride several decades, shattering the rules of television longevity. Together, their creative vision painted vivid pictures for the small screen, pictures rarely equaled in the history of the medium. There are several reasons *Gunsmoke* made an everlasting impact on American culture; one reason began when, and was reinforced, almost every time the writer's typewriter keys struck a piece of twenty pound bond.

Actor Ben Cooper perhaps summed it up best, "Many of the shows are writing down to the audience today. *Gunsmoke* seemed to write for people that were willing to think."

FILMING CARA James Arness and guest star Jorja Cartwright take direction from Robert Stevenson.

GUNSMOKE-THE DIRECTORS

The freshman season of *Gunsmoke* presented a staggering thirty-nine episodes. Even more staggering, in addition to writing and producing, Charles Marquis Warren directed twenty-six of them. Harry Horner directed one, Robert Stevenson and Ted Post, six each. Post has an impressive list of television credits, ranging from *Wagon Train* to *Cagney and Lacey*, in addition to over fifty *Gunsmoke* credits.

"I hold the record for most episodes directed...ninety-five," stated a proud Andrew V. McLaglen. "It's quite an experience to be part of a show that is as well known as *Gunsmoke*."

Born in London, England in 1920, the son of Academy Award winning actor Victor McLaglen, he began his career in 1944, playing an uncredited role in the film *Since You Went Away*. Preferring work behind the camera, which he began in 1948, McLaglen worked on a multitude of projects, including assistant director on *The Quiet Man* for John Ford, and two projects that featured a young James Arness, *Big Jim McClain* and *Hondo*, where he functioned as assistant director and unit production manager, respectively.

SMOKE BREAK *James Arness and director Andrew V. McLaglen take a break during some location filming.*

"I had worked with Jim Arness in 1951 or 1952. He had one year of *Gunsmoke* in 1956 and during his hiatus, I went to United Artists and in five minutes sold them on

THE CHARACTERS WERE VERY TRUE TO LIFE. THEY STRUCK A CHORD WITH THE COMMON MAN.

DIRECTOR HARRY HARRIS, JR. (photo courtesy of Harry Harris, Jr.)

a nice small western with the star of *Gunsmoke* called *Gun the Man Down*. We made the movie, Jim went back to *Gunsmoke* and in the course of time he said to CBS,

'Hey, why don't you have Andrew come and do a couple of episodes. You know, I've worked with him and he might be good,'" recalled McLaglen. "They signed me up for two, and ninety-five *Gunsmoke*'s later..."

McLaglen also directed many episodes of *Have Gun—Will Travel*. "During those days *Gunsmoke* and *Have Gun—Will Travel* were alternating as the number one shows, literally, in the Nielsens." The accomplished director credits many factors for the record- breaking run *Gunsmoke* would set. "John Meston and Norman Macdonnell were the genesis of the whole thing and, very briefly, Charles Marquis Warren. It was just a very homey, warm type of a Western without being necessarily blood and guts."

"I can't say enough about my pal Andy McLaglen," gushed actress Angie Dickinson. "They were smart to do a lot with him. You get in a groove, there is a camaraderie there of character and of person that falls into place and helps the show so much." Dickinson turned in a moving performance in the groundbreaking episode from 1957, *Sins of the Father*. "What I loved, of course," continued Dickinson, "in the part of Andy's direction was the ease of it all. In a half-hour or less not counting commercials, they told so much, so innocently and smoothly. Maybe that was the key to its great success. It was simple and very human. They cared and it showed."

On the subject of McLaglen, actress Suzanne Lloyd gushed, "I adored him! He was wonderful, I can't praise him enough. He knew what he was doing." Frequent *Gunsmoke* guest star Wright King added, "He was a doll. Andy is a great big man, easygoing guy with a wonderful humor about him. You didn't feel rushed or any kind of pressure with him." That wonderful humor was appreciated by actor Robert Donner. "Andy had a penchant for stepping on your toes," recalled the actor. "He used to love to walk over, face you straight on, of course at his height, he's looking right over your head. He'd be standing on your toes. His nickname for me was Hank, 'Where the hell is Hank?!' and of course he's standing on my feet. We had good times."

McLaglen directed his final episode in 1964, which aired in 1965. He went on to a successful career in feature films directing, among others, John Wayne in many classic films including *McClintock*. Assessing McLaglen, actress Karen Sharpe observed, "A solid base. You felt secure when you worked with him." High praise from the actress who was married to producer-director Stanley Kramer.

Harry Harris, Jr. joined the show in late 1960 during the final season of the half hour episodes. As Harris explained, "I started on *Wanted: Dead or Alive*, the Steve McQueen show, and I went on to *Gunsmoke*." When *Gunsmoke* began season seven, the episodes were now an hour in length. It was this transition that prompted Harris to state, "That was the best experience...the people

ON LOCATION *Harry Harris, Jr. on location recently, said of his* GUNSMOKE *years: "That was the best experience..." (photo courtesy of Harry Harris, Jr.)*

that were associated with the show at that time were probably the best of what was around at that time in television. John Meston was in Europe and every week you'd get a script from somewhere. Meston's wife was a lady bullfighter and he followed her all over, particularly in Spain. Norman Macdonnell was probably the nicest

95

human being I ever met in my life and the two of them, Norm and John, had a close bond. John was really the father of that show."

For his take on the popularity of the oater, Harris offered, "It was an anthology of the West...a little town in Kansas where all these people passed through. They went into such depth of character—it wasn't just people shooting people in the streets. They had every kind of problem that people had in those days—sickness, poverty, greed or criminals—attached to this little town. Jim Arness was the epitome of the law, this six-foot-seven guy upholding the law. Doc, this homemade guy, a Doctor. Amanda, the woman in the bar, who did or didn't have anything to do with Matt, who the hell knows? Dennis was a hayseed who was smart and the sidekick. They were all characters that people attached to."

Harris directed actor Michael Forest in two memorable *Gunsmoke* segments, *The Cousin* and *Innocence*. Forest, reflecting on his work with the director, opined, "Harry Harris. Terrific, easygoing guy. Knew what to do and how to get it done with very little effort. Left you to improvise within the scene...nice guy to work with."

Harris truly enjoyed his time on *Gunsmoke* and the creative license he was given by Meston and Macdonnell. He left the show only after the Meston/Macdonnell—Leacock/Mantley shakeup.

In addition to *Gunsmoke* and the aforementioned *Wanted: Dead or Alive*, Harris also directed episodes of *Rawhide* and, for eight years, *In the Heat of the Night*. He

STILL DIRECTING TODAY Mark Rydell has directed some of Hollywood's heaviest hitters throughout his career, ever grateful for his beginnings on GUNSMOKE.

continues his craft today on *7th Heaven*. Another assessment from Karen Sharpe: "I worked with Harry Harris on *Dry Well*—I liked working with him. I'm one of these that likes to bring my own props, so I knew exactly what I

CREATIVE VISION Director Vincent McEveety and executive producer John Mantley confer on location during the CHARLIE NOON shoot in 1969. Future Academy Award winning director Ron Howard played a key role in the segment. (photo courtesy of John and Angela Mantley)

TAKE FIVE Director Vincent McEveety and series star James Arness chat between set ups on location.

picture roster began on television with an episode of *Ben Casey* and then blossomed on *Gunsmoke*.

"I grew up a New York Jew... I brought a Jewish mentality to *Gunsmoke*," laughed Rydell. He was one of the first directors hired by Philip Leacock. "I'm eternally grateful to Philip Leacock and John Mantley for having the prescience to realize that I was a guy who could come and direct *Gunsmoke*. I always watched it, but like any boy from the Bronx, I was watching it as a fantasy. The closest I had ever been to a horse was to a theatre cop in New York City...I had to learn everything."

Rydell truly enjoyed his stint in Dodge City. "Everybody loved working on *Gunsmoke*. The atmosphere was fabulous and much of that had to do with Leacock and Mantley. And Arness made every show, I don't know how he did it after all those years, he came every day with enthusiasm and an attitude—never bored. He loved the character."

"Amanda Blake. Charming, gracious and a friendly woman. Milburn Stone was interesting too...crotchety and difficult, but a wonderful, wonderful old character...much like the character he played. There was a lot of talent

wanted to do; he never told me anything, he just loved everything I did, so I could do anything I damn well pleased! (laughs) Harry and I got along really, really well."

John Wayne in *The Cowboys*. Steve McQueen in *The Reivers*. Bette Midler in *The Rose* and *For the Boys*. Katherine Hepburn and Fonda's Henry and Jane in *On Golden Pond*. Impressive actors in equally impressive films...all directed by Mark Rydell. This A-list motion

involved in making those shows. The sense of family was very strong and once you were accepted, as I became, you worked all the time," Rydell continued.

Echoing sentiments of his peers, Rydell stated, "*Gunsmoke* had a primitive kind of set-up. A heroic marshal of a small town, his close friends Festus, Doc, Kitty...fundamental characters...icons of the legendary West. They were good, they had a nobility, honor and the ethical position taken by Matt Dillon. The heroes and the villains...a realistic comic strip in a way."

Actress Lane Bradbury worked with Rydell in 1965 on the episode *Outlaw's Woman* and stated, "He had worked with me and seen my work at Actor's Studio in New York. I read for him and got the part. He was wonderful...encouraging...knowing when to help. A good director knows when to stay out of the way...you're doing your work and just let you do it. He was terrific to work with." Continuing his praises, actress France Nuyen added, "Mark was a treasure. He was a director who understood what was happening inside the actors and he understood the complexity of emotion, the depths that any performers need even if it is for a five-minute period. You need that understanding and you don't have that anymore. I was lucky to be working with the best."

"I've had a very, very fortunate career. I've worked with stars who will be remembered forever. I did many, many *Gunsmokes* and learned my craft on the show," Rydell reflected.

Director Robert Butler entered the dusty *Gunsmoke* soundstage on only three occasions, capturing lightning in a bottle each time. Helming three of the series standout episodes, including *Prairie Wolfer* in 1967, Butler had the

DIRECTOR AND ACTOR Gunnar Hellstrom, pictured here with Milburn Stone in the episode DEAD MAN'S LAW, was comfortable both behind and in front of the cameras.

opportunity to showcase two up and coming megastars, Jon Voight and Harrison Ford, in early television roles. Established stars Steve Forrest and Alex Cord starred in *Mannon* and *The Sodbusters*, respectively, and under the gentle guidance of Butler, turned in career highlight performances. "He left me pretty much alone but was very supportive, that's what I remember," recalled Alex Cord. "After every take he would come up and say something nice, even if it was just a word, a wink or a pat on your shoulder, whatever. That goes such a long way towards making you feel confident about what you're doing. A real nice work experience."

With a combined total of 100 *Gunsmoke* credits, brothers McEveety, Vincent and Bernard directed some of the best episodes during the program's final decade. Vincent related, "I'm so proud to have been a part of it. Every one of those shows that I had anything to do with taught me something about myself." Of the brothers, actor Robert Pine offered, "Very nice men. Very nice, very capable. They were very good to me, I loved them both. Both really good guys, good family guys."

Vincent has high regards for three actors he has directed during his career. Three actors closely identified with the characters they portrayed...William Shatner as Captain Kirk on *Star Trek*, Peter Falk as *Columbo* and James Arness as Matt Dillon on *Gunsmoke*. "Dear Jim," remembered Vincent, "Without a doubt one of the most unusual, most beautiful people I've ever known. Most, most professional; one of the funniest men I've ever

CECIL B. DE-WEAVER Milburn Stone and Amanda Blake visit the set on their day off as castmate Dennis Weaver, with whip in hand, prepares to direct James Arness.

worked with...always prepared. He said to me once, 'You know, I really like to keep the audience guessing. I don't really like them to know everything I'm thinking.' That's a marvelous quality of a leading character."

As for the other cast members, Vincent went on, "They were all very professional and cared immensely

knew who he was, how he related to Kitty and what he would say to her and what he wouldn't."

"We did those shows in six days and these were big, big shoots...not all talk shows, a lot of action," said Vincent. "At that time we were shooting with one camera...very tough shows." Not all was hard work though. "Every Friday night we always had a beer at the end of the day in the Long Branch. We'd all just gather around—Amanda, Milburn and Kenny would always stay. Jim would never stay, never socialized. Didn't like small talk."

Beverly Garland appeared on *Gunsmoke* four times with three of her segments directed by Vincent. "A good director, the best," reflected Garland. "He'd go along with my suggestions, and I thought he was very good so I went along with what he said. We worked very well together."

"Sometimes you rehearse with a director and there's no room for the performer," stated actress Miriam Colon. "The director has it all figured out and there's only room for his interpretation." Colon, a veteran of countless television and motion picture roles, including several on *Gunsmoke*, continued, "I never got this feeling with Vince. He was gentle and trusting. Therefore, if he had a point to make, he would make it, but you would not feel that he mechanically imposed his conception on you. This made working very pleasant because he's a man that trusts."

Vincent fondly remembers the joking Arness was famous for, with one incident in particular that created a lasting impression: "We went from black and white to color so we had to redo the opening titles. We're on the

RADIO'S MATT DILLON Actor William Conrad directed the televison show a few times.

about what they did in a very loving way...very respectful to one another...a unique experience I've never, since that time, ever experienced anything like it. They knew who they were as characters, they knew how they related. Doc

MULTIPLE TALENT Actor Victor French appeared in many GUNSMOKE episodes and directed a few too, including MATT DILLON MUST DIE! during the final season.

backlot duplicating Dodge. Wide angle shot, Jim in the foreground. A gunfighter then steps out, shoots and Jim turns and falls down dead, right in front of the camera! He just laid there." A stunned crew and director rushed to the bloodied actor. With a strategically placed blood cap,

Arness planned the whole stunt, but couldn't keep a serious face for long and soon broke out laughing. "It's a classic. We couldn't film anymore...we went to lunch," laughed Vincent.

Out of all the *Gunsmoke* directing alum, Vincent is the only member to helm one of the reunion films produced after the series initial twenty-year run. He directed *Gunsmoke: Return to Dodge* in 1987. "It was fun, I loved working with Jim again. I liked the show...very melodramatic."

"I never felt so comfortable in my life filming," recalled Vincent's brother Bernard. "I've directed three to four hundred shows and only three shows, *The Rebel*, *Combat!* and *Gunsmoke* were ideal. The rest were just work. I came on the show in 1967. Nobody on *Gunsmoke* was fighting for screen space, which made it beautiful for a director. All actors have to have an ego but they did not display it on *Gunsmoke*...marvelous camaraderie."

Bernard was very fond of Arness, not only directing him on *Gunsmoke*, but also on his other television series, *How the West Was Won* and *McClain's Law*. His experience on *Gunsmoke* was always his favorite. "What I liked about it was you had a chance. You were dealing with actors, not just action. I like working with actors...you don't teach them how to act but you give them a destination."

"On *Gunsmoke* you felt instrumental along with the writer, producer and actors in telling a story. The work was great satisfaction. Sometimes directing is work and sometimes it is enrapturement. That was *Gunsmoke*."

Bernard earned the trust of many that he worked with, including actress Gwynne Gilford, who recalled Bernard as, "Very easy, very comfortable and provided a very relaxed set. You could really do your work with a certain amount of ease. There wasn't any tension."

Bernard strongly agreed with director Harry Harris, Jr. as to why the program was so different from the multitude of Westerns offered in the sixties and seventies: "It was anthology in the sense that they could tell any kind of story...they were not tied down to the lead characters. Most shows in episodic television have to be tailored to the people that are running characters. But people who watched *Gunsmoke* were satisfied with the way it was. If you saw the Marshal once in awhile, great. Doc, Kitty, Festus...sometimes they played a very integral part, sometimes they were almost bystanders. It gave the writers a lot more freedom and as a director it kept my interest up tremendously."

"In other shows, the characters had to be the good guys and the bad guys. There's an awful lot of greys in *Gunsmoke*," concluded Bernard. At the age of seventy-nine, Bernard died of natural causes on February 2, 2004, in Encino, California.

From 1955 to 1963, Ted Post directed over fifty episodes of *Gunsmoke*, earning the respect and trust of cast and crew alike. In a famous and oft quoted perception of Arness, and ultimately the program itself, Post pointed out in a November 1961 issue of *TV Guide*, "Arness had a lot of Matt Dillon's gutsiness to begin with. But this guy's long suit as an actor is the compassion that

> "ON GUNSMOKE YOU FELT INSTRUMENTAL ALONG WITH THE WRITER, PRODUCER AND ACTORS IN TELLING A STORY. THE WORK WAS GREAT SATISFACTION. SOMETIMES DIRECTING IS WORK AND SOMETIMES IT IS ENRAPTUREMENT. THAT WAS GUNSMOKE."

comes out in a poignant look that I call Weltschmerz—world pain. Gary Cooper had it. So did Bogart. Jimmy Stewart, Henry Fonda, Spencer Tracy, they all have it. Arness has it and he doesn't even know it." In addition to his broad television work, Post directed many motion pictures, including *Beneath the Planet of the Apes* and *Magnum Force*.

Director Joseph Sargent began his association with *Gunsmoke* as an actor in 1957, appearing in the episode *Skid Row*. Five years later he returned to Dodge as a director, eventually helming big-screen thrillers, such as *The Taking of Pelham 1-2-3*, and the war epic *MacArthur*, starring Gregory Peck. John Rich, an Emmy-award winner for his work on *The Dick Van Dyke Show* and *All in the Family*, was one of televisions most reliable directors. His first *Gunsmoke* assignment was the superlative 1957 entry *How to Kill a Woman*, featuring a wonderful performance by Pernell Roberts; his last *Gunsmoke*, the classic from 1969, *The Long Night*, was one of the best episodes out of the show's twenty-year run and perhaps the best hour Rich directed.

Before directing the motion picture classics *Love Story* and *Silver Streak*, Arthur Hiller took on many *Gunsmoke* segments, honing his skill at blending subtle comedy with tense situations seamlessly. *Doc Judge*, from 1960, features standout performances from regulars Dennis Weaver and Milburn Stone, and under the skillful hand of Hiller, it is one of their best efforts.

Two directors from the last decade of the show, Gunnar Helstrom and Robert Totten, took on acting assignments occasionally as well. Helstrom was particularly nasty in the episode *Dead Man's Law*. Totten, or "Rotten Totten" as Amanda Blake affectionately nicknamed him, directed many memorable segments. He was justly proud of the episode *The Newcomers*, which featured a then unknown actor, Jon Voight. A triple-threat, Totten also developed the story for the 1968 episode *Nowhere to Run*. In 1967, Totten was directing the two-part episode *Nitro!* when news reached the set that CBS had cancelled *Gunsmoke*. Although the cancellation was temporary, the news proved traumatic during the shoot.

Warren Vanders worked for Totten many times including *The Wreckers*, which opened season thirteen in 1967. Vanders played a character named Reb and recalled shooting a scene with Amanda Blake, "I'm hiding behind a tree, all of a sudden I hear Totten yell, 'Reb!' I come running, stumbling, and he yells, 'Cut! You dumb son of a bitch!' I said 'What?!' He says, 'Yes, you asshole, what are you doing? You blew your cue!' I said, 'You yelled Reb!' He says 'I yelled Red!' From fifty yards away Reb and Red...he called Amanda 'Red.' Those were the days..." laughed Vanders.

Totten directed the extremely physical and strenuous episode *The Lost*, featuring actress Laurie Prange. "The first take, I was supposed to run across the shore," recalled Prange. "I had studied a lot of ballet as a young girl. I remember him cutting the camera and telling me I was running like a ballerina. He was very direct; I adored him. He was real meat and potatoes. He wanted me to run like an animal. He got me into the physical real fast because he was so physical. He was a real bear of a man, I remember."

Actor Victor French, an avid collector of Western movie memorabilia, was sorting through lobby cards one day at Larry Edmunds Cinema Bookshop in Hollywood. Other collectors recognized the performer and one asked, "What is your favorite Western series?" Before the actor could respond, another collector piped up, "Oh come on, that's easy, *Little House on the Prairie*." French replied, "Well, that would be the obvious answer, but actually my favorite will always be *Gunsmoke*. Great opportunities for an actor, plus they let me direct a time or two, for which I'll always be grateful." French had a wonderful flair for directing, most notably the opener for season twenty, *Matt Dillon Must Die!*

Writer Jim Byrnes had great respect for the directors on *Gunsmoke*, recalling, "The ones I worked with—Vince McEveety, Bernie McEveety and Gunnar Hellstrom, who directed *Island in the Desert*. Terrific directors." Never intimidating, directors on the show made everyone feel welcome, regardless of title, part or function. "They were directing *Gunsmoke* long before I came in," continued Byrnes. "My first day they just welcomed me—Vince McEveety went out of his way to say hello." All in the family.

Series regular Dennis Weaver jumped at the chance to direct his fellow castmates, who presented him a directors chair with the name Cecil B. De-Weaver on the backrest. Actress Susan Gordon had fond memories of Weaver, who directed her in the episode *Little Girl.* "He was very laid back, I didn't feel any tension or the pressure some directors might do. The whole experience was just a lot of fun, I had a great time."

William Conrad, Matt Dillon on the radio version, directed, as did Peter Graves, star of *Mission Impossible* and little brother to series lead, Arness. CBS and the producers of *Gunsmoke* always welcomed new directors into their fold, offering a remarkable training ground for those wishing to spend their time in those familiar folding chairs made of wood and canvas.

THE FAMOUS PRACTICAL JOKE.

THREE PROS "We did a lot of ad-libbing because we were so in tune with the characters."

CHATTIN' WITH CHESTER

AN INTERVIEW WITH DENNIS WEAVER
July 11, 2002

BC: Thank you so much for this interview.

DW: Well, it might be premature...(laughs)

BC: Do you ever get tired of talking about *Gunsmoke*?

DW: Not really. I mean, I would be very ungrateful if I did.

BC: Were you a fan of the show when it was on radio?

DW: No, I've never heard the radio show.

BC: Do you know who you were up against when you were auditioning for the role?

DW: I do know one person who auditioned for it. He was a friend of mine named Guy Williams, who later played *Zorro*. Can you imagine him for that part? I don't know. He was a New Yorker-type. (laughs) I think the reason that he tested, because he and I played brothers in a movie that Charles Marquis Warren directed about six months earlier.

BC: Did Mr. Warren contact you or your agent to have you test?

DW: Well, it's an interesting situation. I was in-between

A GOODE PART Of his role on GUNSMOKE, Weaver stated, "...I loved the character of Chester and I thank God for him everyday..."

agents, and some friend of mine who I met on the street in North Hollywood said, "You know they're doing a Western TV series, a so-called 'adult Western' over at CBS, and Charles Marquis Warren is directing it. There might be something in there..." Well, I was looking for work and obviously had a connection with Charles Marquis Warren—we called him "Bill"—so I called him up. He says, "Where've you been? I've been trying to get ahold of you. There's a part in here you might be right for." He couldn't get me because I didn't have an agent at the time.

BC: Were you the first person cast?

DW: Yeah, I was.

BC: Do you recall any of the actors you tested with who were trying for Matt Dillon?

DW: Yes, there were several actors. The only one I can remember was Royal Dano. Do you know his name? (laughs)

BC: I can't imagine him playing the part.

DW: (still laughing) I can't either! Well, I can't imagine anybody playing it except Jim. Charles Marquis Warren sometimes had odd tastes: He was a little strange sometimes and maybe he thought the idea of casting away from type might be interesting, because Royal Dano made a career out of playing villains and heavies.

BC: I also heard that Denver Pyle was considered.

DW: Denver Pyle was probably considered. They considered a lot of people.

BC: Why do think the show was so popular and still remains popular today?

DENNIS DIRECTS DOC "...I just went to the producer and said, 'Let me direct one.'"

DW: I've got to tell you, if the networks used the same standard then that they're using today to decide whether a show remains on the air or not, we may not have made it. The first half a year, it didn't explode. I remember very distinctly that the first show of the second season, we were number one, and everyone was so excited about that. And we stayed number one for four years straight, never knocked off of that top spot week after week after week. It was incredible. Unheard of.

Why do I think it was so popular? Well, first of all it was a groundbreaker. It was the first "adult" Western. Before *Gunsmoke*, of course, we had Roy Rogers and Gene Autry and the singing cowboy. Those stories weren't based on real relationships or stories that really dealt with problems of real people and real interesting characters. See, *Gunsmoke* in the beginning, during those half-hour shows, we leaned a lot on character study, and we brought onto the screen a lot of interesting characters and interesting situations dealing with the old West that had never been done before.

Also, I think one of the reasons that the show was very successful was that the television family was very interesting. I think it was a great mix of characters. It had a lady saloon keeper, which had never really been done, with a heart as big as a watermelon, and this marshal that stood for no-nonsense law enforcement. He also had a big heart in terms of dealing with people honestly, and those that were guilty, (laughs) he put it to 'em. He had sympathy for others; he had a lot of dimension to him. And, of course, Doc was a very, very interesting character. The relationship that Doc and Chester had was just something that people wanted to tune in and see what the family was doing that Saturday.

BC: I know as a viewer and a fan, I felt that I was part of the family also.

DW: Yeah, well, people did. They identified with it so, so deeply.

BC: It was just cast so perfectly.

DW: It really shows you how important casting is. I know when I directed, I understood that eighty percent of my job was to get the right people to play the parts. You know, the casting was so important. You're absolutely right about that.

BC: Did you enjoy directing?

DW: Oh yeah, I did. It was fun.

BC: Was it your idea to direct?

DW: Yes, I just went to the producer and said, "Let me direct one." (laughs) I had a good relationship at that time with Norm Macdonnell. I had a wonderful relationship with him, and he said sure. It was very, very enjoyable, I really liked it.

BC: It's certainly a testament to your abilities that thousands, maybe millions of people actually thought you were handicapped.

DW: I used to get a lot of sympathetic letters. It's remarkable. I have a lot of lame dogs and cats named after me. (big laugh) You know, one lady wrote in and thanked CBS for giving a veteran an opportunity. We got all kinds of letters like that. There were a couple of doctors at UCLA who had a bet on whether I was really lame or not: One of them said "yes," one of them said "no." They actually wrote a letter to me asking, "OK, tell us which one is right." (laughs)

(We then discussed the live appearances by the

PITCH A favorite card game played between scenes. The above arcade cards were not used in the game.

Sullivan Show. (chuckles) The only time, the only time I ever hit one of them, was on *The Ed Sullivan Show*! (laughs)

BC: Right, in front of millions of people...

DW: But I didn't lose my stiff leg. I kept that. (laughs)

BC: Was it a tough decision for you to leave the show?

DW: Absolutely. It was because I had financial security; my agent and my business manager thought I was nuts. But my wife, Gerry, agreed with me. She knew that in my heart this was awfully good for me, and I loved the character of Chester, and I thank God for him every day because he opened up all the doors for me. But I knew that the doors weren't gonna stay open if I didn't make a move at

Gunsmoke cast. Most of that portion of the interview is in the LIVE! chapter.)

BC: I wish there was a filmed record of one of the live appearances.

DW: Yes, that would be something.

BC: You did do *The Ed Sullivan Show,* correct?

DW: I did the jumping over the hurdles on *The Ed*

some time. I was getting to the age where, if I stayed with the show until the end, that's all I would ever do. So I made the decision, bit the bullet. I quit, left it—but I didn't leave it until I had a bird in the hand. I had twenty-four shows guaranteed to me before I left. It was a good thing I did, for me, for my career. Ben, I think I'm the only actor that ever went from a very, very successful sidekick on a

DENNIS AND JIM The actors still enjoy each other's company fifty years after first working together.

very, very successful television series to a very successful leading man on a very successful television show. I don't think anyone else has made that jump.

BC: Not that I can think of.

DW: No, I can't either.

BC: And nine years is a long time for one show.

DW: Yeah, I pretty much exhausted all the possibilities of the character, and I just wanted to move on to something else, while I had the so-called "golden" opportunity. You

know, I was lucky, Ben, because others have done that and just disappeared. I mean, the guy that left *M*A*S*H*, for instance, and what was his name that left *Bonanza*?

BC: Pernell Roberts.

DW: He just kind of disappeared for a long time. He finally got back on television playing the doctor.

BC: And David Caruso…

DW: Yeah, on *NYPD Blue*. It's a very, very difficult thing to do. I just feel extremely fortunate.

BC: Well, you've got to have the talent to back you up, too.

DW: Well, that's very kind of you.

BC: You've played almost every kind of character.

DW: I've played a lot of different characters, that's for sure.

BC: And there's a belief in your characterizations that started with Chester.

DW: I really became Chester. I felt like I was Chester during *Gunsmoke*, and that's the reason why Doc and I could really improvise. We did a lot of ad-libbing because we were so in tune with the characters. We would ad-lib lines you know, off of the script and as soon as I ad-libbed one, believe me, Doc would pick it up. There was no hesitation, there was no bump in the road, nothing. He would just pitch Doc right into whatever I said as Chester. (laughs)

BC: Milburn Stone seemed to be very professional…

DW: He was extremely professional; he was a good lesson. He wanted everything to be very, very professional. He (laughs)—a lot of times we'd break each other up, and he would actually get so irritated with himself. It didn't bother me that much. We just broke up, if something was funny. We got our funny bone tickled, and we just went. But he was so intent on being professional (laughs).

BC: I've heard that you and Jim Arness have had a few laughs together, too.

DW: Oh my God! I mean, that was a different situation with us. We had so many laughs. I remember one time, we had a scene: He was coming down the boardwalk one way, and I was coming the other way. I was on the run, my stiff leg and everything, and I'm yelling, (as Chester), "Mister Dillon, Mister Dillon, Mister Dillon!" And I'd get up to him, (laughs), we would just crack up. Andy McLaglen was directing. You know this guy was as big as Jim Arness, and he had about a size fourteen shoe. So he'd say, "All right you guys, come on—let's go, do it again!" We do the same thing, do it again, and pretty soon he'd say, "Listen guys, we're on a budget here. We're professional actors here.." Well, the minute he said "We're professional actors," it just made it worse. We'd get up there and just crack up again. Finally, Andy McLaglen with his size 14 foot, just stomped the hell out of me: He'd say "Come on, Dennis!" Then he'd stomp Jim, and say, "You guys, come on now! This is serious!" (laughs) And of course, we got together again, we'd just break up. We'd break up about three feet before we came to our marks!

Finally, he said, "Okay, just do me this. Just get into position without laughing: Just get into position and I'll say 'cut!' Okay? And then we'll go for the close-ups."

We finally managed to get into positions, he said

"cut." (laughs) And then, of course, in my close-up, Jim was off-camera reading lines, and the minute he said anything, I started to laugh. Finally, Andy McLaglen had to have the script girl read the off-camera lines, and Jim had to go off the set, and then when it was his close-up, I went off the set. (laughs) It was hysterical.

BC: I had the pleasure of interviewing Mr. McLaglen.

DW: You did?

BC: He said, "Sometimes I was directing two cowboys, other times I thought I was directing the Little Rascals!"

DW: (laughs) He remembered that. I bet he didn't mention stomping on our feet!

BC: No, he didn't. (laughing) This still brings a smile to your face now.

DW: Oh yeah, by God it does.

BC: You're still close with Mr. Arness, I take it?

DW: Yeah, yeah, I'm close. A&E did his biography not long ago, and I had the honor of being part of that. I was over to his house not too long ago—had a real nice visit with him after the *Biography* was shown. We talk on the telephone quite a bit. I hadn't seen him in person in a couple or three years. Every time we get on the phone, it's the same old jokes, we bring up the same remembrances (laughs) and we just laugh again.

BC: What great memories! It must have been a great time filming *Gunsmoke*.

DW: It was. It was totally magic. You know, Jim and I talk about it quite often. It was different then. He says, "It was like a family. We were like two young guys just having

PERSONAL FAVORITE Weaver with Earle Hodgins in his favorite GUNSMOKE segment, CHESTERLAND from season seven.

fun," and it was absolutely the truth. You know, the sponsor at that time and the actors and the producers of the show had a lot to say about what went on the air, and it wasn't just totally locked in by the network. The networks weren't making the total decisions in connection with the show like they are now.

BC: So if you had a concern, they'd actually listen to you?

DW: Yes, and actually they'd give you a chance to correct it. If they had some problem, they'd talk to the producer and maybe they'd fix it. Now, they give you maybe two shows on the air, and you're off! If you don't hit the bullseye in two shows, they discard you.

BC: It doesn't seem to be a collaborative medium any more.

DW: No, it doesn't. It's so discouraging. These kids are like 24, 25-years-old and they're in executive producing positions? It's just horrible how they've discarded talent that has been proven over the years, and experience that could be extremely valuable. We're so oriented toward youth. I think the shows are suffering because of that.

BC: I agree. Nothing is on the air now that is up to the caliber of *Gunsmoke*.

DW: No, no. And the sitcoms, for the most part, are totally inane as far as I'm concerned. There's no real development of character and interaction of character, there's really no situation that is funny. They depend upon gag lines and pratfalls.

BC: A cheap laugh.

DW: Yeah.

WORKING WITH JAMES ARNESS "It was like a family. We were like two young guys just having fun."

BC: For real laughs, I have a favorite episode of yours: *Chesterland*.

DW: Oh, that's my favorite. I love that show. Oh man, I really love that show.

BC: You can compare your performance to the great Buster Keaton.

DW: Well, (laughs), that's very flattering. It was such a good idea. Didn't Kathleen Hite write that? I think she did.

BC: Yes.

DW: She knew how to write for the character. That was really kind of special for me. I loved it. Do you know that show was originally called *Chesterfields*? (laughs) We had a problem—we were sponsored by Pall Mall (laughs). "You've got to change that," the sponsors said. "You can't do that!"

BC: That could have been the last season for *Gunsmoke*.

DW: Right. (laughs) So it was changed to *Chesterland*. It was one of those moments for me. I just loved that show.

BC: Did you see many of the cast members or did you visit the set after you left?

DW: Yeah, I didn't make a habit of visiting, but I did go the wrap party when it was cancelled after the thirteenth year. I visited with Doc, Milburn Stone and Amanda Blake—I visited with all of them at their homes. I didn't go to the set that much except for the wrap party. You've heard the story of the wrap party: How *Gunsmoke* ended then how it was started again?

BC: Because of Mr. Paley, I believe.

DW: That's exactly right. He came back from vacation and looked at the schedule and says, "Where's *Gunsmoke*?"

BC: That wouldn't happen today either.

DW: No! Absolutely not. It went on for seven more years.

BC: I've heard a lot about the legendary card games on the set.

DW: We had a running card game going on the *Gunsmoke* set: Pitch. I grew up on Pitch, I learned to count playing Pitch. Tiny Nichols, Jim's stand-in, also was a real good Pitch player, and Jim had never played it, so we taught him. (big laugh) Oh God, it was funny. I write about that in my book. We'd play at noontime in his dressing room. He'd (laughs) go over to the cupboard and grab that marble bag full of quarters and slam 'em down on the table and say, "Now get that, you sons a bitches!" (laughs) And before the lunch hour was over, we'd probably have it. Jim told somebody once, "Yeah Den, ol' Den—I paid for his swimming pool."

BC: Pitch paid for the pool!

DW: (laughs) Yeah, that's what he said. We'd play in between takes, between set-ups, on the stage. And of course, Tiny would be playing with us, and at that time, he was Jim's stand-in. I'll tell you what kind of a guy Jim is: Tiny wound up being first assistant director on the show. Jim was extremely loyal. Extremely, extremely giving, also. I know our hairdresser, Patty Whiffing, had cancer, and he made sure that all of her hospital bills were taken care of. He also donated his thousand-acre ranch out in Simi Valley to the Brandeis Institute. That ranch today would be worth, oh God, I don't know, a thousand acres? He had a sailboat called *Seasmoke*, and he donated it to the Sea Scouts, a division of the Boy Scouts. He was very generous. He was just so in love with life, so in love with life.

BC: It's great to hear that you think so highly of him after all these years.

DW: I feel so privileged to have been connected with him and to have worked with him. He's just a guy that wears well. What you see is what you get. Not a phony bone in his body.

BC: If you could sum up *Gunsmoke* with one word, what would it be?

DW: Oh God, how could you do it with one word? (pause) Glorious. It was a glorious time, that's all I can tell you.

BC: That's great. Anything else you'd like to share?

DW: All of the townspeople, you know, that had recurring parts like Dabbs Greer who played the storekeeper, and James Nusser, the town drunk—they were all wonderful.

BC: I remember when my family went to see *The Green Mile* with Tom Hanks at the movies, and Dabbs Greer was in it. People sitting behind us saw him and said, "There's Mr. Jonas from *Gunsmoke*!"

DW: (laughs) How 'bout that.

BC: It's etched in our memories in a positive way.

DW: You betcha.

BC: Well, I thank you very much for your time.

DW: Thank you, and you are certainly welcome.

THE DEAN MARTIN CELEBRITY ROAST OF DENNIS WEAVER

Multi-talented performer Dean Martin was a huge success on television with his variety show and celebrity roasts. In 1976, Producer Greg Garrison managed to get Dennis Weaver in the hot seat with celebrities such as Rich Little, Steve Forrest, Zsa Zsa Gabor, Shelley Winters, Milton Berle, George Hamilton, Red Buttons, Nipsey Russell, J. D. Cannon, William Conrad, Peter Graves, Jim Hutton and from *Gunsmoke*, Amanda Blake and Milburn Stone, to participate in the fun. Here are some selected highlights...

DEAN MARTIN: Dennis, a lot of your friends couldn't be here tonight—boy, are they lucky. So they sent some wires and I'd like to read a few of them...here's one with heart and tender, it says "Dear Dennis, get off my back!" Signed, your horse. Here's another one from your pal Jim Arness, he's six-twelve you know. "Dear Dennis, Never had the opportunity to tell you how much I admire your courage in quitting a show, a hit show, like *Gunsmoke*. I was totally surprised at your leaving, because I just found out about it this morning." Our first guest needs no introduction, so the hell with him! Rolling right along...William Conrad—Cannon!

WILLIAM CONRAD: Because I'm a private detective, I was asked to shadow Dennis Weaver for a whole day and

Weaver stopped at the home of Jim Arness where he wrote obscene Western expressions on the front door...after shadowing Dennis Weaver for eighteen hours, I find his shadow is a hell of a lot more interesting than he is.

SHELLEY WINTERS: In all the years I've known him he's only done one nice thing for me—he didn't get me a part in *Kentucky Jones*.

RED BUTTONS: ...here to solve the greatest mystery of all-times. Why are we honoring Dennis Weaver? Mr. Weaver, I don't know you too well, and I certainly intend to keep it that way! But I have followed your career and I'm familiar, very familiar with your many awards. I remember when you got the Emmy for the best supporting limp. I even know how you got that limp. You once tried to get something from Kitty that didn't come in a shot glass.

MILBURN STONE: Dennis, Amanda, this is really like old times, you know, you sitting around on your duffs and me working. As *Gunsmoke* started to go up in the ratings, it was then the famous Dennis Weaver ego was born. I'll give you an example, a very short time later he came to me and said, "Milburn, I'm gonna have my own show someday." So I humored him. I said, "Okay Dennis, what is it going to be called?" He said, "*Gunsmoke*." It was then that he started his legendary "Dump Arness" campaign.

DINO ROASTS DENNIS Weaver was the man of the hour in 1976 and Dean Martin was the Roastmaster.

find out what he is really like. Here is my report...5:30 am, subject awoke...then did thirty laps in the swimming pool...by the way, the pool was built according to Dennis Weaver's own personality—it's completely shallow. 8:30—

DENNIS WEAVER: Don't believe it Jim. Don't believe it!

MILBURN STONE: He did certain things at first—like he turned out the light while Jim was cleaning his gun...if anybody is wondering why Jim isn't here...Dean asked me to invite him and I did. Jim said, "Well, he'd like to come on the show, but didn't know what to do." I said, "Well all you have to do is come on the show and insult Dennis. Say nasty things about him." And he said, "What show is it? *To Tell the Truth?*" Regretfully, Dennis rode out of Dodge City for the last time. Now for the rest of us on the show— after we polished off all the champagne—we put up a barricade to make sure he didn't change his mind.

NIPSEY RUSSELL: I have totally omitted any reference to the whole *Gunsmoke* thing. There's been a great disservice done to my people in the historical context of all the Westerns on television. Now you know General Custer was black. When he got to Little Big Horn and saw all the Indians in the world waiting for him, then he turned white!

DEAN MARTIN: Ladies and gentlemen, a glamorous lady, a fine actress, the Queen of *Gunsmoke*—Miss Amanda Blake.

AMANDA BLAKE: Thank you, Dean. You know, I always love to do your show here at the MGM Grand. It's really the most magnificent place in Las Vegas. It makes all the other hotels look like the Long Branch. Dennis, of course, created the part of Chester—a slow-witted character with a limp. In doing so, he drew upon his past experiences. The limp he perfected during the war when he appeared before his draft board. That was Chester, slow-witted with a limp. Not to be confused with the real-life Dennis, who does not limp. Of course, Dennis became immensely popular as Chester, but his success didn't change him. He still treated us with the same petty jealousy he always had. For example—Milburn, Jim Arness and I all had air conditioners in our dressing rooms. So Dennis demanded that he wanted one, too. But they turned him down, because they were afraid the horses would catch cold!

PETER GRAVES: I'm happy that tonight, I'm the one who gets to tell you that the Patrolwomen's Benevolent Association has voted you the best looking police officer on television. I was supposed to present you with the award tonight, but they're having trouble getting it back from last year's winner, Karl Malden.

MILTON BERLE: Look at the man of the week—Dennis Weaver who is so old he thinks the Happy Hooker specializes in needlepoint. What is Amanda Blake doing here? I mean, she doesn't need this. She's a very rich woman— she made a fortune endorsing Kitty litter. Here's another one you may not care for...

DENNIS WEAVER: You know, I really, honestly—

I really didn't think it was possible for a group of entertainers like yourself to get together and do funny jokes about me for an hour—and I was right. Milburn Stone, my old friend from *Gunsmoke*, Milburn Stone. You know, I tell you, that Milburn has really got a down-home sense of humor, and I think that's where he left it...and gracing this dais tonight is another alumnus of *Gunsmoke*—Amanda Blake. You came here out of affection—you also came here out of material.

To own the complete Roast on video or DVD, go to www.DeanMartinRoasts.com

A TO Z From Jean Arthur to Anthony Zerbe, most actors from the era wanted to add GUNSMOKE to their resumes.

WELCOME TO DODGE

The Guest Stars Reminisce

From Jean Arthur to Anthony Zerbe, most actors from the era desired a chance to appear on *Gunsmoke*. It was always a prestigious resume credit and one appearance would definitely lead to future employment on other shows. *Gunsmoke* was a springboard for many actors appearing on Broadway hoping to make their television debuts. Hollywood veterans offered their services; future superstars launched their careers.

Character actor extraordinaire, Strother Martin, appeared on virtually every show imaginable, accumulating hundreds of credits. Ten of those were appearances on *Gunsmoke*, with two standing out as personal career highlights. Martin ordered a 16mm print of *Cooter* from the studios for his personal and professional use. He proudly screened the episode to family and friends, and for agents, producers, directors and casting directors as well. His last appearance on the show, a two-parter from 1974, *Island in the Desert*, became the actor's favorite credit during his long career.

STROTHER MARTIN As Ben Snow, another brilliant characterization for the actor, in ISLAND IN THE DESERT, 1974.

MORGAN WOODWARD as Abraham Wakefield "GUNSMOKE was a remarkable part of my show business life," exclaimed a proud Woodward, shown here in MATT DILLON MUST DIE! from the twentieth season.

Regarding his numerous appearances on *Gunsmoke*, Morgan Woodward admitted, "I retired in 1997 after fifty years in theatre, motion pictures and television. *Gunsmoke* was the highlight; the best experience I had in my career. *Gunsmoke* was just a remarkable part of my show business life. There's been no other series that I can think of in my time that could compare with it."

Woodward considered the program unique. "The cast of *Gunsmoke*—Jim, Milburn, Amanda, Buck, Ken— all great people," he recalled fondly. "I can still hear Amanda's laugh. Boy she had the dirtiest laugh you've ever heard in your life. Ol' Jim would get her going with some dirty joke and you could hear her all over the set." His favorite episodes include *Matt Dillon Must Die!*, *Death Train* and *The Sodbusters*. "*Death Train* was my first so-called 'leading man' role with Dana Wynter. I was all spiffed up and dressed beautifully; it was a nice show I thought," recalled Woodward. "*The Sodbusters*, that was one of my favorites. Alex Cord was good in that."

Securing his place in television history with his portrayal of Agent Hobson on *The Untouchables*, actor Paul Picerni always looked forward to appearing on *Gunsmoke*. On *The Untouchables*, Picerni had the pleasure of working with John Mantley as a writer and Vincent McEveety, who was first assistant director. As for his stints on *Gunsmoke*, Picerni stated, "I'd say Vince had something to do with it, but mostly John Mantley. I liked John a lot. He didn't say much, but when he did, he meant it. He was like his hero, the star of the show, Jim

Arness...quiet, Western-type guy...like Gary Cooper." In the segment *The Disciple*, Picerni had the unenviable position of replacing Matt Dillon. "I'm brought in to replace him as the new marshal, and, of course, by the end of the show, everybody hated me and they brought back Dillon."

"Every time I worked on the show it was enjoyable. They always had good actors and nice people behind the camera, the crew," reflected Picerni. "It was a nice set. On *Gunsmoke* everyone had their own moments, their own characters. No one was greedy and they were very easy to work with. Sometimes you get a cast and everyone hates each other and usually the show dies. You don't have a long-running series unless everyone is cooperative. That's one of the reasons *Gunsmoke* went on so long, it was a family."

Oft bad guy Anthony Caruso agreed, "No animosity on the *Gunsmoke* set at all, no arguments." Caruso had two favorite directors, Andrew V. McLaglen and later, Gunnar Hellstrom. "I love Andy, not only the *Gunsmoke* segments, but he did *Have Gun—Will Travel*, I did a lot of them, back to back. You go out on location, you'd do two at once, the half hour shows. Gunnar, towards the end, they'd say, 'We need a heavy', he'd say, 'Get Tony.' That was it. He liked me and I liked him, we got along great. He'd let me do whatever I wanted." His praise continued for the producers, stating, "Macdonnell, I knew him very well, a sweet man, a great guy. He and John Dehner and I were inseparable buddies, always at each other's houses.

SCENE STEALER Actress Jacqueline Scott in a moment from the 1964 segment KITTY CORNERED. (photo courtesy of Jacqueline Scott)

I liked Mantley very much too, he gave me a lot of jobs."

Caruso cited several episodes as favorites, including *Ash, Sarah*, and *A Family of Killers*. "You know, I kind of liked all of them; I knew everybody, they all knew me. It was a happy family," concluded Caruso. His *Sarah* co-star, Anne Francis, enjoyed the episode also. When asked about working with series star James Arness, her beautiful face lit up and Francis stated, "He was adorable."

Veteran character actor James Gregory, best known for his role on *Barney Miller* and for many memorable motion picture turns, including *The Sons of Katie Elder* and *The Manchurian Candidate*, also enjoyed appearing on *Gunsmoke*. He did not, however, enjoy working with Jim Arness. Gregory recalled a scene from a 1965 episode, *The Avengers*, and offered, "I had an emotional scene with Arness; he arrested my son and I was trying to explain the way it was. We shot the scene, just the two of us. We got that. Then the cameraman and director said, 'Get Jim's close-up.' They turned the camera, I fed him my lines, a page and a half of dialogue, cues, from off-camera, which was standard operating procedure. Done. Then they said, 'Back on Jim Gregory.' Took them fifteen, twenty minutes to light, etc. I'm ready, Vince McEveety was the director, and there was this script girl standing on an apple box to simulate Arness' height. I was to play the scene with her reading Arness' lines."

"That was, as you may or may not know," continued Gregory, "very unprofessional and I didn't like it. I said to Vince, 'Where's Jim?' 'Oh, he's tired, he's lying down in his

A FAMILY OF KILLERS Anthony Caruso and Zina Bethune share a lighter momemt on the set in 1974. (photo courtesy of Anthony Caruso)

dressing room.' I said 'Either he'll be here to read his lines off-camera for my close-ups or I'll never be there for his.' I was quite annoyed with it. I remember that vividly

ONE OF HOLLYWOOD'S BEST Character actor William Schallert in the episode TWELFTH NIGHT from the third season. (photo courtesy of William Schallert)

a big star you can do that. I never did that. When I was the star in *Batman* I always stayed for the other performers close-ups—it's a professional courtesy."

On a lighter note, Gregory's sentiments echoed those of Morgan Woodward when the subject of Amanda Blake came up. "Kitty had the most obscene or contagious, raucous laugh that you ever heard," chuckled Gregory. "You couldn't help but join in her mirth when it erupted. Not just from a joke, but from something that struck her funny. I always remembered that about her." By the way, did Arness reappear to read off-camera? "You bet your bottom 'whatever' he did," finished Gregory.

With all due fairness to Arness and the off-camera participation complaints, not many people knew of the almost constant leg pain the actor endured from his injuries suffered in World War II. Arness was not pulling a "star turn" by refusing to work, he simply and quietly retreated when he could. Actor Peter Mark Richman appeared in the episode *Mr. Sam'l* in 1968 and recalled his frustrations, "When I was doing close-ups with Jim Arness, the first time it happened he didn't come to do off-camera. I said, 'Well if Jim doesn't do off-camera you're not going to get me to do on-camera.' That message was relayed to him and he came right out and he was very nice and sweet. I guess it was assumed by the staff, the crew, the A.D.'s that he never does off-camera. Well, that wasn't going to fly with me. He respected that, was a perfect gentleman and he did off-camera and I did off-camera for him." "I remember Arness, he made me laugh," stated

because of the unprofessionalism." TV's Batman Adam West concurred, "Jim Arness never stayed and did close-ups with you. He'd do his and leave. I guess when you're

BEN COOPER Amanda Blake and Ben Cooper in a scene from the March 13, 1965 installment. (photo courtesy of Ben Cooper)

actor William Windom.

With three *Gunsmoke* appearances, Windom adds another dimension to the off-camera techniques employed by Arness. "I'm playing a scene with Arness, just the two of us, me facing him and him facing me. When the camera was on me, an assistant came up to me and said, 'Do you mind if I read Mr. Arness' lines? He's tied up on the phone.' So, we did it, I pretended he was Arness off screen, no problem for me...just like radio," Windom relayed. "When the time came for the camera to be on him, he had torn the page out of his script and was reading as he walked onto the set, chewing gum. I'm standing beside the camera while he's getting all set to go, looking at his lines and chewing gum. He stops chewing the gum and put it on the back of the page and came over and slapped the whole thing on my forehead—the page was hanging down in front of my face while I'm standing next to the camera so he could read it while he's looking at me. I thought it was funny," chuckled Windom.

Appearing many times on the show, William Schallert particularly enjoyed two segments...his first role in *Twelfth Night* and his casting against-type in *Albert* from season fifteen. "*Twelfth Night* I played an okie who came down out of the mountains, and the character was kind of droll," recalled Schallert. A good friend to Dennis and Geri Weaver, Schallert turned to them both for help with his role. "On the show Dennis used a real okie accent, so I got to use that and it was kind of fun."

For his role as killer Jake Spence in *Albert*, Schallert played a character that, "...was literally a psychopath, no sense of right or wrong, no conscience. He'd kill somebody just as easy as he'd cook an egg," offered Schallert. Actor Milton Selzer portrayed the title role, a timid bank teller. Schallert continued, "Conventional casting, I would have played *Albert*." Director Vincent McEveety and

THE DEVIL'S OUTPOST Guest stars Robert Lansing and Warren Vanders. (photo courtesy of Paige Schoolcraft)

casting director Pam Polifroni gave the actor a chance that he relished. "I'm not a physically threatening person. There was something about my attitude that seemed to hold things together. I was glad to have a shot at it because I knew I could do it. Good work—I liked that show a lot." As for the overall success of *Gunsmoke*, Schallert offered, "*Gunsmoke* was a class Western;

Macdonnell and Meston did a really remarkable job. John Meston, his scripts were literate and interesting. It was also very good chemistry in that cast."

In 1970, Loretta Swit began her episodic television career on *Gunsmoke*. She first appeared in *The Pack Rat* and then in *Snow Train*, a two-parter, also broadcast in 1970. Milburn Stone was very impressed with Swit, and urged many of his producing and casting friends to see this new talent. Swit enjoyed both episodes, especially *Snow Train.* "It could have been a full-length movie. The scenery was beautiful; the casting and the music pulled it all together. You looked forward to going to work every day," recalled Swit.

Many guest stars were in awe of the way shooting was scheduled for series star, Arness. As the show went on, most of the regulars wanted to work less, Arness in particular, so scripted appearances were often "book-ended" for him. Writer Jim Byrnes explained, laughing occasionally, "Jim was contracted to appear in every episode. When he wanted to work less, he'd appear in the beginning to say 'I'm taking a prisoner to Hayes City,' and come in at the very end and say 'Hold it!' Actually, it gave the writers some freedom...you could bring in guest characters and revolve stories around them."

David Carradine, was one such guest. The actor, famous for both TV, *Kung Fu*, and movies, *Kill Bill,*

HOLLYWOOD VETERAN Film star John Payne (right) joined James Arness in 1970 for the memorable outing, GENTRY'S LAW.

recalled his 1971 appearance in the episode *Lavery.* "Arness would work two days—bam! —he's gone...but he practically owned the studio. Amanda was great! The anti-violence thing was in; we couldn't shoot or fight—we could push! A great show to do." Carradine and his brothers watched *Gunsmoke* growing up, beginning with their father John's first appearance in 1955. Carradine added, "It was fun to see how Dennis Weaver started out with his goofy character and then to see how he (Carradine puffed out his chest) grew in stature with other roles."

Actress Carol Vogel had her first leading role in the episode *The Angry Land*, one of the last segments filmed. "We shot out on this ranch, near Saugus, California. It was very exciting for me," recalled Vogel, "because everyone was treating me like a star and I was thrilled. They wouldn't have a rehearsal...they'd say get your marks and the most they'd do was two takes! The wardrobe people, the stunt people, the crew, everybody was great, everybody was respectful." Vogel was impressed by her co-star, stating, "Ten minutes before we'd do a scene, Jim Arness would read all his lines, get up and do it without missing a beat! He was incredible. I was at home going 'Oh God, I can't remember this!' in a panic."

Hollywood heavyweight Bette Davis made only one appearance on *Gunsmoke*, however the impression she made was a lasting one. Cast as Etta Stone, the two-time Academy Award winning actress turned in another legendary performance. As reported in the July 30, 1966, issue of *TV Guide*, "...she enjoyed doing the...show which, according to TV custom, was completed in six days. She believes it's one of the best organized programs on TV and that much of the credit should go to the production people. The experience reminded Miss Davis of her early days at Warner Brothers, where feature films were often completed in eight days. 'There is something to be said for

WILD CHILD Laurie Prange starred in the 1971 episode THE LOST.

doing a show quickly,' Miss Davis observed, 'but I think six days is cutting it just a little bit close.'"

Her episode, *The Jailer*, remains a fan favorite and

recently *TV Guide* ranked the episode as number twenty-seven out of the one-hundred Greatest Television episodes of all-time. Of all-time. In 2001, producer John Mantley recalled, "We always had flowers for our guest star's first day. Bette Davis had a reputation for being difficult, but she was very cooperative. A true professional."

"EVERYBODY STROVE FOR A KIND OF EXCELLENCE"

"Out of all the TV shows I've done, I'm always asked, 'What is your favorite?' I always say *Apprentice Doc* because of working with Milburn Stone," stated Ben Cooper. "It was like giving an actor a million dollars for his pocket." Cooper appeared three times on *Gunsmoke* and at one time was considered for a regular role of lawyer Breckenridge Taylor. However, it was his first appearance that had a lasting impression on both the audience and the actor. "I started working when I was eight years old. *Gunsmoke* was the only time in my whole career that I wrote a thank you letter to another actor," Cooper continued. "I wrote Milburn Stone a letter thanking him for the honor of working with him. Later that year we were at a Christmas party and there was Millie and his wife. When we saw each other we just held out our arms and hugged. Millie's wife said to my wife Pamela, 'Do you know what he did with Ben's letter? He put it on the front page of his scrapbook.' A truly fantastic experience, a joy."

Cooper has fond memories of his final scene in *Apprentice Doc* with Stone and Arness, and remembered, "God love her, Amanda drove in on her day off just to watch us work together, that was flattering." The last portion shot was Cooper's death scene. "I grabbed Doc's hand, I died. I'm lying there with my eyes closed, Doc was kneeling beside me, Matt standing in the doorway. Millie was looking at me, puts his hat on, closes his bag, and all the time he was doing that, I could feel his tears landing on my hand. When director Harry Harris finally said cut, he whispered it... 'cut.' Off scene, Amanda started wailing and crying." Cooper truly enjoyed all three of his guest stints. "*Gunsmoke* was already an institution when I did it. You didn't want to go home at the end of the day. They didn't treat you as if you were only there temporarily, they treated you as if you'd just got adopted," reflected the actor.

"Everybody strove for a kind of excellence," recalled Cliff Osmond. "If a fish stinks from the head first...the show smelled nice from the head first. Great pride, from the writing and the producing on down." Osmond appeared in six memorable segments, including the two-parter *Pike* from 1971. *Pike* introduced the character of Dirty Sally, brilliantly portrayed by Jeanette Nolan. Fondly recalling his work with Nolan, Osmond observed, "She was very shrewd—she'd let the other person do their close-up first—and you'd defer to whatever she wanted, she was older. She'd watch what you did and then her close-up just soared—she always saved her best for last.

GIFTED ACTOR AND ARTIST Anthony James played the recurring role of Elbert Moses in several GUNSMOKE episodes. Retired from acting, James now concentrates on his artwork. (photo courtesy of Anthony James)

REAL-LIFE HUSBAND AND WIFE Lane Bradbury and Lou Antonio starred in OUTLAW'S WOMAN from 1965. At the time, the two performers were married.

She was wonderful, a consummate professional." His first appearance on the show occurred in 1968 in an episode entitled *The Victim*. This episode, along with Celia, are his two favorite *Gunsmoke* credits. For his excellent portrayal

of the blacksmith in the latter segment, producer John Mantley submitted Osmond for an Emmy nomination.

Now an accomplished acting teacher, Osmond, assessing series star James Arness, stated, "He knew what he could do and do well. He was very generous, not trying to dominate a scene if it was your scene, per se, emotionally. That would be fine with him, he'd be the counterpuncher. He did that brilliantly well. His generosity was very intelligent; it wasn't coming out of insecurity, but out of great security." He assessed the show itself, remarking, "Of all the other Westerns, it has lasted...I would say it's professionalism with a capital 'P'—the guest star roles were all juicy, wonderful—you always looked forward to working." Reiterating his earlier observation, "That show strove for excellence."

Actor and writer Warren Vanders appeared on the show over a dozen times. Reflecting upon his career, he stated, "I don't know where I would've been in the business without *Gunsmoke*...it opened a lot of doors." Vanders enjoyed the camaraderie found on the set, remembering, "You got to know everybody, wardrobe, make-up, the script supervisor; it was all very friendly, you knew everybody." Vanders, recalling an amusing incident with costumer Alexander Velcoff, shared, "I ripped the ass out of my pants and I'm in the next scene. Alex says, 'Okay, come over here, I'll fix them.' My white jockey shorts are showing, he says, 'Okay, bend over.' I do and all of a sudden I hear 'Pssssssssssh'—he spray painted my jockey shorts! I feel this cold on my ass, he says, 'Ah, nobody'll ever see it.' He laughed, I laughed; that's an indication of the fun on *Gunsmoke*."

Vanders sold his first television script to *Gunsmoke*. "It was *The Lost*. Cal Clements changed it, edited it and I got a story credit on it," Vanders stated. A fan favorite, *The Lost* would become a pivotal episode during the shows run, most notably Amanda Blake's participation in it. The guest cast included Royal Dano, Mercedes McCambridge, Harry Carey, Jr. as well as John Mantley's children, Jon Jason and Maria. But the bulk of the story belonged to

EVIL JUDE BONNER William Smith starred in the memorable 1972 episode HOSTAGE! with Amanda Blake.

Blake and young actress Laurie Prange. Playing the wild child, Prange truly enjoyed the shoot in Kanab, Utah. "It was really invigorating for me, I absolutely loved it," recalled the actress. "It was a wonderful script. The script had so much action written into it, obviously not a lot of dialogue, it was action." The action included a now famous tussle in the river between Prange and Blake. "The water was cold, really cold—there may have been ice. Amanda was such a trouper, she did it take after take, all the coverage and everything."

"We both felt it was kind of a Helen Keller scene, *The Miracle Worker*, taming the young child," Prange continued. Although her time on *Gunsmoke* was brief, Prange formed many strong opinions of her co-stars and crew. "Amanda was a spirited woman. She wasn't a shy, demure type of woman. She was feisty with a hearty sense of humor. The crew felt like a family. Fun too. James Arness set that tone...he was larger than life, just as sweet as can be. Such a sweet spirit. John Mantley, these shows were like his babies. He really put his heart and soul into the series...he really knew what he wanted." Proud of her *Gunsmoke* association, Prange stated, "We're the greatest country in the world and *Gunsmoke* captures the best of our own very short history."

With memorable film roles from *3 Godfathers* in 1948 to *Tombstone* in 1993, Western icon Harry Carey, Jr. originally had a tough time securing employment on *Gunsmoke*. Director Andrew V. McLaglen changed all that. "A lot of television directors were very liberal guys politically—I'm a Democrat—they would not cast me because they thought I was aligned with John Wayne—that's a true fact. I think that's the shits, don't you? Andy always gave me a part," recalled Carey. *Gunsmoke* was on the air four years before he appeared on the program. "It was ahead of its time," stated Carey. "The writing was so well done, the dialogue was crisp, the characters were well defined. The other shows are very dated in comparison; it had a lot more class. They had marvelous actors."

In complete contrast to the experiences shared by actors James Gregory, Adam West and Peter Mark Richman, Carey reflected, "Jim, being the star, wasn't a pain in the ass like so many of them were. Sometimes on some of those shows when you're a freelance actor like I was, you'd do your close-up with a script girl. I don't know if Jim did that with other actors, but he certainly didn't do it with me, he was always right there. That's professionalism."

Jude Bonner. *Hostage!* William Smith. As an actor, Smith has played some of the baddest of the bad, Bonner being no exception. "Yeah that was a good show," offered Smith, "I thought it was one of the best parts I ever had. He was a bad dude." A truly memorable role, that resulted in a memorable first meeting with Miss Kitty, Amanda Blake. "The first day when I walked on the set, I had never done a *Gunsmoke*. I asked where Miss Kitty was, because I have to rape her and all that stuff on that show. 'She's right over there, that's Amanda Blake.' So I walked over and I said, 'Hi Amanda, my name is William Smith and I'm

HILL FOLK Anthony James, Lane Bradbury and Victor French pose on the set of UNCLE FINNEY in 1968. (photo courtesy of Anthony James)

playing Jude Bonner,' and she said, 'Well, I've never been "did" since I've been on this show so do it right.' I was so embarrassed, I almost fainted," laughed Smith. "She turned out to be one of the nicest people I ever worked with. She was just great, she made everything real easy...just a delight. Big Jim was great too."

In the episode, Bonner rapes, beats and then shoots Miss Kitty in the back. On film, Bruce Dern shot John Wayne in the back, killing him, in *The Cowboys*, also from 1972. Dern received an immediate backlash from fans, as did Smith after *Hostage!* first aired. "I almost had two guys punch me out because of it. People out there that watch television think it's real. I had some problems with that...that was years and tears and yesterday," remembered Smith. On a lighter note, Smith recalled Jim Arness arriving at the studio, "He would fly down to Lockheed airport and he would come in, in a car. He didn't slow down at the front gate, he'd come onto the lot at about sixty miles per hour every day. I'm not kidding you. The guard at the gate would say, 'If you see Jim coming, get out of the way!' He's a better pilot than a driver of a car."

"I remember William Smith from *Hostage!*" recalled Arness. "A great actor and a tough hombre." The final fistfight between Smith and Arness is a no holds barred highlight. Out of curiosity, one wonders who would actually win between the two men if the fisticuffs were real? "I would," laughed Smith.

Actress Lane Bradbury did her first *Gunsmoke* in 1965, appearing with her husband, actor turned director Lou Antonio, in the segment entitled *Outlaw's Woman*. "Well, it was just the most fun show to do. The scripts were wonderful and it was a wonderful working atmosphere,"

KICKIN' BACK *Actor-turned-agent Steve Stevens relaxes on the set of SHONA in 1963. He later represented many Western character actors, and was Amanda Blake's final agent. (photo courtesy of Steve Stevens)*

stated Bradbury. "It was all your fantasies—as a child I rode horses and I would practice running across my front lawn and falling off...you know, getting shot and falling off and I actually got to do it on the show! It was my first lead," Bradbury continued. A Broadway actor, Antonio revealed, "I used to come out to California every summer to do guest shots just to support my theatre habit." Among his favorite work are his *Gunsmoke* segments. "The great thing for actors on that show is that the characters were so well written. Really interesting characters and then we had all the comedy stuff later on, we got to play the doofuses."

At first Bradbury was a little intimidated on the show, recalling, "I remember doing a scene with Arness and Roger Ewing. They were both so tall and when I watched it on television, all you could see was the whites of my eyes because I was having to look up so high!" The actress held her own and eventually wound up with a recurring character in several episodes. "I did six of them," stated Bradbury, "the last four I played the same character, Merry Florene. It was during the time when there wasn't a lot violence in the shows." Antonio was impressed with the detail to be found on a *Gunsmoke* set. "I played the goofus with Anthony James in *Gold Town*. When you played these characters, you didn't shave and to make your teeth look gamey, they would put spirit gum on our teeth to make it look like we chewed tobacco or didn't brush our teeth. They really went for authentic. They were very careful about that and the wardrobe people were wonderful."

Regarding her portrayal of Merry Florene, Bradbury related, "I've always loved playing somebody from the wrong side of the tracks because I grew up on the right side of the tracks. It was always fun for me to play someone poor and ignorant...it was much more interesting to me instead of playing the debutante." Anthony James often joined Bradbury and Antonio on these hillbilly outings. "What I remember is how wonderful all the people

were." expressed James. "Not only the main cast, but the directors and the crew and the producer, John Mantley, a wonderful guy." Mantley was very impressed with his work on *Hill Girl* in 1968. "John Mantley put me up for best supporting for an Emmy for that performance. I got a wonderful letter from him regarding that particular episode. He was great to work with."

"I would say most importantly," continued James, "it was just how wonderfully sensitive and caring and dedicated all of the people I worked with were in trying to do something good as opposed to just something that was exploitative and went for the lowest common denominator, you know, aesthetically and artistically. They really worked hard on that." James appreciated the fact that working on the program was truly a team effort, not only allowing input but welcoming it from all involved, including the guest stars. His second *Gunsmoke* segment was the aforementioned *Hill Girl* in 1968, in which he co-starred with Victor French. James remembered, "When Victor and I went to wardrobe for the hillbilly characters they wanted to give us those pointed black hats, like in *Li'l Abner*. We looked at each other and both were thinking the same exact thing—we don't want to be stereotypical hillbillies, we wanted to do something that was reasonable that would set us apart a little."

James elaborated, "We decided that we were the kind of guys that would ambush people so what we wore should be a strange combination of different things that really didn't go together. Because of whoever we robbed or took, that's what we ended up having. It was a very eclectic outfit. I found this old derby and Victor found this old top hat. It was great because all of a sudden it still was within the range of what those people would be wearing, all beaten up, but they were a little more idiosyncratic and gave the character a little more of a personal style...as opposed to two hillbilly guys in pointed hats." The actors' input didn't stop at the wardrobe department.

"It wasn't supposed to be funny, it was a serious thing—we try to rob a store and we wound the guy. It was a very dramatic piece, but Victor and I tended to want to counterpoint things, so we put some funny schtick here and there. They liked the idea after they saw the episode and that's how those two characters became funny," offered James. "Originally they were supposed to be these mean, sadistic characters with no humor about them at all. They went from that to really written for comedy purposes." James also appreciated working with Ken Curtis. "I could go to him and say 'You know, this line sounds a little banal, do you have anything a little more ethnic or regional or something I could translate into it?,' and he would always come up with something. Everybody really worked hard doing something good as opposed to just gliding through it. It showed so much throughout the course of the history of the show." After appearing in Clint Eastwood's *Unforgiven* in 1992, James retired from acting and began concentrating on his artwork full-time. His paintings have been exhibited throughout the United States. James published a book devoted to his art entitled *Language of the Heart* in 1994.

"Out of all the acting things I did," recalled actor-turned-agent Steve Stevens, "for me my dream came true—I got to ride a horse and play cowboy—this was exciting!" Stevens appeared in the beginning of *Shona*, which first aired in 1963. "Every actor will say he can ride a horse—probably ninety-eight to ninety-nine percent of them the only horse they've ever been on is a trail ride at camp." As for the state of the Western genre today, Stevens opined, "You can't do a Western today and call it *Westward Ho 90210*—actors are too pretty." After retiring from acting, Stevens became an agent, representing many familiar Western faces, including Buck Taylor. "I had the honor of representing Miss Kitty," stated a proud Stevens. Sadly, he was Amanda Blake's last agent. As for his time on *Gunsmoke* and the program in general, he offered, "Good actors, good production, good writing, it all starts there. If there is a likeability for the characters, they become part of your family. It wouldn't have happened if it was just Matt Dillon, but it was Matt and Kitty, Doc and Festus—you learned to care about what happened to these people."

Child actress Susan Gordon, so memorable as Danny Kaye's daughter in the 1959 Paramount picture *The Five Pennies*, appeared on *Gunsmoke* once in 1961. Her episode, *Little Girl*, was another one of Dennis Weaver's directing credits. Gordon recalled, "*Gunsmoke* was a special experience because it was the only Western I did." And what of her co-star, Arness? "He was the tallest man

CHILD ACTRESS Susan Gordon and James Arness in a scene from LITTLE GIRL, which debuted in 1961.

FAMILY AFFAIR Dennis Weaver and Wright King with their real-life sons who appeared in the episode LITTLE GIRL. Left to right: Rickie, Robby and Rusty Weaver and Megan, Michael and Rip King.

that I had ever seen and being as small as I was for my age, he was a giant. He was just the kindest, gentlest person—his gentleness made it even more striking to me." Actor Wright King also appeared on that episode, along with his sons and Dennis Weaver's sons. "Dennis was a very good friend of ours, I knew him from New York City—our two families were very close. Very nice to work with."

Wright, who later starred on another television oater, *Wanted: Dead or Alive*, continued, "*Gunsmoke* was pretty close to me because that was early on. I did my first one when I moved out to California in 1955. Jim Arness was great to work with—you don't realize that a star of a TV series is a really tough job. A great deal of responsibility and it is not easy in any category—it takes about twenty-five hours a day."

Beautiful and talented actress Suzanne Lloyd guest-starred in two episodes, *Target*, and *Harriet* from seasons five and six, respectively. She had very fond memories of her time in and around Dodge City. "We were on location—way out in the boonies. I used to love to get up at 4:30 or 5 in the morning and get in the bus or car and arrive on location. The first thing you could smell in that clear, clear air was coffee and bacon and toast cooking so that it would be ready for everybody when we got there. I just thought I was in heaven," laughed Lloyd, "just thought I had died and gone to heaven. The greatest experience of my life. The people—I was just so grateful that I had a chance to meet and to work with them. Those were really the best of times." Lloyd also respected Arness and

NOT YET A CASTAWAY Prior to a famous shipwreck, Russell Johnson appeared as a heavy on several Westerns, including GUNSMOKE.

Weaver, stating, "Both men were very good and I enjoyed working with them."

"I had been such a fan of the show before I actually did the show, I had their characters fixed very strongly in

JOHN SAXON The actor appeared on GUNSMOKE many times, including THE SQUAW in 1975.

my mind. I was surprised, and delightfully so, when I got to know Jim and Dennis and how different they were from the characters that they were playing, which I always found delicious. Dennis, who played this kind of whiny, almost PMS character a lot of the times and because he was a studied, brilliant actor—he was very accessible, but he was also a very pensive, thoughtful actor. With Dennis, there was a lot going on beneath the character that he had worked on." Her praise for her co-stars did not extend to Amanda Blake, however, causing Lloyd to state, "Amanda, on the other hand—I was so looking forward to meeting her—I thought she was one of the most beautiful women on television at the time. I just thought she was going to be this wonderful magnanimous earth-mother character like Miss Kitty—she wasn't like that."

Lloyd met Blake when she filmed *Harriet.* "It was the first day and I was really excited, my second *Gunsmoke,* a heck of a good part. There's a code of ethics when you're working that has to do with being ready on time. If you have to shoot a scene before another actor but another actor is seated in the makeup chair—when you come into the makeup room, the other actor just automatically gets up because you're up first. She wouldn't. She would not get up. It was in hairdressing. She was talking and talking and talking and talking to the hairdresser, and I was becoming more and more panicked because I was the new kid on the block. I was afraid I was going to get blamed for being late. I considered myself a professional—I was never late." Regardless of that awkward situation, Lloyd maintained, "The cast was obviously highly professional and very skilled and very gifted; they knew their craft well."

Prior to being the most famous professor ever to be marooned on an island with an eclectic group of castaways, actor Russell Johnson appeared in several Westerns, both on the little and big screens, often as an impressive heavy. Of his four appearances on *Gunsmoke*, Johnson cites episodes *Bloody Hands* and *The Long Night* as his favorites. "*Bloody Hands* originally ended in a fight with Jim Arness, which was cut—too bloody. *The Long Night*, directed by John Rich was a really good show." Johnson was friends with both Arness and Weaver prior to his work on the show. "Jim is an old friend from before *Gunsmoke*. He has always been a nice guy and a good actor. Dennis is a wonderful man and a fine actor, also an old friend. We were contract players at Universal in 1952 to 1954."

And just when a really good one hour episode is about to end and you know the story cannot be wrapped up in time, these words flash across the screen—To Be Continued, and so...

To Be Continued...

FROM THE CATWALK Typical day of filming in the Long Branch Saloon.

BEHIND THE SCENES

There are so many components involved in making a television series or film, be it successful or not. As actor Gregory Peck once said, "No one sets out to make a bad movie; what looks good on the page doesn't always translate well onto a screen." Truer words never spoken. However, chances are you'll have a memorable product when all of the pieces fit, in front of and behind the camera. *Gunsmoke* always had the best talent onscreen and always managed to have the best behind the scenes also. The well-oiled machine so many celebrities remembered.

All involved were like family. Individuals got to know what a co-worker was thinking or what was needed for a scene usually before one inch of film passed through a camera. Actor and frequent heavy Anthony Caruso observed, "No arguments—directors, producers, the crew. Not on *Gunsmoke*. The crew didn't change I'll bet you two men in ten years. If they didn't die, they didn't change."

When production began on the series in 1955, the crew had already been together for several years. They were hired originally by William Boyd for his *Hopalong Cassidy* series. When Boyd decided to semi-retire and

SNACK TIME Blake and Arness share a popsicle between scenes.

limit his work to personal appearances, he was kind enough to find employment for his all-important behind the scenes gang on various projects, rather than handing everyone a pink slip. Hoppy eventually convinced CBS and Charles Marquis Warren to hire them on for their new adult Western. What a grand gesture that was—practically unheard of in today's entertainment world. Boyd, at best, probably hoped to secure two or three more years of work for his people—never dreaming that some would achieve job security for two decades.

James Arness explained the shooting schedule to *Trail Dust* magazine in 2001: "We had an ideal situation those first few years. We would come in on a Monday afternoon and have a sit-down reading around a table in the office. That's where ideas for a character or the story would be discussed. Then we filmed on Tuesday, Wednesday and Thursday. We had Friday, Saturday and Sunday off. It really was a great week! The one-hour episodes, of course, took a six-day shooting schedule—Monday through Friday, then over into the following Monday."

Glen Alden headed up the makeup department from the very beginning, with Pat Whiffing handling hairdressing. Alden stayed with the show for the entire twenty seasons, becoming a close friend and confidant to series star James Arness on and off the set. Ken Chase assisted Alden in the later years. "It was just a whole different way of working in those days. I was just a young guy and I worked my butt off," Chase recalled. "I loved it. There weren't three or four makeup men to work on twelve

BIRDS-EYE VIEW Blake watches the filming from the camera location with cameraman Fleet Southcott.

actors; there was one make-up man that made up everyone in the entire cast. It was a hard-working environment, but it was a lot of fun for a young guy."

"We'd do a little bit of location work, usually once a year...for three weeks," continued Chase. "There was a lot of challenges for the make up guy—a lot of beards and mustaches and scars and bruises for characters—it was great! It was a great environment. In those days the business was still fun. That was before the training programs and before the production assistants and before cell phones and all the baloney—people then were more interested in having fun." Work always came first, but camaraderie was foremost. "We used to play cards on the set all the time. We used to play a game called 'Liars Poker' with dollar bills—there'd be card games at night on location; Acey-Deucey games at lunchtime—it was just a whole different world."

Chase had great admiration for Alden, stating, "He was a nice old guy. He was really practically retired when I was working. Jim Arness, out of loyalty, used to keep him on the payroll. Glen would just come in the mornings and put Jim's makeup on and go home. It was really a terrific thing. It was great to see somebody treated that way." Loyalty, in addition to talent and professionalism, was an integral part of the continued success during the long run *Gunsmoke* would enjoy.

Was there a downside to working on *Gunsmoke*? "Summers were kind of awful because of all the horse crap—the soundstages really smelled bad. The collection of urine week after week—I don't know how often they cleaned out those stages, that was pretty rough," laughed Chase. Many performers would instruct their agents to book them on *Gunsmoke* at the beginning of the season rather than near a season's end, just for this reason. First assistant cameraman Richard Meinardus remembered, "We had horses on that stage and mules five days a week...it got pretty rank in there." As for the, uh, shall we say, horse remnants? "You could scoop it up, but when they peed on the floor, there was no scooping that up," Meinardus laughed. Actor Will Hutchins summed it up best—"I called the indoor town sets the graveyard of a thousand horse turds."

Meinardus fondly recalled his days working in Dodge. "It was my very first experience on production. I was an assistant cameraman. I started out as a second assistant and after a year I took over as first assistant. That was a career that lasted for about twenty-seven years with Harry Stradling, Jr." Meinardus elaborated, "Harry

CRAFT SERVICES *Amanda Blake and crew members are served lunch on location.*

moved up on *Gunsmoke* from camera operator to director of photography. I joined him on his second year as director of photography—we stayed together as a team for twenty-seven years." Meinardus and Stradling went on to a successful career in motion pictures, which included the films *Little Big Man, McQ, The Way We Were* and *Rooster Cogburn*. Stradling was very grateful for his time spent on *Gunsmoke*, reflecting, "The first film I did was *Welcome to Hard Times* with Henry Fonda. It was a big picture. I got that because Burt Kennedy, who directed that picture, was a follower of *Gunsmoke*. He liked the way it looked and that's how I got the job."

"I was an operator when I first went on *Gunsmoke*," recalled Stradling, "I was working with cinematographer Frank Phillips on *Have Gun—Will Travel*. Then we went to *Gunsmoke*. They wanted Frank to do another show and I became a cinematographer on *Gunsmoke* in 1964. It was very exciting, I was pretty young. It was a great experience." With the brief cancellation of *Gunsmoke* in 1967, Stradling and Meinardus were temporarily unemployed. "We went off to do another Western, *Cimarron Strip*, which only lasted one year," remarked Meinardus. Then the big screen called, and the two pros never looked back. Except for the good times at CBS. "They were all very nice, easy to get along with. We were all very close," Stradling recalled of his *Gunsmoke* co-workers. "I enjoyed the cast and the crew, everyone got along really well, " added Meinardus.

Photographing someone with the height of a James Arness could be a challenge at times, especially when the shoot is on a confined set. "When he got up from behind that desk in the marshal's office it was really something to follow, because he's so tall. When he'd get up, he'd lean way forward then rise up forever, like he was ten feet tall," laughed Meinardus. "It was difficult for me and the operator because there's a big focus change as he leaned forward. He stood up and if you weren't careful he'd take you right off the set. You'd have the microphone in the shot." There wasn't a lot of time for mistakes around Arness either. "Arness always left at six, no matter. It could be right in the middle of a take and if it was six o'clock, he'd leave," chuckled Stradling.

Both men were very protective of their leading lady, Amanda Blake, and her image. Meinardus explained, "I liked Amanda, oh she was great, really great. On Mondays we had to use a lot of diffusion with Amanda...she liked to party on the weekends!" Diffusion meaning softer focus techniques, nothing harsh. "We had to use diffusion so you couldn't see what you weren't supposed to see," laughed Meinardus. Stradling agreed, "I tried very hard to make Amanda Blake look good—she was very appreciative of everything you did for her."

The camera crew obviously had to work closely with the segment directors, and out of this working condition, many friendships were formed. "The McEveety's—they were really characters," recalled Meinardus. "I remember doing a couple of shows in Bishop, California. We did the first one with Vince. He just plum wore us into the ground, and it was real hot there anyways, difficult for everyone because of the heat. He just wore us into the ground. Then, here comes Bernie after lunch to do the next one, (he laughs), and he was piss and vinegar, ready to go, and the crew was just wilted!" The crew had nicknames for most of the directors. "I remember Harry Harris—Captain Midnight," laughed Meinardus. "Harris would go over schedule—we would end up being there on a Friday night until 11:59! Back in those days, after midnight you went into some exorbitant overtime scale. Every time we did a show with Harry—well, that's how he got the name of Captain Midnight."

Performers lucky enough to be cast on *Gunsmoke* always had high praise for the crew behind the scenes. Morgan Woodward, one of the finest actors from his generation, stated, "Well, start with the costumer, Alex Velcoff —wonderful. I mean every one of them—even the craft services guy who swept up after the horses, he was a pro!" Katherine Ross put it simply, "They had top people." And it showed on the finished product.

Music always plays an important part of any program and CBS always hired the best for *Gunsmoke*. Concert organist and composer Rex Koury wrote the theme song originally for the radio series in 1952. It was his first attempt at composing music for a Western, and Koury readily accepted the task. Recalling the creation of

FILMING PREPS *Blake, left, gets ready for filming while Arness, upper right, studies his lines in an unusual place.*

the theme in 1976 for a WAMU-FM radio program out of Washington, DC, honoring *Gunsmoke*, Koury stated, "I had gone to bed the night before...I knew pretty well what I wanted...figuring I could do it quickly in the morning. At eight o'clock...I'm in the middle of shaving...I suddenly realize we haven't written the theme! I grabbed a magazine, a piece of manuscript and a pencil, and sat down in the most convenient spot—and that is where the theme from *Gunsmoke* was actually composed."

In 1955, lyricist Glenn Spencer added words to the music, causing the title to be incorrectly referred to as

GOLD TOWN SET Actress Lane Bradbury prepares for a scene with Ken Curtis, who will provide his lines off camera. (photo courtesy of Lane Bradbury)

THANKFUL PECK of Blake, Stradling stated: "She was very appreciative of everything you did for her." (photo courtesy of Harry Stradling, Jr.)

LOCATION, LOCATION, LOCATION Regarding the crew, actor Anthony Caruso stated: "The crew didn't change I'll bet two men in ten years. If they didn't die, they didn't change."

TAKE FLIGHT Actor Morgan Woodward and casting director Pam Polifroni prepare to take off in Woodward's plane. (photo courtesy of Pam Polifroni)

LOCATION TRUCK Actor Steve Stevens hopped on the hood of the studio transport truck prior to filming his scenes for SHONA in 1963. (photo courtesy of Steve Stevens)

MUSIC MAESTRO Legendary film scorers such as Elmer Bernstein worked on GUNSMOKE throughout the seasons.

QUICK STUDY Arness takes a last look at the scene as crew members and Dennis Weaver prepare to shoot.

BLAKE'S STAND-IN Shirley Wilson not only doubled for Kitty, she was an artist as well, presenting character portraits to Milburn Stone and Ken Curtis in 1967. (photo courtesy of Lucille S. Dillon)

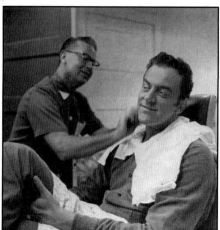

MAKE-UP Like star James Arness, make-up artist Glen Alden, shown applying Arness' sideburns, stayed with GUNSMOKE for twenty seasons.

LOOKING THROUGH THE LENS Blake and cinematographer Harry Stradling, Jr. on location. (photo courtesy of Harry Stradling, Jr.)

EYE FOR TALENT Many performers owe their careers to casting director Pam Polifroni, shown here in 1994. (photo courtesy Pam Polifroni)

Gunsmoke Trail by some. The theme was published by Herman Music, Inc. and sold by Fiesta Music, Inc. out of Hollywood. The television theme arrangement would change almost as often as the cast did throughout the years, beginning with a slow doom-ba-dee-dah doom-ba-dee-dah beat in season one to a rousing guitar and brass version in the latter years. Wisely, the lyrics were never sung or heard over the opening or closing credits. The tune was recorded many times by artists that varied from champagne bandleader Lawrence Welk to guitar rocker Duane Eddy, and from country pianist Floyd Cramer to Arthur Fiedler and the Boston Pops.

Episode scores were handled by some of the best composers Hollywood had to offer, many legends in their field. Bernard Herrmann, Jerry Goldsmith, Wilbur Hatch, Morton Stevens and a Western's best friend, Elmer Bernstein, to name but a few. Hatch and Stevens are remembered primarily for their work on television. Hatch gained fame on *I Love Lucy*, working closely with series star and producer Desi Arnaz. Stevens wrote perhaps one of the most famous television theme songs ever, *Hawaii 5-0*. Director Alfred Hitchcock collaborated with Herrmann on several motion pictures, with his scores for *Vertigo*, *North by Northwest*, and especially *Psycho*, standing out. Goldsmith wrote some of the best film scores ever and was always in high demand. His scores include *Basic Instinct*, *Poltergeist*, *Chinatown*, *Patton* and *Star Trek–The Motion Picture*.

Bernstein, if for nothing else, wrote the definitive

THE CHAIR Arness waits for the next set-up in front of the Long Branch set in 1963.

150

Western tracks in 1960; the rousing and unforgettable theme and score for *The Magnificent Seven*. Bernstein was never typed with his style, and his scores ran the gamut of the world of show business. His work includes *Ghostbusters*, *The Ten Commandments*, *Big Jake* and *Thoroughly Modern Millie*, for which Bernstein won the Academy Award for best score. The entertainment world suffered a great loss in 2004 when both Goldsmith and Bernstein passed away. Their work on the big and little screens will live on forever.

Visitors were often welcomed into the family as well. "My father came out and he'd never been on a set. So I took him down to the set and told the assistant director," remembered writer Jim Byrnes. "Ken Curtis walked over and I said, 'This my Dad,' and Ken just took it from there. He took care of my dad for the rest of the day; introduced him to everybody on the set—Jim Arness, Amanda—always saying, 'This is Jim Byrnes father.' My dad was in heaven, he loved it. He planned on staying an hour and spent all day there. Twelve hours on the set! I'd ask him, 'Do you want to go?' 'No, I want to stay here!'" laughed Byrnes. "It was very nice."

Herman N. Schoenbrun, Clem R. Widrig and Edla Bakke—set decorator, property master and script supervisor—three longtime *Gunsmoke* employees holding positions that frequently changed throughout a season on other shows. Schoenbrun stayed for twenty seasons, Widrig for thirteen and Bakke for nine. The all-important job of casting each episode was initially handled by Lynn Stalmaster. Stalmaster then took on a partner, James Lister, and the two handled the weekly chore. Stalmaster left the series and for a brief time, Lister took over. Some of Lister's methods were not popular with some actors and the network—Lister would go as far as blacklisting certain performers from *Gunsmoke*—making his days in Dodge City numbered. Pam Polifroni was hired and the rest, shall we say, is history. As a child, she lived just up the street from actor Glenn Strange and his family. Little did she know how much this future bartender would figure in her world.

Polifroni had a knack for casting and those who worked on *Gunsmoke* always stated, "she was the best." Polifroni reflected, "I was working as a secretary on *The Loretta Young Show* in the early fifties, and the casting director kept saying, 'I think you've got a flair for this' and he sort of pushed me into it. He took me with him when he went to another show which was *Lineup* with Tom Tully and Warner Anderson—they were cops. Our office was in a little area at this studio...you went through my office to go to a conference room—and that's where the *Gunsmoke* people and the *Have Gun—Will Travel* people rehearsed. I used to see them going through, Andy McLaglen, Jim Arness and all these guys that were eighteen feet tall!" Taking a few years off from the business to adopt a baby, Polifroni was lured back to cast two soap opera style shows, *Day In Court* and *Morning Court*. Casting two complete half hour shows a day, fifty-two weeks a year was quite a challenge.

"It was the best training ground anybody could have because using that many actors—complete new cast every day—was using between seventy-five and eighty actors every week. I got to know all these great character people," remarked Polifroni. One rolodex full of people interviewed quickly turned to four. Soon CBS came calling, as Polifroni explained, "They were looking for someone and someone recommended me. The head of casting called, interviewed me and said, 'when can you start?' I was just assigned shows—*Gunsmoke, Rawhide* and *Gilligan's Island*." Polifroni admitted, "Westerns weren't my thing...I really didn't even know which end of the horse ate! The first script I read of *Gunsmoke* was featuring Festus and it was written in his vernacular—I had no idea what they were talking about half the time. I had to ask, 'What's does this mean? And what's a dogie?' But anyway, I got the hang of it."

"There wasn't a lot of casting on *Gilligan's Island*...but the two Westerns kept me pretty busy—I didn't have a lot of excess time," continued Polifroni. Many future stars owe so much to Polifroni and *Gunsmoke*, with Jon Voight being the perfect example. Polifroni cast him at the suggestion of actor Anthony Zerbe. Voight had done some work in New York before landing a role in the episode *The Newcomers* in 1966. "Here comes this big lanky kid," laughed Polifroni, "adorable. So I said, 'Can you do a Swedish accent?' He said, 'sure.' He was so good in that episode."

Voight made a total of three *Gunsmoke* appearances—returning the final time in 1969 after completing *Midnight Cowboy*, out of gratitude for what the segments had done for his career. Within a year, the actor would receive his first Oscar nomination. Voight would go on to win the Academy Award for Best Actor a little over a decade after his last *Gunsmoke* episode, for his performance in *Coming Home*. "I was so proud of him when he won the Oscar," stated Polifroni.

Others in her debt include David Carradine, Nick Nolte, Gary Busey, Michael Learned, Richard Dreyfuss and Sam Elliott. "Harrison Ford—day player, several times, four-hundred dollars a day. Would he do that now?" laughed Polifroni. "I thought he had something special. Also, Gerald McRaney had something special. Richard Dreyfuss, remember him on *Gunsmoke*? That was a good show. It was fun when we cast people who turned out well—'Oh, I knew him when...!' *Gunsmoke* had been on the air for so many years—nobody ever said 'Oh I won't do *Gunsmoke*!'—it was always prestigious, respected. Everybody enjoyed doing the show. You never heard anybody say, 'It was the worst experience of my life.' Ever."

Actor James Nusser, who portrayed town drunk Louie Pheeters, holds a special place in her heart. "Wasn't he wonderful? There were times when we weren't sure if he could stand or not—but he always came through. And when he had to," recalled Polifroni, "he would break your heart. He was a terrific character actor."

Recalling her years on *Gunsmoke*, Polifroni admitted, "I didn't realize it at the time; it's only in retrospect that I realized it was just the best possible show to work on. Everybody cared; everybody liked everybody else—it was just fun. I looked forward to going to work every day, and I can't say that about my entire career. Everybody did their job—Mantley was a good delegator—as much as he controlled, he was a good delegator. He let the writers do their thing and casting do theirs; directors do their thing."

The job was a demanding one, constantly in motion. As soon as one segment was cast, the next episode was waiting for Polifroni to dissect. "It was a pressure job, everything was yesterday," chuckled Polifroni. "But at the same time it was interesting and exciting because no two days were the same, always something different happening." Polifroni continued her professional relationship with Mantley and Arness, casting *How the West Was Won* and all of the *Gunsmoke* reunion movies. She worked her magic on many other programs including, *Hawaii 5-0*, *All in the Family*, *The Waltons* and *Macgyver*, to name but a few. Her motion picture credits include *Telefon* with Charles Bronson, *Tron* with Bruce Boxleitner and John Wayne's final film, *The Shootist*. She retired in 1994, with the soap opera *Santa Barbara*, her last credit.

Regarding Polifroni, actor Cliff Osmond assessed,

GIVE THE ELEPHANT A BEER On the set of ARIZONA MIDNIGHT, extras watch as Ken Curtis films a scene while the elephant wants a drink from the man seated at far left.

"She had great, great taste—quality oriented—a decent human being, which is a rare combination in people—a personal decency and artistic excellence." Director Vincent McEveety readily agreed, "Pam was an incredible, major contributor. She always knew what chemistry was right. She really, really worked hard." And it paid off every time.

Looking back, summing up, Polifroni, speaking for everyone involved on *Gunsmoke*, stated, "Yeah, it was the best of times as they say."

THE RUN

Charles Marquis Warren may have only stayed with *Gunsmoke* for just a little over one season, but his influence stayed with the show for all twenty seasons and beyond, as we celebrate the fiftieth anniversary of the premiere episode. His attention to casting would become iconic; his four leads would soon become synonymous with their characters, and vice versa. Though the program itself never cracked the top twenty in the final Nielsen ratings during the first season, it was nevertheless popular because it was different.

The hero in this case, Marshal Matt Dillon, was nearly shot to death in the first episode. That's no way to treat a hero—unheard of in the annals of television history—and motion picture history, for that fact. It was a bold move; one that certainly was not planned. Warren decided to air the second episode filmed, *Matt Gets It* first, instead of the pilot, *Hack Prine*. In his foreword to the novel *Blood, Bullets and Buckskin* for Signet in 2005, James Arness stated his opinion on the segment switch: "They chose the more dramatic *Matt Gets It*. What I never told anyone was that I always thought we should have aired *Hack Prine* first. I still feel it was a better show."

THE ORIGINAL CAST *James Arness as Matt Dillon, Amanda Blake as Kitty Russell, Milburn Stone as Doc Adams and Dennis Weaver as Chester Goode.*

STRONG MAN James Arness stayed with the show for twenty seasons—and beyond. This photo is a "Bumper"—used primarily between commercial breaks, broadcast interruptions, and occasionally for magazine and newspaper advertising.

Arness is right, *Hack Prine* is a better episode, but had it been the first episode aired, many may have judged *Gunsmoke* as just another Western, adult or not. *Matt Gets It* set *Gunsmoke* up for a record-breaking, history-making run. You were more or less hooked. As the season progressed, viewer numbers slowly increased.

By season two, Arness, Amanda Blake, Milburn Stone and especially Dennis Weaver, became household names and their little screen counterparts became members of the family. Weaver made such an impact as Chester and was so believable in his portrayal, he became the first breakout star of the show.

Chester proved so popular with the public that sympathy began to generate worldwide for his "disability." Donna Johnson, Emergency Department Director for the Hi-Desert Medical Center in Joshua Tree, California, recently recalled a story from the time she was training to be a nurse: "The story was in a nursing journal. Apparently a mother noticed her four year old was having a great deal of trouble walking—he had a horrible, horrible limp. It really distressed her and she thought it would go away, but as the day went on, it didn't go away. So she took him to the pediatrician."

"The pediatrician walked in and noticed the boy's horrible limp. He checked the boy over and did some preliminary x-rays to see if he could find anything wrong and they couldn't find a thing. He told the mother, 'As young as he is, that is a terrible limp. We've got to find out what's causing it—I recommend that you take him to see an orthopedic specialist to see if they can figure out what is going on.' They made all of the arrangements and the boy went to see an orthopedic surgeon. The boy was given a thorough examination—they ran him through bunches of x-rays, trying find out what caused his limp. Everything came out normal. The surgeon told the mother, 'I just can't understand it—I don't find a thing wrong with your son.' So finally he looked at the little boy and said, 'Son, why are you limping like that?' The little boy says, 'My name is Chester and I work for Mr. Dillon.'"

"I've always loved that story, not just because

I thought it was funny, but because, you know, we nurses, and doctors particularly, don't talk to our patients sometimes and if somebody had just asked the little kid what was wrong, he would have told them." Johnson chuckles, then concluded, "I'm Chester and I work for Mister Dillon." Such was the power of Weaver's characterization, not to mention his wide acceptance with the viewing public.

DENNIS WEAVER as Chester

In 1957, *Gunsmoke* was the number one show in the country. On April 15, 1958, the National Academy of Television Arts and Sciences honored the show as the Best Dramatic Series with Continuing Characters of 1957—becoming the first Western ever to win a major Emmy. The following year, the Academy would bestow Weaver with the Emmy for Best Supporting Actor in a Drama Series.

Memorable guest stars during the seasons first five years included, Keye Luke, John Carradine, James Drury, DeForest Kelley, Charles Bronson, Chuck Connors, Cloris Leachman, Jack Kelly, Robert Vaughn, Barbara Eden, Jack Klugman, June Lockhart, Jack Cassidy, Martin Landau and Marilyn Maxwell.

At the end of season six CBS announced first, that *Gunsmoke* would return for a seventh season, and second, the show would expand from a half hour to an hour per episode. It would keep its Saturday time slot, airing at 10 p.m. The format change was questioned by many, but would ultimately prove successful. The transition, however, was rocky, with early episodes at the new running length seeming awkward and padded, at times. CBS wanted to continue rerunning the half-hour episodes so they immediately repackaged them under the title *Marshal Dillon* and put them into syndication. *Marshal Dillon* would air on Tuesday nights from 7:30 to 8:00, from October 1961 to June 1964 originally.

Awards and fan mail not withstanding, Weaver began to grow restless in Dodge. In December of 1961, *TV*

Guide reported that the actor had the seven-year itch. Weaver was leaving the show to emcee *TV Tonight*, an hour-long variety show for Bob Banner Associates. A pilot was shot but never sold. "I went all through the period of Chester leaving," recalled director Andrew V. McLaglen. "Dennis had *McCloud* later, but he could have gone on for the whole twenty seasons." Weaver made a second attempt to leave Chester behind in a dramatic show called *The Giant Step*, portraying a high school vice-principal. Again, pilot shot—no sell.

In a cover story from July 1963, *TV Guide* reported: "I've exhausted the potential of Chester," he [Weaver] says, and after eight years this is undoubtedly true. But Norman Macdonnell, producer of *Gunsmoke*, sees more to it than that—"Denny wants to be the top man—the star—of his own series, and he won't be happy until he finds out whether he can make it or not." In 2004, director Harry Harris offered, "Dennis was terrific, but he didn't do anything. He'd do a little bit. He kind of moseyed his way through the show—they didn't have a hell of a lot for him..." Harris elaborated, "He was thinking about going off and doing his own thing. He played that same thing over and over and over again—he was second banana and I think he wanted to be first. I think he got bored."

With Weaver in a perpetual revolving door, the production team began thinking of a replacement for Chester. Ben Cooper and Will Hutchins were briefly considered. At the beginning of season eight, a little known actor named Burt Reynolds joined the cast as a half-Indian blacksmith

JAMES ARNESS as Matt

named Quint Asper. The amount of fan mail received by Weaver seemed paltry by comparison to what began arriving at the studio for Reynolds, Dodge City's newest inhabitant. Popularity aside, few could have imagined what

TAKING A STROLL Stone, Blake, Arness and Weaver walked into television history.

can't use him as much." Macdonnell's prophecy would become reality in just a short while.

Third time's a charm they say, and in Weaver's case, his third attempt to leave *Gunsmoke* would stick. He was offered the lead in *Kentucky Jones*. In his 2001 autobiography, *All the World's a Stage*, Weaver stated, "Well, before I left *Gunsmoke* in 1964, I made sure I had a bird in the hand. I had a guarantee of twenty-four shows with NBC for *Kentucky Jones*. I thought it would be a winner...but after we shot the twenty-four shows, they cancelled it. I was in shock. I just assumed that the next series I did would be as successful as *Gunsmoke*, but it wasn't." Weaver began to doubt his decision to leave *Gunsmoke*. Eventually he found great success in movies and other television series, among them *Gentle Ben* and, of course, *McCloud*. To this day, Weaver remains grateful for his time on *Gunsmoke* and for the doors his portrayal of Chester Goode ultimately opened for him.

With Reynolds no longer considered a replacement for Weaver, he instead became an addition to an already powerful cast. In 1963, actor Ken Curtis was cast as scruffy, loveable-yet-deadly when need be, Festus Haggen, and the search for Weaver's replacement was over. Festus, who would become a regular character in 1964, was eased into the storylines as Chester was

would lay in store for Reynolds beyond *Gunsmoke*. Producer Norm Macdonnell had an inkling however, and was quoted in a May 1963 *TV Guide* article about Reynolds: "I think he's a good actor. Innately, he's a leading man, which creates something of a problem for us. We

TWO MAJOR ADDITIONS Burt Reynolds and Ken Curtis, top row, joined Stone, Blake and Arness in 1962 and 1964, respectively.

eased out; Chester eventually disappeared completely without any explanation.

Curtis was welcomed with open arms by his fellow castmates, who became tired and annoyed with Weaver and his many attempts to vacate the role. "Why, on his last show, he hardly even limped!" exclaimed Amanda Blake.

Milburn Stone added, "We had about nine funerals over him." That said and done, Weaver and his castmates remained close friends—friendships that continue even today. Macdonnell also weathered the Chester vs. Festus storm, recalling, "The mail on Festus is either absolutely white or absolutely black. Some people say they can't stand him. Others say they like him better than Chester. They either love him or hate him—but 90 percent say they love him." In the same 1964 *TV Guide* article, Curtis stated, "There are so many good actors that are hurtin', I'm just grateful. I hope *Gunsmoke* goes on for another ten years." Curtis would stay on the show for eleven years and with his character Festus, for the rest of his life.

In 2001, Arness offered his perspective to *Trail Dust* magazine, stating, "Dennis decided to leave *Gunsmoke* after nine seasons...his departure from the series had everyone concerned—his character, Chester Goode had been tremendously popular and a deep part of the show. Then Andy McLaglen, who directed ninety-five episodes of *Gunsmoke*, came up with the idea of replacing Dennis with Ken Curtis, with whom Andy had already worked. That move worked out great for the series and Ken fit right into the character of Festus Haggen—a very smooth transition—and Festus proved to be quite popular for the rest of the series."

"In early 1964, during my second season on *Gunsmoke*," wrote Burt Reynolds in his memoir *My Life*, "my initial enthusiasm for playing Quint was replaced by a gnawing frustration. It wasn't merely that people constantly remarked, 'Oh, you play a half-breed,' and I had to say, 'No, I play a half-Indian.' It was that I really hadn't fulfilled what the show needed, which was someone to take Chester's place. As soon as Ken Curtis guested as Festus, I knew that was what the show needed." Reynolds continued, "The bottom line was the job had become boring. Each week Quint got insulted. Then Jim, after spending six days in Hawaii, would show up on the set and beat up the guy who insulted me." Following the sage advice given to him by co-star Stone, Reynolds left the show and his three-thousand dollar a week salary to pursue a career in motion pictures. Stone felt that movies were the future for Reynolds and that he was simply wasting his time on the series. Doc certainly had the right diagnosis again!

Among the performers of merit that walked through the swinging doors of the Long Branch Saloon from 1960 to 1965 were George Kennedy, Buddy Ebsen, Jeanette Nolan, Lois Nettleton, Leonard Nimoy, Joan Hackett, Richard Jaeckel, Peter Breck, Sheree North, Gilbert Roland, James Broderick, Forrest Tucker, John Drew Barrymore, James Whitmore, Rory Calhoun and Betty Hutton.

The young hunk quotient was filled by relative newcomer Roger Ewing in 1965. First introduced in the episode *Clayton Thaddeus Greenwood*, Ewing would co-star as Thad for the next two seasons. Ewing never quite fit the *Gunsmoke* mold, and his character never really fit in. At times, the character and his acting seemed gangly or awkward, and just like Quint who preceded him, there wasn't a whole lot for the role to present.

WATCHFUL EYE If you were wanted, steer clear of Dodge City and Marshal Matt Dillon.

On September 17, 1966, *Gunsmoke* returned for its twelfth season. The episode was *Snap Decision* and it was the first segment to be presented in color. Even with the show switching to color from black and white, the audience for the seasoned oater was dwindling, as were the rating numbers. Twelve years is a long time for any television show to run, and apparently, *Gunsmoke* was beginning to run its course.

They're Killin' Marshall Dillon—*Gunsmoke* dropped by CBS in 1968 schedule. Headline—*The Hollywood Reporter*, February 23, 1967

CBS Sets 8 New Series; Axes 10—*Gunsmoke* among the victims. Headline—*Daily Variety*, February 23, 1967

Those were the headlines and that is how the cast and crew of *Gunsmoke* first learned of the program's sudden demise. Out on location filming scenes for the two-part episode *Nitro!*, word reached the shoot and stunned everybody there. The next scheduled set-up involved Arness riding his horse from point A to point B, quickly. A shaken Robert Totten directed cast and crew to places. "Action!" A furious Arness spurred his horse on at lightning speed and like a bat out hell, raced across the California landscape that doubled as the Kansas plains. With the camera crew barely able to keep up with the actor and his equine partner, the scene was shot and in the can. Producers Philip Leacock and John Mantley would now convert the annual "end of season" cast party to a "final wrap" celebration.

Nitro! co-star Tom Reese remembered the occasion: "That wrap party. All the bad guys were there—Morgan Woodward, Lee Van Cleef, George Keymas, George Kennedy—they all came—Jack Elam was there. They held it in the Long Branch Saloon. I remember Doc was going to go fishing. Everybody was saying good-bye and crying in their beer."

"Alan Hale, Jr. came into my office," recalled Paul Savage who was story consultant at the time of the

TEN YEARS STRONG Humorous cartoon celebrating an accomplishment that amazed everyone, especially Stone.

162

cancellation. "Big guy, remember? He puts his hand out to mine and said, 'I think it's horrible, it's wrong. If any show should've been cancelled it's that turkey we're doing. For us to stay on and for you to get cancelled, it's wrong and I'm so sorry Paul.'" That turkey Hale referred to was *Gilligan's Island*, of course.

CBS vice-president in charge of programming, Michael Dann, removed *Gunsmoke* from the upcoming 67-68 television schedule, citing "program fatigue." Backed up by the fact that the share-of-audience numbers had dropped recently from forty to thirty, Dann felt he was making a sound business decision that would receive little or no opposition from the network, the affiliates or much less, from the viewers themselves. Numbers be damned! The affiliates began to cry foul; viewers stung the network with irate phone calls and scathing letters; the Kansas State legislature passed a resolution censoring the network for their rash decision. CBS was criticized before Congress by U.S. Senator Byrd on March 2, 1967. The affiliates, the phone calls, the letters, even the Kansas state legislature and the Congress of the United States could be overlooked, but the next voice Dann heard would resonate loud and clear into the vice-president's ears, perhaps even his soul.

William S. Paley was a man of many distinctions. First and foremost, Paley was a huge fan of a little Western called *Gunsmoke*. Second, Paley happened to be CBS's chairman of the board. Paley was on vacation in the Bahamas when Dann had made his decision. Returning to

STATUESQUE BEAUTY Amanda Blake as Miss Kitty welcomed viewers into the Long Branch each week.

the States, Paley learned of the cancellation. At the time, Paley was the most powerful and influential man in

GATHER 'ROUND Arness, Stone, Blake, Curtis and Reynolds.

television, and he immediately ordered his network executives to reinstate *Gunsmoke*. With the new schedule in place, putting the Western back in the lineup meant that something had to go.

The Saturday schedule would have to stay as is, so the search began for a suitable slot. Paley and Tom Dawson, president of the CBS Television Network in New York City, went over the upcoming fall schedule and after careful consideration, found that Monday night from 7:30 to 8:30 was the only possible spot for *Gunsmoke* to air. This meant canceling one established comedy and one new comedy, *Gilligan's Island* and *Doc*, respectively. Paley never cared for the castaways and since *Doc* was untried, they were removed immediately from the fall lineup. There was no vacillation from Paley and against the advice of most of the network underlings, press releases went out on March 8—it was official—*Gunsmoke* was back and on a new night and time.

Savage further recalled, "When the old man, Paley, came back from his vacation and said '*Gunsmoke* is on'—*Gilligan* was cancelled; Hale came back in my office and said, 'Now that's right, that's the way it should be.' Believe it or not. Now that's a personal story. A fact, not second-hand. That's true and that's Alan Hale, Jr. and that's the kind of guy he was. And—what another actor thought of our show."

When the dust settled, most involved were left unscathed—with one notable exception. Inexplicably, Roger Ewing was not asked to return when the show was reinstated. As with the characters Chester and Quint before him, Thad just simply disappeared. Some theorize that had the show not gone through the cancellation attempt, Ewing would have been removed from the cast regardless. "...they had the young kid, Roger Ewing—Thad." recalled Savage. "I remember Jim saying, 'I can't turn over the office to a callow youth!' That was his exact term, 'callow youth,' and he was right, in honesty to the show." Casting director Pam Polifroni stated, "I have no idea whatever happened to Roger Ewing. He was just new on the show when I started. He didn't fit—they tried to make him fit in...nice kid."

Most CBS executives felt that moving the program to Mondays would be the final nail in the coffin for the Western—it would be just a matter of time before Paley would lose his precious program. However, Monday proved to be just the right shot in the arm the show needed. In an August 1970 *TV Guide* cover story, CBS West Coast programming chief, Perry Lafferty, stated, "For no reason you can imagine, the show found a new audience waiting for it in the early time period." Programming executive Martin Dooling added, "Where we have really picked up is in the 18-34 age group. This, combined with a strong influx of early-teens, could account for as many as 10,000,000 additional viewers." Lafferty concluded, "Thirty-five million people tune in. Of course, a lot of people have never seen Arness. Big Jim. He's something else. He's TV's John Wayne."

In the same article, Wayne himself offered, "They

always get back on top of the heap. They represent our folklore. They are understood by the greatest number of people." The Duke continued, "No mystery to me, I always knew *Gunsmoke* was a good thing. Almost did it m'self." Thirty-three years before CBS would debut a reality show that would result in a glut of copycat programming, (purposely avoiding the word entertainment), the network already had a *Survivor.*

1967 and season thirteen would also see the addition of the last major recurring character to amble down Front Street. With Ewing gone, the studio was looking for a replacement character to appeal to the younger set, particularly the ladies. Buck Taylor fit the bill, and after guesting on the two-part episode *Vengeance!* as a heavy early in the season, was cast as Newly O'Brien. Taylor became a regular on November 6, 1967, in the episode *The Pillagers.* Taylor was very impressive in his debut segment, holding his own with the established stars as well as the guest stars—his scenes with the always dependable John Saxon served testament to his acting skills. Taylor as O'Brien made a memorable impression on viewers with just one episode—more than Ewing as Thad could muster in two seasons.

Tom Skerritt, Beau Bridges, Michael Ansara, James MacArthur, Leslie Ann Warren, Carroll O'Connor, John Ireland, William Shatner, James Stacy, John Astin, Ralph Bellamy, Leslie Nielsen, Steve Forrest, Brock Peters, Joan Van Ark and Jack Albertson are but a few of the Hollywood heavyweights that appeared on the dusty CBS soundstages between 1965 and 1970.

With the ratings continuing to ascend, network executives remained astonished. Not only did *Gunsmoke* bounce back, it was getting stronger and gaining momentum with each season. Milburn Stone never expected to portray Doc for more than five years and on several occasions stated, "I've made a bet every year for the last several years and lost them all—that *Gunsmoke* wouldn't be back." Year after year the cantankerous one indeed lost the bet and eventually began to stall come contract time. Pam Polifroni amusingly recalled, "Milburn could be a problem...I'm sure you've heard about the script of Doc dying? We had a script in the files that was about Doc dying. So every season when they'd start negotiating and renegotiating these deals—he would, of course, drag his feet and kick and scream. So they would give that script out and it would make the rounds. It would get back to him—he'd sign on."

Renewing contracts is always a frenetic time in Hollywood, with the cast of *Friends* negotiations coming to mind. Arness and CBS had many memorable contract discussions. "Every time they resigned Jim, he would ask for something," shared director Harry Harris. "There was a ranch he wanted out in the valley—Simi Valley or someplace. He wanted that ranch real bad. He wouldn't sign unless CBS bought it for him and carried the note—about a half a million dollars, and at that time, that was a lot of money. So he finally signed and they carried the note on that piece of property. A couple of years later," continued

NEW LINEUP Arness, Blake, Stone, Curtis, Strange and newcomer, Roger Ewing as Thad, in 1965.

MILBURN STONE as Doc.

TALENTED MAN James Nusser as the loveable Louie—town drunk.

TWO PROS Milburn Stone and Amanda Blake, better known as Doc and Kitty, happily pose together on the outdoor set.

167

SEASON ELEVEN Television viewers tuned in and enjoyed Sam, Matt, Doc, Kitty, Festus and Thad.

dollars for the note, we made a deal with you.' He says, 'Then I'm not coming back.' And he went home and he stayed home."

Arness wouldn't take any calls from the studio, in fact, he didn't answer the phone at all. CBS began to panic and asked Harris to intercede. The director finally made contact with Arness' father and arranged for a meeting with the reluctant star. Harris met with Arness and spoke on behalf of the studio. After spending the afternoon together, the director returned to CBS with his answer. "I went back and said, 'He's not coming back unless you give him the note on the property, and that's final and you will never get a hold of him.' So, as a result, they gave him the note," remembered Harris. "A half a million buck bonus they gave him. He wound up with that property—but then later he wound up donating it to some organization for children or orphans. He was a terrific guy."

For many years, Amanda Blake no longer called Hollywood her home and had relocated to Phoenix, Arizona. Flying to and from the set began to take its toll on the actress, and at times, tensions at work would arise, especially when it involved location work. Blake no longer wanted to leave the Long Branch, and became quite vocal about her desires. Blake and producer Mantley would often square off about anything—from the despised location shoots to the desire for a new wardrobe for Miss Kitty. "We did a show called *The Lost*," recalled Jim Byrnes, "a very difficult show. Amanda hated going on location—most of her shows we did in the Long Branch.

Harris, "when that deal was up, he said, 'I'm not coming back next year.' They said, 'why?' He said, 'I want a new deal.' 'What do you want?' 'I want the note for the property.' They said, 'We're not paying the half million

But that show she had to go on location—she hated it. It was rough." The episode, however, proved to be a very popular chapter in the *Gunsmoke* canon.

As the 1970s began, sixty-five year old Stone would begin to experience bouts of fatigue and would often experience dull chest pains. Mantley insisted that the fictional Doc of Dodge City seek medical attention from a real physician—this request ultimately saved the actor's life. In 1971, Stone underwent open-heart surgery, and would miss several episodes. Blake, always very close to Stone, underwent a terrible sense of loss with Stone gone. At the same time, Blake's personal life was in upheaval—her father was gravely ill, also.

Prior to the surgery, which in those days was much riskier without the advances in medical sciences we have today, Stone contacted his friend Pat Hingle and asked if he would fill in for him while he recuperated. Hingle agreed and stepped in as Dr. Chapman, a New Orleans surgeon. After winning a Golden Boot Award in 2004, Hingle remarked to fans, "In all my many years in the acting profession, *Gunsmoke* was the best organized TV group I have ever had the pleasure of working on. I always liked the show and was excited to now be a part of it."

Hingle appeared in a handful of episodes until Stone reported back to work approximately eight weeks after his operation. In 1992, Hingle would appear in the third television movie based on the series as a heavy in *Gunsmoke: To the Last Man.*

Stone returned triumphantly to the show in the only three-part episode presented in all twenty seasons, *Gold Train: The Bullet.* The three-parter was written by Jim Byrnes and proved to be one of the series best story arcs. Filmed in the Gold Country in Northern, California, this was one occasion where Blake didn't mind the time spent away shooting on location—Stone was back and his operation was a success. Directed by Bernard McEveety, the segments featured many talented performers, including Eric Braeden, Katherine Justice, Harry Carey, Jr., Mills Watson and Jonathan Lippe. "Jim Byrnes was one of my favorite writers—Byrnes stands out in my mind. I liked *Gold Train* very much," stated McEveety. *Gunsmoke* once again seemed indestructible.

It was between the seventeenth and nineteenth seasons that the highly polished and seemingly indestructible veneer that was *Gunsmoke* began to develop a few cracks here and there. At the end of the nineteenth season, Amanda Blake announced that she was leaving the show, citing she was tired of traveling, fatigue, etc. At least that was the spin that the CBS publicists put on it. "What's the word? The official word? She quit?" asked Jim Byrnes. "She didn't quit. Mantley fired her," stated Byrnes matter of factly.

"Yeah, it's true," confirmed Pam Polifroni. "There would be battles on the set between her and Mantley." As the nineteenth season was coming to a close, Paul Savage turned in a script that required location shooting. Rugged location shooting that would be comparable to what Blake experienced while filming *The Lost* in 1971. Savage

169

KEN CURTIS as Festus

PAT HINGLE as Dr. Chapman, Hingle replaced Milburn Stone for a brief time in 1971 while Stone recuperated from open-heart surgery.

STEVE FORREST as Mannon, one of the series best villains.

FAMILIAR CAST Arness, Curtis, Blake, Buck Taylor as Newly and Stone.

remembered, "I had written a two-parter called *The Comancheros* and the story dealt with Kitty and Doc on a stagecoach that's held up and they're taken prisoner along with other passengers." Amanda loudly objected to the idea of another scheduled location shoot and also brought up another sore subject. "Among other things," recalled Savage, "Amanda wanted new gowns. Those gowns were very, very expensive and Mantley didn't want to spend the money for it. So, the producers and the agents went round and round."

In March of 2001, both Mantley and his wife, Angela recalled the troubled times. Mrs. Mantley paid tribute to Blake, stating, "When Amanda entered the *Gunsmoke* set, with that red hair so beautiful—she was absolutely stunning. She could be very ladylike but she had this raucous laugh. She was something else! She was just one big funny person." John Mantley continued, offering, "I always liked Amanda because what you saw was what you got—she was just a genuine person, she really was—and, you'll always remember Miss Kitty." "We remember when she had lion cubs and would bring them to the set," added Mrs. Mantley. Blake was always the well-known animal advocate.

Defending her husband and the decision to let Blake go, Mrs. Mantley stated, "Amanda had been acting up and she wanted to quit. She wouldn't be on the set on time—she was forcing John to let her go." John agreed and added, "She was a bit of a strange woman. I liked her a lot, but she gave me a headache. Every two or three weeks at

the most, she'd say, 'I can't come to work,' and she'd send me a picture of herself with her face all smashed up. She was just a woman who walked with trouble with men." It is terrible to think that Blake possibly suffered any kind of abuse—terrible to think that any woman anywhere should encounter this worst form of cowardice. As her producer, Mantley helped her time and again, allegedly, and concluded, "Amanda really wanted to quit—at the end she did—she'd had it."

"John Mantley couldn't handle strong women," stated Byrnes. Savage continued, "Mantley went to the network and said, 'I either need more money, you know, she wants this—she wants that and da da da...' The network said, 'What do you figure?' And Mantley said, 'As far as I'm concerned, she can go fly!' They fired her!" The episodes were finally filmed as part of season twenty as *The Guns of Cibola Blanca*, sans Blake; sans Miss Kitty. "It was tough, it was tough," reflected Polifroni. "At first they were going to try and replace her and then they discovered that that would never work, especially at that point in time." Blake and Miss Kitty, after nineteen years, had made too great an impact on television viewers and fans. To allow another actress to portray Kitty would have been ludicrous, and most certainly career suicide for anyone foolish enough and willing to try. The script was altered with the addition of another female character for Doc to play against.

"The script is destroyed," continued Savage. "They put another actress in—completely changed the dynamics. I was sick as a dog when I saw what happened to it. And frankly, personally—sicker that Amanda was off the show." Wisely, it was decided to sugarcoat what happened by stating that Blake voluntarily decided to leave the show—a decision that Blake readily agreed with, fearing that negative publicity would hurt the show and much worse, her beloved co-stars. "It was a mistake to let her go," stated associate producer Ron Honthaner, who contributed the firing back to the problems filming *The Lost*. "There was an altercation between them [Mantley and Blake] and because it was done in front of the cast and crew—from that time on, Mantley really wanted to get rid of her." Byrnes summed up the unfortunate event, stating, "Mantley told the network we could do the show without her, had her fired and told publicity that she quit. She was fired. What a shame, she was a nice lady."

Actress Fran Ryan was hired for a few episodes in the twentieth season as the new proprietor of everybody's favorite watering hole, the Long Branch Saloon. Her character, Miss Hannah, was vastly different from Miss Kitty—a wise decision on behalf of the network. Ryan was a nice addition to the cast, but nobody could fill the shoes vacated by Blake, and hordes of fans to this day, will not watch any of the episodes from the twentieth, and final season. "Back to Amanda," added Byrnes, "a lot of people missed her—she'd been on the show so long—people were disappointed to see her gone. I think if the public had found out what happened, there would have been nasty letters. The public never learned it." Blake had class and above all,

dignity. Her handling of the event says a lot about Blake as a person; she was as classy as they come.

The Kittyless season would be the final one for the *Gunsmoke* gang. It would be easy to say that with Blake gone, the show suffered so and was ultimately cancelled. However, that simply isn't true.

The show became earthier, taking on a different feel and a different vibe. Some of the episodes from this season are now considered classics of the genre, including *The Busters, The Fires of Ignorance, Island in the Desert, Matt Dillon Must Die!*, and especially the multiple award-winning *Thirty a Month and Found*. Of the latter segment, series star Arness fondly stated, "*Thirty a Month and Found* is one of the real classics. It has to be in the top ten *Gunsmokes* we ever filmed. A really great episode and a wonderful show."

Yes, Kitty was missed, but *Gunsmoke* also fell out the top twenty in the ratings. Statistics killed *Gunsmoke*. Fred Silverman was running CBS at the time and he never liked Westerns period, regardless of success or not. "Silverman was never fond of Westerns—he was the one who finally had the show cancelled," stated Byrnes. The cancellation in 1975 came as a shock to everyone. Scripts had been ordered for a twenty-first season, in fact, there was even talk that a certain redhead was coming back to Dodge.

Chicago Tribune reporter Gary Deeb had heard that *Gunsmoke* would be cancelled as early as April 1975. Deeb spoke with Mantley, who assured him that he had

LAW AND ORDER Marshal Matt Dillon and Deputy Festus Haggen.

not heard of the cancellation and that he was confident *Gunsmoke* would return for a twenty-first season. Deeb and Mantley made a bet of one-hundred dollars as to whether or not CBS would pull the trigger on the long lasting horse opera. On April 14, Mantley sent Deeb the following letter...

Dear Gary:

I'm delighted to see that you're on the up and up in regard to our bet, and having informed the world that it is in existence, you're going to have to pay up!

I don't know whether you'll be heartened or dismayed by the fact that CBS has, up to now, requested three extensions in order to make up its collective mind about renewal. The fact, however, that the extensions have been requested, when several other shows have already been cancelled, makes me feel that your money is already in my pocket!

All best,
John Mantley

CBS formally cancelled *Gunsmoke* on April 25, 1975. Deeb received another letter from Mantley dated April 29th, along with one-hundred dollars.

Dear Gary:

I had your money in my pocket three times

173

during the last three weeks, but close only counts in horseshoes! In any case, our bet has added a little spice to these last trying weeks and I'm grateful to you for that. In retrospect, CBS might have picked a better day for the cancellation, because Friday, 25th April, was my fifty-fifth birthday and I've had better presents!!

All best wishes,

John Mantley

One would think that the cast and crew would have been notified of the cancellation in a manner befitting their status, being the staple that *Gunsmoke* had become for CBS. However, the news was delivered in typical Hollywood fashion, via the trade papers. Decades later, Arness told *Associated Press* writer Bob Thomas, "We didn't do a final wrap-up show. We finished the twentieth year, we all expected to go on for another season, or two or three. The network never told anybody they were thinking of canceling." Byrnes offered, "I think it could've gone on another five seasons, easy." "The genre just died out—things were changing—attitudes and tastes were changing," stated Honthaner.

The cancellation was met with mixed emotions from all involved. Mantley definitely wanted to continue, as did Arness and Ken Curtis. Stone was beginning to show his age and, by now, definitely wanted to work less. Continuing on probably would have meant much more storylines involving Buck Taylor, which would have been

a welcome, perhaps revitalizing, step.

In a 1995 *TV Times* story, Burt Reynolds told writer Stephen Cox, "When the show finally ended, I asked Jim about the set because I wanted something. God love him, he remembered me. I have the swinging doors to the saloon. They're in Florida at my ranch, where I built a saloon." All involved would gather for another final cast party—this time there would be no last minute reprieve. *Gunsmoke* was gone, leaving an emptiness for fans and for the actors who enjoyed the guest stints and the opportunity to appear with their favorite Western characters.

During the final five seasons *Gunsmoke* attracted talents such as Ricardo Montalban, Vera Miles, Suzanne Pleshette, John Payne, Dack Rambo, Mariette Hartley, Richard Kiley, Harry Morgan, Anthony Zerbe, Kay Lenz, Kurt Russell, Harold Gould, Cameron Mitchell, John Saxon, Lee J. Cobb, Allen Garfield, David Wayne, Gary Busey and Donna Mills, to name but a few.

During the initial run through the subsequent television movies, *Gunsmoke* was never mechanical, garrulous or lackluster, instead becoming one of the most revolutionary, influential, and first and foremost, entertaining Westerns in television history. As a monument to the power of good storytelling, the show reflected the old West while also reflecting each decade in which it aired. Actress Laurie Prange stated, "*Gunsmoke* permeates and has lasted so long—we live through entertainment places like a violin—they stroke the best and the worst in us. Movies today titillate and stroke the worst parts of ourselves and I think *Gunsmoke* strokes the best parts of ourselves."

All television series end. Perhaps the greatest tribute we can pay to those talents in front of and behind the cameras in Dodge is this—after fifty years, over six-hundred episodes and five movies—they've left us wanting more.

MEMORABLE ADDITION Buck Taylor joined GUNSMOKE in 1967.
"It was a shot in the arm for me...It still is!" stated Taylor.

NOTES FROM NEWLY

AN INTERVIEW WITH BUCK TAYLOR
August 26, 2004

BT: My wife Goldie said she had a great talk with you and you got a good book going.
BC: Well, I hope so, I'm trying to do it justice—that's a tall order, but...
BT: You can do it.

BC: Well, thank you.

BT: It's a good topic. (laughs)

BC: Well, it was my favorite show as a kid and I still enjoy it as an adult.

BT: Isn't that something. I appreciate what you're doing and I think a lot of people will—the interest is still certainly there. I'm just so thrilled that I was associated with such a great show.

BC: Well, you were certainly a shot in the arm when you joined the show.

BT: It was a shot in the arm for me. (laughs) It still is! For my artwork, it's amazing, amazing. They put me in concrete a couple of weeks ago in Dodge City. I'll be right next to Jim and Amanda, Ken, Doc and the rest of them.

LEGACY "GUNSMOKE was a great ride—and it's still ridin'—hard and fast."

BC: A show that has truly stood the test of time.

BT: Fifty years. If you'd have told me that, you know, in 1967…I thought in '75, well, it's all over, it's been great. But after fifty years, it keeps going.

BC: Were you offered the role of Danno in *Hawaii 5-0* at the same time you were offered Newly in *Gunsmoke*?

BT: I was, I sure was. I had done some shows with Jack Lord and the director Leonard Freeman. They offered me that, and I had a movie offer, *Hang 'Em High* with Clint Eastwood. I tested for *Gunsmoke*, and I got cast in the part. What do you choose? Well, I wanted to go with *Gunsmoke*. (laughs) It was certainly my way of life, the Western way of life. I was raised around horses, and my dad was an actor in Western movies. Ken Curtis and Milburn Stone—they were the kind of folk I wanted to be around. I was so thrilled that I could.

BC: What can you share about the live performances?

BT: I think I started in the third year. Kenny told me that it takes about three years to kind of get established where people really know you. He said, "Would you be up to going out on the road entertaining? Can you sing, or anything like that?" "Well I sing a little bit, you know, nothing great, and I play the guitar." He said, "Perfect, we'll put you with Joanie and the Frontiersmen and Hi Busse and people like that. It'll be your band, you and Glenn Strange."

BC: By this time Amanda Blake wasn't performing live much.

BT: Jim and Amanda, they didn't do much of that, and Jim never wanted to because of his Howard Hughes/Greta Garbo image. (laughs) He let us go out there and do the footwork, which we were happy to do it. At the time, it's what all the TV series were doing, and there were so many of them—Cheyenne Frontier Days, the Dixie National Final Rodeo, big and small rodeos. Entertainers from television shows such as *Bonanza* and so forth would go out and perform at these different rodeos and fairs. It was pretty lucrative, there was a lot of it, and I think we probably all had the same agent, but nevertheless, they rotated us around.

BC: Did you see any of the shows that Milburn Stone and Ken Curtis put together?

BT: It was just fantastic. They were really professional. I had the opportunity to go out with them a few times, to break me in. In fact, (chuckles) my break-in was at Cheyenne Frontier Days, which was a huge rodeo, I think, 15,000 people in all—and singing wasn't my favorite thing to do. I think they sang in back of me and loud! (laughs) Kenny told me, "Let me tell you something, Buck, if this eases your mind. Just the fact that you're here and you're out in front of those people, that's what they want. Now, if you can sing a little bit, that's fine." Well, it just so happens that Kenny could sing real good (chuckles) and Milburn wasn't bad himself. And, of course, the banter between each other and the jokes were just fantastic.

BC: Dennis Weaver enjoyed the live performances very much.

BT: It was a throwback from the old days when the

studios like Columbia, Monogram, Universal would send their Western stars out on the road. My dad did it. He was the sidekick to Wild Bill Elliott, Tex Ritter and the Durango Kid. You know, like Smiley Burnette and Gabby Hayes. He was Cannonball. They would all go on the road to all the movie theaters, before television, and that's the way the people would get to meet their heroes, the Western stars in those days. So, it was a continuation of that thought and it worked. We had the market on those kind of acts, the family acts, with the fairs and rodeos. Milburn and I would do a lot of the rural rodeos and some of the big ones—Ken would, too.

BC: The *Gunsmoke* performers seemed to have a certain etiquette when it came time for the fans.

BT: I was taught by my dad, you know, if you're going to put yourself in public and be accessible to them, then treat them like family. Milburn Stone told me when I first went on *Gunsmoke* and again when I was getting ready to start touring: "Buck, you're gonna have people come up to ya and wrap their arms around ya and hug ya and look at ya and break into tears and this kind of stuff, because they love the show and they've actually met someone that they allow into their home. They allow you into their bedroom—a private part of their home. And when they see you in person, you're part of their family, and don't disappoint them."

BC: No bad attitudes.

BT: Some actors have attitudes, you know, "I'm not signing an autograph, naw," that kind of stuff. We didn't—

we were real people. I've maintained that ever since. With my artwork, (chuckles) I'm still going to the rodeos and the state fairs, signing the autographs, selling my artwork. I've maintained what they taught me and I know it's been a success for my artwork. I deal one-on-one with people, and a lot of them know me from *Gunsmoke*. I think *Gunsmoke* gave me the start to do what I'm doing now with my artwork across the United States.

BC: That's great.

BT: When I first started selling my artwork, a fellow artist said, "You want to do this and seriously make a living?" And I said, "Yes." He gave me a list on how to market my work and so forth. He says, "Find out where they play *Gunsmoke* the most"—this was 1991 or 1992. "Go to those cities with your artwork. The press will come to you, the people will support you, get some press going for you." And I did, and sure enough it was the *Gunsmoke* people who showed up. As Ken Curtis put it before he passed away regarding my artwork, "It looks like *Gunsmoke* is going to give you another ride." (laughs)

BC: What a great quote.

BT: I'm telling you.

BC: And it worked, huh?

BT: It sure has. It's been wonderful. But it all stems, I believe, from what I was taught on *Gunsmoke*. Accommodate everyone. John Wayne was like that. He was tough to work with. He was a real professional, kind of a tough guy, and all that. But any fan who wanted an autograph from John Wayne got one. He would hold up production—he was famous for that—and his line was, "These are the people that make me; I got time for 'em." Actors do a lot of nice things, some of them do anyway. And baseball players. Football players. A lot of them do things like that, and they should do things like that. That's what it's about—helping people.

BC: You look at it today, the cast of *Deadwood* as opposed to the cast of *Gunsmoke*— they wouldn't have the drawing power.

BT: (big laugh) They'd probably run 'em off in the Midwest! (laughs) I'm sure they would. God Almighty, that is something. I'm sure there was profanity in those days, but not that much. They went overboard. Those words were probably used by some classes of people, but it was also a Victorian age and they spoke pretty good English. Where I live in Texas right now, it's the same kind of people: These are rough, tough cowboys on working ranches—big working ranches—and they don't swear. It's the nicest thing in the world because they don't. They don't have to. They've been raised that way for 150 years. It's not necessary to use all that stuff. The stuff that's coming out of music…it's no wonder our kids talk so tough.

BC: You bet.

BT: It's just horrible in movies with what they're doing. You know, I always thought movies and art were kind of an escape from our reality. (chuckles) The beauty of *For Whom the Bell Tolls*, or Matt and Kitty—I mean, they were lovers! You figure out what they did. They might have had the wildest sex in the world, but that's your business! You don't have to show it. That was the beauty of it. You know, why is the Mona Lisa smiling? Whatever you figure she's smiling for. It gives the audience a chance to create something.

Many great films have been done and hold up on their own without a lot of profanity, a lot of violence and a lot of sex. It's not that we're prudes or anything, it's just that we're kind of educated, we hope, and even socially, it's kind of nice to read between the lines.

BC: Leave it to your interpretation.

BT: Yes, and I think that holds true with *Gunsmoke* to this very day. It was a simple story of the good guy wins and the bad guy loses and justice prevailing. If you do something wrong, you pay for it. And it still holds.

BC: Right.

BT: It was also about a group of people that cared for each other. They would sit in the Long Branch after a day's work, and they were friends that cared for each other and would help each other out in any kind of situation. For me, it was just a wonderful experience being on that show. It still is to this day. Unbelievable. I mean, I don't know how kids recognize me. I'm older, you know, hell, I'm 66. (laughs) I've had a beard and a mustache ever since *Gunsmoke* practically, and they still know me. It depends on where they run the show a lot again, but it's amazing. Little kids, you know, five-year-olds—"We watch you on *Gunsmoke*!" Maybe their folks make 'em watch, but it's amazing that it's still going.

I owe so much to *Gunsmoke*, as far as accolades go,

GREAT RESPECT Taylor has nothing but respect and fond memories of his GUNSMOKE co-stars, especially James Arness and Milburn Stone.

especially to James Arness. He's the guy. He called the shots. Actually, there were two leaders. Jim was the main guy. Milburn Stone was the sage, the wisdom. Jim would honor him and respect him. Milburn was very instrumental. He would put his two cents in if something wasn't right. I'm talking about major decisions, and I know Jim respected that.

That's why I think the whole thing worked so well. There was respect amongst everyone. In eight years, I probably only had four or five conversations with Jim Arness. I was in awe of him and was smart enough to keep my distance because I knew he was a very private person. I didn't want to make mistakes that maybe prior people had, and that's trying to get too close to him.

BC: That's understandable.

BT: When you're working 20 years at the job, you do your job and you go your separate ways. They're not going to be your best friends, although they were dear friends of mine, but I think that's what made it work. I certainly respected Jim's privacy. He reminds me of my dad. I knew my dad growing up and I loved him and respected him and all that, but I didn't get to know him until later. And that's the same way it was with Jim. I guess about eight years ago, I hadn't spoken to him in maybe ten years at the time I got married to a great gal, Goldie, and she asked, "Don't you ever speak to James Arness?" And I said, "Well, no, he's kind of a private guy, and I honor and respect that." She said that he might like to hear from me. So I called up Bruce Boxleitner and got Jim's phone number,

HE KEPT THE LID ON DODGE Taylor's striking tribute to James Arness. ©Copyright Buck Taylor (courtesy of Buck Taylor)

and when I spoke to him it was the best thing I ever did.

BC: Really?

BT: Oh, he was just so thrilled to hear from me. I sent him some photographs of my artwork and so forth, and he called me back. He's a real enthusiastic guy on the phone, he's just wonderful. I've always respected him and I think that's why we got along so well. But in the last few years I got to know him better and it's kinda nice. But I can't say anything but nice things for everyone associated with that show.

BC: That says a lot for the show itself.

BT: I had a great experience working with Burt Reynolds just four years ago. He directed a television movie I worked in, and the whole time we spent working all we did was talk about Jim and *Gunsmoke*.

BC: Burt always said that was the happiest time of his life, when he was on *Gunsmoke*.

BT: Yes, absolutely. He named his son after the character he played. I didn't work with Burt on *Gunsmoke*, but got to know him afterward, and he's just a great guy, a fantastic guy, and I just think the world of him.

BC: When you originally did the show, you played a heavy in the two-parter *Vengeance!* in 1967. At the time, did you have any idea they were considering you for the role of Newly?

BT: Not at all. No. I was doing a lot of work at the time, and it was just another show and a good one. Everyone wanted to work on *Gunsmoke* and everyone did. Any actor, Jon Voight, Katharine Ross, Sam Elliott, all of 'em.

Guys that were destined to become stars. I felt it was a great opportunity to appear on a *Gunsmoke* and play a bad guy, John Ireland's son. I got shot by James Stacy, and Morgan Woodward was in it. It was great, I was very happy to be able to partake in that. Then right after I did the show, they went and tested myself and five other guys. The name of the character was Newly Jorgenson, pronounced "Yorgenson."

BC: Really?

BT: I think they felt that Jim was Nordic, and they figured they needed a guy that was like a young Jim, (chuckles). But a young Buck got it and I'm kind of Irish lookin'. (laughs) So they called him O'Brien. I wasn't quite a Jorgenson. So I was from Pennsylvania, and a gunsmith, and came out West and found a home in Dodge City.

BC: Was Pam Polifroni responsible for your casting?

BT: I'm sure she was. I wish I could remember the other actors who were tested then, but when you're testing for something, you just don't worry about all that stuff. I know it was a scene with Kitty and Vince McEveety directed it.

BC: A delightful man.

BT: Oh, a great guy. Have you talked to him?

BC: Yes, both him and his brother Bernard.

BT: Oh yeah, great guys. What about Gunnar Hellstrom?

BC: Regretfully no, he's passed on.

BT: Are you kidding?

BC: About two years ago in Sweden, I believe.

BT: I'll be damned. He was great. What about Alf Kjellin?

You see, Gunnar and Alf Kjellin were both protégés of Ingmar Bergman. When they came over to direct a *Gunsmoke*, these guys didn't know anything about Westerns, but they knew how to direct a movie. They were pretty good at it. The episode I did called *Patricia* in which I got married and my wife died was directed by Alf Kjellin—a fantastic director. I mean, this guy was something. And Bob Totten was one of my favorites, a dear friend of mine. We did *The Sacketts* and *Pony Express Rider*, a movie he wrote for me. He had me kill Festus in it. (laughs)

BC: I've also talked with Andrew McLaglen.

BT: You know, interestingly enough, Andy recommended me for the part of Quint Asper.

BC: I didn't know that, the part that Burt Reynolds got?

BT: Yes. I was doing a *Have Gun—Will Travel*, and he says, "You know, they're looking for kind of a guy like you with dark hair and could be a half-breed type Indian." So I went over and met Norman Macdonnell. I didn't get the part, but Burt did and then I ended up with a similar part later.

BC: That's interesting, I don't think the fans know that.

BT: No, I don't think they know that one.

BC: He enjoyed his time on *Gunsmoke*.

BT: *Gunsmoke* was a family. It was fun and there was work involved, but not a lot of work. Everyone kind of fell into place. And Jim was the greatest guy in the world to work with because he was so funny. Great sense of humor—sometimes I couldn't look at him. Matt Dillon was this serious guy, and Jim wasn't. Funny sense of

humor—he just makes me laugh to this day. You know Jim, he lost his daughter and I lost a son, it's one of them damned things. And that's something that Jim and I talked about. Unfortunately, we have that in common, but life goes on, and you keep going.

BC: I know what you mean all too well. Did you have any particular episodes that were favorites?

BT: I like the one called *Patricia*. It came out about the time that *Love Story* did, and there was a critique, either in the newspaper or *Variety*. *Love Story* came out first and then the *Gunsmoke* episode, and the writer said the episode stood on its own and maybe even a better show than *Love Story*. I don't know if I believe all that stuff, but they liked it.

BC: Well, with an hour format as opposed to a movie, there's no padding.

BT: Yes, and it turned out to be a good show. The lady's name who played my wife was Jess Walton. I think the world of her—a terrific actress. I was so honored to be a part of it and have her play my wife.

BC: The show was always cast so well. Look at what Glenn Strange did with Sam.

BT: What a guy—I just loved him so much.

BC: He just fit that character.

BT: Well, he was the real deal. He was a cowboy from Weed, New Mexico. He cut hair as a barber on big cattle ranches. He worked as a cowboy, but they always needed a barber. He worked the Matador Ranch, the Four-Sixes, and went on and became a peace officer in Ponca City,

1995 FEATURE Taylor made the cover in a great article about his career and artwork.

Oklahoma, and then joined *Miller's 101 Wild West Show*, which included Will Rogers, Tom Mix, Hoot Gibson, and Buck Jones. Big Boy Williams, remember that name?

BC: Guinn Big Boy Williams, yep.

BT: Guinn Big Boy Williams and Glenn Strange bull-dogged steers off motorcycles. That's an act that they did. And Glenn was this terrific fiddle player, and they all came to Hollywood together. They lived at Universal Studios at the ranch, where they had their horses. They'd get drunk every night and fight each other. (laughs) On the back lot at Universal, isn't that something? Glenn told me some of the greatest stories, how he met Gary Cooper ropin' over at Will Rogers place. Someday I'll probably write some sort of a book, I guess.

BC: I think you should.

BT: I've got so many stories growing up with my dad and all that. We knew Roy Rogers and Yakima Canutt lived right down the street. I grew up with his kids.

BC: I believe one of your paintings is titled *I've Got Lots of Friends?*

BT: Yep.

BC: That would be a great title for your book.

BT: That's not a bad idea. I'd like to do a few stories, a lot of photographs and a lot of paintings, not unlike what you're trying to do with your *Gunsmoke* book. Just a story of my life, my mom and dad.

BC: Did your folks meet during the vaudeville days?

BT: Dad saw her face on the billboard for coming attractions said, "I'm going to marry that woman." My life now?

TWO GIANTS This award presentation between James Arness and John Wayne made quite an impression on Taylor.

This is the best time in my life. I've got this ranch in Texas that I worked real hard to get, and just built a house and I've got cattle and horses. I love to rodeo and rope and try to stay in as good of shape as I can. In fact, I tried out for the Olympics in 1960. It was my goal to make the Olympic team as a gymnast. I didn't quite make it, but I came

close. (laughs)

BC: Dean Smith did a lot of *Gunsmoke* episodes.

BT: He was the real deal, a gold medalist, and a dear friend of mine who lives forty miles from here in Texas. I just love him. He's awesome. I've got to tell you one more story.

BC: Go ahead..

BT: My wife's favorite actor is John Wayne. If there hadn't have been a John Wayne, there wouldn't have been a Jim Arness. Anyway, here's the kind of guy Jim is—John Wayne presented him an award or vice versa and I can't remember what show it was, but I remember they were in tuxedos and it was on television and I watched it. And Duke says, "Well, I want to introduce James Arness," so Jim came walkin' out there, and they kind of came up eye to eye—Jim is six-foot-seven and Duke was about six-four. Duke looks at him and says, "You're bigger than I am." And Jim says, "Taller maybe." (big laugh) That's a good quote there. Hey listen, can I get some books from you after you get these out?

BC: Oh, absolutely.

BT: I'd love some. Would you sign 'em?

BC: I'd be honored.

BT: All right. Hey, Morgan Woodward—have you talked to him?

BC: Yes, he had me down to his home—what a gentleman. While I was there, he said to me, "I hope you don't mind, but my lady friend may be stopping by." I had no idea it was Ann Miller.

BT: (big laugh) Here's the funny thing—Ann Miller played my dad's wife in *You Can't Take it With You*.

BC: That's right, for -. Mr. Woodward has called me a couple of times since we did the interview and says, "I'm just checkin' up on you. Ben. How's the book coming along?"

BT: Isn't it funny how the legacy of *Gunsmoke* kind of lives on? Morgan is a wonderful guy.

BC: That he is.

BT: *Gunsmoke* was a great ride and it's still ridin'—hard and fast.

BC: You bet, you bet. Thank you for your time here.

BT: Thank you sir. I can't thank you enough.

KITTY'S OUTLAW Amanda Blake shared the screen with Ainslie Pryor during this 1957 segment.

WELCOME TO DODGE II

More Guest Stars Reminisce

Veteran character actor Robert Donner still watches *Gunsmoke* on TVLand and The Westerns Channel today. "I watch it now because I want to see what we all looked like as kids," Donner stated. "It's amazing who shows up on it." And that's an understatement. On one episode you may catch a young Jon Voight or perhaps Nick Nolte. Han Solo, Indiana Jones and Jack Ryan himself, Harrison Ford, can be seen as a heavy in two episodes. Ellen Burstyn showed up twice, as well. Prior to television stardom, you could catch Donna Mills or Daniel J. Travanti. It is amazing.

Donner, who refers to Westerns as, "...our fairy tales," recalled, "It was fun to play cowboy. As a character actor, by the time you got cast all of the good horses have been taken. The horse you got, if he had four legs you counted yourself as way ahead of the game. Nobody looked good riding one of those horses." Donner enjoyed the show and James Arness as well. "It was just always a pleasant experience. When it was a heavy show for Jim with a lot of dialogue, he'd like to come over and say, 'What are you

1973 CREDIT Donna Mills in an early appearance in the two-part episode A GAME OF DEATH...AN ACT OF LOVE.

TOUGH GUY Prior to becoming a regular on RAWHIDE, actor Charles Gray made many appearances on GUNSMOKE (photo courtesy of Charles Gray)

piece of script and tape it to your back, so that he could get position, check it out and he was ready. Very easy to work with."

Reliable actor Charles Gray appeared on most of the Western series of the day, recalled, "I knew Charles Marquis Warren, who got *Gunsmoke* off the ground, and later *Rawhide*—he was CBS's golden boy. Warren had a stock company of actors that didn't get too drunk, could get on and off a horse, show up with their lines. I was a member of that stock company. One of the early shows that I did called *The Guitar*—Aaron Spelling, he was a little creepy guy with a guitar." On *Gunsmoke* in general, Gray added, "It was always a nice set to be on. Nice people. They came there to do what they were supposed to do and had a good time doing it."

"*Gunsmoke* was a wonderful show," shared Karen Sharpe, "it had a lot of stature with it...a moral fiber to it. Westerns are a part of our culture." Impressed by *Gunsmoke*, she cited, "The quality of the writing, the quality of the show, the quality of the actors and the quality of the chemistry of the characters." Her favorite episode was *Sweet and Sour* from 1957, when she portrayed dance hall girl Rena Decker. "She was kind of an evil girl, but I played her kind of innocent and sweet," offered Sharpe. "I was told they liked my performance so much, that they composed a special musical score for me—that was really nice and very rare, I think."

Hard Luck Henry from season thirteen, featured newcomer Bo Hopkins. "It was pretty much my first

doing in this?' 'Nothing Jim, I'm just gonna stand right here.' 'Well, you don't mind do you?' He'd take a little

GUEST STAR Ruth Roman was always a welcome addition to any show, including the two-parter WASTE in 1972, shown here with James Arness.

it was just that I wasn't on the friggin' wagon!" Hopkins, who would later gain fame in motion pictures such as *The Wild Bunch* and on television with *Dynasty*, observed series star Arness: "James Arness was just like a John Wayne hero to me—he was the man. It was fun to watch him—he was strictly business, but he was nice."

During lunch in Beverly Hills one day, actresses and friends France Nuyen and Barbara Luna shared their favorite memories of *Gunsmoke*. There was a lot of spirited conversation, laughter and a few tears, but mostly fun reminiscences. Nuyen started, "Fond memories. I remember it being very professional, very concise. It was my first time on a Western. There was a feeling of elegance, even though it was a Western—an elegant production, run with ethics; a gentle attitude on the set. Every show had something to say to make the world better." *Gunfighter R.I.P.* was her favorite of two appearances on the show, with co-star Darren McGavin, one of her favorite performers. "Marvelous, sensitive actor, seemed able to do everything without any effort. So at ease. Dignity. The values we don't have anymore." Luna landed a memorable guest

pretty good speaking part. I played Festus' cousin," said the actor. "I was driving a wagon with Mayf Nutter, so they wanted to come in for the close-ups. Because I'm supposed to be bouncing around they put me on a ladder and a guy was shaking it—I kept blowing my lines. I must have done that damn thing five times. I knew all the lines,

shot on *He Learned About Women* in 1962, playing half-breed Chavela. "It was a great, wonderful experience and educational. A relaxed set, they were kind."

Relaxed until an accident befell series star Amanda Blake. Luna recalled, "Amanda had punctured her eye by putting on mascara and separating her lashes with a straight pin or safety pin. She was having the most difficult time and she was crying." This did not happen at the studio, but out in the middle of nowhere on location. Cooler heads prevailed and the set and Amanda was soon back in working order. Luna compared *Gunsmoke* with another, more recent show. "They just seemed to have this family thing going, chemistry—it's the one thing that makes a show work. It's like the chemistry that the kids have on the show *Friends*—the chemistry is so good." Luna enjoyed her time with Dennis Weaver and co-stars Claude Akins and Miriam Colon. "I loved Miriam Colon—such a wonderful actress."

Actor Chris Alcaide made many trips to Dodge City, with the episode *Doc's Revenge* his personal favorite. Alcaide stated, "It was the best part I ever had. Doc sees me come into town and wants to kill me. The best thing I ever did on that show." The episode features a standout performance by series regular Milburn Stone. "He was a cuddly, cuddly guy. A pro all the way—I don't think I ever saw Milburn do two takes," offered Alcaide. "The whole thing felt rich; when you came in on that show, you felt like you were dealing with a class 'A' outfit. I always found Arness to be a very likeable, very pleasant guy."

SWEET AND SOUR *Actress Karen Sharpe made quite an impression with her 1957 guest shot.*

Long before *The Karate Kid* films and television's *Cagney and Lacey*, Martin Kove 'cowboyed up' on the CBS series. "It was the first Western that I had done," stated Kove, "it was heaven, just great to do a Western in Hollywood with Matt Dillon. I had a great time galloping around the set on my lunch hour."

Child star Dawn Lyn, famous for her role as Dodie on *My Three Sons*, appeared on *Gunsmoke* three times. Her first credit was *The Sodbusters* in 1972 and her second and third was the two-part episode *Women for Sale*, which kicked off the nineteenth season in 1973. "I remember Jim Arness, he and I became great buddies. Really a

MEMORABLE TEAM Darren McGavin and France Nuyen were memorably paired in GUNFIGHTER R.I.P. during season twelve.

truly nice guy, one of the all-time nice ones," recalled Lyn. "He has a bad leg and I would notice sometimes that it would be hurting more and he would be limping. Usually he could walk without a limp during the scene. I noticed one time he was sitting there rubbing his knee, so I went over to him and sat down on the ground in front of him and started rubbing his knee for him. He appreciated that." *The Sodbusters* was a memorable episode for the actress, allowing her to share screen time with her real-life brother, Leif Garrett. "My brother was in that episode and our mom was there, and Jim took the three of us out to dinner one night, and it was so silly, it was so much fun."

"We filmed in Tucson, Arizona, and the streets just rolled up at nine o'clock; it was that kind of town. We had gone to this restaurant a block or two from the hotel we stayed at, and after dinner we were walking back and all of a sudden we started playing tag—running down the middle of the street in Tucson playing tag with Marshal Dillon!" laughed Lyn. "He was just wonderful, we had so much fun with him." Lyn also enjoyed working with co-star Alex Cord. "Alex was a nice person. He was kind of quiet, like, 'still waters run deep'—that expression comes to mind. A man of few words." As for *Gunsmoke* being what it is, Lyn offered, "The good conquering evil; that kind of positive message. It's the same thing I hear about *My Three Sons*, it's the old-fashioned values."

Robert Pine and his wife Gwynne Gilford both had fond *Gunsmoke* memories, Pine appearing four times and

TV'S GREEN HORNET Van Williams was just one of the many ingredients that helped make the episode THIRTY A MONTH AND FOUND a classic.

Gilford, once. Pine recalled, "I always loved doing the show because it was a very character-driven show and the stories were very important. There were wonderful guest star roles on it. You really don't find that too much anymore." Pine continued, "I thought it was the most solid Western on the air. The people were terrific; all the people I worked with on that show were well-oiled and professional." Gilford agreed, "It was a very well constructed show and every character was so clear. The Old West presented in a way that families could enjoy it. Kids could watch it and yet it had the sophistication of Miss Kitty and it had the sophistication of the relationship that they [Matt and Kitty] had...and the wonderful humor between the Doc and Festus characters. It offered a lot for everybody."

"I always got a kick when James Arness would come on the set," stated Pine. "I don't think he ever looked at the lines; he'd just take his pages out of his back pocket, look it over just before we were shooting it, wad 'em up and throw 'em away, and deliver a great scene. I'd be working days on my part! He was wonderful." Gilford, who also teaches acting, enjoyed working with Ken Curtis on *The Tycoon.* "My character was opposite Festus—he was so fun. Ken Curtis really had that character down; he inhabited him and was delightful."

As a teacher, Gilford offers yet another take on the Arness/close-up debacle: "I had a close-up with James Arness and his contract specified that he left at a certain time. By the time that my close-up came, I spoke to a ladder; I talked to the ladder and the script supervisor spoke his lines off camera. When I was teaching acting I would use this as an example of how important it is to be able to use substitution in who you're talking to because you often don't get the real person there to talk to." Did Arness offend the actress? "No, because he'd done the show probably 15 years or so and I figured he had every right to leave when he wanted to leave—it wasn't up to him to be off-camera. A lot of stars don't do their off-camera. It was

DOC'S REVENGE Chris Alcaide was a popular heavy in several television Westerns.

an example of the technique as an actor one really needs to know because you rely on being able to act with a person, even if it is your close-up. Substitution is part of the acting process and generally when it comes to close-ups, that really is technical."

"I remember sitting on the set one time, I was probably twenty-four, and the two guys I went to college with, my closest friends; one was in medical school, one was an oceanographer, very successful, but here I am sitting with a real six-gun on my hip, great chaps, boots, the horse— I'm just having the time of my life saying, 'Does it just get any better than this? I never have to grow up.' These friends of mine are just working their ass off, the books, sixteen hours a day, and I'm out here playing!" laughed Pine. "And being paid a lot of money for it. It was great." Being cast on *Lyle's Kid* in 1968 was a major advancement for Pine and his career. "John Mantley was terrific," stated Pine. "They were going to do a spin-off and I had been cast and John Gavin was cast as the sheriff—I was the deputy sheriff. They were going to do an episode on *Gunsmoke* and use that as the pilot, then CBS bailed out on it. I was bitterly disappointed. John Mantley was going to produce."

Appearing on *Gunsmoke* made a permanent impression on several performers—it didn't matter if they were just starting out or were seasoned veterans. Early in his professional career, Stuart Whitman was assigned a guest role on the show in 1956. The episode was *Cholera*, and Whitman played a heavy working for Paul Fix. Whitman stated, "Dennis Weaver got me the job. We were at Universal Studios under contract to them. You'd learn how to swordfight and to dance—do all the things you've got to do. Dennis mentioned that I should do *Gunsmoke*." Working with Arness struck a positive chord with Whitman, who recalled, "Arness was the biggest guy I ever met in stature, six foot seven or something like that, God bless him. Later on I guess I duplicated him when I played Marshal Jim Crown on *Cimarron Strip*. He made a lasting impression on me, and Dennis was special. It had a big influence on my life."

Actress Angie Dickinson echoed Whitman's sentiments. Her episode, *Sins of the Father*, is one of the best out of six-hundred plus segments the show would present in twenty seasons. The year was 1957 and Dickinson was only in the business for two years. "*Gunsmoke* really played an important part; a stepping stone for me and one of the reasons I got to where I got." *Sins of the Father* dealt with racism, mixed marriages, and illiteracy. "*Gunsmoke* was very, very brave. The good writing, to have all that in one twenty-five minute episode, and not hurried. Very, very clever. It gave television real class." The story showed how situations can get out of hand, with rumors and insinuations fueling hatred and mob mentalities. Dickinson played an Indian married to a white man. "What I found, she's so loving and the husband is so sweet. Very succinctly they put across that he couldn't read or write; not so subtle you missed it, just so naturally—that's what struck me—the naturalness of the show."

After a violent confrontation, the accusers realize their error. "When she says, 'I don't blame anyone.' The hotel keeper—so innocently fervent in his hatred for what her father did and then so lovingly apologetic," stated Dickinson. "It's a lovely moment isn't it? Very well written. For me it was just a wonderful experience and great to have a leading role like that. I don't have any other adjectives for it except wonderful. Westerns have honesty and simplicity that holds up, and that's what *Gunsmoke* has; the simplicity of the West but the sincerity of the characters." Angie Dickinson went on to a huge career, highlights including *Rio Bravo* opposite John Wayne and later starring on television, with the series *Police Woman*. Earl Holliman co-starred with Dickinson on *Police Woman* and made a few memorable trips into the Long Branch Saloon himself. "Vince McEveety was a terrific director; he brought me to *Gunsmoke* the first time," explained Holliman.

"It was a terrific anthology show, it was one of those things where you went on and James Arness was in the beginning scene and usually at the end scene," remarked Holliman. "Really, it was turned over to Festus and the guest star. It offered a lot of actors wonderful parts. I remember when *Gunsmoke* first started when I was doing my first series, *Hotel De Paree*—we were right on the adjoining stage. I was taking dance lessons...I was surprised one time to walk in and find in the dressing room, Jim Arness. He had just finished; he was taking lessons. He was with kids and he was taking a movement class, a jazz class. I had great respect for him doing that."

DRAW! Martin Kove tries to get the drop on James Arness in a scene from IN PERFORMANCE OF DUTY, 1974. (photo courtesy of Martin Kove)

INDIAN WIFE Beautiful Angie Dickinson gave a fantastic performance as Rose Daggit in SINS OF THE FATHER, a role she considered a stepping stone for her unmeasured success to come.

CHOLERA Stuart Whitman played a rare heavy in this 1956 installment, shown here with Paul Fix.

HELPING HAND Dawn Lyn and James Arness in the 1973 two-parter WOMEN FOR SALE, which was originally titled VALLEY OF TEARS.

Holliman appeared on three segments during the initial series run, and also co-starred in the first reunion movie in 1987. *Hackett* was his favorite episode; one that cast him and co-star Morgan Woodward against type. "*Hackett* was interesting because Morgan Woodward always played heavies—it was Vince's idea to have Morgan play the weakling and have me play the heavy. He thought the casting switch would be good and it was. They had written this wonderful six-minute scene—Hackett walking into the saloon late at night and terrorizing Miss Kitty and Sam, the bartender. A really good scene. That was my favorite role on *Gunsmoke*, I loved that part and working with Morgan Woodward and Jennifer West. Hackett was a rotten scoundrel. A mean son-of-a-bitch. Great fun to play." As President of Actors And Others For Animals, a non-profit charitable organization benefiting animal welfare, Holliman and Amanda Blake became friends. "She was always quite involved with it; she was great fun," remarked Holliman.

Actor Paul Carr offered this observation: "Jim Arness was a very laid back kind of guy, as opposed to Chuck Connors, who was very unhappy about being on the series *The Rifleman* after a couple of years because he wanted to be a big movie star." As for the

initial and continuing popularity of *Gunsmoke*, Carr stated, "Their regular cast was just fabulous, Arness, Dennis Weaver, one of the better actors around town. Milburn Stone, wonderful character actor. Amanda, wonderful. Those people had a lot of respect for each other, in

THE DAGGITS Angie Dickinson and Peter Whitney shared the screen in the 1957 episode SINS OF THE FATHER.

the casual way that they dealt with each other all the time. It was obvious that they had a connection, and that connection broadcast itself—you could see it on the screen. You always felt comfortable on the show as a guest. Hurry

EARL HOLLIMAN Shown here in the reunion movie GUNSMOKE: RETURN TO DODGE, made many memorable appearances on the series as well.

1965, Forest almost lost his head, literally. Blocking a fist-fight scene with actor R.G. Armstrong, the stunt guys warned Forest that Armstrong was awkward. Armstrong was supposed to take a roundhouse swing at Forest, who would duck, then fire back with a right and left to his opponent's gut. "We did it once, it didn't look good. I said 'Look R.G., just aim at my head and make a big round-house swing, etc.' The cameras start, I ducked down and he hit me right on the top of the head. Flattened me, I went down like a sack. He had a knot on his knuckles, I had one on my head like an egg. I was out. My bell had been rung. I'm glad he didn't hit me in the middle of my face, he would have changed my whole appearance," recalled Forest painfully. "Oh God, he hit me hard."

Known to millions as Eddie Munster, child actor Butch Patrick left 1313 Mockingbird Lane for Front Street on a couple of occasions. Patrick shared, "I remember the giant rocking chair that James Arness had and I remember Ken Curtis seemed to be the class clown. I liked meeting James Arness because of the fact that he had done *The Thing*— I thought that was really cool." How appropriately Munsterish. Patrick commented, "Once *Gunsmoke* got rollin' it maintained a juggernaut effect—it established a huge foothold and never relinquished it. It established itself almost like a Western Soap Opera; Miss Kitty, Matt Dillon. They were having a love affair without having a love affair. People kept tuning in almost to see if they're ever gonna pop the question." Patrick also enjoyed the opening segment, with Dillon facing the bad guy in the

is the middle name of Hollywood. *Gunsmoke* had time to do things good and right. Everyone worked towards that goal."

"So many television shows lacked storylines and were one-dimensional; at least with *Gunsmoke*, it had a little more depth to it than the usual run of Westerns," declared actor Michael Forest. While filming *The Lady* in

MAD DOG In this episode from 1967, child-star Butch Patrick joined Ken Curtis and a four-legged friend.

street. "People loved that opening, like *High Noon*, over and over again."

"It was all different back then, so different," opined actress turned teacher Kim Darby regarding her work on the show in the sixties. "You felt you belonged. It's important for an actor to feel like they're being embraced and that they're cared about. I noticed how relaxed I was in it—I wasn't uptight or self-conscious. I didn't have to twist myself into a pretzel to be something that they thought would work. It was glorious." Darby was particularly impressed with Amanda Blake. "She was just wonderful, just wonderful. A terrific lady, larger than life, incredibly nice. I remember having a wonderful, wonderful experience."

Will Hutchins only appeared on *Gunsmoke* once, but his recollections are vivid. "It was the first show I did after I left Warner's. I'd been set out to pasture by Warner Brothers, the only job I could get was a play in Hollywood at the—ironically named—Horseshoe Theatre. After six months, an agent saw me and suggested me for *Gunsmoke*." The episode was entitled *Blind Man's Bluff*, which first aired on February 23, 1963. "Ted Post, the director, barely mentioned in passing that the part I was playing, Billy Poe, was in essence, a working audition for Chester's replacement. It could become a running part." Two instances stand out in the actors mind. "That scene with the Irish maid, a terrific actress, [Natalie Norwick]. When I was doing that scene, it was my big scene as I recall, one of the guys up in the catwalk fell asleep and

SUGARFOOT IN DODGE Actor Will Hutchins was briefly considered as a replacement for Dennis Weaver when he appeared on the show in 1963.

started snoring. I thought, oh my God, the critics are following me right on to the set here," laughed Hutchins, or Hutch, as he likes to be called.

"I loved working with Glenn Strange on that show," continued Hutch. "He played an Indian chief on one of the best *Sugarfoot* shows we did. It was great seeing him again. He was just a real gregarious, funny guy. Milburn Stone is my all-time favorite actor." Hutch recalled watching Stone film a promo or teaser scene for the show. All that was required of Stone was to walk down the street from point A to point B. Action. Stone began his walk, stopped, looked up at a clock, took out his pocket watch, adjusted the time, placed the watch back in his pocket, tugged his ear, and moved on—all just as natural as can be. "He was the greatest."

Actor turned author Alex Cord, whose latest novel *A Feather in the Rain* was published in 2005 by Five Star Publications, Inc., also appeared on *Gunsmoke* once in a very memorable episode, *The Sodbusters*. Cord commented, "I loved the Westerns and the cowboy life. Of course, *Gunsmoke*, as you know as well as I do, is a classic. Just to have the opportunity to work on that show I thought was just great. To be able to play a heroic cowboy character like that, it was wonderful. It was part of an era where the Western was king, and yet all the others fell by the wayside and *Gunsmoke* never did—it was the one that survived among all of them." Cord, who has been on hundreds of sets throughout his career, recalled, "There was great harmony all the way through, from the grips to

GOOD BAD GUY Actor Tom Reese made many memorable visits to Dodge City, as both a hero as in TALL TRAPPER, and a villain, as in NITRO! (photo courtesy of Tom Reese)

the costumes to the makeup; I always had the feeling that they were like a family, all the people that worked on the show. I think they all knew in some way that they were a part of something that was special."

A future superstar shared screen time with Cord. "Harrison Ford had such a small part in it—I knocked him over a bar or something," remembered Cord. "Whoever would have dreamed that Harrison Ford would become the huge star that he did. That's part of his charm, he's very modest about his success." Cord turned in a great performance as Pete Brown in a story that is reminiscent of the classic film *Shane* starring Alan Ladd.

Tom Reese appeared in several episodes, playing a heavy almost every time. But *Gunsmoke*, unlike most other shows airing at the time, often would cast against type, giving actors a chance to try something different. Reese got that opportunity in 1961 on the episode *Tall Trapper*. "I got to play the good guy, Strother Martin was the heavy. *Tall Trapper* was my favorite, one of my best." In 1967, Reese appeared in a two-part episode, *Nitro!*, co-starring David Canary. "*Nitro!* was probably the best thing I'd done, that was a good part. Robert Totten, God rest his soul, was a good director. David Canary got *Bonanza* from those episodes. It was originally a one-parter and they ran over, they couldn't finish it in a week."

Reese always enjoyed working on the show, especially with Arness. "Arness wrapped at 6pm. 6pm, finished with a shot or not, he wrapped, that was it. He'd unbuckle his gun belt and drop it, the prop man would catch it before it hit the floor. 'Goodnight everybody.'" Reese continued, "They wanted quick study actors—reliable, don't come drunk. After we wrapped, that's different, across the street with the wranglers and stunt men." As for employment on the series, Reese remembered, "If they liked you, you were always called back. I was very flattered that they accepted me into the group."

"Well, there was something kind of wonderful about

Jim Arness and Amanda Blake," stated actress Beverly Garland, "they became really good friends of mine, good working friends. They treated me just so wonderful. I loved working on *Gunsmoke*—it was my favorite Western to work; it was the best." Garland would appear

MIRIAM COLON *The accomplished actress, seen here in CHATO, 1970, who appeared many times on GUNSMOKE, stated, "Why don't they make more television like that anymore?"*

GUNFIGHTER *Actor Steve Forrest turned up several times on* GUNSMOKE, *including this 1973 appearance in* THE WIDOWMAKER.

on *Gunsmoke* a total of four times. "I always envied Amanda because I always thought wouldn't it be wonderful to play Kitty for so many years? Now, when you talked to Amanda, she didn't feel that way because she never had a chance to play anything else. She was always Kitty—but she did a lot with that." Garland has appeared on countless television shows, always adding a touch of class and professionalism with each credit, including her roles on *My Three Sons* and *Scarecrow and Mrs. King.* "When I was called to do a *Gunsmoke*, that was a very special thing to me. I just loved it. Working with those people to me was the best."

She cites an example from 1969 when she appeared on the segment *Time of the Jackals*: "Jim Arness was so good to me. I remember one of the shows I did, I run out to the path and somebody shoots me and I fall down. Now, I'm probably four or five months pregnant, Jim says, 'No, no, no—you can't do that.' I said, 'Oh Jim, of course I can do that, I'm just going to fall down in the street.' 'No, no-we've-got-to-have-a-stunt-double-for-Beverly-please!' Very protective." As for the success and longevity of the show, Garland offered, "They all underplayed and played it very honestly I felt, and I think that's why it lasted. Jim had that kind of easy quality—you never thought he was acting. You never thought Amanda was acting. It was an honest piece and it was very well written."

For Jonathan Goldsmith Lippe, *Gunsmoke* offered, "Some of the best Westerns I've ever seen on television. It set the bar for Westerns. It was a joy to go to work—just a fun set. It was like being with a bunch of friends. Like old shoes—it just felt good." Lippe continued, "I had done thirteen or fourteen episodes. My favorite was with Jack Albertson, *Cowtown Hustler*, which Jimmy Byrnes—a superb writer—wrote." Albertson and Lippe, always reliable, professional performers—worked very well togeth-

SEASONED VETERAN After a long career in motion pictures, Lew Ayres appeared in the episode THE PRODIGAL in 1967.

er, resulting in another memorable episode in the *Gunsmoke* canon. Lippe was fond of Arness and relayed a humorous anecdote: "Every time Arness killed one of the bad guys, he'd blow the smoke away from the top of his gun and he'd say, 'Well, he's with Jesus now.'" A sly chuckle turns into a hearty laugh.

Stunt man/actor Dean Smith worked on *Gunsmoke* many times. "I've been watching some of these shows on the Westerns Channel and hell, they're holding up good. I enjoy watching 'em. The stories are good." Smith, who has probably worked on most of the television Westerns ever broadcast, stated, "*Gunsmoke* was the one that lasted the longest due to the fact, I think, that it was so down to earth. They played it very realistic. They had a great cast. Jim Arness was perfect for Marshal Dillon. Milburn, Amanda, Dennis, Buck, Ken, Burt—they were all just perfect for their parts." His praise continued to the guest stars. "They got guys like Morgan Woodward, a gentle soul, a terrific actor; and Royal Dano and all the good characters worked on that show. Real believable, nothing hokey."

"Everything I remember is positive," recalled actress Miriam Colon. Colon appeared on *Gunsmoke* many times, with every turn a memorable one. "It was like returning home—it was always a very gentle atmosphere—a family. The high tensions of other studios, you know, some kind of vibrations sometimes you sense in going to various sets was not there at all. I wish it were like that all the time. Why don't they make more television like that anymore?"

Colon has had a long and distinguished career in television and motion pictures and on the stage also. "I was always very happy when they called me to do *Gunsmoke*. It's a piece of American history and American folklore. I feel very proud that I was a part of that and they liked me enough that they kept calling me." In 1972, Colon appeared in a two-part episode that opened season eighteen. Filming *The River* holds a special place in Colon's heart. "They took us to Oregon. I had never seen that part of America, where you see almost virginal grounds."

"I don't know what I was going through in my life, but I was very, very tense. Suddenly, to be informed they want you for this *Gunsmoke* and you've got to go on location so you've got to move fast. Since you've done some work for them before, there's not going to be auditions or anything. There's gonna be a departure and they're talking to your agent. I said, 'Oh my God, I have to leave town?' So I did." Upon reflection, Colon was grateful that it all happened so fast. "It was like lifting me over such a very tense situation. I was so unhappy, I was so tired and suddenly, like magic, to be put on a plane and fly there, arrive late and then the next morning wake up in the woods."

"Then I would hear in the distance a noise and I realize it was a river passing in the near distance. It was like a dream, like I was transported to a Technicolor dream. I remember everybody lived there and there were wood cabins. They were preparing breakfast—lusty breakfast. I could smell toasted bread and bacon—oh it was so wonderful. And I would eat and eat as if I were on vacation at

BEVERLY GARLAND *Talented and beautiful, Garland graced many GUNSMOKE episodes.*

some country estate. It was glorious, it was wonderful. And I get paid for this too?" laughed Colon. "It was like somebody wanted to save me from self-destruction.

They put me in a paradise environment; I became healthy again. It was so soothing; it helped to bring me back to health. *The River*. It was a happy episode for me. The color of the water was greenish—so beautiful. I was very thankful. And James Arness. What a sweetheart, what a gentleman."

2001: A Space Odyssey star Gary Lockwood appeared in the excellent two-part episode *The Raid* from season eleven. Lockwood recalled, "The show was mostly me and my gang. My character was very well conceived—it got me the movie *Firecreek* with Jimmy Stewart, Henry Fonda and Jack Elam—they just took my character and kind of re-tooled it." Lockwood was impressed with the *Gunsmoke* company, stating, "It was a lot of fun to do. There was a good structure to the writing—the good hats and the bad hats. They were stories then—what do you watch now?"

Accomplished actress Katharine Ross revealed, "I had sort of grown up with *Gunsmoke*, so it was like a fantasy to be on it for me. It was thrilling to work with those people who've been around a long time." Ross, who had guest-starred on almost all of the Westerns running at the time, made her first appearance on *Gunsmoke* in 1964. The episode, *Crooked Mile*, was a huge stepping stone in her career. "I worked with Andy McLaglen on the first one and that led to me doing my very first movie that Andy directed, *Shenandoah*. So *Gunsmoke* has a special place in my heart." McLaglen cast Ross in the film with no reading and no audition based on the strength of her performance in *Crooked Mile*. She made her second appearance in Dodge in 1965 opposite Eileen Heckart in *The Lady*. Her role in this segment was a complete three-sixty from her first *Gunsmoke* assignment. "It was kind of fun playing, you know, kind of a not such a nice person. Those are always more fun," laughed Ross.

"Yes, it was television and yes, it was in the sixties, but you know, they were well written. The parts that I played, for the time, had some substance to them," offered Ross. "It was a pretty well-oiled machine. Incredible cast—incredible people did those shows," Ross continued. "It was good. I think there is a core of people that love Westerns—in Westerns there's good and there's bad—there's moral and immoral. It's also, really, totally American." Ross reflected on the star of the show: "The few scenes that I had with him—Jim Arness—who is about a hundred feet tall—I mean, I came up to his belt buckle; they always had him sitting on the edge of the desk or something so there wasn't this disparity in height."

As for Amanda Blake and Kitty, Ross stated, "I have a horse that I named after her. It's a quarter horse and she's out of a horse called Mr. Gunsmoke. She had a registered name, but I call her Miss Kitty. She's red." Ross has left an indelible mark in the world of entertainment, with her involvement in the Western genre time well spent.

Lance Le Gault appeared in *A Town in Chains* during the twentieth season and found the experience unique. "It was a great show to do. The only television show where we went on location, went a day early and had a complete guest cast rehearsal at the hotel in Tucson—went through the whole script with Bernie McEveety directing. It was more like theatre. Jim Arness was a day or two behind. So big Jim flew in to Tucson for half a days work, knelt down at a campfire and said, 'Hmm, they were here yesterday,' and went home! Then he came in again for another half a day and captured us at a bank just in time to wing me and take us away in chains," remembered Le Gault.

Le Gault was impressed by Arness and his concern for his fellow performers. "I'll never forget—he was leading me away, Jim turned around and said, 'Are you really tied to that saddle horn?' And I said, 'No sir.' I had my hands tied and it looked like I was tied to the saddle horn. He was worried that if, should something happen, I'm dead meat," recalled Le Gault. "Very good show to do, it was a wonderful thing to do." Le Gault also did the narration for the episode *Thirty a Month and Found*. "Mantley was very proud of that episode," stated Le Gault.

A guest shot on *Gunsmoke* meant so much to so many. Actor Robert Pine summed it up best: "I feel very grateful and blessed that I was a part of it."

A TALENTED TRIO Dennis Weaver, Milburn Stone and Amanda Blake, better known as Chester, Doc and Miss Kitty, coming soon to a venue near you! This photo was used to announce dates for the 1960 Rodeo Circuit Tour.

GUNSMOKE - LIVE!

In the forties and fifties, moviegoers could be treated to a pre-screening appearance of their heroes in person—stars such as Johnny Mack Brown, Monte Hale, Dub Taylor and Sunset Carson, to name a few, would stroll down the aisle, six-guns blazing—much to the delight of young and old fans alike. Bela Lugosi would show up in full Dracula regalia while Dean Martin and Jerry Lewis often appeared live before their films, causing attendance records to triple.

With the rise in popularity of the television medium, especially the small screen oaters, series stars quickly came in demand for public appearances, sometimes performing as well.

The folks from Dodge City were no exception. James Arness led many a parade and opened several rodeos in the late fifties through the early sixties. But the big-ticket headliners were Dennis Weaver, Amanda Blake and Milburn Stone.

Chester, Kitty and Doc would guarantee any benefit a success and shatter attendance records for established annual shows and programs.

The trio performances were the brainchild of Milburn

ANOTHER OPENIN', ANOTHER SHOW The three popular GUNSMOKE stars pose in the auditorium of their latest live appearance, circa 1958.

"IT WAS JUST INCREDIBLE, TOTALLY MAGIC— A REAL THRILL, A REAL KICK."

Stone, who never lost his love for live performing. In a January 1960 *TV Guide* article, Stone related, "We broke the new act in at Long Beach, California and it was disastrous. We kept changing and finally came up with something—well, it's a boff wherever we go."

"You know, Milburn was a good singer—he started out in vaudeville. He loved to sing. He was the one who

UNITED CEREBRAL PALSY TELETHON Dennis Weaver, Amanda Blake and Milburn Stone lead the crowd in a rousing rendition of the song, "He's Got the Whole World In His Hands," the finale used in most of their live shows.

RUN RABBIT, RUN Chester and Doc stop bickering long enough to make music during a performance in Jacksonville, Florida.

really put the act together. He had the idea to do these performances," remembered Dennis Weaver.

The appearances were simple but packed a wallop wherever staged. Rodeos were popular events for the talented castmates. Weaver continued, "It was just incredible, totally magic—a real thrill, a real kick. First of all, Doc would come out and he'd stroll out to the middle of the arena, and get on a small stage that they'd constructed. He'd kinda suck on his teeth and do something with a toothpick, tip his hat forward, which was a trademark of the character. Then he'd say, 'All right, I'm gonna sing one for all us old folks,' then he would sing *When You and I Were Young, Maggie*—and I'll tell you there wasn't a dry eye in the house when he got finished with that."

Enter Miss Kitty. "He'd bring Amanda out and they'd do a little patter and a few jokes and whatnot," Weaver remembered. Cue Chester.

"I've never had such an introduction in my life as I had when we were doing rodeos," reflected Weaver. "They had chutes all set up for the horses. Doc would say 'Okay, we know who you're waitin' for—and here he is ladies and gentlemen, out of chute number one, our Chester!' The chute would open up and everybody would expect me to come ridin' out of there on a horse just goin' lickety-split, and instead of that I came running out limping (laughs) and we had hurdles set up. I'd jump over two of them stiff-legged and then up onto the stage and the applause was absolutely thunderous...brought a chill up and down my spine every night. I could hardly wait because I knew when I'd come out the place would explode—and it did."

Finding a proper song for the First Lady of Dodge proved no small task, with actor William Schallert saving

SEPTEMBER 1959 Milburn Stone, Amanda Blake and Dennis Weaver pose in front of the real Long Branch Saloon in Dodge City, Kansas.

the day. "Dennis and Milburn were both very creative guys," recalled Schallert. "Milburn was very droll, he could make stuff up and write things. Amanda had a very good presence. They'd go out and perform every weekend—very lucrative because people paid a lot to see them. Dennis was talking about having a song for Kitty. So I went home...I actually studied composing—I could play the piano and make up tunes—had an idea for a song, *Long Branch Blues*. So I played around with it for a couple of days. I was at Dennis and Gerry's, played it for them and Gerry just fell in love with it. I made an arrangement with them where they paid me one hundred bucks or something like that to let them have the rights, and Amanda used it on the road." In 1971 Amanda performed the ditty on *Hee Haw*, causing Schallert to join ASCAP. "I'm a member of ASCAP on the basis of that one song," laughed Schallert.

These appearances became so popular that during some seasons, the performers made more money on the road than they did with their CBS contracts. During the initial performances, the trio would hire local bands or orchestras to accompany the act, but without proper rehearsal time, the combination rarely gelled. A country group known as The Frontier Boys and Joanie soon joined the *Gunsmoke* gang and began performing with them at all of their bookings. The shows, much to everyone's surprise and delight, became even more popular, breaking attendance records from California to Florida. Doc, Kitty and Chester were soon breaking records they had established themselves the prior year.

Crowds of fans would gather at airports and train stations to catch a glimpse of their heroes when they arrived in town, sometimes numbering up to two thousand well-wishers. "Audiences regard us as old friends," says Stone, again from *TV Guide*, "because of the intimacy of the TV show. They nearly always call us by our stage names: Doc, Chester, Kitty. And more than likely their questions—and there are plenty of them—will be about the TV characters, not about us actors who play them."

When Weaver began hinting about leaving

SHERIFF PAT GARRETT'S BUGGY Milburn Stone and Amanda Blake ride the real deal in the Truth Or Consequences Fiesta Parade in New Mexico, 1958. (Photo courtesy of the Geronimo Springs Museum, Truth Or Consequences, New Mexico)

Gunsmoke, Blake began to tire of the constant traveling and slowly curtailed her involvement in the act. Stone needn't worry about future bookings—when Ken Curtis joined *Gunsmoke* as Festus, he became the perfect foil for the crusty Doc, be it onscreen or onstage. Together, their live performances continued to set records everywhere and they became personal appearance agent Michael

SNAPPY PATTER, DANCE & SONG Dennis, Amanda and Milburn broke attendance records wherever they appeared throughout the United States and Canada.

North's top act.

Curtis and Stone became fast friends and performed together for several years—even after *Gunsmoke* left the air in 1975. Writer Paul Savage fondly remembered the Doc/Festus shows..."They worked so wonderfully together.

My wife Laurie and I went with Milburn and Kenny a couple of times on these personal appearances. Milburn did his single, at the end of which he starts to introduce Festus as 'The only kindergarten dropout in the history of schooling...' Pin spot picks up Festus walking up, great applause, they have a couple of lines together, Milburn leaves and Kenny does his Festus stuff. 'Now if you don't mind, now that Doc ain't here to rag me on it, I'd like to

THE GUNSMOKE GANG, PERHAPS MORE THAN ANY OTHER SHOW AT THE TIME, BECAME FAMILY...

sing you a song.' Audience laughs, ha ha ha. He'd break into song and the house would become absolute silence. Not even breathing. They couldn't believe it. Phenomenal voice."

Series regular Buck Taylor confirmed, "Doc and Festus were probably one of the greatest rodeo acts for a television series ever. They were just unbelievable and the people loved them."

Ken was the singer that Big Band leader Tommy Dorsey hired when singers Jack Leonard and Frank Sinatra left his employ. Festus replaced Frankie? That is the caliber of voice Curtis was blessed with. A voice that made him a member of The Sons Of The Pioneers, singing many memorable songs on the big screen—most notably in John Ford's *Rio Grande* in 1950.

"We went to a rodeo in San Francisco, Milburn and

MR. DILLON, MR. DILLON! James Arness is mobbed by fans after a personal appearance in 1958. The stars of GUNSMOKE always accommodated those who wanted autographs and pictures.

Kenny were performing," recalled Laurie Savage. "We were sitting by some young girls and out come Milburn and Kenny in regular suits. These girls were saying, 'Wow! That's Festus?! He's good looking!'"

These beloved characters were in our living rooms at least once a week since the radio debut in 1952—the *Gunsmoke* gang, perhaps more than any other show at the time, became family...and when the opportunity arose to meet them in person, fans flocked to these "family reunions."

Ken Curtis would stay and sign autographs and pose for pictures with fans—often more than two hours at a time. Actors And Others For Animals could always count on the participation of Amanda Blake to meet and greet fans at their fundraisers. Burt Reynolds has been known to miss flights to accommodate fans—a trait that began during his tenure as Quint Asper.

"They were real people, no pretense about them. They were the salt of the earth. Basic, you know—they loved people," stressed Laurie Savage.

Agent Michael North also represented Newly and Sam, Buck Taylor and Glenn Strange respectively, for their joint live appearances at State Fairs and Rodeos. Ken Curtis inspired this latest *Gunsmoke* pairing. "I always refer to it as the 'B' team—Ken and Milburn were the 'A' team," mused Buck Taylor. "I sing a little bit, nothing great, and I play the guitar. Glenn Strange, Sam the bartender, was a fiddle player, and a good one." Buck and Glenn began touring with Ken and Milburn, breaking

GRAND MARSHAL DILLON *James Arness led the parade for the 15th Annual Sheriffs Rodeo at the Los Angeles Memorial Coliseum, August 23, 1959.*

in their act and refining bits of business under the watchful eyes and guiding hands of the arena veterans. An appreciative Taylor remembered, "We worked in slowly and developed a pretty good act ourselves. I followed Milburn and Kenny's instructions as far as how they treat people and what they did and we did the same thing—tell

A LIVE APPEARANCE BY ANY OF THE GUNSMOKE STARS WAS ALWAYS SO MUCH MORE THAN JUST PERFORMING.

WALNUT STREET TO GUNSMOKE STREET Series star James Arness officially changes the street signs, downtown Dodge City, Kansas, in 1958. Amanda Blake and Milburn Stone, partially hidden, proudly look on. (photo courtesy of Boot Hill Museum, Inc)

COMING SOON *The ad says it all!*

a few jokes...pertaining to *Gunsmoke* and Sam and I would have some dialogue back and forth."

From the very first performance made by the *Gunsmoke* alum, a strict work ethic and respect for the audience and venue was stressed. "You know, the rodeo is about cowboys and cowgirls and we would always thank the real heroes of the day," added Taylor. "At the end of it—our performance, we'd always get on a couple of horses and go all around the inside of the arena and shake hands with kids. Then we would set up a table and sign autographs and we'd stay there 'til the last kid was gone. That's the way Doc and Festus did it, and that's the way Glenn and I did it."

A live appearance by any of the *Gunsmoke* stars was always so much more than just performing. Prior to an advertised date, cast members would show up sometimes two or three days early and research the schools and hospitals in the town and surrounding areas. After

WJBK TV STUDIOS DETROIT, Michigan television personality Ted Lloyd, better known as Sagebrush Shorty, poses with Milburn Stone, Amanda Blake and Dennis Weaver in the early sixties.

handling the press and television promotional work, they would visit the children at schools for the deaf, blind or handicapped and visit with people of all age groups in the local hospitals. Those who couldn't attend the fair or rodeo were treated to personal visits by Kitty, Doc, Festus, Chester, Newly, Sam and, on rare occasions, Marshal Matt Dillon himself.

One such personal visit changed lives. Buck Taylor shared, "It was during Vietnam and Kenny and I were in San Antonio, Texas. It was a big military hospital. We were there in our outfits—the Newly outfit and the Festus outfit—we walked into these rooms and these kids—God, their eyes would light up."

"We were leaving and a mother and father came to us and their son had just got back from Vietnam and he was in ICU—he was unconscious and wounded pretty bad. *Gunsmoke* was his favorite show and they said, 'Would you mind, could you please go in there and see if you could say anything to him? It might help.' The Doctor asked us also, so we went in there and God Almighty, tears come to my eyes—I don't know if I can say anything—it's hard for me to say it now—but Kenny started talking to this kid and it was something like (Festus voice) 'Ya know, ya ought to feel real lucky thet yer where yer at cuz ya could be in Doc Adams office right now and by golly'—you know that kind of stuff."

"The kid opens his eyes and smiles! I tell you, things like that would happen—great moments you know, what you can do for other people. And of course,

FESTUS MEETS THE PRESS Ken Curtis talks shop with the media in Cincinnati, Ohio before an appearance in the sixties.

mom and dad are thrilled, you pulled this kid out of his coma!" Truly a visit they would never forget. "I won't either!" reflected Taylor. "It gave me chills. It's never easy for me to tell that story."

These appearances by the show's lead characters throughout the country helped solidify the success of *Gunsmoke* and enhanced the popularity of an already popular show. "The success of *Gunsmoke* was not only great, quality shows and the written word and the material of the show—but it was the fact that Doc and Festus

THE KIDS LOVE 'EM Agent Michael North's daughters, Tracy and Wendy pose with dad's top clients, Doc and Festus, Milburn Stone and Ken Curtis, respectively. (photo courtesy of Tracy North)

mainly, and what little part Glenn and I had to do—went on the road and touched hands with the people—kept it going for so long," stated Taylor.

Giving a human side to our heroes? "Absolutely," Taylor concurred.

TRADE ANNOUNCEMENT Booking ad for one of Agent Michael North's most popular acts, Buck Taylor and Glenn Strange.

Collector's Edition and
Official Souvenir Program 50¢

101 RANCH RODEO

75th Anniversary Cherokee Strip Celebration
September 13-14-15-16, 1968 - Ponca City, Oklahoma
Starring *"Doc"* and *"Festus"* Stars of *"Gunsmoke"*

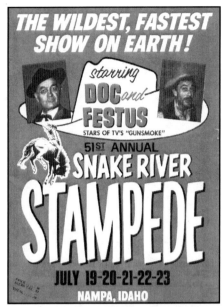

THE WILDEST, FASTEST
SHOW ON EARTH!

starring
DOC and FESTUS
STARS OF TV'S "GUNSMOKE"

51ST ANNUAL
SNAKE RIVER
STAMPEDE

JULY 19-20-21-22-23
NAMPA, IDAHO

"Chester"   "Miss Kitty"   "Doc"

SEE "GUNSMOKE TRIO" IN PERSON

"CAROLINA JUBILEE HORSE SHOW"
Greensboro Coliseum   November 27, 28, 29

223

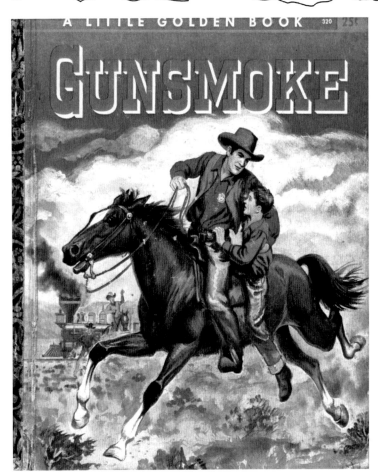

A LITTLE GOLDEN BOOK

THE MEMORABILIA

Entertainment-related trinkets and memorabilia are as old as the various mediums themselves. From the early days, with a Charlie Chaplin doll, to today, with a *Star Wars*, well, everything, fans and collectors never seem to get enough.

Beginning with William S. Hart, cowboy collectibles have always been popular. Tom Mix was the first cowboy star to meet mass production. However, three stars would raise the bar for entertainment marketing, expanding their lucrative images when they entered the foray of television. Gene Autry, Roy Rogers, and especially Hoppy himself, William Boyd, were champions both of the west and self-promotion. Toothbrushes, bed sheets, flashlights, bicycles, cap guns, decoders, potato chips, wristwatches, comic books and record players are just a small sampling of the products fans snapped up.

Although Martians never invaded the United States, TV Westerns did, and in the fifties and sixties, product tie-ins hit an all-time high. Virtually every small screen cowboy had at least one cap pistol and one issue of a comic book based on their character and show. Other shows, based on popularity, ran the gamut of products

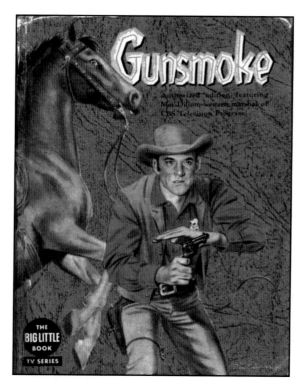

BIG LITTLE BOOK

BOARD GAME

that America's children of the era carried to school, played with at home or dressed like when delivering justice to the bad guys they found in their front yards or basements.

Gunsmoke, the longest-running Western, was rarely out of the Top 10 where ratings were concerned, and produced its fair share of memorabilia. It has been over twenty-five years since a first-run episode of the show was produced and aired, with items still created and released today.

In no particular order, here is a sampling of wares from Front Street that would make Mr. Jonas proud...

Aladdin produced five different *Gunsmoke* lunchboxes between 1959 to 1973, with one actually being a mistake. The mistake version was also the first released and had the word marshal misspelled with two "L's" on the front and back of the box. A correctly spelled version came out almost immediately, staying on the market for close to three years.

Several cap pistol and holster sets were made by three toy companies...Halco, Leslie-Henry and Hubley, with the latter producing a Marshal pistol series that was often included in the gun and holster sets. At least ten different sets of pistols were made, with the boxed set from Halco being the nicest and most sought after today. RC Cola placed an ad on the back of some of the Halco belts. The nicest Leslie-Henry set featured black horse grips and conchos shaped into a bust of Matt Dillon. Fun-N-Play John Henry Products produced

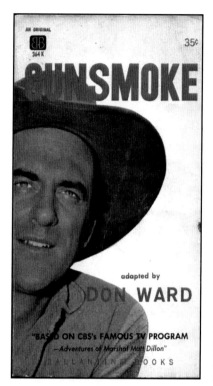  

BOOKS Novels and short stories based on GUNSMOKE are still published today.

a mini-pistol and holster set that included a color photo mask of James Arness.

TV show comic books were always popular and most were based on the Westerns. Dell comics released twenty-seven *Gunsmoke* issues from 1955 to 1961, all featuring a full color photograph of Arness as Matt Dillon.

Doc, Kitty or Chester never graced a Dell cover, but were featured in the stories found within. In 1969 Gold Key Comics released its first *Gunsmoke* issue with all four characters, which now included Festus, in photographs on the cover. Six issues were produced, with the last released in February of 1970. Foreign comic markets honoring the show included Australia, with pocket-sized editions and from Great Britain, hard cover annuals with colorful covers.

Between 1957 and 1971, *Gunsmoke* graced the cover of *TV Guide* a total of thirteen times, featuring photos by the likes of Mario Casilli and Leo Fuchs, and artwork by James Hill and Jack Davis, to name a few. Articles on the show were featured in countless issues of *TV Guide*, and the show or its stars were featured on the covers of hundreds of local television booklets found in newspapers on a weekly basis. With titles ranging from *TV Prevues*, *TV Times* and *TV Week*, these were found in the *Seattle Post-Intelligencer*, the *Winnipeg Tribune* and the *Chicago Tribune*, respectively.

One of the shows earliest sponsors was L&M Cigarettes, also known as the Liggett and Myers Tobacco Company. In the late fifties, the company produced several cardboard advertising signs, ranging in sizes from 21" by 21" to a life-sized standup of Arness as Marshal Matt Dillon. These ads were also utilized in print campaigns,

COLORING BOOK

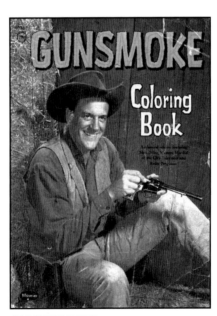

COLORING BOOK

DOC on TVUE

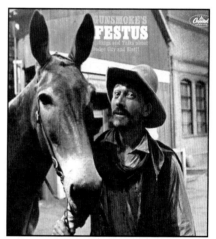

FIRST GUNSMOKE ALBUM Ken Curtis and Capitol Records.

MERRY CHRISTMAS Gifts from cast members, include candy dishes from Ken Curtis and Milburn Stone, and a mug from James Arness.

POPULAR ITEM Viewmaster reels by GAF

L&M CIGARETTE AD

POSTCARDS *Through the years, postcards featured paintings from the Cowboy Hall of Fame and a watercolor from Buck Taylor.*

MATT DILLON
(JAMES ARNESS)

Howdy from "Doc & Festus"

FESTUS HAGGEN
(KEN CURTIS)

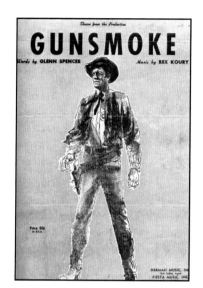

SHEET MUSIC

SPIEGEL AD 1964 Mom, Dad! Tell Santa...

WHITMAN TRAY PUZZLE

WHITMAN CHILDREN'S
BOOK 1958

TOY GUN Mask included!

WHITMAN BOXED PUZZLES

showing up on the backs of various magazines and Broadway programs.

Tobacco and especially bubble gum cards were always popular with collectors, often causing playground and neighborhood trading frenzies. In 1958 a card set entitled TV Westerns offered seventy-one different cards honoring various shows including *Have Gun—Will Travel* and *Wagon Train*, dedicating fifteen cards of the set to the denizens of Dodge. Pacific Trading Cards, Inc. released a set of one-hundred and ten *Gunsmoke* TV trading cards that featured the original radio and television shows, as well as the first reunion movie, *Gunsmoke: Return to Dodge*. Both the Topps and Pacific sets featured Matt Dillon on their wrappers.

Whitman produced two coloring books and two storybook editions beginning in 1958. *Gunsmoke* was also featured in editions published by both Little Golden Books and the ever-popular Big Little Books. Adult reading was covered in paperback novels at least three times during the initial twenty-year run. Ballantine Books released a collection of ten short stories adapted by Don Ward in 1957. Chris Stratton offered his stories in 1970 via

TABLETS More popular school items.

RALPH MARLIN TIE

VINYL WALLETS Two styles from 1960.

LUNCHBOXES from ALADDIN

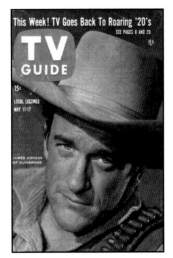

TV GUIDE May 1957

TV GUIDE March 1958

TV GUIDE January 1960

TV GUIDE December 1960

TV GUIDE November 1961

TV GUIDE July 1963

TV GUIDE January 1964

TV GUIDE June 1964

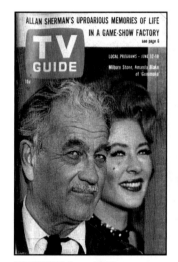

TV GUIDE June 1965

TV GUIDE December 1966

TV GUIDE August 1968

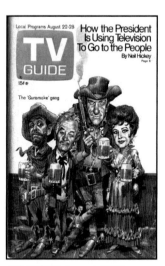

TV GUIDE August 1970

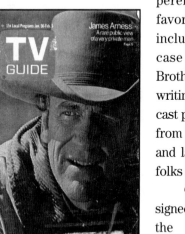

TV GUIDE January 1971

Popular Library and Award Books presented adaptions by Jackson Flynn in 1974. Author Gary McCarthy penned three original stories published by Berkley Boulevard in 1998 and 1999, with titles including *Marshal Festus*. In 2005, Signet published yet another *Gunsmoke* paperback novel titled *Blood, Bullets and Buckskin*. The work, by Joseph A. West, featured a foreword by Arness and a striking color cover.

Puzzles, also from Whitman, were made from 1957 to 1969 in both frame tray inlay and boxed formats. A highly collectible board game was released by the Lowell Toy Manufacturing Company in 1958. Ben Cooper Costumes offered masks and vinyl gowns for Matt, Doc, Chester and Kitty beginning in 1956, which became perennial Halloween favorites. School supplies included a colorful pencil case from Hassenfeld Brothers, Inc. and several writing tablets with color cast photos for covers, first from Penworthy in 1957, and later from the reliable folks at Whitman.

Capitol Records signed Ken Curtis to record the album *Gunsmoke's Festus* in 1965, with the platter reissued in 1968 on

PENCIL CASE A popular school item from Hassenfeld Brothers, Inc., 1961.

the Hilltop label, and again by Pickwick in 1976. Curtis also recorded *Festus Calls Out Ken Curtis* in 1969 for the Dot label. Buck Taylor released a collection of folk and country songs in 1978 for JPL. *That Man From Gunsmoke* featured a striking photo of Taylor as Newly on the front cover. Dennis Weaver released a single for Cascade Records in 1959, *Girls (Wuz Made to be Loved)* backed with *Michael Finnigan*, both novelty tunes. Several versions of the *Gunsmoke* theme song were recorded by artists ranging from bandleader Lawrence Welk to guitarist Duane Eddy. It is truly a shame that no one thought to record the material that Weaver, Stone and Blake toured with, and later Stone and Curtis. It would be nice to have a stereo recorded version of *Long Branch Blues*.

Other items from the show produced during its heyday include vinyl wallets in 1960, arcade cards, pin back

Topps 1

Topps 2

Topps 3

Topps 4

Topps 5

Topps 7

Topps 8

Topps 9

237

Topps 10

Topps 11

Topps 13

CIGARETTE CARD

Topps 14

Topps 15

BRITISH CARD

CIGARETTE CARD

Topps 6

Topps 12

buttons, badges and handcuffs, shirts, boots, vests and gloves. In 1972 GAF released two Viewmaster sets, one regular and one talking, that featured the episode *The Drummer*, co-starring Victor French.

Christmas was always a special time for the cast and crew, and gifts they exchanged now show up in antique shops and especially on the Internet through eBay. Arness was fond of giving out white mugs with various images on them. He, along with producer John Mantley, hired Western Artist Al Shelton to produce brass buckles and luggage tags featuring the opening showdown sequence in striking relief. The Motion Picture Stuntman's Association was so impressed with Shelton's work they made him an honorary member. Blake would give out handsome personalized pewter tankards. Stone had beautiful drinking glasses and candy dishes emblazoned with his horse and buggy or other Dodge City symbols. Curtis gave out various items, including a candy dish with a full color cast photo in the center and a notepad holder, belt buckle and glass mugs with a caricature of Festus adorning them.

Post production items include Spanera Tobacco cigars and cigar bands in 1985; a set of six collector plates honoring the program's fortieth anniversary in 1995 from Franklin Mint; a Best of the West Matt doll from Exclusive Premiere in 1997; a sepia-toned necktie from Ralph Marlin the following year. In 2003, the Leanin' Tree Company released a series of greeting cards featuring various cast members.

DELL 1955 #679

DELL 1956 #720

DELL 1956 #769

DELL 1957 #797

DELL 1957 #844

DELL 1958 #6

DELL 1958 #7

DELL 1958 #8

DELL 1958 #9

DELL 1958 #10

DELL 1958 #11

DELL 1958 #12

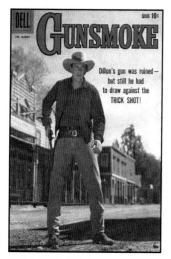

DELL 1959 #12

DELL 1959 #13

DELL 1959 #14

DELL 1959 #15

DELL 1959 #17

DELL 1959 #18

DELL 1960 #19

DELL 1960 #20

DELL 1960 #21

DELL 1960 #22

DELL 1960 #23

DELL 1961 #24

242

DELL 1961 #25

DELL 1961 #26

DELL 1961 #27

GOLD KEY 1969 #01

GOLD KEY 1969 #02

GOLD KEY 1969 #03

GOLD KEY 1969 #04

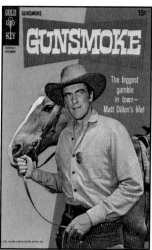

GOLD KEY 1969 #05

Gunsmoke episodes were available for home use in various formats, beginning with VHS tapes in 1990 from CBS Video. *Gunsmoke: Return to Dodge* was released by Fox Video in 1992, with the remaining reunion films following suit in 1996 from Star Maker Video. The premiere episode was available on laserdisc in 1992. First and second season episodes became available on DVD in 2003, with most of the reunion movies released on the same format the following year. DVD volumes are still being released with formerly unavailable episodes throughout 2005.

High-end collectibles hit the market in the year 2001. A firearms company, America Remembers, produced two stunning limited-edition tributes to Arness...a Colt single action revolver and a Winchester Model 94 rifle, both decorated in 24-karat gold and nickel and both with a production limit of two-hundred fifty each. A tribute rifle honoring Dennis Weaver followed a year later. Legendary holster maker John Bianchi offered three tributes to Arness...a professional leather gun belt and rifle scabbard modeled after those the actor used on the show, and a U.S. Marshal badge, perfectly replicated to match what Matt Dillon wore for many seasons.

Numerous toys, tributes and memorabilia have been sold because of the seemingly indestructible popularity *Gunsmoke* has enjoyed. What will spring forth from the minds of merchandisers remains to be seen, but it's a sure bet fans and collectors alike will snap up whatever appears. Two outstanding publications are available and

GOLD KEY 1970 #06

recommended for fans of all westerns and toy collectors... *Hakes Guide to Cowboy Character Collectibles* by Ted Hake, published in 1994 by the Wallace-Homestead Book Company and *Television's Cowboys, Gunfighters and Cap Pistols* by Rudy A. D'Angelo, published in 1999 by Antique Trader Books.

LONG BRANCH BLUES (photo courtesy of William Schallert)

TOP MOVIE STAR Burt Reynolds

Q & A WITH QUINT

AN INTERVIEW WITH BURT REYNOLDS
March 8, 2005

Interview Conducted by Janette Anderson
Questions Provided by Ben Costello

Q: How did you get the role of Quint Asper?

BR: When I did the role, no one told me that it was going to be a recurring role. It was just a wonderful part. I was doing a lot of Indians in those days. And, of course, everybody wanted to do *Gunsmoke.* Every actor in town loved doing the show because it was a family, and it was—now that I think back about it—I don't think anybody in town, before or since, ever had the generosity of spirit that they had on that show in terms of being an ensemble group, where it was Kitty's turn or Doc's turn or Chester's turn or whoever's turn. It was a great place for young actors to learn some manners and behave, because, number one—Jim and Milburn wouldn't put up with it. Milburn had a much more crotchety, wonderful, funny, old way. Jim would just quietly walk away (chuckles) and the guys would figure it out that they

READY TO WORK Reynolds was perfect for the role of half-Indian blacksmith Quint Asper.

were not behaving well.

I did the show, and then my agent got a call that they were interested in bringing the character back. I was very flattered. I think the whole kind of Indian, half-Indian thing brought all kinds of dramatic possibilities—also having the blacksmith shop in town, all that sort of stuff. Being half-Indian, he knew how to track a little bit better than the average guy. The character was, in retrospect, like Nevada Smith in *The Carpetbaggers*—raised by one Indian parent and who really thought of himself as more of an Indian than a white man. Then we could deal with the prejudice and all that kind of stuff that was going on at the time in those days.

When Ken came on the show and did Festus, I immediately knew that if they were looking for a replacement for Chester that he was much better suited for that than I was—all the things he could do with Doc that Chester did, with the comedy, and so on. My character wasn't a leading man—he wasn't somebody you could have a great deal of fun with, you know. Indians don't get a lot of funny lines. (laughs) That's another way we messed them over—we gave them no funny lines!

Q: Is it true that Milburn Stone advised you to leave the show?

BR: I had such a wonderful, almost father and son relationship with Millie, and Jim and I were very, very close; with everybody, actually. I spoke to them about leaving, and Jim was convinced that I could go off and have a movie career. I was very flattered by that but I also thought that this was a terrific show to be on. And quite honestly, and I didn't know it then, some of the happiest years of my life were on that show, because of the time I spent sitting around the Long Branch Saloon porch with Milburn talking about Fred Stone, who was this huge, huge vaudeville star and all the routines that he did.

I had made friends with Eddie Foy and one great evening, I had a party at my house and had Eddie Foy over. Millie and he were doing Eddie Foy and Fred Stone routines together. It was absolutely amazing. Millie could do a little dance, a little juggling, a little this, a little that and had 900 stories and jokes. It was wonderful for a young actor like me to be around storytellers like that who were from another era, an era that I wish I could've been a part of. It was wonderful to sit out on that porch every day and listen to Millie tell stories. It usually was Amanda and myself, Doc and Matt and the guest star that week, whoever that person was, while they were lighting the scene. Unlike a lot of shows where you'd probably be running your lines, we would be listening to these great stories.

Q: Like a family?

BR: It was a family. It was tremendously like a family. Again, I wasn't sure about leaving and Jim said—I'll never forget it—he said, "You know, we've been on seven years and hell, we've probably only got another year." It was still in black and white—I thought well, okay, I had done it for almost three years, so I said I'll strike out on my own and they made a deal with Ken and then it went on for another eight or nine years. (laughs) Quite honestly, in spite of the fact that I had an incredible, very lucky motion picture career, I've often wondered what would have happened had I stayed for the whole run of the show. There's a lot to

STROTHER MARTIN Reynolds enjoyed working with Martin on GUNSMOKE and later in the movie THE END from 1978.

be said for peace of mind and the fun and just being part of this whole legend of that show.

Q: It really is a legend.

BR: Well, it deserves to be because it works on every level. There was Norman Macdonnell who was our producer and even Charles Marquis Warren who ended up over at *Rawhide*. Clint Eastwood was doing *Rawhide* when I was doing *Gunsmoke*, and every day at lunch we would meet. We were working out with this guy who was an extra and who was teaching karate. As only Clint could say, (after I saw the guy kick a light bulb out, which was a little unbelievable to see because he was shorter than both of us) Clint said, "He's pretty good." And I said, "Yeah, I think he is." Well, this extra was Bruce Lee. I went to a couple morning classes. Steve McQueen was there. Kareem Abdul Jabbar was there and I thought, I don't mind being kicked, but I don't want to be kicked a block away, not by a guy who's seven feet tall. So I didn't go back to the morning classes, I went to the lunchtime classes with Clint.

As you know, when you look at the shows, you'll see Jon Voight doing his first piece of film. Here are all these

TIGHT GROUP Milburn Stone, Ken Curtis and Reynolds.

unbelievable, incredible actors. You couldn't name all the actors. I mean, there's Strother Martin, who I was crazy about, who I think did three or four shows a year. There was Slim Pickens, all the guys that we were all crazed to work with, funny and wonderful. I always say when I am working with young actors, "We don't get paid for what's printed on the page, we get paid for the white spaces, what we do with the white spaces." What Strother Martin did with the white spaces was incredible. Same with Slim Pickens and Dub Taylor.

I did a show, which I was watching the other night. Somebody said "*Gunsmoke*'s on." I flipped it on. I had absolutely no recollection of that film. After doing a hundred movies and live television, they do kind of get all jumbled up. But here I was with Katherine Ross. She was my love interest, which wasn't bad, and the heavy was George Kennedy. He was the technical advisor on *Sgt. Bilko*, and then they hired him as an actor. He played her father. There never really was anybody that I can remember that came on the show and was a stinker. It just didn't happen.

Q: Did you have a favorite director on the show?

BR: Andy McLaglen was great fun. Harry Harris I adored. Harry was just one of the kindest, sweetest guys. Harry did most of the shows that I did. I loved working with Harry.

Q: You used to leap on your horse a lot and swing off onto the ground. Was that your idea?

BR: I was a pretty good athlete in college, played college football, and I wanted to put in something a little more Indian. I figured this guy probably didn't have a saddle and really didn't know how to ride that well on a saddle. Norman, I think, thought I was the worst horseman in the world, until he realized what the hell I was doing...finally I stopped leaping into the saddle so much and getting on like a cowboy by the second year. The first year I was jumping every time I had a chance. I remember Jim would be standing there talking and all of a sudden I'd be sitting beside him on the horse, and he'd turn around and say, "How the hell did you get here?" (laughs)

I look at the show and I feel that I really hadn't learned my craft yet, but I was working on it. The hardest thing in the world for an actor to learn is to listen. I learned to listen. They were not afraid on that show to play the silences. Where someone says something and there's a moment where everybody kind of reacts, or Milburn would maybe have a long speech and go on and on and on. Learning how to listen is a great lesson, not only as an actor but in life

Q: Did you have a favorite episode?

BR: The first show I did was kind of the showiest one I suppose, and many years later, I wished I could have done it over when I was a much better actor. The one that was my favorite was the one in which the idea was mine. One of Festus' relations was coming to town because when he was young, Festus had bit the earlobe off him. [*Eliab's Alm*, February 27, 1965] That was all my dialogue. It was such fun to see it come to life and to be a part of that. Because of the look that I had, I never ever was given any comedies to do, so at least I had a chance to write some. I wrote it on the sly. It was a funny episode, and Kenny was brilliant as always.

Q: Can you share any thoughts about Amanda Blake?

BR: Amanda was just heaven, and I say this with the greatest respect. She was a great dame in the old-fashioned sense of a dame, where you could take her to the fights, you could take her to the Governor's Ball, you could play poker with her and the guys, and she was still a great dame. And great fun and stunning. Her skin was like…I never saw skin before or since that was that beautiful—white—like forever amber. She was a dear, dear lady, and I adored her. I remember years and years later, I was doing rather well in pictures, and I was in Arizona and was asked to get up on stage and do something. I was talking and all of a sudden, I just stopped and went,

"AMANDA WAS JUST HEAVEN, AND I SAY THIS WITH THE GREATEST RESPECT."

"Amanda?" and she was sitting in the front row and just looked gorgeous. She said hello, and I ran down, knelt down and kissed her hand, and everybody applauded, and then I told the audience how special she was. To work with somebody like that who was just, everyday, kind and wonderful.

Jim had Tiny Nichols who originally started out as his stand-in. He was this great big huge guy. I don't know if this story has been told, but it's a wonderful story—He must have weighed close to 400 pounds, and he was tall, as tall as Jim. He drove a pink Cadillac.

He got promoted from stand-in to second assistant. So he started coming through the front gate and the guys at the gate would stop him. Well, this went on for about three weeks, and finally—Tiny stuttered—after about the third week, the guard asked, "So who are you?" And he said, "Can I-I ask you a q-q-q-q-q-question?" The guard said, "Sure." "How many g-g-g-g-guys do you get coming t-t-through here that weigh f-f-f-four-hundred pounds and drive a p-p-p-p-p-pink Cadillac?" (big laugh)

Q: Why do you think the show lasted for twenty seasons?

BR: We had wonderful writers. There was never a show that I can remember about which you'd say, "This is really a stinky one, you got to get past this one." Every one of them had moments that no other show had. And the moments were what we call now relationship humor or relationship dialogue. The dialogue comes from the relationship, and that's the way it should be. They really started it, truthfully, back when the show was on the radio.

I'm sure you've heard the stories about who they tested for Matt Dillon. I actually saw the tests—they were hysterical! The funniest was what happened to Bill Conrad who played Matt Dillon on the radio. They tested Robert Stack, Raymond Burr, Hugh O'Brian, a couple of other people, but Conrad had this magnificent voice.

Everything was going along perfect and then he stood up, and the chair stuck to his ass. (big laugh) He took about four steps with it stuck there, and that wasn't gonna work for Matt Dillon.

Q: Why is *Gunsmoke* still popular today?

BR: It was as authentic as it could have been under the circumstances. For television, it was a show that was important, an important show for actors to do. There was *Playhouse 90* which had tremendous prestige and all that, but if you were going to do drama in spite of the fact that it was in the Western era—and it doesn't matter who gives a damn what era it is, which we found out when Clint did so well with *Unforgiven*. But on *Gunsmoke*, the main and supporting cast readily supported you on the show. You realized right away that the guest shots were tremendously generous to the actors that came on the show. Everybody had a real shot to show their wares.

If you watch the show over a period of years you keep seeing these same wonderful, wonderful character actors, these wonderful young actors who became friends of mine—Bruce Dern, Tom Simcox, I could go on and on—Jimmy Hampton and I became close friends—he ended up doing six or seven movies with me. James Best. Jean Arthur did a *Gunsmoke* and just blew our socks off. She was just an amazing woman—so sweet and funny and no bigger than a minute. A lot of people of that stature did the show. Chill Wills—three or four times. You couldn't refuse them if they asked you to come back.

Q: Any other *Gunsmoke* stories you'd like to share?

BR: I remember the guy who drove the stagecoach. Richard Farnsworth. He was the only guy in town who could drive a six-up. He was in probably twenty-five of

"THEY WERE VERY, VERY, HAPPY, WONDERFUL YEARS—I'M GLAD TO TALK ABOUT IT."

them. When they gave him dialogue, I remember thinking, "Damn, this guy's good!" Hollywood didn't really give him a part until he was fifty-five years old and did *Comes a Horseman*, for which he was nominated for an Academy Award.

Q: Thanks so much for your time.

BR: They were very, very, happy, wonderful years—I'm glad to talk about it.

MATT GETS IT September 10, 1955. James Arness as Marshal Matt Dillon.

THE TELEVISION EPISODES

This listing reflects the billing style used by CBS for twenty seasons—staying as true to their credits as possible. One season the director was listed first, then the writer, etc. The following season, it could be the opposite. This list follows the spirit of the actual credits, season to season, bad grammar included.

SEASON ONE

Black and white - half hour episodes.
Shown on Saturday night at 10pm.

Produced by Charles Marquis Warren

001. MATT GETS IT
Original air date: September 10, 1955
Produced and directed by Charles Marquis Warren
Screenplay by Charles Marquis Warren
Story by John Meston
Starring:
Paul Richards - Dan Grat
Robert Anderson - Jim Hill
Malcolm Atterbury - Bird

MAGNUS December 12, 1955. James Arness and Amanda Blake.

Howard Culver - Hotel Clerk

Dan Grat (Paul Richards) is a notorious gunman landing in Dodge City. With no respect for the law, he'll shoot anyone who dares his defiance, including Marshal Dillon. Grat seriously wounds Matt, who, during his recovery, figures Grat's weakness before their final confrontation.

Production # 502

002. HOT SPELL
Original air date: September 17, 1955
Produced and directed by Charles Marquis Warren
Story and screenplay by E. Jack Neuman
Starring:
John Dehner - Cope Borden
James Westerfield - Rance Bradley
Marvin Bryan - Jason Bradley

After saving Cope Borden (John Dehner) from a lynch mob, Matt is put in the middle of a vicious tug of war between the denizens of Dodge City and the unsavory ex-con.

Production #503

003. WORD OF HONOR
Original air date: October 1, 1955
Produced and directed by Charles Marquis Warren
Screenplay by Charles Marquis Warren
Story by John Meston
Starring:
Robert Middleton - Jake Worth
Claude Akins - Harry
Dick Paxton - Rudy
Thom Carney - Jack

REED SURVIVES December 31, 1955. James Arness and John Carradine.

Ray Boyle - Jeff Worth
Will J. White - Ed Worth

Doc, a witness to murder, becomes the man in the middle with family members of the deceased and those who killed him.

Production #504

REED SURVIVES December 31, 1955. James Arness and Lola Albright.

004. **HOME SURGERY**

Original air date: October 8, 1955
Produced and directed by Charles Marquis Warren
Story and screenplay by John Meston
Starring:
Joe De Santis - Mr. Hawtree
Gloria Talbott - Holly Hawtree
Wright King - Ben Walling

Matt and Chester find Mr. Hawtree (Joe De Santis) dying from gangrene due to a supposed accidental injury. Was the injury caused by Holly Hawtree (Gloria Talbot) or Ben Walling (Wright King)?

Production #505

005. **OBIE TATER**

Original air date: October 15, 1955
Produced and directed by Charles Marquis Warren
Screenplay by Charles Marquis Warren
Story by John Meston
Starring:
Royal Dano - Obie Tater
Kathy Adams - Ella Mills
Jon Shepodd - Mitch
Pat Conway - Quade

Former prospector Obie Tater (Royal Dano) is beaten by a gang who suspects he has hoards of gold hidden on his property. Obie marries Ella (Kathy Adams) who is actually a part of the gang, seeking to get rich quick.

Production #507

006. **NIGHT INCIDENT**

Original air date October 29, 1955
Produced and directed by Charles Marquis Warren
Story and screenplay by Charles Marquis Warren
Starring:
Peter Votrian - Timmy
Robert Foulk - Hinton
Amzie Strickland - Mrs. Hinton
Anne Warren - White Fawn
Lance Warren - Maggie

Jeanne Bates - Mrs. Wyatt
Lou Vernon - Cal Ross

Young Timmy (Peter Votrian) is a teller of tall tales. In a twist on *The Boy Who Cried Wolf* he tells the disbelievers in Dodge of impending robberies. Reluctantly, Matt checks out his stories.
Production #511

007. **SMOKING OUT THE NOLANS**
Original air date: November 5, 1955
Produced and directed by Charles Marquis Warren
Screenplay by Charles Marquis Warren
Story by John Meston
Starring:
John Larch - Clay
Ainslie Pryor - Josh Nolan
Jeannie Bates - Mrs. Nolan
Ed Platt - Mr. Burgess

Marshal Dillon tries to avert a range war between a wealthy landowner (Ed Platt) and Mr. and Mrs. Nolan (Ainslie Pryor and Jeannie Bates), who have homesteaded his property.
Production #506

008. **KITE'S REWARD**
Original air date: November 12, 1955
Produced and directed by Charles Marquis Warren
Story and screenplay by John Meston
Starring:
Adam Kennedy - Andy Travis
James Griffith - Joe Kite
Herbert Lytton - Jake Crowell
George Selk - Moss Grimmick

Joe Locke - Beecher
Chris Alcaide - Barnes

A reformed outlaw, Andy Travis (Adam Kennedy), must defend himself from a ruthless bounty hunter, Joe Kite (James Griffith).
Production #508

009. **THE HUNTER**
Original air date: November 26, 1955
Produced and directed by Charles Marquis Warren
Story and screenplay by John Dunkel
Starring:
Peter Whitney - Jase Murdock
Richard Gilden - Golden Calf
Lou Vernon - Cal Ross
Robert Keene - Dude

Jase Murdock (Peter Whitney) is a psychotic buffalo hunter who arouses Indian wrath when he breaks a government treaty by entering sacred hunting grounds.
Production #510

010. **THE QUEUE**
Original air date: December 3, 1955
Produced and directed by Charles Marquis Warren
Screenplay by Sam Peckinpah
Story by John Meston
Starring:
Keye Luke - Chen
Sebastian Cabot - Bailey
Robert Gist - Rabb
Devlin McCarthy - Howard

HELPING HAND March 17, 1956. Amanda Blake, James Arness and Brett Halsey.

20-20 February 25, 1956. Wilton Graff and James Arness.

INDIAN SCOUT March 31, 1956. Pat Hogan and James Arness.

THE BIG BROAD April 28, 1956. James Arness and Dee J. Thompson.

In a tale of racial prejudice, Chen (Keye Luke) is roughed up by two brothers, Howard and Rabb (Devlin McCarthy and Robert Gist), who disgrace the man into a life changing decision.
Production #513

011. **GENERAL PARSLEY SMITH**
Original air date: December 10, 1955
Produced and directed by Charles Marquis Warren

Screenplay by John Dunkel
Story by John Meston
Starring:
Raymond Bailey - General Parsley Smith
James O'Rear - Drew Holt
John Alderson - Nash
Wilfrid Knapp - Mr. Botkin

Parsley Smith (Raymond Bailey) arrives in Dodge spreading rumors about the new banker and his concerns about the residents' money.
Production #517

012. **MAGNUS**
Original air date: December 24, 1955
Produced and directed by Charles Marquis Warren
Story and screenplay by John Meston
Starring:
Robert Easton - Magnus
James Anderson - Lucifer
Than Wyenn - Dealer
Tim Graham - Cowboy
Dorothy Schuyler - Olive

Chester's brother Magnus (Robert Easton) arrives in Dodge just in time for the Christmas holidays.
Production #512

013. **REED SURVIVES**
Original air date: December 31, 1955
Produced and directed by Charles Marquis Warren
Story and screenplay by Les Crutchfield
Starring:

Miss Amanda Blake

Dennis Weaver and James Arness

GUNSMOKE

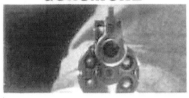

Dodge City– where the law is ten feet tall.

Gunsmoke. 7:30 pm.
James Arness, Milburn
Stone, Amanda Blake, Ken
Curtis—they aim to please.

WSBC-TV⊙2
A CBS Affiliate

COLOR AD SLICK

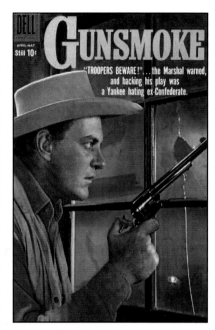

COMIC BOOK COVER

*NEW ZEALAND GUIDE Cover
features Milburn Stone, Ken Curtis
and Burt Reynolds.*

OLD RELIABLES This photo of the supporting cast ran in the March 18, 1972 TV GUIDE. Top row: Roy Roberts, Ted Jordan, Tom Brown, John Harper; middle row: Howard Culver, Charles Wagenheim; front row: Hank Patterson, Charles Seel, Woodrow Chambliss and Sarah Selby.

DRAGO Buddy Ebsen guest-starred memorably as the title character. (photo courtesy of Jim Byrnes)

ARNESS VS. DAVIS One of the fondest remembered episodes during the twenty-year run. THE JAILER.

ACTION James Arness in THE BADGE. (photo courtesy of Jim Byrnes)

HOSTAGE! William Smith starred as Jude Bonner.

IN THE PHOTO STUDIO James Arness and Ken Curtis pose for the still camera.

KILLER Steve Forrest as the cold-blooded Mannon.

REGULARS Ted Jordan as Burke, Glenn Strange as Sam and Buck Taylor as Newly.

THE GANG Four of the most recognizable performers and characters in the history of television.

Season's Greetings!!

You and your guest are cordially invited to attend the Twentieth Annual GUNSMOKE Christmas Party on Friday evening, December 20th, at 7:00 PM, to be held on Stage 3, CBS Studio Center.

The Longbranch will dispense "spirits", there will be an orchestra for dancing, and a buffet dinner will be served upon presentation of the enclosed tickets.

We hope that we will see you there!

CHRISTMAS PARTY

*TV MOVIE Richard Kiley and James Arness in a scene from THE
LAST APACHE.*

BUCK TAYLOR ART A beautiful example of his artwork, DAD AND ME, features the talented actor and artist with his father Dub Taylor, a memorable performer in several Westerns including GUNSMOKE. ©Copyright Buck Taylor (courtesy of Buck Taylor)

KEN CURTIS as Festus Haggen

FRIENDS SURROUND ARNESS Bruce Boxleitner, Buck Taylor, Arness, Jim Byrnes and Laurie Prange. (photo courtesy of Mary Jo Barlow)

John Carradine - Ephraim Hunt
Lola Albright - Lucy Hunt
James Drury - Booth Rider
Virginia Arness - Gypsy

After marrying an older man (John Carradine), young and attractive Lucy (Lola Albright) falls in love with another man and together, they plot her husband's demise.

Production #520

014. **PROFESSOR LUTE BONE**

Original air date: January 7, 1956
Produced and directed by Charles Marquis Warren
Screenplay by David Victor and Herbert Little, Jr.
Story by John Meston
Starring:
John Abbott - Professor Lute Bone
Jester Hairston - Wellington
Gloria Castillo - Mrs. Ringle
Don Gardner - Mr. Ringle
Strother Martin - Mr. Stooler
Sally Corner - Mrs. Stooler

When a cure-all elixir almost kills an infant, Doc and the folks of Dodge City want to run Professor Lute Bone (John Abbott) out of town.

Production #515

015. **NO HANDCUFFS**

Original air date: January 21, 1956
Produced and directed by Charles Marquis Warren
Screenplay by Les Crutchfield
Story by John Meston

Starring:
Victor Perrin - Hank
Mort Mills - Brake
Marjorie Owens - Woman
Herbert Lytton - Hunter
Cyril Delevanti - Turnkey
Charles Gray - Sheriff

HACK PRINE May 12, 1956. Hal Baylor and James Arness.

COOTER May 19, 1956. Amanda Blake and Strother Martin.

THE PREACHER June 16, 1956. Dennis Weaver throws water in the face of Chuck Connors.

THE KILLER May 26, 1956. Charles Bronson, James Arness and Dennis Weaver.

Hank (Victor Perrin) is an innocent man arrested to cover up evidence for a crooked lawman (Charles Gray). Matt is convinced of Hank's innocence and is ultimately forced to challenge his colleague.

Production #519

016. **REWARD FOR MATT**

Original air date: January 28, 1956
Produced and directed by Charles Marquis Warren
Screenplay by David Victor and Herbert Little, Jr.
Story by John Meston
Starring:
Val Dufour - Day Barrett
Helen Wallace - Mrs. Stoner
Paul Newlan - Mr. Stoner
Jean Inness - Mrs. Reeves
John G. Lee - Young Farmer

Widow woman Stoner (Helen Wallace) offers a reward to anyone who will kill Marshal Dillon. Matt was forced to kill her husband (Paul Newlan) during his attempted arrest of the murderer.

Production #516

017. **ROBIN HOOD**

Original air date: February 4, 1956
Produced and directed by Charles Marquis Warren
Screenplay by Daniel B. Ullman
Story by John Meston
Starring:
William Hopper - John Henry Jordan
Barry Atwater - Mr. Bowen
Nora Marlowe - Mrs. Bowen
James McCallion - Vince Butler

Wilfrid Knapp - Mr. Botkin
S. John Launer - Judge

A highwayman who robs only the rich, John Henry Jordan (William Hopper), runs the law and courts ragged when witnesses refuse to testify against the notorious outlaw.

Production #518

018. **YORKY**

Original air date: February 18, 1956
Produced and directed by Charles Marquis Warren
Screenplay by Sam Peckinpah
Story by John Meston
Starring:
Jeff Silver - Yorky
Howard Petrie - Brant
Dennis Cross - Tom
Malcolm Atterbury - Seldon
Mary Gregory - Mrs. Seldon

Indian raised white boy Yorky (Jeff Silver) seeks revenge against the horse thieves who attempt to frame him for their crimes.

Production #514

019. **20-20**

Original air date: February 25, 1956
Produced and directed by Charles Marquis Warren
Screenplay by David Victor and Herbert Little, Jr.
Story by John Meston
Starring:
Wilton Graff - Troy Carver
Martin Kingsley - Lee Polen
Pitt Hebert - Dealer
George Selk - Moss Grimmick

Retired lawman Troy Carver (Wilton Graff) attempts to keep his failing eyesight hidden from his numerous enemies.
Production #522

020. REUNION '78
Original air date: March 3, 1956
Produced and directed by Charles Marquis Warren
Story and Screenplay by Harold Swanton
Starring:
Val Dufour - Jerry Shand
Marion Brash - Belle
Maurice Manson - Andy Culley
Joe Perry - Witness
Mason Curry - Marty

Revenge is the motive when a cowboy, Jerry Shand (Val Dufour), arrives in Dodge gunning for Andy Culley (Maurice Manson).
Production #526

021. HELPING HAND
Original air date: March 17, 1956
Produced and directed by Charles Marquis Warren
Screenplay by David Victor and Herbert Little, Jr.
Story by John Meston
Starring:
Brett Halsey - Elser
Ken L. Smith - Pence
Russ Thorson - Bowers
Michael Granger - Hander

Accused of cattle rustling, Elser (Brett Halsey), is rescued from those wanting to lynch him by a sympathetic Miss Kitty. He

HOW TO DIE FOR NOTHING June 23, 1956. Mort Mills and James Arness.

turns into a would-be tough guy and causes trouble for all involved, including Matt.
Production #509

022. TAP DAY FOR KITTY

Original air date: March 24, 1956
Produced and directed by Charles Marquis Warren
Screenplay by John Dunkel
Story by John Meston
Starring:
John Dehner - Nip Cullers
John Patrick - Jonas
Mary Adams - Nettie
Evelyn Scott - Olive
Dorothy Schuyler - Kate
Charlene Brooks - Blossom

    Elderly rancher Nip Cullers arrives in Dodge City looking for a wife and who fits the bill better than Kitty Russell? After an attempt on his life, Kitty becomes suspect number one.
    Production #521

023. INDIAN SCOUT

Original air date: March 31, 1956
Produced and directed by Charles Marquis Warren
Story and screenplay by John Dunkel
Starring:
Eduard Franz - Amos Cartwright
DeForrest Kelley - Will Bailey
William Vaughan - Twitchell
Tommy Hart - Clay
Pat Hogan - Buffalo Tongue

    Matt and Chester trail accused criminal Amos Cartwright (Eduard Franz) deep into Comanche territory.
    Production #524

024. THE PEST HOLE

Original air date April 14, 1956
Produced and directed by Charles Marquis Warren
Story and screenplay by David Victor and Herbert Little, Jr.
Starring:
Howard McNear - Bradley
Patrick O'Moore - Matthews
Evelyn Scott - Olive
Norbert Schiller - Franz Betzer
Phil Rich - Townsman
Gordon Mills - Burkleman
Lisa Golm - Mrs. Saur

    Dodge City is hit hard with an outbreak of typhoid fever amongst the German inhabitants. Panic stricken citizens begin to flee, causing Doc to put not only his life on the line, but Chester's as well while trying to find and cure the carrier.
    Production #525

025. THE BIG BROAD

Original air date: April 28, 1956
Produced and directed by Charles Marquis Warren
Screenplay by David Victor and Herbert Little, Jr.
Story by John Meston
Starring:
Dee J. Thompson - Lena Wave
Joel Ashley - Nate
Terry Becker - Emmett
Heinie Brock - Drummer
Howard Culver - Hotel Clerk

    Six-foot tall two-hundred pound Lena Wave (Dee J. Thompson) becomes Matt's adversary when she arrives in town

with meek gambler Emmett Fitzgerald (Terry Becker).
Production # 523

026. HACK PRINE
Original air date: May 12, 1956
Produced and directed by Charles Marquis Warren
Story and screenplay by John Meston
Starring:
Leo Gordon - Hack Prine
George Wallace - Dolph Timble
Hal Baylor - Lee Timble
Wally Cassell - Oley

Dillon's former friend Hack Prine (Leo Gordon) is now a hired killer and has been offered a large sum of money to kill the marshal.
Production #501

027. COOTER
Original air date: May 19, 1956
Directed by Robert Stevenson
Screenplay by Sam Peckinpah
Story by John Meston
Produced by Charles Marquis Warren
Starring:
Strother Martin - Cooter
Vinton Hayworth - Sissle
Brett King - Pate
Robert Vaughn - Kid

A simple man named Cooter (Strother Martin) is hired by a crooked gambler (Vinton Hayworth) to goad Matt into a gunfight.
Production #527

028. THE KILLER
Original air date: May 26, 1956
Directed by Robert Stevenson
Screenplay by John Dunkel
Story by John Meston
Produced by Charles Marquis Warren
Starring:
Charles Bronson - Crego
David Chapman - Jesse
James Nusser - Man
Dabbs Greer - Jonas

Crego (Charles Bronson) is a new face in Dodge but proves to be no stranger to trouble. He has a penchant for pushing innocents to violence—then cites "self-defense" upon killing them.
Production #528

029. DOC'S REVENGE
Original air date: June 9, 1956
Directed by Ted Post
Story and screenplay by John Dunkel
Produced by Charles Marquis Warren
Starring:
Chris Alcaide - Clem Maddow
Ainslie Pryor - George Maddow
Harry Bartell - Ben Bartlett
Bert Rumsey - Bartender

A stranger named Clem Maddow (Chris Alcaide) rides into town causing Doc to grab his gun and threaten to kill the man on sight. When Clem is shot, Doc becomes the obvious suspect.
Production #530

PRAIRIE HAPPY July 7, 1956. James Arness, Robert Ellenstein and Anne Barton.

030. **THE PREACHER**
Original air date: June 16, 1956
Directed by Robert Stevenson
Screenplay by John Dunkel
Story by John Meston
Produced by Charles Marquis Warren
Starring:
Royal Dano - Seth Tandy

Chuck Connors - Sam Keeler
Paul Dubov - Humbert
Jim Hyland - Stage driver
George Selk - Moss Grimmick

Boxer "Roaring" Sam Keeler (Chuck Connors) bullies helpless newcomer Seth Tandy (Royal Dano) until Matt steps in and the real fight begins.
Production #529

031. **HOW TO DIE FOR NOTHING**
Original air date: June 23, 1956
Directed by Ted Post
Screenplay by Sam Peckinpah
Story by John Meston
Produced by Charles Marquis Warren
Starring:
Mort Mills - Howard Bulow
Maurice Manson - Riesling
Lawrence Dobkin - Jacklin
James Nolan - Zack
Bill White, Jr. - Ned
Herbert Lytton - Stranger

Matt is marked for death by the brother (James Nolan) of a man (Bill White, Jr.) he killed in an earlier altercation.
Production #531

032. **DUTCH GEORGE**
Original air date: June 30, 1956
Directed by Robert Stevenson
Produced by Charles Marquis Warren
Story and screenplay by John Dunkel

CARA July 28, 1956. James Arness and Jorja Cartwright.

Starring:
Robert Middleton - Dutch George
Tom Pittman - Jimmy McQueen

Richard Warren - Hack
George Selk - Moss Grimmick

Matt is forced to arrest his childhood idol, Dutch George (Robert Middleton) who now leads a brutal band of horse thieves.
Production #532

033. PRAIRIE HAPPY
Original air date: July 7, 1956
Directed by Ted Post
Produced by Charles Marquis Warren
Screenplay by David Victor and Herbert Little, Jr.
Story by John Meston
Starring:
Robert Ellenstein - Tewksbury
Dabbs Greer - Jonas
Anne Barton - Quiet One
Wilfred Knapp - Botkin
Tyler McVey - Father
Bruce Holland - Boy
Jack Holland - Danvers
Roy Engle - Citizen

Tewksbury (Robert Ellenstein) is a bitter old man who, through calculated lies, arouses the citizens of Dodge to action preparing for a supposed Indian uprising.
Production #534

034. CHESTER'S MAIL ORDER BRIDE
Original air date: July 14, 1956
Directed by Robert Stevenson
Produced by Charles Marquis Warren
Story and Screenplay by David Victor and Herbert Little, Jr.

Starring:
Mary Carver - Ann
Joel Ashley - Linus
Russ Thorson - Brady
William Hamel - Customer
Bert Rumsey - Sam

Chester changes his mind regarding marriage when Miss Ann Southwright (Mary Carver)—his mail-order bride—arrives in town.
Production #535

035. **THE GUITAR**
Original air date: July 21, 1956
Directed by Harry Horner
Produced by Charles Marquis Warren
Screenplay by Sam Peckinpah
Story by John Meston
Starring:
Aaron Spelling - Weed Pindle
Jacques Aubuchon - Short
Charles Gray - Tyler
Duane Thorsen - Delmer
Bill Hale - Tom
Joseph Mell - Pence

Coaxed by two diehard rebels (Jacques Aubuchon and Charles Gray), meek and mild former Union soldier Weed Pindle (Aaron Spelling) resorts to violence to avoid being lynched.
Production #533

036. **CARA**
Original air date: July 28, 1956
Directed by Robert Stevenson
Produced by Charles Marquis Warren
Screenplay by David Victor and Herbert Little, Jr,
Story by John Meston
Starring:
Jorja Cartwright - Cara
Charles Webster - Sheriff Benson
Douglas Odney - Tolliver
Wilfrid Knapp - Mr. Botkin
Howard Culver - Mr. Uzzel

Former girlfriend Cara (Jorja Cartwright) crosses paths with Matt, who realizes she is now on the wrong side of the law.
Production #536

037. **MR. AND MRS. AMBER**
Original air date: August 4, 1956
Directed by Ted Post
Produced by Charles Marquis Warren
Screenplay by David Victor and Herbert Little, Jr.
Story by John Meston
Starring:
Paul Richards - Neal Amber
Ainslie Pryor - Peak Fletcher
Gloria McGhee - Mrs. Amber
Dabbs Greer - Jonas
Bing Russell - Simon Fletcher

A self-proclaimed religious prophet Peak Fletcher (Ainslie Pryor) begins making life miserable for his family members.
Production #537

038. **UNMARKED GRAVE**
Original air date: August 18, 1956

Directed by Ted Post
Story and screenplay by David Victor and Herbert Little, Jr.
Produced by Charles Marquis Warren
Starring:
Ron Hagerthy - Rusty
Helen Kleeb - Mrs. Randolph
William Hopper - Tasker
Than Wyenn - Darcy
Joe Scudero - Munro
Boyd Stockman - Stage Driver

A young outlaw (Ron Hagerthy) gains the confidence of elderly Mrs. Randolph (Helen Kleeb) in a desperate attempt to gain his independence.
Production #538

039. ALARM AT PLEASANT VALLEY
Original air date: August 25, 1956
Directed by Ted Post
Produced by Charles Marquis Warren
Story and screenplay by John Dunkel
Starring:
Lew Brown - Sam Fraser
Helen Wallace - Ma Fraser
Dorothy Schuyler - Alice Fraser
Bill White, Jr. - Tad Fraser
Dan Blocker - Lieutenant

Renegade Indians ambush homesteaders en route to Dodge City. When his wife goes into labor, Sam Fraser (Lew Brown) is forced to stand his ground and fight.
Production #539

SEASON TWO

Producer (12 episodes) - Charles Marquis Warren
Associate Producer (12 episodes) Norman Macdonnell (Producer remainder of season)

040. COW DOCTOR
Original air date: September 8, 1956
Directed by Andrew V. McLaglen
Produced by Charles Marquis Warren
Screenplay by John Dunkel
Story by John Meston
Starring:
Robert H. Harris - Ben Pitcher
Dorothy Adams - Mrs. Pitcher
Tommy Kirk - Jerry Pitcher

Farmer Ben Pitcher (Robert H. Harris) sends for Doc who hurries to his ranch, only to find his emergency is an ailing cow. In the meantime, a female patient back in Dodge dies during Doc's absence.
Production #541

041. BRUSH AT ELKADER
Original air date: September 15, 1956
Directed by Ted Post
Produced by Charles Marquis Warren
Screenplay by Les Crutchfield
Story by John Meston
Starring:
Gage Clark - Hinkle
Alfred Linder - Clerk

COW DOCTOR September 8, 1956. Milburn Stone and James Arness.

Dennis Cross - Bartender
Malcolm Atterbury - Liveryman
Paul Lambert - Lou Shippen

Matt and Chester travel to Elkader to arrest a man responsible for murder. The pair soon find the citizens there rather uncooperative, making their task next to impossible.
Production #542

042. CUSTER

Original air date: September 22, 1956
Directed by Ted Post
Produced by Charles Marquis Warren
Screenplay by Gil Doud
Story by John Meston
Starring:
Brian Hutton - Joe Trimble
Richard Keith - Major Banker
Herbert Lytton - Judge

Fate plays an ironic trick on deserter, rustler, murderer Joe Trimble (Brian Hutton) who is in Matt's custody but is set free due to insufficient evidence. Major Banker (Richard Keith) is forced to re-recruit the scum to join up with General Custer, and the rest as they say, is history.
Production #540

043. THE ROUND UP

Original air date: September 29, 1956
Directed by Ted Post
Screenplay by Sam Peckinpah
Story by John Meston
Produced by Charles Marquis Warren

CUSTER September 22, 1956. James Arness and Amanda Blake.

Starring:
Jacques Aubuchon - Torp
Michael Hinn - Zel
Barney Phillips - Summers
John Dierkes - Rydell

Mason Curry - Jake
John Patrick - Dad

Dodge City merchants ask for Matt's protection against the onslaught of rough and rowdy cowhands coming to town. When he closes Front Street, Matt has to face a riotous mob alone.
Production #544

044. YOUNG MAN WITH A GUN
Original air date: October 20, 1956
Directed Christian Nyby
Screenplay by Winston Miller
Story by John Meston
Produced by Charles Marquis Warren
Starring:
Jack Dimond - Peyt
Fredd Wayne - Sam Kertcher
Clegg Hoyt - Jack Rynning
Sid Clute - Spencer
Bert Rumsey - Bartender

When Matt kills his outlaw brother, young Peyt (Jack Dimond) arrives in Dodge with one thing on his mind—revenge.
Production #545

045. INDIAN WHITE
Original air date: October 27, 1956
Directed by Ted Post
Produced by Charles Marquis Warren
Screenplay by David Victor and Herbert Little, Jr.
Story by Tom Hanley, Jr.
Starring:
Peter Votrian - Dennis

Marian Seldes - Mrs. Cullen
Alexander Lockwood - Col. Honeyman
Abel Fernanadez - Little Wolf
Stanley Adams - Ross
Clegg Hoyt - Dutchholder
Kenneth Alton - Cowboy
George Archambeault - Citizen

A young white boy (Abel Fernandez) raised by the Cheyennes, must adjust to life with his own people after his rescue by the cavalry.
Production #546

046. HOW TO CURE A FRIEND
Original air date: November 10, 1956
Directed by Ted Post
Produced by Charles Marquis Warren
Screenplay by Winston Miller
Story by John Meston
Starring:
Andrew Duggan - Nick Search
Simon Oakland - Enoch Mills
Jess Kirkpatrick - Mr. Teeters
Joseph Mell - Bill Pence

Nick Search (Andrew Duggan) uses his friendship with Matt to launch a con game on the unsuspecting folks of Dodge City.
Production # 550

047. LEGAL REVENGE
Original air date: November 17, 1956
Directed by Andrew V. McLaglen
Screenplay by Sam Peckinpah

Story by John Meston
Produced by Charles Marquis Warren
Starring:
Cloris Leachman - Flory Tibbs
Philip Bourneuf - George Bassett
Robert Strong - Clerk

An exhausted man and woman are found in a far off cabin by Doc Adams, each fearing one will kill the other.
Production #547

048. **THE MISTAKE**
Original air date: November 24, 1956
Directed by Andrew V. McLaglen
Produced by Charles Marquis Warren
Screenplay by Gil Doud
Story by John Meston
Starring:
Touch Connors - Bostick
Gene O'Donnell - Haney
Cyril Delevanti - Driver
Robert Hinkle - Rider
Bert Rumsey - Bartender

The prime suspect to a murder claims Doc as his alibi. With Doc out of town, his statement cannot be confirmed. When the suspect escapes, Matt must set out after him, leaving Dodge unprotected from the real killer.
Production #543

049. **GREATER LOVE**
Original air date: December 1, 1956
Directed by Ted Post

Screenplay by Winston Miller
Story by John Meston
Produced by Charles Marquis Warren
Starring:
Frank DeKova - Tobeel
Amzie Strickland - Mrs. Bryant
Claude Akins - Jed Butler
Ray Bennett - Hank

Jed Butler (Claude Akins) threatens to kill Doc if he is unable to save his wounded partner. Matt puts himself in harm's way to save his friend.
Production #548

050. **NO INDIANS**
Original air date: December 8, 1956
Directed by Ted Post
Produced by Norman Macdonnell
Screenplay by John Dunkel
Story by John Meston
Starring:
Herbert Rudley - Capt. Starr
Dick Rich - Sam Butler
Mickey Simpson - Stapp
Fintan - Meyler - Arie O'Dell
Joel Ashley - Jake
K. L. Smith - Cran

Matt and Chester become decoys to uncover a group of cowboys masquerading as attacking Indians—inciting the wrath of the citizens of Dodge.
Production #554

051. **SPRING TERM**

Original air date: December 15, 1956
Directed by Ted Post
Produced by Charles Marquis Warren
Screenplay by William F. Leicester
Story by John Meston
Starring:
Harry Townes - Bill Lee
Howard Culver - Mr. Uzzell
Stanley Adams - Bartender
Paul Newlan - Danch
Ross Ford - Dane Shaw
Clayton Post - Citizen
Jack Kruschen - Jed
H. M. Wynant - Barker

Dane Shaw (Ross Ford) is gunned down in Dodge City. After investigating the crime, Matt realizes that he himself was the intended target.
Production #552

052. **POOR PEARL**

Original air date: December 22, 1956
Directed by Andrew V. McLaglen
Produced by Charles Marquis Warren
Screenplay by Sam Peckinpah
Story by John Meston
Starring:
Constance Ford - Pearl Bender
Denver Pyle - Willie Calhoun
Michael Emmett - Webb Thorne
Jess Kirkpatrick - Frank Teeters
Bert Rumsey - Bartender

YOUNG MAN WITH A GUN October 20, 1956. Dennis Weaver, Milburn Stone, James Arness and Jack Diamond.

275

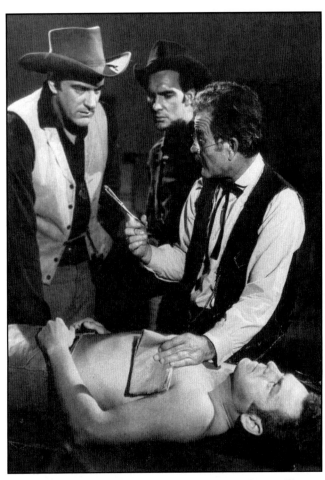

SPRING TERM December 15, 1956. James Arness, Dennis Weaver, Milburn Stone and Ross Ford.

John Hamilton - Big John
Johnny McGough - Jimmie

Matt must halt a showdown between two would-be suitors Webb (Michael Emmett) and Willie (Denver Pyle). The object of their affection—Pearl Bender (Constance Ford).
Production # 551

053. **CHOLERA**
Original air date: December 29, 1956
Directed by Andrew V. McLaglen
Produced by Norman Macdonnell
Screenplay by Les Crutchfield
Story by John Meston
Starring:
Peg Hillias - Jenny
Paul Fix - McCready
Bartlett Robinson - Gabriel
Stuart Whitman - Bart
Gordon Gebert - Billy
John Smith - David

Tragedy, violence and death result when an unscrupulous landowner (Paul Fix) attempts to evict a homesteader (Bartlett Robinson) and his family.
Production #553

054. **PUCKET'S NEW YEAR**
Original air date: January 5, 1957
Directed by Andrew V. McLaglen
Produced by Norman Macdonnell
Story and screenplay by John Meston
Starring:
Edger Stehli - Ira Pucket
Grant Withers - Jed Larner
Richard Deacon - Botkin
Rocky Shahan - Jim
Bert Rumsey - Bartender

Matt and Chester find Ira Pucket (Edger Stehli), an old buffalo hunter, left to die on the freezing Kansas plains by his partner Jed Larner (Grant Withers). Ira later searches for the cowardly Jed in Dodge, much to Matt's dismay.

Production #555

055. THE COVER UP

Original air date: January 12, 1957
Directed by William D. Russell
Produced by Norman Macdonnell
Screenplay by William N. Robson
Story by John Meston
Starring:
Tyler McVey - Sam Baxton
Vivi Janiss - Sara Baxton
Ted Marcuse - Zack Ritter
Malcolm Atterbury - Jed Bates
Roy Engel - Hoffer

Matt searches for the mysterious killer targeting homesteaders—the weapon of choice? A deadly shotgun used to commit the crimes in the victims' own homes.

Production #558

056. SINS OF THE FATHER

Original air date: January 19, 1957
Directed by Andrew V. McLaglen
Produced by Norman Macdonnell
Screenplay by John Dunkel
Story by John Meston
Starring:
Angie Dickinson - Rose Daggitt
Peter Whitney - Big Dan Daggitt

Gage Clark - Dobie
Paul Wexler - Rodin

An excellent episode that centers around the arrival of Dan Daggitt (Peter Whitney) and his Indian wife, Rose (Angie Dickinson—in a stand-out performance)—and the prejudice and hatred that surrounds them.

Production #557

057. KICK ME

Original air date: January 26, 1957
Directed by Andrew V. McLaglen
Produced by Charles Marquis Warren
Screenplay by Endre Bohem and Louis Vittes
Story by John Meston
Starring:
Robert H. Harris - Fred Myers
Frank DeKova - Tobeel
Julie Van Zandt - Jennifer Myers
Paul Lambert - Harry Bent

Bank Robber Fred Myers (Robert H. Harris) kidnaps Miss Kitty but is halted in his attempt by Tobeel (Frank DeKova), an Indian who was a victim of an earlier cruel joke from the criminal.

Production #549

058. EXECUTIONER

Original air date: February 2, 1957
Directed by Andrew V. Mclaglen
Produced by Norman Macdonnell
Screenplay by Gil Doud
Story By John Meston
Starring:

Michael Hinn - Morgan Curry
Liam Sullivan - Tom Clegg
Robert Keys - Abe Curry

A ruthless young man (Liam Sullivan) kills elderly farmer Abe Curry (Robert Keys) while trying to establish his reputation with a gun.
Production #559

059. **GONE STRAIGHT**
Original air date: February 9, 1957
Directed by Ted Post
Produced by Norman Macdonnell
Screenplay by Les Crutchfield
Story by John Meston
Starring:
Carl Betz - Nate Timble
Marianne Stewart - Mrs. Timble
Joe De Santis - Gunter
Tige Andrews - Mike Postil
Ward Wood - Parker
John Dierkes - Ace

Nate Timble (Carl Betz) is a reformed outlaw and now a respected member of a small town where his neighbors now protect his former identity, much to the dismay of Matt and Chester. When former partners in crime plan an ambush, Matt sides with Timble and allows him to continue his new life.
Production #562

060. **BLOODY HANDS**
Original air date: February 16, 1957

Directed by Andrew V. McLaglen
Produced by Norman Macdonnell
Story and screenplay by John Meston
Starring:
Russell Johnson - Stanger
Lawrence Dobkin - Brand
Gloria Marshall - Linda
Harvey Grant - Billy
David Saber - Tom

After a particularly violent gunfight, a tortured Matt Dillon decides to turn in his badge.
Production #561

061. **SKID ROW**
Original air date: February 23, 1957
Directed by Ted Post
Produced by Norman Macdonnell
Screenplay by Gil Doud
Story by John Meston
Starring:
Joseph Sargent - Shomer
Susan Morrow - Ann
Gwinn Williams - Groat (Note: first name misspelled in credits, actually Guinn, often billed as Guinn "Big Boy" Williams.)

An Eastern girl named Ann (Susan Morrow) arrives in Dodge to marry Shomer (Joseph Sargent), who is now flat broke and uninterested in matrimony. Heartbroken, the naive young woman falls prey to a vicious man named Groat (Guinn Williams).
Production #564

THE PHOTOGRAPHER April 6, 1957. James Arness and Sebastian Cabot.

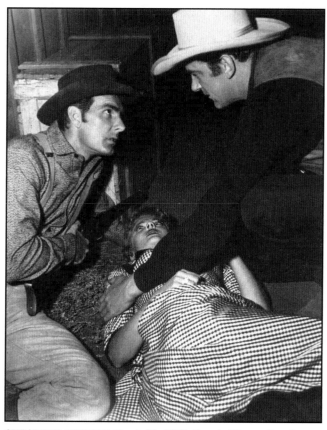

CHESTER'S MURDER March 30, 1957. Dennis Weaver, Peggie Castle and James Arness.

279

062. SWEET AND SOUR

Original air date: March 2, 1957
Directed by Andrew V. McLaglen
Produced by Norman Macdonnell
Story and screenplay by John Meston
Starring:
Karen Sharpe - Rena Decker
John Alderson - Ab Laster
Walter Reed - Joe Garrett
John Mitchum - Joe
Ken Mayer - Hank
George Archambeault - Agent

Dance hall girl Rena Decker has a peculiar hobby—provoking her many male admirers into gunfights over her affections.
Production #569

063. CAIN

Original air date: March 9, 1957
Directed by Ted Post
Produced by Norman Macdonnell
Story and screenplay by John Meston
Starring:
Harry Bartell - Cain Vestal
Mark Roberts - Adams
Paul Dubov - Pritchard
Dan Riss - Mike
Howard Ledig - Pete
Gorday Clifton - Cowboy

Rancher Adams (Mark Roberts) is revealed to be a former gunfighter after he is challenged to a showdown.
Production #566

WRONG MAN April 13, 1957. Catherine McLeod, Dennis Weaver, Don Keefer and James Arness.

064. BUREAUCRAT

Original air date: March 16, 1957
Directed by Ted Post
Story by John Meston

Teleplay by William F. Leicester
Produced by Norman Macdonnell
Starring:
John Hoyt - Rex Procter
Ken Lynch - Will Stroud
Ned Glass - Husk
Richard Avonde - Nick Fane
William Bryant - Charlie Frost
Alfred Toigo - Ben Lawrence

A high muckey-muck from Washington, D.C. arrives in Dodge City with one thing in mind—reforming the lawless ways of the citizens and Marshal Dillon.
Production #570

065. LAST FLING
Original air date: March 23, 1957
Directed by Andrew V. McLaglen
Written by John Meston
Produced by Norman Macdonnell
Starring:
Florenz Ames - John Peavy
Frank DeKova - Mulligan Rives
Anne O'Neal - Sabina Peavy
Susan Morrow - Melanie

Old farmers John Peavy (Florenz Ames) and Mulligan Rives (Frank DeKova) head into Dodge for one last fling. Miss Kitty becomes the object of their affections and sternly lets them know to leave her alone. When one of the sodbusters is shot, Kitty becomes the prime suspect.
Production #571

066. CHESTER'S MURDER
Original air date: March 30, 1957
Directed by Ted Post
Written by John Meston
Produced by Norman Macdonnell
Starring:
Peggie Castle - Nita Tucker
Murray Hamilton - Jake Buley
Gage Clarke - Jim Dobie
Tom Greenway - Ned Pickard
Tim Graham - Jonas
Charles Conrad - Man

Chester is accused of murdering a cowboy who previously threatened him publicly. Bowing to pressure and trying to avoid mob justice, Matt must place Chester into his custody while trying to solve the crime and clear his friend's name.
Production #568

067. THE PHOTOGRAPHER
Original air date: April 6, 1957
Directed by William D. Russell
Produced by Norman Macdonnell
Story and screenplay by John Dunkel
Starring:
Sebastian Cabot - Professor Jacoby
Norman Fredric - Gart
Ned Glass - Grubby
Charles Horvath - Left Hand
Howard Culver - Citizen
Dorothy Schuyler - Kate

Eastern photographer Professor Jacoby (Sebastian Cabot)

ignores Matt's advice and warnings when he trespasses on sacred Indian grounds.

Production #556

068. WRONG MAN

Original air date: April 13, 1957
Directed by Andrew V. McLaglen
Produced By Norman Macdonnell
Story and screenplay by John Meston
Starring:
Catherine McLeod - Letty
Don Keefer - Rickers
Robert Griffin - Catlin

Rickers (Don Keefer) shoots and kills a man he believes to be a wanted criminal. This killing leads to another as revenge takes over all involved.

Production #563

069. BIG GIRL LOST

Original air date: April 20, 1957
Directed by Ted Post
Produced by Norman Macdonnell
Story and screenplay by John Meston
Starring:
Gloria McGhee - Laura
Michael Pate - Locke
Judson Pratt - Bill Pence
Gerald Milton - Doolin

Locke (Michael Pate) arrives from Philadelphia searching for his former fiancee Laura (Gloria McGhee) who now works in the Long Branch. Covering up her vocation almost leads to

murder—with Matt stuck in the middle.

Production #560

070. WHAT THE WHISKEY DRUMMER HEARD

Original air date: April 27, 1957
Directed by Andrew V. McLaglen
Story by John Meston
Teleplay by Gil Doud
Produced by Norman Macdonnell
Starring:
Vic Perrin - Wilbur Hawkins
Robert Burton - Sheriff
Robert Karnes - Roberts
Bert Rumsey - Sam

Loose talk and rumors lead Marshal Dillon to believe that he has become the target of an unknown assassin.

Production #572

071. CHEAP LABOR

Original air date: May 4, 1957
Directed by Andrew V. McLaglen
Story and screenplay by John Meston
Produced by Norman Macdonnell
Starring:
Andrew Duggan - Fos Capper
Peggy Webber - Flora Stancil
Robert F. Simon - Ben Stancil
Susan Morrow - Melanie
James Nusser - Bum

Fos Capper (Andrew Duggan) is a reformed gunman who invokes the ire of Ben Stancil (Robert F. Simon) when he falls in

JEALOUSY July 6, 1957. James Arness and Joan Tetzel.

love with his sister Flora (Peggy Weber). Fos no longer carries a gun, but is eventually forced into a gunfight with the jealous sibling.

Production #567

072. **MOON**

Original air date: May 11, 1957

Directed by William D. Russell
Produced by Norman Macdonnell
Story and screenplay by John Meston
Starring:
Phillip Pine - Vint
Rebecca Welles - Nan
Stafford Repp - Brewer
Thomas Palmer - Jack Salter
Jane Ray - Vickie

Successful gambler Brewer (Stafford Repp) is beaten and killed and poker dealer Vint (Phillip Pine) becomes the prime suspect.

Production #575

073. **WHO LIVES BY THE SWORD**

Original air date: May 18, 1957

Directed by Andrew V. McLaglen
Story and screenplay by John Meston
Produced by Norman Macdonnell
Starring:
Harold J. Stone - Joe Delk
Steven Terrell - Billy Baxter
Robert C. Ross - Lew Baxter
Harry Woods - Snyder
Sheila Noonan - Mrs. Baxter
Hal Baylor - Mike

Shooting men in self defense is the modus operandi for killer Joe Delk (Harold J. Stone). Matt is unable to arrest Delk, but challenges him to a fist fight, reducing the murderer to an almost cowardly condition.

Production #573

074. UNCLE OLIVER
Original air date: May 25, 1957
Directed by Andrew V. McLaglen
Produced by Norman Macdonnell
Story and screenplay by John Meston
Starring:
Earle Hodgins - Uncle Oliver
Paul Wexler - Viney

After Chester is ambushed and wounded, Matt must use him and Doc as decoys to flush out the assailant.
Production #574

075. DADDY-O
Original air date: June 1, 1957
Directed by Andrew V. McLaglen
Produced by Norman Macdonnell
Story and screenplay by John Meston
Starring:
John Dehner - Wayne Russell
Judson Pratt - Bill Pence
Cyril Delevanti - Messenger

Kitty's father, Wayne Russell (John Dehner), arrives in Dodge and tries to convince her to return with him to New Orleans, Louisiana.
Production #565

076. THE MAN WHO WOULD BE MARSHAL
Original air date: June 15, 1957
Directed by William B. Russell
Produced by Norman Macdonnell
Screenplay by David Victor and Herbert Little, Jr.
Story by John Meston
Starring:
Herbert Rudley - Emmett Egan
Alex Sharp - Jeff Willoughby
Kelly Thordsen - Wilson Willoughby
Walter Barnes - Mr. Odell
Kirby Smith - Mr. Botkin
Clancy Cooper - Bozeman
June Carter - Clarise
Ned Glass - Mr. Pibbs
George Selk - Moss Grimmick
Rusty Westcoatt - Gere (unbilled)

Retired army officer Emmett Egan (Herbert Rudley) longs for the glory he once earned as an officer and would now like to have Matt's job, along with respect he feels that comes with the badge.
Production #577

077. LIAR FROM BLACKHAWK
Original air date: June 22, 1957
Directed by Andrew V. McLaglen
Produced by Norman Macdonnell
Story and screenplay by John Meston
Starring:
Denver Pyle - Hank Shinn
Strother Martin - Ed Davey
John Doucette - Al Janes
Fred Graham - Cowboy
Howard Culver - Hotel Clerk
Bert Rumsey - Sam

Braggart Hank Shinn (Denver Pyle) has the reputation of a

fast gun until someone tires of his tall tales and calls his bluff.
    Production #576

078. JEALOUSY
Original air date: July 6, 1957
Directed by Andrew V. McLaglen
Produced by Norman Macdonnell
Screenplay by Sam Peckinpah
Story by John Meston
Starring:
Jack Kelly - Cam Durbin
Joan Tetzel - Tilda Durbin
Than Wyenn - Lonnie Pike
Jack Mann - Jack Davis
Kenn Drake - Cowboy
Barbara Dodd - Waitress

    Lonnie Pike (Than Wyenn) causes a major problem when he convinces Cam Durbin (Jack Kelly) that Matt is having an affair with his wife Tilda (Joan Tetzel).
    Production #578

SEASON THREE

Producer Norman Macdonnell

079. CRACK-UP
Original air date: September 14, 1957
Directed by Ted Post
Written by John Meston

Starring:
John Dehner - Nate Springer
Jess Kirkpatrick - Mr. Teeters
Howard Culver - Jim Uzzell
Preston Hanson - Jess
Brick Sullivan - Bartender
Jean Vaughn - Girl (unbilled)

    Hired assassin Nate Springer (John Dehner) arrives in Dodge City and Matt wants to know who hired him, and more importantly, why?
    Production #585

080. GUN FOR CHESTER
Original air date: September 21, 1957
Directed by Louis King
Written by John Meston
Starring:
Thomas Coley - Asa Ledbetter
George Selk - Moss Grimmick
Howard Culver - Hotel Clerk
Clayton Post - Man

    Asa Ledbetter (Thomas Coley) once vowed to kill Chester if their paths ever again crossed. Ledbetter arrives in town, denies even knowing Chester, who further complicates matters by refusing to explain what is behind the original alleged threat.
    Production #579

081. BLOOD MONEY
Original air date: September 28, 1957
Directed by Louis King

GUN FOR CHESTER September 21, 1957. Dennis Weaver.

Written by John Meston
Starring:
Vinton Hayworth - Harry Spencer
James Dobson - Joe Sharpe
Lawrence Green - Smith
George Selk - Moss Grimmick
Robert Nash - Grant
Allan Nixon - Adams

Joe Sharpe (James Dobson) rescues Harry Spencer (Vinton Hayworth) from injuries after being thrown from his horse. Spencer learns that Sharpe is a wanted man and decides to collect the reward money offered for the outlaw.
Production # 580

082. KITTY'S OUTLAW
Original air date: October 5, 1957
Directed by Andrew V. McLaglen
Screenplay by Kathleen Hite
Story by John Meston
Starring:
Ainslie Pryor - Cole Yankton
Dabbs Greer - Mr. Jonas
Chris Alcaide - Cowboy
Howard Culver - Hotel Clerk
Jack Mann - First Man

Kitty is implicated when her former boyfriend Cole Yankton (Ainslie Pryor) and his cohorts rob a bank in Dodge.
Production #582

083. POTATO ROAD
Original air date: October 12, 1957

Directed by Ted Post
Written by John Meston
Starring:
Robert Simon - Pa Grilk
Tom Pittman - Budge Grilk
Jeanette Nolan - Ma Grilk
Morgan Woodward - Calhoun

Young Budge Grilk (Tom Pittman) reports his father (Robert Simon) to Marshal Dillon—for murder. Matt realizes he has entered an elaborate scheme allowing the elder Grilk to rob the bank.
Production #586

084. JESSE
Original air date: October 19, 1957
Directed by Andrew V. McLaglen
Written by John Meston
Starring:
George Brenlin - Jesse Pruett
Edward Binns - Bill Stapp
James Maloney - Karl
Brick Sullivan - Bartender

Matt tries to calm Jesse Pruett (George Brenlin) who has ventured to Dodge searching for the party responsible for his father's death.
Production #581

085. MAVIS MCCLOUD
Original air date: October 26, 1957
Directed by Buzz Kulik
Screenplay by Kathleen Hite

Story by John Meston
Starring:
Fay Spain - Mavis McCloud
Casey Adams - Barney Wales
Robert Cornthwaite - Lou Staley
Kelly Thordsen - Link
Howard Culver - Hotel Clerk
Dan Sheridan - Stage Driver

Eastern lady Mavis McCloud (Fay Spain) heads to Dodge for a taste of life in the wild and woolly West. She marries one man (Casey Adams) while another (Robert Cornthwaite), who she jilted in the past, wants to kill her.
Production #584

086. **BORN TO HANG**
Original air date: November 2, 1957
Directed by Buzz Kulik
Written by John Meston
Starring:
Wright King - Joe Digger
Anthony Caruso - Hank
Mort Mills - Robie
Ken Lynch - Ed Glick
Dorothy Adams - Mrs. Glick

Drifter Joe Digger (Wright King) swears revenge on those who tried to hang him for horse theft.
Production #583

087. **ROMEO**
Original air date: November 9, 1957

Directed by Ted Post
Written by John Meston
Starring:
Robert Vaughn - Andy Bowers
Barry Kelly - Jake Pierce
Barbara Eden - Judy Pierce
Robert McQueeney - Pete Knight
Tyler McVey - Emmett Bowers
Bill McGraw - Ab Drain
William Erwin - Preacher

Matt has his hands full averting a range war when the son (Robert Vaughn) and daughter (Barbara Eden) of rival cattlemen fall in love and plan to marry.
Production #588

088. **NEVER PESTER CHESTER**
Original air date: November 16, 1957
Directed by Richard B. Whorf
Story and screenplay by John Meston
Starring:
Buddy Baer - Stobo
Woodrow Chambliss - Shiloh
Tom Greenway - Trevitt
Paul Birch - Boss
Gary Vinson - Jim

Chester is beaten and dragged behind a horse by bullies Stobo (Buddy Baer) and Trevitt (Tom Greenway). With his friend near death, Matt proves that his badge is not squeaky clean and pursues the pair with a vengeance.
Production #590

KITTY'S OUTLAW October 5, 1957. Amanda Blake and Ainslie Pryor.

NEVER PESTER CHESTER November 16, 1957. Tom Greenway, Dennis Weaver and Buddy Baer.

MAVIS MCCLOUD October 26, 1957. Milburn Stone, Dennis Weaver, Amanda Blake and James Arness.

089. FINGERED

Original air date: November 23, 1957
Directed by James Sheldon
Written by John Meston
Starring:
John Larch - Jim Cobbett
Karl Swenson - Hank Luz
Virginia Christine - Lila
John Launer - Jim Dobie

When his first wife disappeared, the people of Dodge became suspicious of Jim Cobbett—now his second wife has vanished also and a freshly dug grave is discovered on his property.
Production #589

090. HOW TO KILL A WOMAN

Original air date: November 30, 1957
Directed by John Rich
Screenplay by David S. Peckinpah
Story by John Meston
Starring:
Barry Atwater - Jesse Daggett
Pernell Roberts - Nat Pilcher
Robert Brubaker - Jim Buck
John Parrish - Elderly Rancher
Jolene Brand - Young Bride
George Cisar - Whiskey Drummer

Matt and Chester investigate a stagecoach robbery that resulted in the death of two passengers.
Production #591

DOC'S REWARD December 14, 1957. Amanda Blake.

091. COWS AND CRIBS

Original air date: December 7, 1957
Directed by Richard B. Whorf
Screenplay by Kathleen Hite
Story by John Meston

THE TWELFTH NIGHT December 28, 1957. James Griffith and William Schallert as two feuding hillbillies. (photo courtesy of William Schallert)

Starring:
Bartlett Robinson - Bowers
Mabel Albertson - Ma Smalley
Anne Barton - Mrs. Nadler
Val Avery - Joe Nadler
Dabbs Greer - Mr. Jonas
Cathy Browne - Mrs. Thorpe
Judson Taylor - Ed Thorpe

Unable to provide for his family, drunken dirt farmer Joe Nadler (Val Avery) becomes a suspect in recent cattle rustlings and murder.

Production # 592

092. DOC'S REWARD

Original air date: December 14, 1957
Directed by Richard B. Whorf
Written by John Meston
Starring:
Jack Lord - Myles/Nate Brandell
Bruce Wendell - Joe
Netta Packer - First Lady
Jean Fenwick - Second Lady
Brick Sullivan - Bartender

Myles Brandell (Jack Lord) threatens Doc and shoots his horse, causing Doc to take defense, killing Myles. Now his brother, Nate Brandell (Jack Lord) demands that Doc is arrested and tried for murder.

Production #593

093. KITTY LOST

Original air date: December 21, 1957
Directed by Ted Post

BUFFALO MAN January 11, 1958. John Anderson and James Arness.

WILD WEST February 15, 1958. Phyllis Coates and James Arness.

DIRT March 1, 1958. June Lockhart as Beulah.

THE CABIN February 22, 1958. James Arness.

Story and screenplay by John Meston
Starring:
Warren Stevens - Rackmil
Gage Clarke - Dobie (Clark misspelled in credits)
Brett King - Pete
Stephen Ellsworth - Pence
George Selk - Moss Grimmick

Eastern suitor Rackmil (Warren Stevens) deserts Kitty on a desolate Kansas plain.
Production #404

094. TWELFTH NIGHT

Original air date: December 28, 1957
Directed by John Rich
Story and screenplay by John Meston
Starring:
William Schallert - Eben Hakes
Rose Marie - Mrs. Monger
James Griffith - Joth Monger
Dick Rich - Farmer

The last members of two Ozark families, Eben Hakes (William Schallert) and Joth Monger (James Griffith) meet face to face in Dodge City and plan to settle their long standing feud.
Production #403

095. JOE PHY

Original air date: January 4, 1958
Directed by Ted Post
Story and screenplay by John Meston
Starring:

Morey Amsterdam - Cicero Grimes
Paul Richards - Joe Phy
William Kendis - Carey Post
Jack Reitzen - Bartender
Ken Becker - Cowboy

Matt is convinced that lawman Joe Phy (Paul Richards) in the nearby town of Elkader is a phony.
Production #402

096. BUFFALO MAN

Original air date: January 11, 1958
Directed by Ted Post
Screenplay by Les Crutchfield
Story by John Meston
Starring:
Patricia Smith - Abby
Jack Klugman - Earl Ticks
John Anderson - Ben Siple
Abel Fernandez - Indian

Matt and Chester are caught in the middle of a skirmish between Indians and two crazed buffalo hunters (Jack Klugman and John Anderson).
Production #594

097. KITTY CAUGHT

Original air date: January 18, 1958
Directed by Richard Whorf
Written by John Meston
Starring:
Bruce Gordon - Jed Gunther

TEXAS COWBOYS April 5, 1958. Allan "Rocky" Lane as Kin Talley.

Pat Conway - Billy Gunther
John Compton - Blain
William Keene - Mr. Botkin
Charles Tannen - Cashier

The Gunther brothers (Bruce Gordon and Pat Conway) rob the bank and take Miss Kitty hostage. Matt and Chester,

knowing Kitty could be killed at any moment, carefully track the ruthless duo.
    Production #595

098. **CLAUSTROPHOBIA**
Original air date: January 25, 1958
Directed by Ted Post
Story and screenplay by John Meston
Starring:
Vaughn Taylor - Olie Ridgers
Joe Maross - Jim Branch
Willard Sage - Dever
James Winslow - Giles
Lynn Shubert - Hank
Jason Johnson - Judge

Two vicious landgrabbers will stop at nothing to get what they want—including murder. They get more than they bargained for when they cross farmer Olie Ridgers (Vaughn Taylor).
    Production #596

099. **MA TENNIS**
Original air date: February 1, 1958
Directed by Buzz Kulik
Story and screenplay by John Meston
Starring:
Nina Varela - Ma Tennis
Ron Hagerthy - Andy Tennis
Corey Allen - Ben Tennis

Ma Tennis (Nina Varela) tries to stop Matt from arresting her son Andy (Ron Hagerthy), who is charged with murder.
    Production #598

100. SUNDAY SUPPLEMENT
Original air date: February 8, 1958
Directed by Richard Whorf
Story and screenplay by John Meston

Starring:
Werner Klemperer - Clifton Bunker
Jack Weston - Samuel Spring
David Whorf - Jack
Theodore Newton - Major
George Selk Moss Grimmick
Eddie Little Sky - Chief Little Hawk
K. L. Smith - Karl

Two troublemaking journalists from the East arrive to report the lawlessness in Dodge City. When the news isn't as exciting as they hoped for, they begin to fabricate stories that soon cause trouble for all concerned.
Production #599

101. WILD WEST
Original air date: February 15, 1958
Directed by Richard Whorf
Story and screenplay by John Meston
Starring:
Philip Bourneuf - Mr. Kelly
Phyllis Coates - Hattie Kelly
Paul Engle - Yorky Kelly
Murray Hamilton - Cutter
Robert Gist - Rourke

Yorky (Paul Engle) informs Matt that his father (Philip Bourneuf) has been kidnapped. To make matters worse, the boy implicates his stepmother (Phyllis Coates) as the mastermind of the crime.

Production #597

102. THE CABIN
Original air date: February 22, 1958
Directed by John Rich
Story and screenplay by John Meston
Starring:
Claude Akins - Hack
Patricia Barry - Belle
Dean Stanton - Alvy (later known as Harry Dean Stanton)

During a blizzard, Matt seeks shelter in a secluded prairie cabin. Inside he finds killers Hack and Alvy (Claude Akins and Dean Stanton) and their abused hostage Belle (Patricia Barry).
Production #417

103. DIRT
Original air date: March 1, 1958
Directed by Ted Post
Screenplay by David S. Peckinpah
Story by John Meston
Starring:
June Lockhart - Beulah
Wayne Morris - Nat
Ian MacDonald - Mr. Troyman
Gail Kobe - Polly Troyman
Barry McGuire - Henry Troyman

The happiness of wedding bells turn to the sadness of a funeral toll when new groom Nat (Wayne Morris) is killed. Several suspects abound, including his former lover Beulah (June Lockhart) and his future brother-in-law.
Production #400

104. DOOLEY SURRENDERS

Original air date: March 8, 1958
Directed by John Rich
Story and screenplay by John Meston
Starring:
Strother Martin - Dooley
Ken Lynch - Colpitt
James Maloney - Faber
Ben Wright - Mr. Ross
George Selk - Moss Grimmick
James Nusser - Nelson

Awakening after a drunken evening, buffalo hunter Dooley (Strother Martin) fears he killed his companion. He turns himself over to Matt—who doesn't believe the man is capable of murder.
Production #401

105. JOKE'S ON US

Original air date: March 15, 1958
Directed by Ted Post
Story and screenplay by John Meston
Starring:
Virginia Gregg - Mrs. Tilman
Bartlett Robinson - Jake Kaiser
Michael Hinn - Frank Tilman
James Kevin - Clabe Tilman
Kevin Hagen - Bill Jennings
Herbert C. Lytton - Tom Benson
Craig Duncan - Jim Duval

Mrs. Tilman (Virginia Gregg) and family seek revenge on those responsible for the lynching of her son Frank (Michael Hinn).
Production #406

106. BOTTLEMAN

Original air date: March 22, 1958
Directed by John Rich
Screenplay and story by John Meston
Starring:
John Dehner - Tom Cassidy
Ross Martin - Dan Clell
Peggy McKay - Fiora Clell

Town drunk Tom Cassidy (John Dehner) is a harmless man—until Dan Clell (Ross Martin) arrives in Dodge City.
Production #413

107. LAUGHING GAS

Original air date: March 29, 1958
Directed by Ted Post
Story and screenplay by James Fonda
Starring:
June Dayton - Mrs. Stafford
Dean Harens - Stafford
Val Benedict - Cloud Marsh
Cyril Delevanti - Old Man
Jess Kirkpatrick - Mr. Teeters
James Nusser - Saloon Customer (unbilled)

Former gunfighter Stafford (Dean Harens) now runs a medicine show but finds his old ways with a gun haunting him as bullies try to provoke him.
Production #414

108. TEXAS COWBOYS

Original air date: April 5, 1958
Directed by John Rich

HANGING MAN April 19, 1958. James Arness and Luis Van Rooten.

Story and screenplay by John Meston
Starring:
Allan "Rocky" Lane - Kin Talley
Clark Gordon - Gil Choate
Ned Glass - Sam Peeples
Stafford Repp - Mr. Hightower
John Mitchum - Bob

The pals of a murderous Texan decide to hide his identity

and take the law into their own hands. Meanwhile, Matt threatens to close down most of Dodge until the cowboys turn over the real culprit—an action that upsets the merchants, residents and visitors.
Production #407

109. **AMY'S GOOD DEED**
Original air date: April 12, 1958
Directed by John Rich
Screenplay by Kathleen Hite
Story by John Meston
Starring:
Jeanette Nolan - Amy
Lou Krugman - Emmett Gold

Amy Slater (Jeanette Nolan) arrives in Dodge bent on killing Matt to avenge her brother's death. The brother's former partner, Emmett Gold (Lou Krugman), has the same idea.
Production #411

110. **HANGING MAN**
Original air date: April 19, 1958
Directed by John Rich
Screenplay by Kathleen Hite
Story by John Meston
Starring:
Luis Van Rooten - Mel Tucker
Robert Osterloh - Dan Dresslar
Zina Provendie - Cora Bell
Helen Kleeb - Mrs. Sawyer
Dick Rich - Hank
K. L. Smith - Jim

Merchant Harp Sawyer is found hanged in his office and

only Matt believes the crime to be murder and not suicide.

Production #415

111. **INNOCENT BROAD**

Original air date: April 26, 1958
Directed by John Rich
Screenplay by Kathleen Hite
Story by John Meston
Starring:
Ed Kemmer - Lou Paxton
Myrna Fahey - Linda Bell
Aaron Saxon - Joe Bassett

Linda Bell (Myrna Fahey) is part of a bizarre triangle that includes her hot-tempered fiancee (Ed Kemmer) and a supposed stranger (Aaron Saxon).

Production #405

112. **THE BIG CON**

Original air date: May 3, 1958
Directed by John Rich
Story and screenplay by John Meston
Starring:
Joe Kearns - Banker Papp
Alan Dexter - Hook
Gordon Mills - Varden
Raymond Bailey - Shane

Three men (Alan Dexter, Gordon Mills and Raymond Bailey) steal twenty-thousand dollars from the bank and flee Doge City with Doc as their hostage.

Production #409

113. **WIDOW'S MITE**

Original air date: May 10, 1958
Directed by Ted Post

CARMEN *May 24, 1958. Ruta Lee and James Arness.*

Story and screenplay by John Meston
Starring:
Katharine Bard - Ada Morton
Marshall Thompson - Leach Fields
Ken Mayer - Zack Morton

After shooting robber Zack Morton (Ken Mayer), Leach

Fields (Marshall Thompson) harasses widow Morton (Katharine Bard) in hopes of finding stolen money.

Production #408

114. CHESTER'S HANGING

Original air date: May 17, 1958
Directed by Ted Post
Story and screenplay by John Meston
Starring:
Charles Cooper - Jim Cando
Sam Edwards - Lee Binders
Walter Barnes - Jack Haney

A murder arrest leads to a violent confrontation between Matt and the guilty party's associates—a confrontation that may cost Chester his life.

Production #412

115. CARMEN

Original air date: May 24, 1958
Directed by Ted Post
Story and screenplay by John Meston
Starring:
Ruta Lee - Jennie Lane
Robert Patten - Nate Brand
Tommy Farrell - Pfc. Atwood
Ray Teal - Sgt. Jones
Alan Gifford - Major Harris

When three cavalry soldiers are murdered and the army payroll is stolen, Major Harris (Alan Gifford) threatens to put Dodge City under martial law, much to the chagrin of Matt Dillon.

Production #410

116. OVERLAND EXPRESS

Original air date: May 31, 1958
Directed by Seymour Berns
Story and screenplay by John Meston
Starring:
Simon Oakland - Jim Nation
Peter Mamakos - Art Carp
Clem Bevens - Fly
James Gavin - Wells
Forrest Stanley - Griffin
Jan Arvan - Station Man
Jimmy Cross - Hank
Alfred Hopson -Bill

Matt and Chester are transporting suspected murderer Jim Nation (Simon Oakland) on the stagecoach. The travelers are then held up by outlaw Art Carp (Peter Mamakos).

Production #587

117. THE GENTLEMAN

Original air date: June 7, 1958
Directed by Ted Post
Story and screenplay by John Meston
Starring:
Jack Cassidy - Marcus France
Virginia Baker - Boni Damon
Timothy Carey - Tiller Evans
Henry Corden - Butler

Boni Damon (Virginia Baker) and Marcus France (Jack Cassidy) fall in love—much to the dismay of Boni's former boyfriend Tiller Evans (Timothy Carey).

Production #416

SEASON FOUR

Produced by Norman Macdonnell

118. MATT FOR MURDER
Original air date: September 13, 1958
Directed by Richard Whorf
Story and screenplay by John Meston
Starring:
Bruce Gordon -Tom Samples
Robert J. Wilke - Hickock
Elisha Cook - Huggins
Adam Howe - McCall
Martin Balk - Reeves

Crooked gambler Samples (Bruce Gordon) frames Matt for murder and Wild Bill Hickock (Robert Wilke) is sent to arrest him.
Production #418

119. THE PATSY
Original air date: September 20, 1958
Directed by Richard Whorf
Screenplay by Les Crutchfield
Story by John Meston
Starring:
Teleplay by Les Crutchfield
Story by John Meston
Martin Landau - Thorp
Peter Breck - Fly Hoyt
Ken Lynch - Jim Cavanaugh
Jan Harrison - Holly Fanshaw
John Alderman - Dave

Fly Hoyt (Peter Breck) is accused of murder by saloon girl Holly Fanshaw (Jan Harrison).
Production #419

120. GUNSMUGGLER
Original air date: September 27, 1958
Directed by Richard Whorf
Teleplay by Les Crutchfield
Story by John Meston
Starring:
Frank DeKova - Tobeel
Paul Langton - Major Evans
Dabbs Greer - Jonas
Sam Edwards - Cowboy
Lou Krugman - Smuggler

When a family is massacred, Matt and Major Evans (Paul Langton) disagree on who will be responsible to find those who are selling weapons to the Indians.
Production #423

121. MONOPOLY
Original air date: October 4, 1958
Directed by Seymour Berns
Screenplay by Les Crutchfield
Story by John Meston
Starring:
Harry Townes - Ivy
J. Pat O'Malley - Trimble
Robert Gist -Cam Speegle
Clegg Hoyt - Bob Adams

A stranger named Ivy (Harry Townes) buys up the Dodge City freight lines. When one freighter refuses to sell out, violence

MATT FOR MURDER September 13, 1958. Robert Wilke and James Arness between scenes.

becomes the tool of persuasion.
Production #426

122. LETTER OF THE LAW
Original air date: October 11, 1958
Directed by Richard Whorf
Teleplay by Les Crutchfield
Story by John Meston
Starring:
Harold J. Stone - Judge Rambeau
Clifton James - Teek
Bartlett Robinson - Lee Sprague
Mary Carver - Sarah
Al Ruscio - Haley
Fred Kruger - Straker

Matt is ordered to evict Teek (Clifton James) and his wife Sarah (Mary Carver) from their home.
Production #422

123. THOROUGHBREDS
Original air date: October 18, 1958
Directed by Richard Whorf
Story and screenplay by John Meston
Starring:
Ron Randell - Portis
Walter Barnes - Burke
Dan Blocker - Keller

Slick and attractive Portis (Ron Randell) comes to Dodge and soon becomes a favorite with the townfolk. However, Matt has him pegged for trouble.
Production #420

124. STAGE HOLD-UP
Original air date: October 25, 1958
Directed by Ted Post
Screenplay by Les Crutchfield
Story by John Meston
Starring:
John Anderson - Yermo
Charles Aidman - Verd
Sandy Kenyon - Green
Robert Brubaker - Jim Buck
Bob Morgan - Charley

Matt and Chester are among the passengers in a stagecoach that is held up by bandits. Later in Dodge, a man asking Doc's help for an injured friend is believed by Matt to be one of the robbers.
Production #421

125. LOST RIFLE
Original air date: November 1, 1958
Directed by Richard Whorf
Story and screenplay by John Meston
Starring:
Charles Bronson - Ben Tiple
Paul Engle - Andy Spangler
Lew Gallo - Joe Spangler
Tom Greenway - Will Gibbs

Though all clues point to Ben Tiple (Charles Bronson) for the murder of a cowboy, he maintains his innocence and relies on his friend Matt to sort things out.
Production #430

126. **LAND DEAL**
Original air date: November 8, 1958
Directed by Ted Post
Screenplay by Les Crutchfield
Story by John Meston
Starring:
Nita Talbot - Sidna
Murray Hamilton - Calhoun
Ross Martin - Keppert
Dennis Patrick - Trumbill

With offers seemingly too good to be true, Matt becomes suspicious of a land agent's generous promises to provide settlers with railroad land.
Production #428

127. **LYNCHING MAN**
Original air date: November 15, 1958
Directed by Richard Whorf
Story and screenplay by John Meston
Starring:
George MacReady - Charlie Drain
Bing Russell - Ed Shelby
Charles Gray - Bob Gringle
O. Z. Whitehead - Hank Blenis
Chuck Hayward - Jake
Michael Hinn - Gil Mather
Robert Montgomery, Jr. - Billy Drico

As a child, Charlie Drain (George MacReady) witnessed the lynching of his father. Now with townspeople in an uproar over murderous horse thieves, Drain must relive his childhood nightmare all over again.
Production #438

128. **HOW TO KILL A FRIEND**
Original air date: November 22, 1958
Directed by Richard Whorf
Story and screenplay by John Meston
Starring:
Philip Abbott - Ben Corder
Pat Conway - Toque Morlan
James Westerfield - Harry Duggan

STAGE HOLD-UP October 25, 1958. Sandy Kenyon, James Arness, Robert Brubaker and Dennis Weaver.

303

Matt has to run two crooked gamblers Duggan (James Westerfield) and Corder (Philip Abbott) out of town, only to have them return with hired killer Toque Morlan (Pat Conway).

Production #429

129. GRASS

Original air date: November 29, 1958
Directed by Richard Whorf
Story and screenplay by John Meston
Starring:
Phil Coolidge - Harry Pope
Chris Alcaide - Ned Curry
Charles Fredericks - Earl Brant

Arming himself against possible Indian raids, farmer Harry Pope (Phil Coolidge) accidentally kills a trailhand.

Production #434

130. THE CAST

Original air date: December 6, 1958
Directed by Jesse Hibbs
Written by John Meston
Starring:
Robert F. Simon - Shell Tucker
Ben Carruthers - Rufe Tucker

Shell Tucker (Robert F. Simon) hates doctors—even more so after Doc is unsuccessful in saving his wife's life. Tucker swears revenge and wants to kill Doc.

Production # 433

131. ROBBER BRIDEGROOM

December 13, 1958

LAND DEAL November 8, 1958. James Arness and Nita Talbot.

Directed by Richard Whorf
Written by John Meston
Starring:
Burt Douglas - Jack Fitch
Jan Harrison - Laura Church
Donald Randolph - Reeves
Frank Maxwell - Stage Driver
Dan Sheridan - Hank
Clem Fuller - Joe
Tex Terry - Pete

Laura Church (Jan Harrison) is abducted by Jack Fitch (Burt Douglas). After her release, she refuses to testify against the man—stating she has fallen in love with him.
Production #439

132. SNAKEBITE
Original air date: December 20, 1958
Directed by Ted Post
Written by John Meston
Starring:
Andy Clyde - Poney Thompson
Warren Oates - Jed Hakes
Charles Maxwell - Walt Moorman

When his dog is killed, Poney Thompson (Andy Clyde) becomes a murder suspect when one of his beloved pet's attackers is found dead.
Production #437

133. GYPSUM HILLS FEUD
Original air date: December 27, 1958
Directed by Richard Whorf

Screenplay by Les Crutchfield
Story by John Meston
Starring:
Anne Barton - Lize Peavy
William Schallert - Alben Peavy
Albert Linville - Jack Cade
Hope Summers - Ellen Cade
Sam Edwards - Ben Cade

Matt and Chester find themselves in the middle of a bloody feud as the Cade family fights the Peavy clan.
Production #424

134. YOUNG LOVE
Original air date: January 3, 1959
Directed by Seymour Berns
Written by John Meston
Starring:
Joan Taylor - Anna Wheat
Jon Lormer - Jesse Wheat
Wesley Lau - Rod Allison
Charles Cooper - Jim Box
Stephen Chase - Enoch Miller

Jesse Wheat (Jon Lormer) is murdered and to make matters worse, his young widow (Joan Taylor) has fallen in love with the suspected killer.
Production #425

135. MARSHAL PROUDFOOT
Original air date: January 10, 1959
Directed by Jesse Hibbs
Story by Tom Hanley

Teleplay by John Meston
Starring:
Dabbs Greer - Uncle Wesley
Charles Fredericks - Pargo
Earl Parker - Ben
Howard Culver - Howard
George Selk - Moss Grimmick

Uncle Wesley (Dabbs Greer) arrives in Dodge thinking nephew Chester is the marshal. With Matt sick and bedridden, Doc and Kitty scheme to make Chester look like the hero his uncle believes him to be.
Production #445

136. PASSIVE RESISTANCE
Original air date: January 17, 1959
Directed by Ted Post
Written by John Meston
Starring:
Carl Benton Reid - Gideon Seek
Alfred Ryder - Hank Boyles
Read Morgan - Joe Kell

Non-violent Gideon Seek (Carl Benton Reid) refuses to fight or even take action against the cattlemen who have burned his home and slaughtered his herd of sheep.
Production #427

137. LOVE OF A GOOD WOMAN
Original air date: January 24, 1959
Directed by Arthur Hiller
Screenplay by Les Crutchfield
Story by John Meston

Starring:
Kevin Hagen - Coney Thorn
Jacqueline Scott - Abby

Paroled convict Coney Thorn (Kevin Hagen) swears to kill Matt. When he is taken ill and put under the care of Abby (Jacqueline Scott), she hopes to calm his wicked ways.
Production #447

138. JAYHAWKERS
Original air date: January 31, 1959
Directed by Andrew V. McLaglen
Written by John Meston
Starring:
Jack Elam - Dolph Quince
Ken Curtis - Phil Jacks
Lane Bradford - Jay
Chuck Hayward - Studer
Earl Parker - Snyder
Cliff Ketchum - Cowboy
Brad Payne - Cook

Jayhawkers threaten a cattle drive from Texas to Kansas and Matt must help his friend Dolph Quince (Jack Elam) safely complete the task.
Production #441

139. KITTY'S REBELLION
Original air date: February 7, 1959
Directed by Jesse Hibbs
Story by Marian Clark
Teleplay by John Meston
Starring:

Barry McGuire - Billy
Addison Powell - Tal
Richard Rust - Weeb
Robert Brubaker - Jim Buck
Tom Greenway - Joe Hines
Ben Wright - Drummer
Howard Culver - Howard

Southern gentleman Billy Chris (Barry McGuire) zealously tries to protect Miss Kitty and defend her honor at every waking moment—after all, the Long Branch is no place for a lady!
Production #446

140. SKY
Original air date: February 14, 1959
Directed by Ted Post
Teleplay by Les Crutchfield
Story by John Meston
Starring:
Allen Case - Billy Daunt
Olive Blakeney - Ma Torvet
Roy Barcroft - Luke
Patricia Huston - Woman
Linda Watkins - Kate
Charles Thompson - Clabe

Matt and Chester track Billy Daunt (Allen Case) who is accused of killing his girlfriend Kate (Linda Watkins).
Production #443

141. DOC QUITS
Original air date: February 21, 1959
Directed by Edward Ludlum

Written by John Meston
Starring:
Wendell Holmes - Betchel
Bartlett Robinson - Jake Wirth
Jack Younger - Cullen
Fiona Hale - Mrs. Crummley
Jack Grinnage - Andy Wirth
Bert Rumsey - Sam

Doctor Betchel (Wendell Holmes) arrives in Dodge and when Doc announces his competition is a quack, the citizens accuse him of petty jealousy.
Production #442

142. THE BEAR
February 28, 1959
Directed by Jesse Hibbs
Written by John Meston
Starring:
Grant Williams - Joe Plummer
Norma Crane - Tilda
Denver Pyle - Mike Blocker
Russell Johnson - Harry Webb
Guy Wilkerson - Pete Wilkins

Practical jokes turn deadly as rancher Mike Blocker (Denver Pyle) prepares to marry the lovely Tilda (Norma Crane).
Production #432

143. THE COWARD
Original air date: March 7, 1959
Directed by Jesse Hibbs

Written by John Meston
Starring:
Barry Atwater - Ed Eby
Jim Beck - Jack Massey
House Peters, Jr. - Nat Swan
William Phipps - Lou
Barney Phillips - Pence
John Close - Pete
Sheldon Allman - Bill

A rancher who closely resembles Marshal Dillon becomes the victim of a planned attempt on the lawman's life.
Production #448

144. **THE F.U.**
Original air date: March 14, 1959
Directed by Andrew V. McLaglen
Written by John Meston
Starring:
Bert Freed - Al Clovis
Fay Roope - Botkin
Joe Flynn - Onie Becker
Steve Raines - 1st Cowboy
Ed Faulkner - 2nd Cowboy

Al Clovis (Bert Freed) is accused of killing Onie Becker (Joe Flynn) after the two men quarrel. Matt and Chester trail the fleeing Clovis.
Production #440

145. **WIND**
Original air date: March 21, 1959
Directed by Arthur Hiller

Written by John Meston
Starring:
Mark Miller - Frank Paris
Whitney Blake - Dolly Varden
Roy Engle - Jed Garvey
Dabbs Greer - Jonas
Walter Burke - Bystander
Allen Lurie - Singer
Stephen Roberts - Hank
George Douglas - Man
Guy Teague - Norman
Robert Swan - John

Long Branch hostess Dolly Varden (Whitney Blake) partners with crooked dealer Frank Paris (Mark Miller) and fool everyone—except Marshal Dillon.
Production #449

146. **FAWN**
Original air date: April 4, 1959
Directed by Andrew V. McLaglen
Written by John Meston
Starring:
Peggy Stewart - Mrs. Philips
Wendy Stuart - Fawn
Robert Karnes - Jep Hunter
Robert Rockwell - Roger Philips
Charles Fredericks - Band
Phil Harvey - Henry
Raymond Guth - Lou
Mike Gibson - Bert
Joe Kearns - Dobie

GYPSUM HILLS FEUD December 27, 1958. James Arness and William Schallert between scenes. (photo courtesy of William Schallert)

Released after years of Cherokee captivity, a white woman (Peggy Stewart) and her half-Indian daughter Fawn (Wendy Stuart) must now face prejudice with seemingly only one champion for their cause—Matt Dillon.

Production # 451

147. RENEGADE WHITE

Original air date: April 11, 1959
Directed by Andrew V. McLaglen
Screenplay by Les Crutchfield
Story by John Meston
Starring:
Michael Pate - Wild Hog
Barney Phillips - Ord Spencer
Robert Brubaker - Jim Buck
Hank Patterson - Jake

While tracking Ord Spencer (Barney Phillips) who is selling rifles to renegade Indians—Matt is captured by a group of the hostiles.

Production #455

148. MURDER WARRANT

Original air date: April 18, 1959
Directed by Andrew V. McLaglen
Written by John Meston
Starring:
Ed Nelson - Lee Prentice
Mort Mills - Jake Harbin
Onslow Stevens - Sheriff Ben Goddard
Fay Roope - Botkin
Joe Kearns - Dobie
George Selk - Moss Grimmick

Lee Prentice (Ed Nelson) is an innocent man charged with murder as part of a scheme to cover up for a crooked sheriff (Onslow Stevens) in Baker City.

Production #454

WIND March 21, 1959. Whitney Blake and James Arness.

149. CHANGE OF HEART

Original air date: April 25, 1959
Directed by Andrew V. McLaglen
Written by John Meston
Starring:
Lucy Marlowe - Bella Grant
James Drury - Jerry Cass
Ken Curtis - Briscoe Cass
Fay Roope - Botkin

Jerry Cass (James Drury), his brother Briscoe (Ken Curtis), and the lovely Bella Gant (Lucy Marlowe) are tangled in a web of love, deceit and deception.
Production #452

150. BUFFALO HUNTER

Original air date: May 2, 1959
Directed by Ted Post
Written by John Meston
Starring:
Harold J. Stone - Gatluf
Garry Walberg - Tobe
Lou Krugman - Tom Mercer
William Meigs - Agent
Sam Buffington - Cook
Tom Holland - Alvin
Bret King - Duff
Scott Stevens - Pate

Matt and Chester cross paths with evil incarnate Gatluf (Harold J. Stone)—a ruthless, bloody buffalo hunter who will kill a man as easy as any beast.
Production #444

151. THE CHOICE

Original air date:May 9, 1959
Directed by Ted Post
Written by John Meston
Starring:
Darryl Hickman - Andy Hill
Robert Brubaker - Jim Buck
Charles Maxwell - Kerrick
Dick Rich - Tough

Andy Hill (Darryl Hickman) defends Kitty's honor and shoots a man in self defense. Matt is uneasy about the situation and would prefer that Andy leave town, however, the young man is hired to ride shotgun for the stage line.
Production #431

152. THERE WAS NEVER A HORSE

Original air date: May 16, 1959
Directed by Andrew V. McLaglen
Written by John Meston
Starring:
Jack Lambert - Kin Creed
Joe Sargent - Drunk
Bill Wellman, Jr. - Roy

Gunman Kin Creed (Jack Lambert) promptly kills a man upon arriving in Dodge in what seems to be self defense. The next victim on his wish list—Marshal Matt Dillon.
Production #453

153. PRINT ASPER

Original air date: May 23, 1959
Directed by Ted Post
Written by John Meston
Starring:
J. Pat O'Malley - Print Asper
Ted Knight - Jay Rabb
Lew Brown - Will Asper
Robert Ivers - Johnny Asper

Crooked attorney Jay Rabb (Ted Knight) is hired to deed Print Asper's (J. Pat O'Malley) ranch to his sons, but through clever deception, takes the title himself.
Production #435

154. THE CONSTABLE

Original air date: May 30, 1959
Directed by Arthur Hiller
Written by John Meston
Starring:
John Larch - Rance
Strother Martin - Dillard Band
Pitt Herbert - Green
William Bryant - Ist Cowboy
Joel Ashley - 2nd Cowboy
Scott Peters - Pete
Joe Kearns - Botkin
Joseph Breen - Mike
Dan Sheridan - Dobie
John Mitchum - Joe
Lee Winters - Bob
Vic Lundin - Hank
Robert DeCost - Carl

Ill-advised merchants in Dodge hire a constable, Dillard Band (Strother Martin) to apply the law in the city limits, forcing

Matt's jurisdiction to the outskirts of town.
Production #450

155. BLUE HORSE
Original air date: June 6, 1959
Directed by Andrew V. McLaglen
Story by Marian Clark
Teleplay by John Meston
Starring:
Gene Nelson - Hob Cannon
Michael Pate - Blue Horse
William Murphy - Lt. Edlridge
Monte Hale - Sgt.

Matt breaks his leg while returning to Dodge with his prisoner Hob Cannon (Gene Nelson). Chester leaves to find help and soon thereafter Matt is overcome by Hob and left to die. Blue Horse (Michael Pate), on the lam from the army, saves the marshal, placing him in an awkward situation later with the cavalry.
Production #456

156. CHEYENNES
Original air date: June 13, 1959
Directed by Ted Post
Written by John Meston
Starring:
Walter Brooke - Capt. Nichols
Ralph Moody - Long Robe
Chuck Roberson - Sgt. Keller
Tom Brown - Major
Eddie Little Sky - Warrior
Dennis Cross - Jim
Connie Buck - Daughter
Edward Robinson, Jr. - Brown

Ambitious Captain Nichols (Walter Brooke) proves to be a problem for Matt who is trying desperately to avoid any more confrontations between settlers and the Cheyenne tribe.
Production #436

SEASON FIVE

Produced by Norman Macdonnell
Associate producer - James Arness

157. TARGET
Original air date: September 5, 1959
Directed by Andrew V. McLaglen
Screenplay by John Meston
Starring:
Story by Les Crutchfield
Darryl Hickman - Danny
Suzanne Lloyd - Nayomi
John Carradine - Kater
Frank DeKova - Gypsy Chief

The romance between Danny (Darryl Hickman) and a young gypsy woman Nayomi (Suzanne Lloyd) is bitterly opposed by their respective families.
Production #160

158. KITTY'S INJURY
Original air date: September 19, 1959
Directed by Buzz Kulik
Story by Marian Clark
Teleplay by John Meston

TARGET September 5, 1959. Suzanne Lloyd and James Arness.

Starring:
Don Dubbins - Lootie
Anne Seymour - Cora
Karl Swenson - Raff

Kitty is thrown from her horse and injured while out riding with Matt, who is forced to seek help from the rude and possibly dangerous occupants of a nearby cabin.
Production #161

159. HORSE DEAL
Original air date: September 26, 1959
Directed by Andrew V. McLaglen
Written by John Meston
Starring:
Bart Robinson - Bowers
Harry Carey, Jr. - Deesha
Trevor Bardette - Slim
Michael Hinn - Worth
Fred Grossinger - Harper
Bill Catching - Joe

Ranchers are sold stolen horses and Matt is somewhat lackadaisical about finding and arresting the responsible thieves.
Production #159

160. JOHNNY RED
Original air date: October 3, 1959
Directed by Buzz Kulik
Teleplay by John Meston
Story by Les Crutchfield
Starring:
James Drury - Johnny Red

Josephine Hutchinson - Mrs. Crale
Abel Fernandez - Nate
Dennis McMullen - Ponca City Kid
Robert Brubaker - Jim Buck

THE BOOTS November 14, 1959. Dennis Weaver and Richard Eyer.

Matt believes that a newcomer to Dodge City, Johnny Red (James Drury), is an outlaw—but has no concrete evidence to back his suspicions.

Production #162

161. KANGAROO

Original air date: October 10, 1959
Directed by Andrew V. McLaglen
Written by John Meston
Starring:
Peter Whitney - Ira
Richard Rust - Dal
John Crawford - Hod
Lew Brown - Jim Bride

Chester's life is in danger after he and Matt cross paths with the crazed Surlock family—with the patriarch (Peter Whitney) most dangerous of all.

Production #164

162. TAIL TO THE WIND

Original air date: October 17, 1959
Directed by Christian Nyby
Story by Les Crutchfield
Teleplay by John Meston
Starring:
Harry Townes - Pezzy
Alice Backes - Cora
Harry Swoger - Burke
Alan Reed, Jr. - Harlow

Rancher Pezzy (Harry Townes) refuses assistance from Matt even though he receives constant threats of violence from Burke (Harry Swoger) and his son.

Production #166

163. ANNIE OAKLEY

Original air date: October 24, 1959
Directed by Jesse Hibbs
Written by John Meston
Starring:
Florence MacMichael - Kate Kinsman
George Mitchell - Jeff Kinsman
John Anderson - Dolliver

Kate Kinsman (Florence MacMichael) is a neglected wife who tricks her husband Jeff (George Mitchell) into a fight with neighbor Dolliver (John Anderson).

Production #158

164. SALUDOS

Original air date: October 31, 1959
Directed by Andrew V. McLaglen
Story by Les Crutchfield
Teleplay by John Meston
Starring:
Gene Nelson - Foss
Robert J. Wilke - Pegger
Jack Elam - Steed
Connie Buck - Sochi

Three cowboys (Gene Nelson, Jack Elam and Robert Wilke) are arrested for wounding a young Indian girl named Sochi (Connie Buck) and killing her husband.

Production #163

165. BROTHER WHELP

Original air date: November 7, 1959
Directed by R. G. Springsteen
Story by Les Crutchfield
Teleplay by John Meston
Starring:
Lew Gallo - Sted
Ellen Clark - Tassy
John Clarke - Tom
Dabbs Greer - Jonas
Clem Fuller - Clem

Sted (Lew Gallo) is released from prison only to find that his brother Tom (John Clarke) now runs the family ranch and has married Tassy (Ellen Clark)—Sted's former fiance.
Production #169

166. THE BOOTS

Original air date: November 14, 1959
Directed by Jesse Hibbs
Written by John Meston
Starring:
John Larch - Zeno
Wynn Pearce - Hank Fergus
Richard Eyer - Tommy

Reputations are both on the line and hidden as young Tommy (Richard Eyer) must face the facts about his friend and idol, Zeno (John Larch), once a feared gun, now the town drunk.
Production #157

167. ODD MAN OUT

Original air date: November 21, 1959
Directed by Andrew V. McLaglen
Story by Les Crutchfield
Teleplay by John Meston
Starring:
Elisha Cook, Jr. - Cyrus Tucker
William Phipps - Hody Peel
Dabbs Greer - Jonas
Elizabeth York - Mrs. Peel
George Selk - Moss Grimmick
Dallas Mitchell - Cowboy
Clem Fuller - Clem

Matt suspects foul play when farmer Cyrus Tucker (Elisha Cook, Jr.) announces his wife has left him after many years of marriage.
Production #168

168. MIGUEL'S DAUGHTER

Original air date: November 28, 1959
Directed by Andrew V. McLaglen
Story by Marian Clark
Teleplay by John Meston
Starring:
Simon Oakland - Miguel
Fintan Meyler - Chavela
Wesley Lau - Ab
Ed Nelson - Rusk

Chavela (Fintan Meyler) is molested by two ruthless trail hands, who should pray that Matt finds them before her vengeful father (Simon Oakland) does.
Production #171

169. **BOX O' ROCKS**

Original air date: December 5, 1959
Directed by R.G. Springsteen
Written by Les Crutchfield
Starring:
Howard McNear - Pete
Vaughan Taylor - Reverend Blouze
Larry Blake - Jed Crooder
William Fawcett - Packy Roundtree
Gertrude Flynn - Mrs. Blouze

At a funeral, Matt discovers that a coffin supposedly holding Packy Roundtree (William Fawcett) actually contains rocks.
Production #173

170. **FALSE WITNESS**

Original air date: December 12, 1959
Directed by Ted Post
Story by Marian Clark
Teleplay by John Meston
Starring:
Wright King - Romey
Wayne Rogers - Tom
Robert Griffin - Judge
Len Hendry - Hank
Richard Sinatra - Bob
Clem Fuller - Clem
Norman Sturgis - Jake
Brad Trumball - Sawyer
Harold Goodwin - Clerk

Matt believes that perjury was committed by murder

THE EX-URBANITES April 9, 1960. Dennis Weaver and Milburn Stone.

witness Romey (Wright King), resulting in the hanging of an innocent man.
Production #179

171. **TAG, YOU'RE IT**

Original air date: December 19, 1959
Directed by Jesse Hibbs
Written by Les Crutchfield

317

Starring:
Paul Langton - Karl Killion
Madlyn Rhue - Rusty
Gregg Stewart - Tex
Clem Fuller - Clem
Harold Goodwin - Clerk

Notorious shootist Karl Killion (Paul Langton) arrives in Dodge causing the townfolk to panic—who will the next notch on his six-gun stand for?
Production #176

172. THICK 'N' THIN
Original air date: December 26, 1959
Directed by Stuart Heisler
Story by Les Crutchfield
Teleplay by John Meston
Starring:
Robert Emhardt - Brace McCoy
Percy Helton - Otie
Tina Menard - Summer Dove

Brace and Otie (Robert Emhardt and Percy Helton) are long time ranching partners who suddenly have a mysterious falling out.
Production #165

173. GROAT'S GRUDGE
Original air date: January 2, 1960
Directed by Andrew V. McLaglen
Story by Marian Clark
Teleplay by John Meston
Starring:
Ross Elliott - Lee Grayson

Thomas Coley - Tom Haskett

Lee Grayson (Ross Elliott) is an ex-Confederate soldier who has vowed to avenge the death of his wife. He thinks cowboy Tom Haskett (Thomas Coley) killed her and he intends to settle things once and for all.
Production #172

174. BIG TOM
Original air date: January 9, 1960
Directed by Andrew V. McLaglen
Stroy by Marian Clark
Teleplay by John Meston
Starring:
Don Megowan - Hob Creel
Robert J. Wilke - Tom Burr
Harry Lauter - Clay Cran
Howard Caine - Brady
Gregg Palmer - Harry
Rand Harper - Jim

An unethical boxing promoter arranges a deadly one-sided match between Hob Creel (Don Megowan) and Tom Burr (Robert Wilke). Matt steps in to protect the ailing Burr and the real fight begins.
Production #180

175. TILL DEATH DO US
Original air date: January 16, 1960
Directed by Jean Yarbrough
Written by Les Crutchfield
Starring:
Milton Selzer - Jezra Cobb
Mary Field - Minerva Cobb

Rayford Barnes - Puggy Rado

Could it be that some of the Long Branch ladies have hired a killer to take the lives of eccentric Jezra and Minerva Cobb (Milton Selzer and Mary Field)?
Production #178

176. THE TRAGEDIAN
Original air date: January 23, 1960
Directed by Arthur Hiller
Stroy by Les Crutchfield
Teleplay by John Meston
Starring:
John Abbott -Edward Vanderman
Howard McNear - Joe
Harry Woods - Ben
Stanley Clements - Brad

Down on his luck actor Edward Vanderman (John Abbott) trades Shakespeare for marked cards and his luck begins to change—for a while.
Production #182

177. HINKA DO
Original air date: January 30, 1960
Directed by Andrew V. McLaglen
Written by Les Crutchfield
Starring:
Nina Varela - Mamie
Walter Burke - Herman
Mike Green - Cowboy
Richard Reeves - Drunk
Ric Roman - Manuel

Bob Hopkins - Pete

Dodge City and the Lady Gay Saloon welcome a new saloon-keeper, Mamie (Nina Varela), who is as tough as any man and handy with a gun
Production #177

178. DOC JUDGE
Original air date: February 6, 1960
Directed by Arthur Hiller
Written by John Meston
Starring:
Barry Atwater - Harp
Dennis Cross - Bob
Dabbs Greer - Jonas
George Selk - Moss Grimmick

Mistaken for a judge from Wyoming, Doc finds that his life is in jeopardy when Harp (Barry Atwater) swears to kill him. Matt is out of town, which leaves Chester as Doc's only protection.
Production #183

179. MOO MOO RAID
Original air date: February 13, 1960
Directed by Andrew V. McLaglen
Story by Les Crutchfield
Teleplay by John Meston
Starring:
Raymond Hatton - Onie
Robert Karnes - Bert
Lane Bradford - Tush
Tyler McVey - Gib
Ron Hayes - Cary

RENEGADE WHITE April 11, 1959. James Arness and Michael Pate.

John Close - Joe
Clem Fuller - Clem

A range war is threatened between two trail bosses and the rights to a river crossing.
Production #167

180. **KITTY'S KILLING**
Original air date: February 20, 1960
Directed by Arthur Hiller
Teleplay by John Meston
Starring:
Story by Marian Clark
Abraham Sofaer - Leech
John Pickard - Ollie
Clem Fuller - Clem

Kitty puts her life in danger to save Ollie (John Pickard) from his crazed former father-in-law Leech (Abraham Sofaer), who has sworn to kill him.
Production #186

181. **JAILBAIT JANET**
Original air date: February 27, 1960
Directed by Jesse Hibbs
Written by Les Crutchfield
Starring:
John Larch - Dan
Nan Peterson - Janet
Bartlett Robinson - Krocker
Steve Terrell - Jerry
Jon Lormer - Clerk

A bandit's children uphold the family tradition as they assist in the latest crime spree—a train robbery—that turns to murder when a clerk is killed.
Production #175

182. UNWANTED DEPUTY

Original air date: March 5, 1960
Directed by Andrew V. McLaglen
Teleplay by John Meston
Story by Marian Clark
Starring:
Charles Aidman - Vince Walsh
Mary Carver - Maise
Marlowe Jenson - Dave Walsh
Dick Rich - Rudd
Ed Faulkner - Harry
Dick London - Tourney
Craig Fox - Lee
Bob Wiensko - Bob
Joe Haworth - Charlie

Vince Walsh (Charles Aidman), brother to convicted killer Dave (Marlowe Jenson), plans on destroying Matt—first by damaging his reputation and second by challenging him in a gunfight.
Production #181

183. WHERE'D THEY GO

Original air date: March 12, 1960
Directed by Jesse Hibbs
Teleplay by John Meston
Story by Les Crutchfield
Starring:
Jack Elam - Clint Dodie
Betty Harford - Medora
Dabbs Greer - Jonas

Clint Dodie is wanted for robbing Mr. Jonas' store. Matt and Chester set out to arrest him, but before they do, Dodie enlists

them to complete his chores around his ranch.
Production #187

184. CROWBAIT BOB

Original air date: March 26, 1960
Directed by Andrew V. McLaglen
Written by Les Crutchfield
Starring:
Hank Patterson - Crowbait
Ned Glass - Elbin
Shirley O'Hara - Martha
John Apone - Ace

In a bizarre story, Kitty is named sole heir in the will of elderly prospector Crowbait (Hank Patterson). With this news, greedy relatives demand their share of the "estate."
Production #191

185. COLLEEN SO GREEN

Original air date: April 2, 1960
Directed by Jean Yarbrough
Teleplay by John Meston
Story by Les Crutchfield
Starring:
Joanna Moore - Colleen
Harry Swoger - Bull
Dabbs Greer - Jonas
Robert Brubaker - Jim Buck
Perry Ivins - Employee
Clem Fuller - Clem
Harold Goodwin - Clerk

Buffalo skinner Bull (Harry Swoger), as well as Doc and

Chester, empty their pockets to care for Southern belle Colleen (Joanna Moore).

Production #188

186. THE EX-URBANITES
Original air date: April 9, 1960
Directed by Andrew V. McLaglen
Written by John Meston
Starring:
Robert Wilke - Pitt
Ken Curtis - Jesse
Lew Brown - Nage

Two outlaws, Pitt (Robert Wilke) and Jesse (Ken Curtis) seriously wound Doc and pin him and Chester down on the prairie. Chester must protect, nurse and feed Doc while the crazed duo plan on killing them both.

Production #195

187. I THEE WED
Original air date:April 16, 1960
Directed by Jesse Hibbs
Teleplay by John Meston
Story by Les Crutchfield
Starring:
Allan Josyln - Sam
Alice Frost - Hester
Hank Patterson - Judge

Sam (Allan Joslyn) continuously abuses his wife Hester (Alice Frost) who enables his horrid behavior—much to the discouragement of Marshal Dillon.

Production #184

188. THE LADY KILLER
Original air date: April 23, 1960
Directed by Andrew V. McLaglen
Written by John Meston
Starring:
Jan Harrison - Mae
Harry Lauter - Sy
Ross Elliott - Grant
George Selk - Moss Grimmick
Charles Sterrett - Cowboy
Clem Fuller - Clem

Mystery surrounds the new dance-hall girl Mae (Jan Harrison) and her shooting of a cowboy named Grant (Ross Elliott).

Production #193

189. GENTLEMAN'S DISAGREEMENT
Original air date: April 30, 1960
Directed by Jesse Hibbs
Written by Les Crutchfield
Starring:
Adam Kennedy - Bert Wells
Fintan Meyler - Jeanne Wells
Val Dufour - Ed Beaudry
Tom Reese - Tulsa
Joseph Hamilton - Pete

A lover's triangle results in murder—Bert and Jeanne Wells (Adam Kennedy and Fintan Meyler) versus Ed Beaudry (Val Dufour).

Production #189

190. **SPEAK ME FAIR**
Original air date: May 7, 1960
Directed by Andrew V. McLaglen
Written by Les Crutchfield
Starring:
Douglas Kennedy - Traych
Ken Curtis - Scout
Chuck Roberson - Driver
Perry Cook - Gunner

Matt and Chester happen upon a severely beaten Indian boy. Matt becomes relentless in his pursuit of the assailants.
Production #194

191. **BELLE'S BACK**
Original air date: May 14, 1960
Directed by Jesse Hibbs
Written by Les Crutchfield
Starring:
Nita Talbot - Belle
Nancy Rennick - Phyllis
Gage Clark - Dobie
Daniel White - Ainsley

Belle (Nita Talbot) returns to Dodge City after running away with a known criminal. Her reception is hardly a friendly or welcome one.
Production #185

192. **THE BOBSY TWINS**
Original air date: May 21, 1960
Directed by Jesse Hibbs

OLD FLAME May 28, 1960. James Arness and Marilyn Maxwell.

Written by John Meston
Starring:
Morris Ankrum - Merle
Ralph Moody - Harvey
Buck Young - Bud Grant

Jean Howell - Lavinia
John O'Malley - Man
Charles McArthur - Taylor
Richard Chamberlain - Pete
Paul Hahn - Les
Hank Patterson - Carl
Clem Fuller - Clem

Crazed, psychotic brothers Merle (Morris Ankrum) and Harvey (Ralph Moody) show up in Dodge with one thing on their minds—killing Indians.
Production #170

193. OLD FLAME

Original air date: May 28, 1960
Directed by Jesse Hibbs
Teleplay by John Meston
Story by Marian Clark
Starring:
Marilyn Maxwell - Dolly
Lee Van Cleef - Rad
Peggy Stewart - Mary
Hal Smith - Dobie
Clem Fuller - Clem

Matt's former girlfriend Dolly (Marilyn Maxwell) arrives in Dodge seeking protection from the marshal—she claims her husband (Lee Van Cleef) wants to kill her.
Production #190

194. THE DESERTER

Original air date: June 4, 1960
Directed by Arthur Hiller
Story by Marian Clark
Teleplay by John Meston
Starring:
Rudy Solari - Cpl. Lurie
Joe Perry - Radin
Henry Brandon - Major
Charles Fredericks - Sgt. Strate
Harry Bartell - Jed
Jean Inness - Maddie

Corporal Lurie (Rudy Solari) teams with civilian Radin (Joe Perry) and plans to steal the army payroll.
Production #174

195. CHERRY RED

Original air date: June 11, 1960
Directed by Andrew V. McLaglen
Written by Les Crutchfield
Starring:
Joanna Moore - Cherry O'Dell
Arthur Franz - Red Larned
Douglas Kennedy - Yancey
Cliff Ketchum - Nighshirt

Red Larned (Arthur Franz) pursues beautiful widow Cherry O'Dell (Joanna Moore). Matt and Cherry are certain that Red robbed a stagecoach and took the life of her husband.
Production #192

SEASON SIX

Produced by Norman Macdonnell
Associate Producer - James Arness

196. FRIEND'S PAY-OFF
Original air date: September 3, 1960
Directed by Jesse Hibbs
Teleplay by John Meston
Story by Marian Clark
Starring:
Mike Road - Ab Butler
Tom Reese - Joe Leeds
George Selk - Moss Grimmick
Jay Hector - Boy
Clem Fuller - Clem

Matt must shoot Joe Leeds (Tom Reese) in order to save his friend Ab Butler (Mike Road). Before dying, Leeds informs the marshal that Butler is both a bank robber and killer.
Production #30156 (154-201)

197. THE BLACKSMITH
Original air date: September 17, 1960
Directed by Andrew V. McLaglen
Teleplay by John Meston
Story by Norman Macdonnell
Starring:
George Kennedy - Emil
Anna-Lisa - Gretchen
Bob Anderson - Tolman

Wesley Lau - Willy
Herb Patterson - Spooner

Good natured blacksmith Emil (George Kennedy) marries a mail-order bride Gretchen (Anna-Lisa)—but happiness proves short-lived as he is pushed to violence by Tolman (Bob Anderson).
Production #301161 (154-206)

198. SMALL WATER
Original air date: September 24, 1960
Directed by Andrew V. McLaglen
Teleplay by John Meston
Story by Norman Macdonnell
Starring:
Trevor Bardette - Finn
Rex Holman - Leroy
Warren Oates - Seth

Matt must arrest old man Pickett (Trevor Bardette) and while he and Chester escort their prisoner back to town, his sons Leroy and Seth (Rex Holman and Warren Oates) have other plans.
Production #30162 (154-207)

199. SAY UNCLE
Original air date: October 1, 1960
Directed by Andrew V. McLaglen
Written by John Meston
Starring:
Richard Rust - Lee Nagel
Gene Nelson - Hutch
Harry Lauter - Martin Nagel
Dorothy Green - Nancy Nagel

THE PEACE OFFICER October 15, 1960. Susan Cummings and Dennis Weaver.

Roy Barcroft - George Farr

Uncle Hutch (Gene Nelson) is suspected by his nephew Lee Nagel (Richard Rust) of fratricide, especially when Hutch begins courting his widowed mother Nancy (Dorothy Green).
Production #30152 (154-197)

200. **SHOOTING STOPOVER**

Original air date: October 8, 1960
Directed by Andrew V. McLaglen
Teleplay by John Meston
Story by Marian Clark
Starring:
Patricia Barry - Laura
Anthony Caruso - Gurney
Paul Guilfoyle - Reverend
Robert Brubaker - Jim Buck

Matt and Chester are trapped at a waystation after their stagecoach is attacked by robbers. With them—a preacher, a young schoolteacher, a wanted killer, a large gold shipment and no water.
Production #30157 (154-202)

201. **THE PEACE OFFICER**

Original air date: October 15, 1960
Directed by Jesse Hibbs
Teleplay by John Meston
Story by Norman Macdonnell
Starring:
Susan Cummings - Stella
Lane Bradford - Clegg Rawlins
John Zaccaro - Ponce
Arthur Peterson, Jr. - Parks

John Close - Lighter
Gilman Rankin - Shay
Stafford Repp - Atyles
James Nusser - Crowe

With reports of misconduct, Tascosa sheriff Clegg Rawlins (Lane Bradford) is removed from duty and swears revenge on the deliverer of the news—Matt Dillon.
Production #30160 (154-205)

202. **DON MATTEO**

Original air date: October 22, 1960
Directed by Jesse Hibbs
Teleplay by John Meston
Story by Marian Clark
Starring:
Lawrence Dobkin - Esteban
Bing Russell - Grave
Ben Wright - Calmers
Anne Whitfield - Trudy
Barney Phillips - Bill Pence
Roy Engle - Grimes

Esteban (Lawrence Dobkin) is living the day for one reason only—killing the man (Bing Russell) who stole his wife.
Production #30155 (154-200)

203. **THE WORM**

Original air date: October 29, 1960
Directed by Arthur Hiller
Written by John Meston
Starring:
Kenneth Tobey - Spadden

H. M. Wynant - Cornet
Ned Glass - Ritchie
Stewart Bradley - Archer
Gage Clark - Judge
Howard Culver - Clerk

Vicious buffalo hunter Spadden (Kenneth Tobey) spends time in the Dodge City jail for fighting. Upon his release, his tortured cook (Ned Glass) plots revenge.
Production #30158 (154-203)

204. **THE BADGE**
Original air date: November 12, 1960
Directed by Andrew V. McLaglen
Teleplay by John Meston
Story by Marian Clark
Starring:
John Dehner - Rack
Conlan Carter - Augie
Harry Swoger - Ike
Allan Lane - Mac
Michael Mikler - Charlie

While escaping a posse, crazed outlaw Rack (John Dehner) and foolish Augie (Conlan Carter) wound Matt and take him prisoner.
Production #30151 (154-196)

205. **DISTANT DRUMMER**
Original air date: November 19, 1960
Directed by Arthur Hiller
Teleplay by John Meston
Story by Marian Clark
Starring:
Bruce Gordon - Sloat
Jack Grinnage - Raffie
George Mitchell - Grade
George Selk - Moss Grimmick
William Newell - Green
Phil Chambers - Hugo

Abusive mule skinners harass army drummer Raffie (Jack Grinnage) and when one of them is found dead, all clues point towards the service man.
Production #30164 (154-209)

206. **BEN TOLLIVER'S STUD**
Original air date: November 26, 1960
Directed by Andrew V. McLaglen
Teleplay by John Meston
Story by Norman Macdonnell
Starring:
John Lupton - Ben Tolliver
Jean Ingram - Nancy Creed
Roy Barcroft - Jake Creed
Hank Patterson - Carl

After an argument between rancher Jake Creed (Roy Barcroft) and his hired hand Ben (John Lupton) over his daughter Nancy Creed (Jean Ingram)—Ben is accused of horse theft.
Production #30154 (154-199)

207. **NO CHIP**
Original air date: December 3, 1960
Directed by Jean Yarbrough

THE PEACE OFFICER October 15, 1960. Susan Cummings and Dennis Weaver.

Written by John Meston
Starring:
John Hoyt - Jeff

Leo Gordon - Hutch
Rex Holman - Pete
Mark Allen - Grant
Guy Stockwell - Lee

Violence erupts when Dolan cattle graze on Mossman property. Jeff Mossman (John Hoyt) wants to fight, but his son Pete (Rex Holman) wants no part of it.
Production #30167 (154-212)

208. **THE WAKE**
Original air date: December 10, 1960
Directed by Gerald H. Mayer
Written by John Meston
Starring:
Denver Pyle - Gus
Anne Seymour - Mrs. Boggs
Michael Hinn - Joe Brant
George Selk - Moss Grimmick

Mystery surrounds the corpse of Orson Boggs and the so-called friend who brings him into town—a drifter named Gus (Denver Pyle).
Production #30165 (154-210)

209. **THE COOK**
Original air date: December 17, 1960
Directed by Ted Post
Written by John Meston
Starring:
Guy Stockwell - Sandy King
Sue Randall - Effie
John Pickard - Jack Purdy

BEN TOLLIVER'S STUD November 26, 1960. Dennis Weaver and Jean Ingram.

Ken Mayer - Ed Fisher
Tom Greenway - Gus
Harry Swoger - Hank Green

John Milford - Joe Grisim
Gene Benton - Waiter
Brad Trumbull - Pete
Craig Duncan - Joe
Sam Woody - Cowboy

Sandy King (Guy Stockwell) begins to cook at Delmonico's and patrons begin to line up down the street for his meals. When he accidentally kills crazy Ed Fisher (Ken Mayer), Matt must arrest him but faces a mob that isn't hungry for justice, but for the young kid's good cooking.
Production #30171 (154-216)

210. OLD FOOL
Original air date: December 24, 1960
Directed by Ted Post
Written by John Meston
Starring:
Buddy Ebsen - Hannibal
Hope Summers - Della
Linda Watkins - Elsie
Hampton Fancher - Dunc

Widow Elsie Hedgepeth (Linda Watkins) tries to break up the happy marriage of Hannibal and Della (Buddy Ebsen and Hope Summers).
Production #30166 (154-211)

211. BROTHER LOVE
Original air date: December 31, 1960
Directed by Franklin Adreon
Written by John Meston

Starring:
Lurene Tuttle - Mrs. Cumbers
Kevin Hagen - Nate Cumbers
Gene Lyons - Frank Cumbers
Jack Grinnage - Gus
Jan Harrison - Polly
Dabbs Greer - Jonas
Clem Fuller - Clem

A dying shopkeeper identifies his killer by last name only—Cumbers. Mrs. Cumbers (Lurene Tuttle) takes the law into her own hands while trying to figure out which one of her boys is guilty.
Production #30163 (154-208)

212. BAD SHERIFF
Original air date: January 7, 1961
Directed by Andrew V. McLaglen
Written by John Meston
Starring:
Russell Arms - Hark
Harry Carey, Jr. - Turloe
Kenneth Lynch - Gance
Don Keefer - Chet
Lane Chandler - Sam

Desperadoes Hark and Turloe (Russell Arms and Harry Carey, Jr.) ambush outlaw Gance (Kenneth Lynch) then pose as lawmen when Matt and Chester arrive.
Production #30153 (154-198)

213. UNLOADED GUN
Original air date: January 14, 1961
Directed by Jesse Hibbs
Teleplay by John Meston
Story by Marian Clark
Starring:
William Redfield - Joe Lime
Lew Brown - Red Lime
Hank Patterson - Carl Miller
Gregg Dunn - Bob Carter
James Malcolm - Harry
Clem Fuller - Clem
Bobby Goodwins - Boy
Rik Nervik - Townman

Matt is pursuing the Lime brothers (William Redfield and Lew Brown)—he manages to kill one before becoming seriously ill. Recuperating in Dodge, he must face the surviving brother bent on avenging his sibling's death.
Production #30159 (154-204)

214. TALL TRAPPER
Original air date: January 21, 1961
Directed by Harry Harris, Jr.
Teleplay by John Meston
Story by Marian Clark
Starring:
Strother Martin - Rowley
Tom Reese - Ben
Jan Shepard - Tassie
George Selk - Moss Grimmick

Trapper Ben (Tom Reese) offers shelter to Rowley (Strother Martin) and his wife Tassie (Jan Shepard). Jealousy drives Rowley to kill his wife and put the blame on Ben.
Production #30175 (154-220)

215. **LOVE THY NEIGHBOR**
Original air date: January 28, 1961
Directed by Dennis Weaver
Written by John Meston
Starring:
Jeanette Nolan - Rose
Jack Elam - Ben
Dean Stanton - Harley
Kenneth Lynch - Leroy
Warren Oates - Jep
Nora Marlowe - Jennie
David Kent - Peter
Cyril Delevanti - Sy Tewksbury
Wayne West - Man

A sack of potatoes is the cause for a tragic feud between Rose (Jeanette Nolan) and Jennie (Nora Marlowe) and their respective families.
Production #30169 (154-214)

216. **BAD SEED**
Original air date: February 4, 1961
Directed by Harry Harris, Jr.
Teleplay by John Meston
Story by Norman Macdonnell
Starring:
Anne Helm - Trudy
Roy Barcroft - Asa
Burt Douglas - Gar

After rescuing young Trudy (Anne Helm) from her abusive father, Matt becomes the object of her affections and later, her vicious lies.
Production #30177 (154-222)

217. **KITTY SHOT**
Original air date: February 11, 1961
Directed by Andrew V. McLaglen
Written by John Meston
Starring:
George Kennedy - Bayloe
Rayford Barnes - Helm
Joseph Mell - Bill Pence

Jake Bayloe (George Kennedy) is in a gunfight where Kitty is shot and seriously wounded. Enraged, Matt sets out to track him down, with a mysterious third party in hot pursuit.
Production #30170 (154-215)

218. **ABOUT CHESTER**
Original air date: February 25, 1961
Directed by Alan Crosland, Jr.
Teleplay by John Meston
Story by Frank Paris
Starring:
Charles Aidman - Dack
Mary Munday - Lilymae
Harry Shannon - Bowers
House Peters, Jr. - Jake
George Eldredge - Cluney

While searching for Doc, who has been missing for four days, Chester stumbles upon a horse thief and now faces death.
Production #30176 (154-221)

219. **HARRIET**
Original air date: March 4, 1961
Directed by Gene Fowler, Jr.

Written by John Meston
Starring:
Suzanne Lloyd - Harriet Horne
Tom Reese - Dan Scorp
Ron Hayes - Hoagler
Howard Culver - Howard
Joseph Hamilton - James Horne

Harriet Horne (Suzanne Lloyd) witnesses the brutal murder of her father and upon reaching Dodge, swears revenge on his killers, including Dan Scorp (Tom Reese).
Production #30172 (154-217)

220. **POTSHOT**
Original air date: March 11, 1961
Directed by Harry Harris, Jr.
Written by John Meston
Starring:
Karl Swenson - Hutch
Gage Clarke - Botkin
Wallace Rooney - Peters
Joseph Mell - Pence
Dallas Mitchell - Bert
Barton Heyman - Joe
Michael Harris - Harve
John Harmon - Carl
Quentin Sondergaard - Cowboy
Alex Sharp - Bud

Mystery surrounds the unseen shooting of Chester, who is seriously wounded.
Production #30185 (154-230)

BAD SEED February 4, 1961. Anne Helm and James Arness.

221. **OLD FACES**
Original air date: March 18, 1961
Directed by Harry Harris, Jr.
Written by John Meston

HARD VIRTUE May 6, 1961. Chester directs Doc for a change.

Starring:
James Drury - Tom Cook
Jan Shepard - Tilda Cook
George Keymas - Ed Ivers
Ron Hayes - Milt
Robert Brubaker - Jim Buck
Glenn Strange - Sam

Tom Cook (James Drury) defends his wife Tilda (Jan Shepard) after disparaging remarks are made about her.
Production #30184 (154-229)

222. BIG MAN
Original air date: March 25, 1961
Directed by Gerald Mayer
Written by John Meston
Starring:
George Kennedy - Pat Swarner
John McLiam - Jud Sloan
Chris Alcaide - Mike
Sandy Kenyon - Ak
Rayford Barnes - Harry
Barney Phillips - Pence
Steve Warren - Cowboy
James Nusser - Dick
Matthew McCue - Joe

Pat Swarner (George Kennedy) has his eyes on Miss Kitty and when he is found beaten to death, Matt is accused of murder.
Production #30188 (154-233)

223. LITTLE GIRL
Original air date: April 1, 1961
Directed by Dennis Weaver
Teleplay by John Meston
Story by Kathleen Hite
Starring:
Susan Gordon - Charity
Wright King - Hi Stevens
Bill McLean - Rafe
Doc Lucas - Albie

Ann Morrison - Mrs. Henry
Ricky, Bobby and Rusty Weaver (unbilled)
Megan, Michael and Rip King (unbilled)

Matt becomes a father figure to little Charity (Susan Gordon) after he and Chester find her outside the burnt ruins of her home.
Production #30179 (89) (154-224)

224. **STOLEN HORSES**
Original air date: April 8, 1961
Directed by Andrew V. McLaglen
Teleplay by John Meston
Story by Norman Macdonnell
Starring:
Buck Young - Jim Redigo
Shirley O'Hara - Mrs. Kurtch
Jack Lambert - Tebow
Guy Raymond - Abe
Henry Brandon - Chief Quick Knife
Charles Seel - Jed Cuff
Alex Sharp - Acker
Eddie Little Sky - Brave

Matt and Chester track a notorious horse thief and killer. The job at hand becomes more serious when a hostage is taken.
Production #30174 (154-219)

225. **MINNIE**
Original air date: April 15, 1961
Directed by Harry Harris, Jr.
Written by John Meston
Starring:

Virginia Gregg - Minnie
Alan Hale - Jake
George Selk - Moss Grimmick
Joseph Mell - Pence
Barry Cahill - Pete
Robert Human - Hank
Matthew McCue - Joe

Wounded Minnie (Virginia Gregg) is treated by Doc and falls in love with him. Her husband Jake (Alan Hales) arrives vowing to kill Doc. With Matt out of town, Chester tries his best to protect Doc.
Production #30183 (154-228)

226. **BLESS ME TILL I DIE**
Original air date: April 22, 1961
Directed by Ted Post
Teleplay by John Meston
Story by Ray Kemper
Starring:
Ronald Foster - Cole Treadwell
Phyllis Love - Beth Treadwell
Vic Perrin - Nate Bush
Dabbs Greer - Jonas

Cole and Beth Treadwell (Ronald Foster and Phyllis Love) meet nothing but resistance from Nate Bush (Vic Perrin) when they attempt to settle in Dodge City.
Production #30186 (154-231)

227. **LONG HOURS, SHORT PAY**
Original air date: April 29, 1961

Directed by Andrew V. McLaglen
Written by John Meston
Starring:
John Larch - Serpa
Lalo Rios - Little Fox
Frank Sentry - Crooked Knife
Allan Lane - Capt. Graves
Dawn Little Sky - Squaw
Steve Warren - Sergeant
Fred McDougall - Tracker

Hot on the trail of gunrunner Serpa (John Larch), Matt is captured by the same Indians who are asked to buy the deadly wares.
Production #30173 (154-218)

228. HARD VIRTUE
Original air date: May 6, 1961
Directed by Dennis Weaver
Written by John Meston
Starring:
Lew Brown - Andy Coe
Lia Waggner - Millie Coe
Robert Karnes - Ed Fallon
James Maloney - Jenkins
George Selk - Moss Grimmick

Jealous husband Andy Coe (Lew Brown) promises to kill the man vying for the affections of his wife (Lia Waggner).
Production # 30178 (154-223)

229. THE IMPOSTER
Original air date: May 13, 1961
Directed by Byron Paul
Teleplay by John Meston

Story by Kathleen Hite
Starring:
Virginia Gregg - Mrs. Curtin
Harp McGuire - Ab Stringer
Paul Langton - Rob Curtin
Garry Walberg - Harve Peters

Ab Stringer (Harp McGuire) arrives in Dodge claiming to be a Texas sheriff. The man he is trailing turns out to be respected Rob Curtin (Paul Langton) and Matts begins to doubt the lawman's story.
Production #30180(90) (154-225)

230. CHESTER'S DILEMMA
Original air date: May 20, 1961
Directed by Ted Post
Teleplay by John Meston
Story by Vic Perrin
Patricia Smith - Edna
John Van Dreelen - Gruber
Dabbs Greer - Jonas

Poor Chester falls for pretty and mysterious Edna (Patricia Smith) whose only concern is retrieving a letter that is on the way to Marshal Dillon.
Production #30187 (154-232)

231. THE LOVE OF MONEY
Original air date: May 27, 1961
Directed by Ted Post
Written by John Meston
Starring:
Cloris Leachman - Boni
Warren Kemmerling - Nate

Michael Ford - Pete
Tod Andrews - Myles Cody

Long Branch hostess Boni (Cloris Leachman) wants to help Matt solve the murder of a retired lawman—her motive? Money.
Production #30182 (154-227)

232. MELINDA MILES
Original air date: June 3, 1961
Directed by William Dario Faralla
Written by John Meston
Starring:
Burt Douglas - Tom Potter
Diana Millay - Melinda Miles
Walter Sande - Harry Miles
Charles Gray - Ray Tayloe
Rand Brooks - Rand
George Selk - Moss Grimmick
Glenn Strange - Man

Melinda (Diana Millay) and Tom (Burt Douglas) want to marry, but her father and his foreman Ray (Charles Gray) have other plans.
Production #30181 (154-226)

233. COLORADO SHERIFF
Original air date: June 17, 1961
Directed by Jesse Hibbs
Written by John Meston
Starring:
Wright King - Rod
Robert Karnes - Ben
Kelton Garwood - Sam Jones

Woodrow Chambliss - Myles

Matt is put in an awkward position when a sheriff from Colorado determines not to yield his stance on arresting a wounded man without a warrant.
Production #30168 (154-213)

SEASON SEVEN

Black and white - One hour episodes
Air day and start time remained the same.

Produced by Norman Macdonnell
Associate producer - Frank Paris

234. PERCE
Original air date: September 30, 1961
Written by John Meston
Directed by Harry Harris, Jr.
Starring:
Norma Crane - Ida
Ed Nelson - Perce
Kenneth Lynch - Seeber
Robert Brubaker - Jim Buck
James Nusser - Louie Pheeters
John Mitchum - Norm
Chuck Hayward - Kemp
Baynes Barron - Vicks
Alex Sharp - Nickols
Chuck Bail - Withers
Ted Jordan - Del

PERCE September 30, 1961. Ed Nelson, Norma Crane and James Arness.

Former outlaw Perce (Ed Nelson) comes to the aid of Matt during a gunfight with several gunmen. When Perce later falls in love with Ida (Norma Crane) Matt knows trouble will soon follow.
Production #31004

235. OLD YELLOW BOOTS
Original air date: October 7, 1961
Written by John Meston
Directed by Ted Post
Starring:
Joanne Linville - Beulah
Warren Stevens - Cassidy
Steve Brodie - Welch
Bing Russell - Head
Dean Stanton - Leroy
James Nusser - Louie Pheeters
Dabbs Greer - Mr. Jonas
Charles Thompson - Milton
Dick Rich - Big John
Howard Wright - Smythe
James Logan - Ezra
Charles Tannen - Hill

Rancher Cassidy (Warren Stevens) is killed and his sister Beulah (Joanne Linville) takes over the property. A cowboy named Leroy (Dean Stanton) comes courting and arouses suspicion—is he the murderer?
Production #31005

236. MISS KITTY
Original air date: October 14, 1961
Written by Kathleen Hite
Directed by Harry Harris, Jr.

Starring:
Harold Stone - Horace
Linda Watkins - Mattie
John Lasell - Tucker
Frank Sutton - Charlie
Roger Mobley - Thad
Dabbs Greer - Mr. Jonas
George Selk - Moss Grimmick
Joseph Breen - Driver
Andy Albin - Proprietor
Glenn Strange - Sam

Kitty leaves Dodge early one morning and meets up with a young boy at a nearby stage stop. Matt, Doc and Chester want to know who he is and where the pair disappeared to.
Production #31002

237. HARPER'S BLOOD
Original air date: October 21, 1961
Written by John Meston
Directed by Andrew V. McLaglen
Starring:
Peter Whitney - Cooley
Evan Evans - Jenny
Dan Stafford - Kyle
Conlan Carter - Jeff
Warren Kemmerling - Carr
Moria Turner - Sarah
Chris Hughes - Jeff
Ricky Kelman - Kyle

A father (Peter Whitney) believes his sons (Dan Stafford and Conlan Carter) have inherited bad blood from their murderous

great grandfather.
    Production #31007

238. ALL THAT
Original air date: October 28, 1961
Written by John Meston
Directed by Harry Harris, Jr.
Starring:
John Larch - Shanks
Buddy Ebsen - Quimby
Guy Raymond - Redfield
Frances Helm - Clara
Harry Lauter - Terry
Herbert Patterson - Len
Harry Swoger - Hank Green
Gage Clarke - Mr. Botkin
George Selk - Moss Grimmick
Harold Innocent - Clerk
Tim Frawley - Mike
Howard Wright - Harry
Glenn Strange - Sam

    After losing everything, Shanks (John Larch) must attempt prospecting and joins his old friend Quimby (Buddy Ebsen).
    Production # 31013

239. LONG, LONG TRAIL
Original air date: November 4, 1961
Written by Kathleen Hite
Directed by Andrew V. McLaglen
Starring:
Barbara Lord - Sarah Drew
Mabel Albertson - Gody Baines
Alan Baxter - Lou Hacker

Peggy Stewart - Fan Hacker
Robert Dix - Jamie

    Matt escorts pretty Sarah Drew (Barbara Lord) on a treacherous trip across deserted plains all the while facing many obstacles.
    Production #31015

240. THE SQUAW
Original air date: November 11, 1961
Written by John Dunkel
Directed by Gerald Mayer
Starring:
John Dehner - Hardy Tate
Paul Carr - Cully Tate
Vitina Marcus - Natacea
Bob Hastings - Bill Craig
Jet MacDonald - Sal
Bill Erwin - Rev Tucker
Jack Orrison - Shopkeeper
John Culwell - Bystander

    Fun-loving well-to-do widower Hardy Tate (John Dehner) takes Natacea (Vitina Marcus), a young Indian woman for his second wife—much to the dismay of his son Cully (Paul Carr).
    Production #31008

241. CHESTERLAND
Original air date: November 18, 1961
Written by Kathleen Hite
Directed by Ted Post
Starring:
Sondra Kerr - Miss Daisy
Earle Hodgins - Tubby
Sarah Selby - Ma Smalley

LONG, LONG TRAIL November 4, 1961. James Arness and Barbara Lord.

Harold Innocent - William
Arthur Peterson, Jr. - Arny

If he can provide a proper home, Daisy Fair (Sondra Kerry) will accept Chester's marriage proposal and become Mrs. Goode.
Production # 31006

242. **MILLY**

Original air date: November 25, 1961
Teleplay by John Meston
Story by Hal Moffett
Directed by Richard Whorf
Starring:
Jena Engstrom - Milly
Malcolm Atterbury - Glover
Billy Hughes - Joey
Don Dubbins - Potts
James Griffith - Tillman
Harry Swoger - Lawson
Sue Randall - Laura

To provide for herself and her little brother Joey (Billy Hughes), Milly (Jena Engstrom) wants to marry the first available bachelor she can get her hands on.
Production #31003

243. **INDIAN FORD**

Original air date: December 2, 1961
Written by John Dunkel
Directed by Andrew V. McLaglen
Starring:
Pippa Scott - Mary Tabor
R. G. Armstrong - Capt. Benter
Roy Roberts - Tabor
Anthony Caruso - Lone Eagle
Robert Dix - Spotted Wolf
John Newton - Sgt. Cromwell
Lane Chandler - Trumbull
Dawn Little Sky - Indian Woman

CHESTERLAND November 18, 1961.
Sondra Kerr and Dennis Weaver.

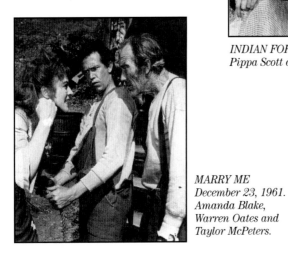

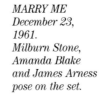

MARRY ME
December 23, 1961.
Amanda Blake,
Warren Oates and
Taylor McPeters.

INDIAN FORD December 2, 1961.
Pippa Scott and Robert Dix.

MARRY ME December 23, 1961.
Amanda Blake.

MARRY ME
December 23,
1961.
Milburn Stone,
Amanda Blake
and James Arness
pose on the set.

A MAN A DAY December 30, 1961. Dennis Weaver and Fay Spain.

CODY'S CODE January 20, 1962. Gloria Talbot and Milburn Stone.

HALF STRAIGHT February 17, 1962. Elizabeth MacRae.

THE WIDOW March 24, 1962. Amanda Blake checks the water temp before filming the next scene. (photo courtesy of Sydney Kent)

DURHAM BULL March 31, 1962. James Arness and Ricky Kelman.

Matt and Chester try to prevent a blood bath during the attempted rescue of Mary Tabor (Pippa Scott) from Spotted Wolf (Robert Dix) and his tribe of Indians.

Production #31001

244. APPRENTICE DOC

Original air date: December 9, 1961
Written by Kathleen Hite
Directed by Harry Harris, Jr.
Starring:
Ben Cooper - Pitt
Crahan Denton - Clint
Robert Sorrells - Angie

Doc is abducted to treat a wounded outlaw and finds that one member of the gang, Pitt (Ben Cooper), has an amazing knowledge of medicine.

Production #31009

245. NINA'S REVENGE

Original air date: December 16, 1961
Written by John Meston
Directed by Tay Garnett
Starring:
Lois Nettleton - Nina Sharkey
William Windom - Lee Sharkey
Ron Foster - Jim Garza
Glenn Strange - Sam
Quentin Sondergaard - Friend
Johnny Seven - Harry Blucher

Lee Sharkey (William Windom) plots to frame his wife (Lois Nettleton) and ranch hand Jim Garza (Ron Foster) for extortion—his plans are working out fine until his wife and Jim presumably fall in love.

Production #31010

246. MARRY ME

Original air date: December 23, 1961
Written by Kathleen Hite
Directed by Dennis Weaver
Starring:
Don Dubbins - Orkey
Warren Oates - Sweet Billy
Taylor McPeters - Pa
Glenn Strange - Sam

Orkey (Don Dubbins) arrives in Dodge City looking for a bride and soon settles his sights on the loveliest woman in town—Miss Kitty Russell.

Production #31016

247. A MAN A DAY

Original air date: December 30, 1961
Written by John Meston
Directed by Harry Harris, Jr.
Starring:
Fay Spain - Bessie
Val Dufour - Cooner
Roy Wright - Carver
Leonard Nimoy - Grice
Glenn Strange - Sam
George Selk - Moss Grimmick
Anne Morell - Ana
James Nusser - Louie Pheeters

WAGON GIRLS April 7, 1962. Ellen McRae (Burstyn), Joan Marshall and James Arness.

Garry Walberg - Hatcher
Tom Fadden - Enoch
Arthur Peterson, Jr. - Sam Frazer
Ben Wright - Dan Binny
Jim Drake - Morgan

A bloody edict comes down—an ruthless band of outlaws will kill one man per day until Matt leaves Dodge City, leaving a large gold shipment for their taking.
Production #31019

248. **THE DO-BADDER**
Original air date: January 6, 1962
Written by John Meston
Directed by Andrew V. McLaglen
Starring:
Abraham Sofaer - Harvey Easter
Strother Martin - Gene Bunch
Adam Williams - Slim Trent
Warren Oates - Chris Kelly
James Nusser - Louie Pheeters
H. M. Wynant - Sam Smith
Harry Bartell - Charlie Fess
Mercedes Shirley - Mary Pickett
James Anderson - Bert Case
Roy Engel - Ed Greeley
Shug Fisher - Harry Obie
Richard Reeves - Red
Craig Duncan - Pete
Glenn Strange - Sam

Prospector Harvey Easter (Abraham Sofaer) crusades into Dodge hoping to reform the citizens. Two saddle bums have other plans for Harvey and his poke.
Production #31012

249. **LACEY**
Original air date: January 13, 1962
Written by Kathleen Hite
Directed by Harry Harris, Jr.
Starring:
Jeremy Slate - Jess

THE SUMMONS April 21, 1962 Bethel Leslie and James Arness. (photo courtesy of Doug Abbott)

Sherry Jackson - Lacey
Dorothy Green - Ellen
Sarah Selby - Ma Smalley
Oliver McGowan - Cyrus
Nora Hayden - Bessie

Lacey Parcher (Sherry Jackson) confesses to the cold-blooded killing of her domineering father Cyrus Parcher (Oliver McGowan).
Production #31017

250. CODY'S CODE
Original air date: January 20, 1962
Written by John Meston
Directed by Andrew V. McLaglen
Starring:
Gloria Talbott - Rose
Anthony Caruso - Cody
Wayne Rogers - Brack
Robert Knapp - Dukes
Ken Becker - Koger
Ollie O'Toole - Postmaster
Robert Gravage - Citizen

Respected citizen Cody (Anthony Caruso) gives haven to wounded outlaw Brack (Wayne Rogers) who then casts a shadow on the romance between Cody and Rose (Gloria Talbott).
Production #31023

251. OLD DAN
Original air date: January 27, 1962
Written by Kathleen Hite
Directed by Andrew V. McLaglen

Starring:
Edgar Buchanan - Dan
William Campbell - Luke
Phil Coolidge - Lom
Dabbs Greer - Mr. Jonas
Hugh Sanders - Thede
Dorothy Neumann - Mrs. Bales
Joe Haworth - Gates

Doc has his hands full when he tries to sober up old alcoholic Dan Witter (Edgar Buchanan). Dan takes a job as a hired hand but runs afoul of the rancher's good for nothing son Luke (William Campbell).
Production #31022

252. CATAWOMPER
Original air date: February 10, 1962
Teleplay by John Meston
Story by James Favor
Starring:
Dick Sargent - Bud
Sue Ane Langdon - Kate
Frank Sutton - Olie
Roy Wright - Bert
Robert Brubaker - Lt.
Harold Innocent - George
Quentin Sondergaard - Hank
Warren Vanders - Pete
Joe Devlin - Jester
Jay Overholts - Sgt.
Robert Gravage - Wit

Kate Tassel (Sue Ane Langdon) uses Chester in a scheme to make her boyfriend Bud (Dick Sargent) jealous.
Production #31020

253. HALF STRAIGHT
Original air date: February 17, 1962
Written by John Meston
Directed by Ted Post
Starring:
John Kerr - Lute
J. Edward McKinley - Hatcher
Elizabeth MacRae - Fanny
William Bramley - Browder
Howard Clulver - Howard
(last name misspelled in credits - Culver is correct)
Lee Sabinson - Barkeep

Originally hired to kill Matt, gunny Lute (John Kerr) contracts a third party to do the job for him when he falls in love with a beautiful woman named Fanny (Elizabeth MacRae).
Production #31026

254. HE LEARNED ABOUT WOMEN
Original air date: February 24, 1962
Teleplay by John Meston
Story by John Rosser
Directed by Tay Garnett
Starring:
Claude Akins - Solis
Barbara Luna - Chavela
Ted de Corsia - Garvy
Robert Wilke - Ab Rankin
Miriam Colon -Kisla
Jeff de Benning - Red

Susan Petrone - Ru
Val Ruffino - Guard
Andy Romano - Jose
Joseph Ferrante - Juan
Miguel d'Anda - Pepe

Chester, with the help of lovely Chavela (Barbara Luna), escape from a gang of ruthless comancheros. Their leader Solis (Claude Akins) is hot on their trail.
Production #31014

255. **THE GALLOWS**
Original air date: March 3, 1962
Written by John Meston
Directed by Andrew V. McLaglen
Starring:
Jeremy Slate - Pruit
Joseph Ruskin - Judge
Robert J. Stevenson - Ax
Richard Shannon - Gamer
James Nusser - Louie Pheeters
Orville Sherman - Sheriff
William Challee - Feist
Nancy Walters - Gal
Ollie O'Toole - Milt
Robert Gravage - Hangman

Pruit (Jeremy Slate) saves Matt's life, however, Matt must arrest the man for alleged charges of murder. Matt believes Pruit is innocent even after he is sentenced to hang.
Production #31028

256. **REPRISAL**
Original air date: March 10, 1962
Written by John Meston
Directed by Harry Harris, Jr.
Starring:
Dianne Foster - Cornelia
Jason Evers - Ben
Tom Reese - Wellman
Brad Trumbull - Ives
George Lambert - Oren
Grace Lee Whitney - Pearl
Joe DeReda - Blake
Billy Hughes - Tommy
Harold Innocent - Teller
Harry Antrim - Mr. Botkin
Gene Benton - Green
Joe Devlin - Dan Binney

Matt is forced to kill Oren (George Lambert) in a gunfight, and his widow Cornelia (Dianne Foster) swears revenge by hiring a man to kill the marshal.
Production #31027

257. **COVENTRY**
Original air date: March 17, 1962
Written by John Meston
Directed by Christian Nyby
Starring:
Joe Maross - Beard
Don Keefer - Rankin
Paul Birch - Jessie
Mary Field - Clara
John Harmon - Judge

Helen Wallace - Hedda
George Selk - Moss Grimmick
James Anderson - Hager
Harold Innocent - Mr. Botkin
Buck Young - Carl
William Boyett - Harry

THE DREAMERS *April 28, 1962. Amanda Blake, Liam Redmond, J. Pat O'Malley.*

When no conviction can be reached for a killer named Beard (Joe Maross), Matt comes up with an idea that is just as punishing for the man.

Production #31021

258. THE WIDOW

Original air date: March 24, 1962
Written by John Dunkel
Directed by Ted Post
Starring:
Joan Hackett - Mady

Alan Reed, Jr. - Corp. Jennings
J. Edward McKinley - Emil
Alexander Lockwood - Colonel
Rodd Redwing - Little Bear
Howard Culver - Howard
Robert Brubaker - Jim Buck

When her husband is killed in an Indian uprising, Mady (Joan Hackett) arrives in Dodge intent on retrieving her husband's body—even if she has to enter hostile territory to do it.

Production #31025

259. DURHAM BULL

Original air date: March 31, 1962
Teleplay by John Meston
Story by Jack Shettlesworth
Directed by Harry Harris, Jr.
Starring:
Andy Clyde - Henry
Ricky Kelman - Little Bit
John Kellogg - Silva
Gilbert Green - Rudd

George Keymas - Polk
Will Corry - Wade
Ted Jordan - Kearny
Richard Keene - Dan Binny

Hank Patterson - Cowboy
George Selk - Moss Grimmick
Howard Culver - Howard
Ted Jacques - Brakeman
Roger Torrey - Downey

Henry (Andy Clyde) and his grandson Little Bit (Ricky Kelman) turn the tables on a group of outlaws intent on stealing their cattle.
Production #31011

260. WAGON GIRLS
Original air date: April 7, 1962
Written by John Meston
Directed by Andrew V. McLaglen
Starring:
Constance Ford - Florida
Ellen McRae (better known as Ellen Burstyn) - Polly
Arch Johnson - Feester
Joan Marshall - Emma
Kevin Hagen - Bowman
William Schallert - Capt. Grant
Ben Wright - Sgt. Pickens
Dabbs Greer - Mr. Jonas
Rayford Barnes - Lee
Joseph Perry - Harve
William Wellman, Jr. - Pvt. King
Buck Young - Cpl. Stone
Gilman Rankin - Chief Red Knife

Matt must rescue a group of ladies, including Florida, Polly and Emma (Constance Ford, Ellen Burstyn and Joan Marshall), from a tyrannical wagon master.
Production #31018

CALE May 5, 1962. Amanda Blake and Carl Reindel.

261. THE DEALER
Original air date: April 14, 1962
Television Story and teleplay by John Dunkel
Based on a story by Les Crutchfield
Directed by Harry Harris, Jr.
Starring:
Judi Meredith - Lily

George Mathews - Champ
Gary Clarke - Johnny
Roy Roberts - Billy
Baynes Barron - Sheriff
Jess Kirkpatrick - Barney
Ted Jordan - Cheater

Against Matt's advice, Kitty hires attractive Lily (Judi Meredith) to deal faro at the Long Branch.
Production #31029

262. THE SUMMONS

Original air date: April 21, 1962
Teleplay by Kathleen Hite
Story by Marian Clark
Directed by Andrew V. McLaglen
Starring:
Bethel Leslie - Rose Ellen
John Crawford - Loy
Myron Healey - Moseley
Robert J. Stevenson - Cape
Cal Bolder - Dawkins
Shug Fisher - Telegrapher
Michael Hinn - Deputy
Cyril Delevanti - Old
Percy Helton - Duffer
Howard Culver - Dobie
William B. Corrie - Clerk

Blood thirsty outlaw Loy (John Crawford) kills a fellow gunman for the bounty on his head. Unable to collect the reward, he lures Matt into a ambush, with the help of Rose-Ellen (Bethel Leslie).
Production #31020

263. THE DREAMERS

Original air date: April 28, 1962
Written by John Meston
Directed by Andrew V. McLaglen
Starring:
Liam Redmond - Cairn
J. Pat O'Malley - Fogle
Valerie Allen - Annie
Cece Whitney - Julia
Gage Clarke - Mr. Botkin
Shug Fisher - Obie
Perry Cook - Barkeep

When Kitty rebuffs the advances of grubby miner Cairn (Liam Redmond), he decides to use his new found wealth to destroy her and her business.
Production #31032

264. CALE

Original air date: May 5, 1962
Written by Kathleen Hite
Directed by Harry Harris, Jr.
Starring:
Carl Reindel - Cale
Peter Ashley - Will
Joseph Hamilton - Nick
Hank Patterson - Hank Miller
Robert Karnes - Sterret
Glenn Strange - Sam

Cale (Carl Reindel) is wounded, left to die on the prairie and found by Matt. Cale is blind in his anger, swearing revenge on Sterret (Robert Karnes), the man responsible for his situation.
Production #31034

265. CHESTER'S INDIAN

Original air date: May 12, 1962
Written by Kathleen Hite
Directed by Joseph Sargent
Starring:
Jena Engstrom - Callie
Karl Swenson - Adam
Eddie Little Sky - Indian
Lew Brown - Frank
Garry Walberg - Simeon
Michael Barrier - Cowboy
Shug Fisher - Obie
Gene Benton - Waiter

Over protective father (Karl Swenson) tries to prevent his daughter Callie (Jena Engstrom) from any contact with men. Nevertheless, she befriends a wounded Indian (Eddie Little Sky) and puts Chester in the unenviable position between them and her father.
Production #31024

266. THE PRISONER

Original air date: May 19, 1962
Written by Robert E. Thompson
Directed by Andrew V. McLaglen
Starring:
Andrew Prine - Billy Joe
Nancy Gates - Sarah
Conrad Nagel - Major
Ed Nelson - Seth
Dabbs Greer - Mr. Jonas
Rayford Barnes - Jellicoe
William Phipps - Ham
Charles Fredericks - Hunk

William Corrie - Waiter
Dorothy Neumann - Mrs. Pierson
Cathy Merchant - Sally
Ollie O'Toole - Postmaster
Chris Whitman - Mrs. Thurmon
John Close - Turner

Vengeance is on the minds of a Major (Conrad Nagel) and his son Seth (Ed Nelson) towards Billy Joe Arlen (Andrew Prine), suspected of murdering the Major's other son, Ham (William Phipps).
Production #31033

267. THE BOYS

Original air date: May 26, 1962
Written by John Meston
Directed by Harry Harris, Jr.
Starring:
Malcolm Atterbury - Professor Eliot
George Kennedy - Hug
Dean Stanton - Nate
Harry Swoger - Hank Green
Gage Clark - Mr. Botkin
Michael Parks - Park
Arthur Malet - Farnum
Dabbs Greer - Mr. Jonas
James Nusser - Louie Pheeters
William Newell - Conductor
Joe Devlin - Drummer
Hank Patterson - Hank
May Heatherly - Molly
Harp McGuire - Guard
Hal Needham - Ed
Glenn Strange - Sam

Professor Eliot (Malcolm Atterbury) is revealed to be a phony by the folks in Dodge City, he plans revenge by ordering his three sons Hug, Nate and Park (George Kennedy, Dean Stanton and Michael Parks) to rob the stagecoach.

Production #31031

SEASON EIGHT

Produced by Norman Macdonnell
Associate producer - Frank Paris

268. THE SEARCH
Original air date: September 15, 1962
Written by Kathleen Hite
Directed by Harry Harris, Jr.
Starring:
Ford Rainey - Tate
Virginia Gregg - Ess Cutler
Carl Reindel - Cale
Hank Patterson - Hank Miller
Raymond Guth - Sam Cutler
Leonard Nimoy - Arnie
Mike Ragan - Frank
Fred Coby - Horn
Mickey Morton - Coot

Cale (Carl Reindel) is suspected of stealing a horse and is seriously injured from a fall from his mount. While hiding from his pursuers, the young man struggles to stay alive.

Production #31208

269. CALL ME DODIE
Original air date: September 22, 1962
Written by Kathleen Hite
Directed by Harry Harris, Jr.
Starring:
Joby Baker - Ky
Diane Mountford - Lady
Carol Seflinger - Marth
Dennis Cross - Norm
Buck Young - John
Jack Searl - Floyd
Mary Patton - Addie
Wallace Rooney - Dan Binny
Dal McKennon - Jake
Guy Wilkerson - Waiter
Bob Hastings - Whip
Nesdon Booth - Bartender
and Kathy Nolan as Dodie

Dodie (Kathy Nolan) escapes from a prison-like orphanage and with Matt's help, makes those responsible pay for their crimes.

Production #31206

270. QUINT ASPER COMES HOME
Original air date: September 29, 1962
Written by John Meston
Directed by Andrew V. McLaglen
Starring:
Burt Reynolds - Quint
Angela Clarke - Topsanah
Michael Keep - Chief
William Zuckert - John Asper

Myron Healey - Mike
Harry Carey, Jr. - Grant
Lane Bradford - Bob
Earle Hodgins - Dobie
Dabbs Greer - Mr. Jonas
Robert Hinkle - Cowboy
Foster Brooks - Ed
Michael Barrier - Brave
Henry Beckman - Duff
John Vari - Leader
James Doohan - Davit
Ed Peck - Semple
Robert Gravage - Charlie
Glenn Strange - Sam

After white men kill his father (William Zuckert), half Indian Quint Asper (Burt Reynolds) seeks his mother (Angela Clarke) and rejoins her Comanche tribe. Later wounded, Quint is nursed back to health—much to the dismay of the townspeople and Quint himself.

Production #31035

271. ROOT DOWN
Original air date: October 6, 1962
Written by Kathleen Hite
Directed by Sobey Martin
Starring:
John Dehner - Luke
Sherry Jackson - Aggie
Robert Doyle - Grudie
Howard McNear - Howard
George Selk - Moss Grimmick
Michael Carr - Cowboy
Ollie O'Toole - Clerk

Aggie (Sherry Jackson) goes husband hunting and tries to catch Chester, all the while arousing the ire of her father Luke (John Dehner).

Production #31210

272. JENNY
Original air date: October 13, 1962
Written by John Meston
Directed by Andrew V. McLaglen
Starring:
Ruta Lee - Jenny
Ron Hayes - Zel
John Duke - Flack
James Nusser - Louie Pheeters
Barry Cahill - Chuck
Ken Hudgins - Pete
Monte Montana, Jr. - Joe

Matt learns all too well about "hell hath no fury like a woman scorned" when Jenny (Ruta Lee) battles the marshal on many fronts after her boyfriend is arrested.

Production #31207

273. COLLIE'S FREE
Original air date: October 20, 1962
Written by Kathleen Hite
Directed by Harry Harris, Jr.
Starring:
Jason Evers - Collie
Jacqueline Scott - Francie
William Bramley - Davis Henry
James Halferty - Rob

THE SEARCH September 15, 1962. James Arness and Carl Reindel.

Richard Bull - Nort
Glenn Strange - Sam
Dennis Cross - Dutton
Mary Castle - Saloon Girl
Orville Sherman - Warden
Barry Cahill - Abel
Henry Rowland - Smithy
Pat McCaffrie - Barkeep

Bitter after eight years in prison, Collie (Jason Evers) finds the road home is well traveled with vengeance—and that road slowly leads to Matt.
Production #31204

274. THE DITCH
Original air date: October 27, 1962
Written by Les Crutchfield
Directed by Harry Harris, Jr.
Starring:
Joanne Linville - Susan
Jay Lanin - Trent
Christopher Dark - Crider
Dehl Berti - Waco
Hardie Albright - Peckett
Ted Jordan - Foreman
Gail Bonney - Mrs. Hawkins
Miguel deAnda - Boss

Susan Bart (Joanne Linville) plans to divert the water on her property—an action that causes her neighbors to protest loudly. A hired gun further arouses anger and a range war is threatened.
Production #31212

JENNY October 13, 1962. James Arness and Ruta Lee.

275. THE TRAPPERS
Original air date: November 3, 1962
Written by John Dunkel
Directed by Andrew V. McLaglen
Starring:
Strother Martin - Billy
Richard Shannon - Tug
Doris Singleton - Irma

PHOEBE STRUNK November 10, 1962. Virginia Gregg and Joan Freeman.

Robert Lowery - Idaho
Lane Chandler - Luke
Chal Johnson - Tom
Robert Brubaker - Jim Buck
Glenn Strange - Sam

A friendship dissolves when trapper Billy (Strother Martin)

leaves his partner Tug (Richard Shannon) for dead after he is viciously attacked.

Production #31209

276. **PHOEBE STRUNK**

Original air date: November 10, 1962
Written by John Meston
Directed by Andrew V. McLaglen
Starring:
Virginia Gregg - Phoebe
Joan Freeman - Annie
Don Megowan - Oliver
Phyllis Coates - Rose
Gregg Palmer - Hulett
Harry Raybould - Casper
Dick Peabody - Simsie
John McLiam - Sam Kinney
Phil Chambers - Ned
Marilyn Harvey - Mary
Glenn Strange - Sam

Annie (Joan Freeman) is kidnapped by the murderous Phoebe Strunk (Virginia Gregg) and her loathsome clan. Matt and Quint set out to free the girl and end the cycle of robberies and murder.

Production #31213

277. **THE HUNGER**

Original air date: November 17, 1962
Written by Jack Curtis
Directed by Harry Harris, Jr.
Starring:
Elen Willard - Althea
Robert Middleton - Dorf

Joe Flynn - Drummer
Linda Watkins - Mrs. Dorf
Sarah Selby - Ma Smalley
Dabbs Greer - Mr. Jonas
Hampton Fancher - Clem
Byron Foulger - Dooley
Kelton Garwood - Fred
Henrietta Moore - Dolly
Robert McQuain - Cowboy
Sue Casey - Martha
Glenn Strange - Sam

Doc saves young Althea (Elen Willard) from the clutches of her brutal tyrant of a father (Robert Middleton). Doc is the first provider of kindness she has received and she falls in love with him.
Production #31036

278. ABE BLOCKER
Original air date: November 24, 1962
Written by John Meston
Directed by Andrew V. McLaglen
Starring:
Chill Wills - Abe Blocker
Wright King - Bud
Dabbs Greer - Mr. Jonas
Harry Carey, Jr. - Jake
Miranda Jones - Mary
Robert Adler - Emmett
Marshall Reed - Sam Vestal
Lane Bradford - Gant
Wallace Rooney - Dan Binney
Chuck Roberson - Joe

Glenn Strange - Sam

Abe Blocker (Chill Wills) is an old friend of Matt's but now has become mentally deranged and begins waging a private war against all homesteaders.
Production #31215

279. THE WAY IT IS
Original air date: December 1, 1962
Written by Kathleen Hite
Directed by Harry Harris, Jr.
Starring:
Claude Akins - Ad
Garry Walberg - Bent
Virginia Lewis - Annie
George Selk - Moss Grimmick
Glenn Strange - Sam
Duane Grey - Rancher
Bob Murphy - Slim

Matt breaks yet another date with Kitty and she has had enough. On a trip she encounters an injured man, Ad (Claude Akins), and nurses him back to health. Kitty soon discovers that his fits of jealousy could turn deadly.
Production # 31214

280. US HAGGENS
Original air date: December 8, 1962
Written by Les Crutchfield
Directed by Andrew V. McLaglen
Starring:
Ken Curtis - Festus

THE HUNGER *November 17, 1962.*
Robert Middleton and Elen Willard.

ABE BLOCKER *November 24, 1962.*
Chill Wills and James Arness.

THE WAY IT IS *December 1, 1962.*
Amanda Blake and Claude Akins.

US HAGGENS
December 8, 1962.
Denver Pyle and
James Arness.

US HAGGENS
December 8, 1962.
James Arness and
Elizabeth MacRae.

THE RENEGADES January 12, 1963. Audrey Dalton and Burt Reynolds.

Denver Pyle - Haggen
Elizabeth MacRae - April
Billy Hughes - Timmy
Howard Wright - Dietzer

Black Jack Haggen (Denver Pyle) is a wanted murderer, and Matt is joined in his pursuit of the scoundrel by Jack's nephew

Festus Haggen (Ken Curtis).
Production #31205

281. UNCLE SUNDAY

Original air date: December 15, 1962
Written by John Meston
Directed by Joseph Sargent
Starring:
Henry Beckman - Uncle Sunday
Joyce Bulifant - Ellie
Ed Neslon - Burt Cury
Dabbs Greer - Mr. Jonas
Gage Clarke - Mr. Botkin
Wallace Rooney - Dan Binney
Nora Marlowe - Mrs. Perkins
Glenn Strange - Sam

Uncle Sunday (Henry Beckman) is a burr under nephew Chester's hide when he decides to visit Dodge City. He arrives with "niece" Ellie (Joyce Bulifant) and Chester believes they are plotting to rob the bank.
Production #31218

282. FALSE FRONT

Original air date: December 22, 1962
Teleplay by John Meston
Story by Hal Moffett
Directed by Andrew V. McLaglen
Starring:
Andrew Prine - Clay
William Windom - Hill
Art Lund - Heber

Charles Fredericks - Senator
Shary Marshall - Rita
Wallace Rooney - Dan Binney
Robert Fortier - Ray Costa
Brett King - Hank
K. L. Smith - Pete
William Bryant - Joe
Roy Thinnes - Harry
Michael Mikler - Bill

Journalist/gambler Hill (William Windom) engineers a huge bet that unassuming Clay (Andrew Prine), who has never fired a gun, can pass for a notorious gunman.
Production #31201

283. OLD COMRADE
Original air date: December 29, 1962
Written by John Dunkel
Directed by Harry Harris, Jr.
Starring:
Frank Sutton - Billy
J. Pat O'Malley - Gabe
Roy Roberts - Mr. Dobie
Ralph Moody - Kip
Vitina Marcus - Missy
Wayne Heffley - Lem
Wayne Treadway - Mr. Green
John Reed King - Townsman
Dick Whittinghill - Jason
Billy Baucom - Photographer
Norman Leavitt - Orderly
Ted Jordan - Lounger

Kip (Ralph Moody) is dying and wants to be reunited with his son Billy (Frank Sutton) who is a fall guy around Dodge.
Production #31217

284. LOUIE PHEETERS
Original air date: January 5, 1963
Written by John Meston
Directed by Harry Harris, Jr.
Starring:
John Larkin - Murph
Gloria McGehee - Clara
James Nusser - Louie Pheeters
Woodrow Parfey - Tom
Larry Ward - Bart
Ted Jordan - Gus Thompson

A murder is committed in Dodge City and town drunk Louie Pheeters (James Nusser) is the only witness.
Production #31202

285. THE RENEGADES
Original air date: January 12, 1963
Written by John Meston
Directed by Andrew V. McLaglen
Starring:
Audrey Dalton - Lavinia
Ben Wright - Colonel
Jack Lambert - Brice
Donald Barry - McIver
John Pickard - Poole
Ed Faulkner - Sergeant
Linda Hutchins - Ruth
Bob Steele - Sam Gordon

Alan Dexter - Trask
Joseph Bassett - Leader

Quint and Lavinia (Audrey Dalton) find themselves hunted by renegade white people and her father's army troops.
Production #31211

286. COTTER'S GIRL
Original air date: January 19, 1963
Written by Kathleen Hite
Directed by Harry Harris, Jr.
Starring:
Mariette Hartley - Clarey
Roy Barcroft - Cotter
John Clarke - Mackle
Jesslyn Fax - Proprietress
Sarah Selby - Ma Smalley

Matt delivers an inheritance to Clarey Cotter (Mariette Hartley) and finds himself in a frontier version of PYGMALION.
Production #31219

287. THE BAD ONE
Original air date: January 26, 1963
Written by Gwen Bagni Gielgud
Directed by Sobey Martin
Starring:
Chris Robinson - Jett
Dolores Sutton - Jenny
Booth Colman - Gant
Dabbs Greer - Mr. Jonas
Michael Mikler - Cowpoke

Ken Kenopka - Clancy
Gil Lamb - Porter
Sue Casey - Saloon Gal
Glenn Strange - Sam
Robert Gravage - Telegrapher

Matt must uncover the reason that Jenny (Dolores Sutton) will not identify the stagecoach robber (Chris Robinson) she witnessed.
Production #31216

288. THE COUSIN
Original air date: February 2, 1963
Teleplay by Kathleen Hite
Story by Marian Clark
Directed by Harry Harris, Jr.
Starring:
Michael Forest - Chance
Gloria Talbot - Hallie
John Anderson - Cheevers
Joseph Perry - Moran
Lew Brown - Gates
James Nusser - Louie Pheeters
Jackie Blanchard - Saloon Girl
George Selk - Moss Grimmick
Helen Wallace - Woman
James Drake - Man
Glenn Strange - Sam

Ex-convict Chance (Michael Forest) is Matt's foster brother. When he arrives in Dodge, the situation leads to a difficult decision for the marshal
Production #31221

SHONA February 9, 1963. Bart Burns, Steve Stevens, John Crawford and Robert Palmer. (photo courtesy of Steve Stevens)

289. SHONA

Original air date: February 9, 1963
Written by John Meston
Directed by Ted Post
Starring:
Robert Bray - Gib Dawson
Miriam Colon - Shona
John Crawford - Torbert
Bart Burns - Riser
Robert Palmer - Rud

Roy Roberts - Dobie
Sarah Selby - Ma Smalley
George Selk - Moss Grimmick

Gib Dawson (Robert Bray) must bring his ailing Indian wife Shona (Miriam Colon) into Dodge. Prejudice and hatred turns to violence as mob mentalities take over the townspeople.
Production #31220

290. ASH

Original air date: February 16, 1963
Written by John Meston
Directed by Harry Harris, Jr.
Starring:
John Dehner - Ben
Anthony Caruso - Ash
Dee Hartford - Tillie
Adam West - Emmett
Sheldon Allman - Murdock
William Fawcett - Hawkins
Robert Bice - Driver
Richard Bartell - Harry
Michael Mikler - Frank
Glenn Strange - Sam

After suffering a head injury, mild mannered Ben (John Dehner) turns into a murderous troublemaker. When he goes after Tillie (Dee Hartford), his best friend Ash (Anthony Caruso) must step in.
Production #31223

291. BLIND MAN'S BLUFF

Original air date: February 23, 1963
Written by John Meston
Directed by Ted Post
Starring:
Will Hutchins - Billy Poe
John Alderson - Canby
Crahan Denton - Walker
Judson Pratt - Dano
Herbert C. Lytton - Hays
Natalie Norwick - Maid
Leonard Stone - Davey
Michael Mikler - Cowboy
John Rodney - Barkeep
Gregg Palmer - Wells
Darlene Fields - Saloon Girl
I. Stanford Jolley - Harry
Ted Jordan - Pete
Hank Ladd - Dave

   While trailing suspected murderer Billy Poe (Will Hutchins), Matt is attacked, causing his eyesight to be impaired. Billy helps the disabled marshal and later at trial, Matt tries to clear his name.
   Production #31222

292. QUINT'S INDIAN

Original air date: March 2, 1963
Teleplay by John Meston
Story by Marian Clark
Directed by Fred Jackman
Starring:
Will Corry - Stope
Patrick McVey - Houser

ASH February 16, 1963. Anthony Caruso, Dee Hartford and James Arness.

James Brown - Feeney
James Griffith - Bettis
James Nusser - Louie Pheeters
Michael Hinn - Jake Sooner
Michael Keep - Leader
Mark Murray - Jimmy
Raymond Guth - Grissom

Ruth Phillips - Mary
Roy Engel - Syker
Shug Fisher - Barkeep
Glenn Strange - Sam
Eddie Little Sky - Brave
Matthew McCue - Waiter

Quint is severely beaten by vigilantes in town when he is falsely accused of a crime he did not commit. Quint leaves town and Matt rides into danger to bring him back.
Production #31224

293. ANYBODY CAN KILL A MARSHAL
Original air date: March 9, 1963
Written by Kathleen Hite
Directed by Harry Harris, Jr.
Starring:
Milton Selzer - Painter
Joyce Van Patten - Molly
James Westerfield - Cleed
Warren Stevens - Lucas
James Nusser - Louie Pheeters
Howard McNear - Howard
Brenda Scott - Betsy
George Selk - Moss Grimmick
Tom Lutz - Cowboy

When the efforts of two outlaws are unsuccessful, they hire a drifter named Painter (Milton Selzer) to kill Marshal Matt Dillon.
Production #31225

294. TWO OF A KIND
Original air date: March 16, 1963
Written by Merwin Gerard

Directed by Andrew V. McLaglen
Starring:
Richard Jaeckel - O'Ryan
Michael Higgins - Finnegan
Kent Smith - Bealton
Earle Hodgins - Judge
Ben Wright - Harris
Garry Walberg - Anson
John Mitchum - Wills
Glenn Strange - Sam
Bee Tompkins - Girl

Two Irish business partners O'Ryan and Finnegan (Richard Jaeckel and Michael Higgins) begin to feud and Matt must figure out a way to keep peace between them.
Production #31226

295. I CALL HIM WONDER
Original air date: March 23, 1963
Written by Kathleen Hite
Directed by Harry Harris, Jr.
Starring:
Ron Hayes - Jud
Sandy Kenyon - Docker
Edmund Vargas - Wonder
Harry Bartell - Colonel
Leonard Nimoy - Holt
Duane Grey - Keogh
William Zuckert - Enoch
Gilman Rankin - Waiter
Eddie Little Sky - Charlie
George Selk - Moss Grimmick
Alex Sharp - Cook

Bigotry takes center stage when a drifter (Ron Hayes) unwillingly teams up with an Indian boy named Wonder (Edmund Vargas).

Production #31227

296. WITH A SMILE

Original air date: March 30, 1963
Teleplay by John Meston
Based on a story by Bud Furillo and George Main
Directed by Andrew V. McLaglen
Starring:
James Best - Dal
R. G. Armstrong - Major
Sharon Farrell - Lottie
Lindon Chiles - Pat
Dick Foran - Sheriff
Dan Stafford - Kelly
Robert J. Stevenson - Foy
Gilman Rankin - Waiter
James Nusser - Louie Pheeters
Jay Della - Cowboy

Major Creed (R. G. Armstrong) comes to the sad realization that his son Dal (James Best) is a cold-blooded killer and must pay for his horrid crimes.

Production #31228

297. THE FAR PLACES

Original air date: April 6, 1963
Written by John Dunkel
Directed by Harry Harris, Jr.
Starring:
Angela Clarke - Carrie

TWO OF A KIND March 16, 1963. Richard Jaeckel, Bee Tompkins and Michael Higgins.

Rees Vaughn - Jeff
Bennye Gatteys - Millie
Dennis Cross - Colley
Orville Sherman - Wib
Richard Jury - Humphreys
Sailor Billy Vincent - Client

PANACEA SYKES April 13, 1963. Nellie Burt and Amanda Blake.

Matt tries to stop the conflict between a domineering mother (Angela Clarke) and her son (Rees Vaughn) from escalating to violence.

Production #31229

298. **PANACEA SYKES**

Original air date: April 13, 1963
Written by Kathleen Hite
Directed by William Conrad
Starring:
Nellie Burt - Panacea
Dan Tobin - Foote
Charles Watts - Little
Charlie Briggs - Driver
John Clarke - Young Man
Jan Brooks - Ethel
George Selk - Moss Grimmick
James Nusser - Louie Pheeters
Carl Prickett - Agent
Charles Seal - One
Robert Nash - Two
John Lawrence - Other
Ollie O'toole - Telegrapher

Panacea Sykes (Nellie Burt) raised Kitty as a child and now shows up in Dodge with a little larceny in her heart.

Production #31203

299. **TELL CHESTER**

Original air date: April 20, 1963
Written by Frank Paris
Directed by Joseph Sargent
Starring:
Lonny Chapman - Wade
Mitzi Hoag - Polly
Lew Brown - Nace
Jo Helton - Wendy

Sara Taft - Tao
Robert Gibbons - Donahue
Ray Galvin - Barkeep

Chester's former girlfriend Polly (Mitzi Hoag) falls in love with and marries an already married man—and Chester is once again stuck in the middle of things.
Production #31231

300. QUINT-CIDENT
Original air date: April 27, 1963
Written by Kathleen Hite
Directed by Andrew V. McLaglen
Starring:
Mary La Roche - Willa
Ben Johnson - Ben Crown
Don Keefer - Nally
Catherine McLeod - Lizzy
Ollie O'Toole - Telegrapher

Quint is the object of revenge when a widow named Willa (Mary La Roche) accuses him of attacking her—placing Matt in a bad situation where the law is concerned.
Production #31230

301. OLD YORK
Original air date: May 4, 1963
Written by John Meston
Directed by Harry Harris, Jr.
Starring:
Edgar Buchanan - York
Michael Constantine - Baca
H. M. Wynant - Sage

Robert Knapp - Clayton
Dabbs Greer - Mr. Jonas
Roy Roberts - Mr. Botkin
Edward Madden - Taylor
Howard Culver - Clerk
Dorothy Neumann - Mrs. Finney
Lou Krugman - Barkeep
Don Spruance - Jim
Robert S. White - Milt

Matt's life was once saved by outlaw Dan York (Edgar Buchanan), and now the aged man and his partner Baca (Michael Constantine) arrive in Dodge City.
Production #31233

302. DADDY WENT AWAY
Original air date: May 11, 1963
Teleplay by Kathleen Hite
Story by John Rosser
Directed by Joseph Sargent
Starring:
Mary Carver - Lucy
William Schallert - Jess
Suzanne Cupito - Jessica
Dabbs Greer - Mr. Jonas

Chester once again falls in love—this time with seamstress Lucy Damon (Mary Carver) who responds favorably to his attentions.
Production #31232

303. THE ODYSSEY OF JUBAL TANNER
Original air date: May 18, 1963

Written by Paul Savage
Directed by Andrew V. McLaglen
Starring:
Beverly Garland - Leah
Peter Breck - Jubal
Denver Pyle - Aaron
Kevin Hagen - Hobie
Gregg Palmer - Fletcher
George Selk - Moss Grimmick
Hal Needham - Cowboy

Saloon girl Leah (Beverly Garland) and Jubal (Peter Breck) team up to to find the man who killed Leah's fiance and shot Jubal before stealing his horse.
Production #31234

304. **JEB**
Original air date: May 25, 1963
Written by Paul Savage
Directed by Harry Harris, Jr.
Starring:
Emile Genest - Chouteau
Roy Thinnes - Ab
Jim Hampton - Jeb
William Hunt - Codge
Duane Grey - Thad
Glenn Strange - Sam
Rand Brooks - Man
Dennis Cross - Brave
Buck Young - Andy

Ab Singleton (Roy Thinnes) makes a tragic mistake when

DADDY WENT AWAY May 18, 1963. Mary Carver and Dennis Weaver.

buys a horse that Jeb (Jim Hampton) has found. Ab is mistaken for a horse thief and killed.
Production #31235

305. **THE QUEST FOR ASA JANIN**
Original air date: June 1, 1963
Written by Paul Savage

Directed by Andrew V. McLaglen
Starring:
Anthony Caruso - Macklin
Richard Devon - Janin
Jack Lambert - Scotsman
George Keymas - Pardee
Joseph Sirola - Leroy
James Nusser - Louie Pheeters
Gene Darfler - Dave
Harry Carey, Jr. - Colridge
Lane Chandler - Warden
Ed Faulkner - Deputy
Pedro Gonzalez-Gonzalez - Bartender

Dave Ingalls (Gene Darfler) is sentenced to hang for killing his girlfriend. Matt knows that his friend is innocent and sets out to find the real killer before it is too late.
Production #31236

SEASON NINE

Produced by Norman Macdonnell
Associate producer - Frank Paris

306. KATE HELLER
Original air date: September 28, 1963
Written by Kathleen Hite
Directed by Harry Harris, Jr.
Starring:
Mabel Albertson - Kate
Tom Lowell - Andy

Betsy Jones-Moreland - Tess
Harry Bartell - Gus
Robert Knapp - Driver
Ted Jordan - Bo
Duane Grey - Shotgun

Greed drives young Andy (Tom Lowell) to murder. He ambushes Matt, who is rescued by a passing stage and taken to Andy's grandmother's (Mabel Albertson) relay station to recuperate.
Production #7102

307. LOVER BOY
Original air date: October 5, 1963
Written by John Meston
Directed by Andrew V. McLaglen
Starring:
Sheree North - Avis
Ken Curtis - Kyle
Alan Baxter - Ab
Carol Byron - Terry
Richard Coogan - Luke
Allan Hunt - Boy

Kyle (Ken Curtis) mixes it up with the much married Avis (Sheree North) and when her husband Ab (Alan Baxter) catches on—tragedy is in order.
Production #7107

308. LEGENDS DON'T SLEEP
Original air date: October 12, 1963
Written by Kathleen Hite
Directed by Harry Harris, Jr.
Starring:

Scott Marlowe - Britt
William Talman - Race
Hope Summers - Jen
James Nusser - Louie Pheeters
Robert Bice - Filler
Alan Dexter - Grosset
Ken Kenopka - Barkeep
Don Haggerty - Sheriff

Race (William Talman) is released from prison after serving five years. He meets up with Britt (Scott Marlowe) a wanna be tough guy who is anxious to learn the ways of the legendary gunfighter.
    Production #7106

309. **TOBE**
Original air date: October 19, 1963
Written by Paul Savage
Directed by John English
Starring:
Harry Townes - Tobe
Mary LaRoche - Mae
Philip Abbott - Frank
L. Q. Jones - Skinner
Sarah Selby - Ma Smalley
Dean Stanton - Young Man
Bud Osborne - Man
John Newton - Cowman
S. John Launer - Townsman

Tobe (Harry Townes), a saloon girl (Mary LaRoche) and a gambler named Frank (Philip Abbott) form a deadly lovers triangle.
    Production #7109

310. **EASY COME**
Original air date: October 26, 1963
Written by John Meston
Directed by Andrew V. McLaglen
Starring:
Andrew Prine - Sippy
Carl Reindel - Calhoun
George Wallace - Tobin
Dave Willock - Clerk
Charles Briggs - Riley
Orville Sherman - Wib Smith
Chubby Johnson - Barr
David Manley - Parks
Sam Edwards - Morff
K. L. Smith - King
James Nusser - Louie Pheeters
Dallas Mitchell - Cowboy
Shug Fisher - Harry
Peggy Rea - Lady

A man named Sippy (Andrew Prine) has an easy going manner and good looks that are quite deceiving—he's actually a dangerous outlaw.
    Production #7103

311. **MY SISTER'S KEEPER**
Original air date: November 2, 1963
Written by Kathleen Hite
Directed by Harry Harris, Jr.
Starring:
Nancy Wickwire - Nell
James Broderick - Pete
Jennifer Billingsley - Leah

LEGENDS DON'T SLEEP October 12, 1963. Milburn Stone and William Talman.

Gage Clarke - Mr. Botkin
Fred Coby - Barkeep
Lisa Seagram - Saloon Girl
Glenn Strange - Sam

Pete (James Broderick) is grief-stricken after the death of his wife and takes a job as a hired hand for two spinsters (Nancy Wickwire and Jennifer Billingsley).
Production #7110

312. QUINT'S TRAIL
Original air date: November 9, 1963
Written by Kathleen Hite
Directed by Harry Harris, Jr.
Starring:
Everett Sloane - Cyrus
Sharon Farrell - Belle
Shirley O'Hara - Florie
Don Haggerty - Clardy
George Selk - Moss Grimmick
Charles Seel - Finch

Quint agrees to guide the down-on-their-luck Neff family (Everett Sloane, Sharon Farrell and Shirley O'Hara) when they relocate to Oregon.
Production #7112

313. CARTER CAPER
Original air date: November 16, 1963
Written by John Meston
Directed by Jerry Hopper
Starring:
Jeremy Slate - Billy

William Phipps - Stark
Anjanette Comer - Cara
Rayford Barnes - Flack
I. Stanford Jolley - Mims
Barney Phillips - Smith
George Selk - Moss Grimmick
Glenn Strange - Sam
Michael Fox - Waiter
William Fawcett - Turner
Jacque Shelton - Carter
Dennis Cross - Bud

Billy (Jeremy Slate) catches Stark (William Phipps) attempting to steal his horse. Billy gives the would be thief a good beating and now Stark plans to even the score.
Production #7111

314. EX-CON
Original air date: November 30, 1963
Written by John Meston
Directed by Thomas Carr
Starring:
Jeanne Cooper - Lily
John Kellogg - Lee
Richard Devon - Pitts
Howard Wendell - Judge
Roy Roberts - Mr. Botkin
Raymond Guth - Clabe
Harry Lauter - Kelly
Tommy Alexander - Kid

Ex-convict Pitts (Richard Devon) arrives in Dodge with a new bride (Jeanne Cooper), stolen gold and a bullet with Marshal

Matt Dillon's name on it.
Production #7117

315. **EXTRADITION - PART I**
Original air date: December 7, 1963
Special guest star Gilbert Roland
Written by Antony Ellis
Directed by John English
Starring:
Gilbert Roland - Julio Chavez
Gene Evans - Hacker
Anna Navarro - Marguerita
Alex Montoya - Diaz
Walter Burke - Willie
Miguel Landa - Rivera
Pepe Hern - Miguel
Lisa Seagram - Girl
Ricky Vera - Boy

Matt tracks a murderer named Hacker (Gene Evans) into Mexico and picks up Julio Chavez (Gilbert Roland) and his lady friend Marguerita (Anna Navarro) along the way.
Production # 7115

316. **EXTRADITION - PART II**
Original air date: December 14, 1963
Special Guest Star Gilbert Roland
Written by Antony Ellis
Directed by John English
Starring:
Gilbert Roland - Julio Chavez
Gene Evans - Hacker
Anna Navarro - Marguerita
Alex Montoya - Diaz

Rico Alaniz - El Pinon
Miguel Landa - Rivera
Pepe Hern - Miguel

Matt and his prisoner Hacker (Gene Evans) become guests in a Mexican jail courtesy of a corrupt army captain named Diaz (Alex Montoya).
Production #7116

317. **THE MAGICIAN**
Original air date: December 21, 1963
Written by John A. Kneubuhl
Directed by Harry Harris, Jr.
Starring:
Lloyd Corrigan - Jeremiah
Tom Simcox - Tom
Barry Kelley - Wells
Brooke Bundy - Alice
Sheldon Allman - Banks
William Zuckert - Ned
James Nusser - Louie Pheeters
Ken Tilles - Sy

A medicine man (Lloyd Corrigan) and his daughter (Brooke Bundy) arrive in Dodge and are quickly labeled card sharks.
Production #7104

318. **PA HACK'S BROOD**
Original air date: December 28, 1963
Written by Paul Savage
Directed by Jerry Hopper
Starring:
Milton Selzer - Pa Hack
Lynn Loring - Maybelle

MY SISTER'S KEEPER November 2, 1963. Jennifer Billingsley and James Broderick.

Marianna Hill - Annie
George Lindsey - Orville
Jim Hampton - Jeb
Russell Thorson - Pa Willis

Charles Kuenstle - Lonnie
James Nusser - Louie Pheeters

Pa Hack (Milton Selzer) wants the life of luxury but won't work for it. Instead, he kidnaps rancher (Jim Hampton) and tries to force him into marrying his daughter (Lynn Loring).
Production #7108

319. **THE GLORY AND THE MUD**
Original air date: January 4, 1964
Written by Gwen Bagni
Directed by Jerry Hopper
Starring:
Kent Smith - Dakota
Marsha Hunt - Sarah
James Best - Beal
Robert Sorrells - Cloudy
Joseph Hamilton - Dan Binney
Rick Murray - Young Buck
Jenny Lee Arness - Amy

Retired gunfighter and wild west show star Dakota (Kent Smith) arrives in Dodge and Sam Beal (James Best) is eager to prove his prowess with a gun.
Production #7113

320. **DRY WELL**
Original air date: January 11, 1964
Written by John Meston
Directed by Harry Harris, Jr.
Starring:
Karen Sharpe - Yuma

Ned Glass - Ira
Tom Simcox - Web
John Hanek - Jeff
Bill Henry - Dave
Glenn Strange - Sam

Yuma and Dave have recently married but that doesn't stop her flirtations with cowhands Web (Tom Simcox) and Jeff (John Hanek).
Production #7120

321. PRAIRIE WOLFER
Original air date: January 18, 1964
Written by John Dunkel
Directed by Andrew V. McLaglen
Starring:
Ken Curtis - Festus
Noah Beery, Jr. - Nate
Don Dubbins - Wendt
Holly McIntire - Sarah
Fred Coby - Charlie
Glenn Strange - Sam
James Drake - Dude

Festus is the only reputable member of the Haggen family and is making a living hunting wolves, both for pelt money and bounty from the cattleman's association.
Production #7119

322. FRIEND
Original air date: January 25, 1964
Written by Kathleen Hite
Directed by Harry Harris, Jr.

EXTRADITION December 7 & 14, 1963. Gilbert Roland and James Arness.

Starring:
Tom Reese - Judd
Jan Shepard - Marge
Ben Wright - Father Tom
Butch Patrick - Runt
George Keymas - Gore

Ralph Moody - Finley
Glenn Strange - Sam
Frank Kreig - Barkeep

Matt travels to a nearby town to investigate the death of his friend Judd Nellis (Tom Reese), who saved the marshal's life years earlier.

Production #7122

323. **ONCE A HAGGEN**
Original air date: February 1, 1964
Written by Les Crutchfield
Directed by Andrew V. McLaglen
Starring:
Slim Pickens - Bucko
Elizabeth MacRae - April
John Hudson - Curly
Kenneth Tobey - Fickett
Roy Barcroft - Pop
Howard Wendell - Judge

Festus and Bucko (Slim Pickens) lose everything in a poker game then turn to the bottle to commiserate. When the game winner is found dead, Bucko becomes the prime suspect.

Production #7118

324. **NO HANDS**
Original air date: February 8, 1964
Written by John Meston
Directed by Andrew V. McLaglen
Starring:
Denver Pyle - Pa
Strother Martin - Timble
Kevin Hagen - Emmett

Rayford Barnes - Jess
Conlan Carter - Ben
Wright King - Lon
Orville Sherman - Wib Smith
James Nusser - Louie Pheeters
Shug Fisher - Barkeep
Mark Murray - Boy
Glenn Strange - Sam

While treating Timble (Strother Martin) for an eye injury, Doc is interrupted by the boisterous Ginnis bunch, with Pa (Denver Pyle) insisting that his son's broken leg is tended to first.

Production #7101

325. **MAY BLOSSOM**
Original air date: February 15, 1964
Written by Kathleen Hite
Directed by Andrew V. McLaglen
Starring:
Lauri Peters - Mayblossom
Charles Gray - Lon
Richard X. Slattery - Greer
Sarah Selby - Ma Smalley
Roger Torrey - Feeder

Mayblossom, (Lauri Peters), cousin to Festus, arrives in town to court her marriage-shy relative. While Festus is away, she is roughed up by Lon (Charles Gray) and Festus sets out after the man.

Production #7123

326. **THE BASSOPS**
Original air date: February 22, 1964
Written by Tom Hanley

NO HANDS February 8, 1964. Amanda Blake and James Arness on the set.

COMANCHES IS SOFT March 7, 1964. Kathy Nolan and Ken Curtis.

FATHER'S LOVE March 14, 1964. Hickman Hill and Amanda Blake.

KITTY CORNERED April 18, 1964. Amanda Blake, James Arness and Jacqueline Scott. (photo courtesy of Jacqueline Scott)

KITTY CORNERED April 18, 1964. Jacqueline Scott. (photo courtesy of Jacqueline Scott)

Directed by Andrew V. McLaglen
Starring:
Robert Wilke - Kelby
Warren Oates - Deke
Mickey Sholdar - Tommy
James Griffith - Harford
Eunice Pollis - Mellie
James Nusser - Louie Pheeters
Ollie O'Toole - Telegrapher
Robert Bice - Wilson
Glenn Strange - Sam
Patricia Joyce - Donna Lee

During a struggle with prisoner Kelby (Robert Wilke), Matt loses his badge and gunbelt. Deke and his wife Mellie (Warren Oates and Eunice Pollis) find the two handcuffed together, with both men claiming to be the law.
Production #7121

327. THE KITE

Original air date: February 29, 1964
Written by John Meston
Directed by Andrew V. McLaglen
Starring:
Lyle Bettger - Polk
Michael Higgins - Cassidy
Allyson Ames - Clara
Betsy Hale - Letty
Sarah Selby - Ma Smalley
Burt Douglas - Bryan
Glenn Strange - Sam

Matt tries to prevent a murderer (Lyle Bettger) from learning that his latest victim's daughter Letty (Betsy Hale) witnessed

his cold-blooded crime.
Production #7124

328. COMANCHES IS SOFT

Original air date: March 7, 1964
Written By Kathleen Hite
Directed by Harry Harris, Jr.
Starring:
Don Megowan - Hardy
James Nusser - Louie Pheeters
Richard Reeves - Heavy
Nesdon Booth - Barkeep
Dean Stanton Leader
Rex Holman - Brother
and Kathy Nolan - Liz

Quint and Festus enjoy a wild night in Wichita and later welcome the attentions of pretty saloon girl Liz (Kathy Nolan)—until her boyfriend Hardy (Don Megowan) steps in.
Production #7126

329. FATHER'S LOVE

Original air date: March 14, 1964
Written by John Meston
Directed by Harry Harris, Jr.
Starring:
Ed Nelson - Tom
Shary Marshall - Cora
Robert F. Simon - Jesse
Anthony Caruso - Sims
Edith Evanson - Nell
Ben Wright - Mr. Ross
Hickman Hill - Hank

Lovely Cora (Shary Marshall) wants nothing to do with Jesse (Robert F. Simon). Later, she marries Tom (Ed Nelson) and discovers that Jesse is his uncle.

Production #7125

330. NOW THAT APRIL'S HERE
Original air date: March 21, 1964
Written by Les Crutchfield
Directed by Andrew V. McLaglen
Starring:
Elizabeth MacRae - April
Royal Dano - Bender
Hal Baylor - Grody
Vic Perrin - Argus
Glenn Strange - Sam

No one believes that beautiful April (Elizabeth MacRae) is an eyewitness to murder—with the exception of the murderers themselves.

Production #7127

331. CALEB
Original air date: March 28, 1964
Written by Paul Savage
Directed by Harry Harris, Jr.
Starring:
John Dehner - Caleb
Dorothy Green - Julie
Lane Bradford - Lige
Ann Loos - Dorcas
Dabbs Greer - Mr. Jonas
George Selk - Moss Grimmick
Vickie Cos - Betsy

Christopher Barrey - George
Dennis Robertson - Stable Boy
Ted Jordan - Chad
Glenn Strange - Sam

Dirt farmer Caleb (John Dehner) is disgusted with his existence and throws it all away to enjoy city life, with little or no regard for his wife Dorcas (Ann Loos).

Production #7128

332. OWNEY TUPPER HAD A DAUGHTER
Original air date: April 4, 1964
Written by Paul Savage
Directed by Jerry Hopper
Starring:
Jay C. Flippen - Owney
Noreen Corcoran - Ellen
Andrea Darvi - Amity
James Seay - Jay
Howard Wendall - Judge
Orville Sherman - Wib Smith
Hank Patterson - Hank Miller
Dolores Quinton - Clara
Vernon Rich - Art
Berkeley Harris - Mal
Steve Gaynor - Clay

Owney (Jay C. Flippen) is a widower who loses custody of his daughter (Andrea Darvi). To prove he can provide for the child, he accepts a job as hangman, to provide money needed for new crops. This decision proves unpopular with neighbors.

Production #7105

THE PROMOTER April 25, 1964. Wilhelm Von Homburg, Vic Perrin and Johnny Newman.

333. **BENTLY**
Original air date: April 11, 1964
Written by John A. Kneubuhl
Directed by Harry Harris, Jr.
Starring:
Charles McGraw - Calvin
June Dayton - Emily
Gene Lyons - Fletcher
Bill Erwin - Ned

Jan Clayton - Clara Wright

Refusing to believe the deathbed murder confession of Ned (Bill Erwin), Chester sets out to find the real culprit and clear his friend's name, and possibly save the life of his widow (Jan Clayton). *(This segment was Dennis Weaver's final Gunsmoke credit)*
Production #7114

334. **KITTY CORNERED**
Original air date: April 18, 1964
Written by Kathleen Hite
Directed by John Brahm
Starring:
Jacqueline Scott - Stella
Joseph Sirola - Eddie
Vici Raaf - Fay
Betty Keeney - Aggie
Shug Fisher - Obie
Glenn Strange - Sam

Stella (Jacqueline Scott) bursts onto the scene with the intention of putting Kitty out of business—she opens the biggest and flashiest saloon Dodge has ever seen.
Production #7131

335. **THE PROMOTER**
Original air date: April 25, 1964
Written by John Meston
Directed by Andrew V. McLaglen
Starring:
Vic Perrin - Huckaby

Allen Case - Lieutenant
Robert Fortier - Sergeant
Don Collier - Price
Larry Blake - Shell
Peggy Stewart - Daisy
Gregg Palmer - Jake
Wilhelm Von Homburg - Otto
John Newman - Towers
James Nusser - Louie Pheeters
Shug Fisher - Obie
Hank Patterson - Hank

Henry Huckaby (Vic Perrin) hopes by promoting a prize fight he will be able to turn his bad luck into good and poverty into fortune.
Production #7129

336. **TRIP WEST**
Original air date: May 2, 1964
Written by John Dunkel
Directed by Harry Harris, Jr.
Starring:
Herbert Anderson - Elwood
Sharon Farrell - Annie
H. M. Wynant - Meade
Percy Helton - Arbuckle
Vinton Hayworth - Ramsay
Elizabeth Shaw - Lucille
Henry Rowland - Frank
Angela Clarke - Mrs. Crabbe

Believing he has only a short time to live, meek Elwood

(Herbert Anderson) plans to live it up and changes his personality radically.
Production #7132

TRIP WEST May 2, 1964. James Arness, Amanda Blake and Milburn Stone rehearse.

337. **SCOT FREE**
Original air date: May 9, 1964
Written by Kathleen Hite
Directed by Harry Harris, Jr.
Starring:
Patricia Owens - Nora

382

Jay Lanin - Rob
Hunt Powers - Cowboy
Julie Sommars - Gert
Ann Barton - Millie
Harry Bartell - Harper
Robert Bice - Jim

Matt and Festus find a body on land now owned by Nora (Patricia Owens), who claims no knowledge of the corpse identity. Her hired hand Rob (Jay Lanin) is her lover and the body is actually her husband.
Production #7130

338. **THE WARDEN**
Original air date: May 16, 1964
Written by Les Crutchfield
Directed by Andrew V. McLaglen
Starring:
George Kennedy - Stark
Anthony Caruso - Bull Foot
Julie Parrish - Cool Dawn
Chris Connelly - Trainey
Ollie O'Toole - Telegrapher

Stark (George Kennedy) buys Cool Dawn (Julie Parrish) from her father Bull Foot (Anthony Caruso).
Production # 7133

339. **HOMECOMING**
Original air date: May 23, 1964
Written by Shimon Bar-David

Directed by Harry Harris, Jr.

Starring:
Phyllis Coates - Edna
Jack Elam - Hector
Harold J. Stone - Orval
Emile Genest - Frisbie
Tom Lowell - Ethan
Howard Culver - Clerk

Hector (Jack Elam) is confronted by Orval (Harold J. Stone), the ex-husband of his wife Edna (Phyllis Coates), who may or may not be legally divorced from him.
Production #7134

340. **THE OTHER HALF**
Original air date: May 30, 1964
Written by John Dunkel
Directed by Andrew V. McLaglen
Starring:
Lee Kinsolving - Jay Bartell and Jess Bartell
Donna Anderson - Nancy
Paul Fix - Sam Bartell
Patric Knowles - MacIntosh
Larry Blake - Mr. Hoover
Dave Cass - Minister
Robert Gravage - Barney

Jess and Jay Bartell (Lee Kinsolving) are twins who care for their disabled father's feed store. A tragic love triangle develops when the boys fall in love with the same girl (Donna Anderson) resulting in Jess' murder.
Production #7135

341. JOURNEY FOR THREE
Original air date: June 6, 1964
Written by Frank Paris
Directed by Harry Harris, Jr.
Starring:
Mark Goddard - Boyd
Michael J. Pollard - Cyrus
William Arvin - Adam
James Nusser - Louie Pheeters
Margaret Bly - Girl
Ollie O'Toole - Telegrapher

While traveling to California, Adam (William Arvin) does not care for the influence Boyd (Mark Goddard) has on his brother Cyrus (Michael J. Pollard). His suspicions prove correct when Boyd kills a girl (Margaret Bly) while trying to molest her.
Production #7136

SEASON TEN

Produced by Norman Macdonnell (13 episodes) and
Philip Leacock (remainder)
Associate producer - Frank Paris
Story consultant - John Mantley, when Leacock was hired.

342. BLUE HEAVEN
Original air date: September 26, 1964
Written by Les Crutchfield
Directed by Michael O'Herlihy
Starring:
Kurt Russell - Packy
Tim O'Connor - Kip

Diane Ladd - Elena
Karl Swenson - Tabe
John McLiam - Stableman
Eddie Hice - Duster
Ernie Anderson - Man
Jan Merlin - Ed Sykes

On the run, fugitive Kip (Tom O'Connor) and young runaway Packy (Kurt Russell) join forces to elude their pursuers, which include Matt and Festus.
Production #1615-0410

343. CROOKED MILE
Original air date: October 3, 1964
Written by Les Crutchfield
Directed by Andrew V. McLaglen
Starring:
George Kennedy - Cyrus
Royal Dano - Praylie
Katharine Ross - Susan

Domineering and bigoted Cyrus (George Kennedy) refuses to allow his daughter Susan (Katharine Ross) to see Quint—a situation that turns violent and deadly for all concerned.
Production #1615-0401

344. OLD MAN
Original air date: October 10, 1964
Written by John Meston
Directed by Harry Harris, Jr.
Starring:
Ned Glass - Old Man
Robert Hogan - Danny

CROOKED MILE October 3, 1964. Ken Curtis, Burt Reynolds and James Arness.

Ed Peck - Silva
Rayford Barnes - Litton
Howard Wendell - Judge
Al Schottelkotte - Bailiff
Gilman Rankin - Waiter
Bryan O'Byrne - Clerk
Harry Bartell - Sheriff
Arthur Peterson, Jr. - Doctor
Robert Gravage - Hangman
Glenn Strange - Sam

An old man (Ned Glass) is found on the prairie. Nursed back to health, he soon becomes the prime suspect for the murder of Silva (Ed Peck). (*This episode features a horrible, hammy performance by Ned Glass as the Old Man—so bad it's funny.*)
Production #1615-0409

345. **THE VIOLATORS**
Original air date: October 17, 1963
Written by John Dunkel
Directed by Harry Harris, Jr.
Starring:
Denver Pyle - Caleb
James Anderson - Hewitt
Michael Pate - Buffalo Calf
Amzie Strickland - Mrs. Hewitt
Garry Walberg - Scroggs
Lee Phillip - Mrs. Bell
Douglas Kennedy - Talbot
Martin Blaine - Colonel
Arthur Batanides - Harv Foster

HELP ME KITTY November 7, 1964. Amanda Blake and Betty Conner.

The scalping of a man sets off a chain reaction of violent events that may result in a full-scale war between homesteaders and the Indians.
Production #1615-0413

346. DOCTOR'S WIFE
Original air date: October 24, 1964
Written by George Eckstein
Directed by Harry Harris, Jr.
Starring:
Phyllis Love - Jennifer
James Broderick - Wes
Harold Gould - Boake
Ann Barton - Mrs. Boake
Helen Kleeb - Mrs. Gort
James Nusser - Louie Pheeters
Robert Biheller - Jared
Dorothy Neumann - Old Woman
Howard Culver - Clerk
Jewel Jaffe - Martha Lou
Buck Young - Carney
Glenn Strange - Sam

Doc becomes the victim of a heartless smear campaign engineered by the wife (Phyllis Love) of a newly arrived doctor (James Broderick).
Production #1615-0406

347. TAKE HER, SHE'S CHEAP
Original air date: October 31, 1964
Written by Kathleen Hite
Directed by Harry Harris, Jr.

Starring:
Lauri Peters - Allie
Malcolm Atterbury - Duggan
Linda Watkins - Ma
Willard Sage - Mel

Dean Stanton - Rainey
Mort Mills - Loren
Ray Lane - Man

To repay a favor, Duggan (Malcolm Atterbury) offers his daughter Allie (Lauri Peters) to Marshal Dillon as a bride.
Production #1615-0411

348. HELP ME KITTY
Original air date: November 7, 1964
Written by Kathleen Hite
Directed by Harry Harris, Jr.
Starring:
Jack Elam - Specter
Betty Conner - Hope
James Frawley - Furnas
Larry Blake - Man
Joe Conley - Carl
Burt Douglas - Ed
Peggy Stewart - Nettie

After surviving an attack on their stagecoach, Kitty and expectant mother Hope (Betty Conner) are stranded and forced to continue their journey by foot.
Production #1615-0414

349. HUNG HIGH
Original air date: November 14, 1964
Written by John Meston
Directed by Mark Rydell
Starring:
Special Guest Robert Culp - Joe
George Lindsey - Bud

Elisha Cook - George
Michael Conrad - Dick
and Edward Asner - Sgt. Wilks
Scott Marlowe - Tony Serpa
Harold J. Stone - Jim Downey

Matt arrests Tony Serpa (Scott Marlowe) and while heading back to Dodge, the pair are ambushed by crazed Joe Costa (Robert Culp).
Production #1615-0416

350. JONAH HUTCHINSON
Original air date: November 21, 1964
Written by Calvin Clements
Directed by Harry Harris, Jr.
Starring:
Robert F. Simon - Jonah
Richard Anderson - Samuel
June Dayton - Phoebe
Tommy Alexander - Franklin
Claude Johnson - Aaron
David Macklin - Steven
Roy Barcroft - Roy
William Fawcett - Lefferts
Charles Seel - Gorth
Glenn Strange - Sam
Rocky Shahan - Stage Driver
Jacque Shelton - 2nd Rancher
Jason Johnson - 1st Rancher

After serving a long prison term, Jonah Hutchinson (Robert F. Simon) returns to Dodge determined to rebuild his cattle empire at any cost.

Production #1615-0404

351. BIG MAN, BIG TARGET
Original air date: November 28, 1964
Written by John Mantley
Directed by Michael O'Herlihy
Starring:
Special Guest J. D. Cannon - Pike
Harry Lauter - Leach
John McLiam - Delphos
Frank Ferguson - Enoch
Glenn Strange - Sam
and Mike Road - Joe Merchant
Mariette Hartley - Ellie

Pike (J. D. Cannon) will stop at nothing in his conquest for Ellie (Mariette Hartley)—including framing her husband Joe (Mike Road) for stealing a horse.
Production #1615-0417

352. CHICKEN
Original air date: December 5, 1964
Written by John Meston
Directed by Andrew V. McLaglen
Starring:
Glenn Corbett - Dan
Gigi Perreau - Lucy
John Lupton - Carl
L. Q. Jones - Brady
Lane Chandler - Morgan
Dave Willock - Becker
Lane Bradford - Davis
Chubby Johnson - Rogers

HUNG HIGH November 14, 1964. James Arness and Scott Marlowe.

Roy Barcroft - Roy
Michael Keep - Willis
John Pickard - Phelps
Bob Steele - Coe

Meek and peaceful Dan (Glenn Corbett) is mistakenly credited with the killing of four notorious outlaws. This situation ultimately leads to another showdown, one that Dan must participate in.
Production #1615-0417

353. **INNOCENCE**
Original air date: December 12, 1964
Written by John Meston
Directed by Harry Harris, Jr.
Starring:
Special Guest Bethel Leslie - Elsa Poe
Jason Evers - Charlie Ross
Michael Forest - Bob Sullins
Jacque Shelton - Joe Rogers
Lee Krieger - Carl Beck
Ric Roman - Sims
Don Brice - Cowboy #1
Claude Akins - Art McLane

Long-time aversion between Art (Claude Akins) and Bob (Michael Forest) intensifies when they both fall for the pretty new Long Branch hostess Elsa Poe (Bethel Leslie).
Production #1615-0418

354. **AUNT THEDE**
Original air date: December 19, 1964
Written by Kathleen Hite
Directed by Sutton Roley
Starring:
Jeanette Nolan - Aunt Thede
Dyan Cannon - Ivy
Frank Cady - Webb
James Stacy - George
Howard McNear - Howard
Hap Glaudi - Townsman

JONAH HUTCHINSON November 21, 1964. Tommy Alexander and Robert F. Simon.

Jenny Lee Aurness (James Arness' daughter) - Laurie

Festus' Aunt Thede (Jeanette Nolan) comes to Dodge City to find herself a man—and instead finds herself plenty of trouble when she mixes moonshine with marryin'.

Production #1615-0412

355. **HAMMERHEAD**

Original air date: December 26, 1964
Written by Antony Ellis
Directed by Christian Nyby
Starring:
John Fiedler - Fitch
Arch Johnson - Ponder
Linda Foster - Carrie
Chubby Johnson - Wohaw
Don Briggs - Deggers
William Henry - Feeney
Peter Dunn - Squatty
Tommy Richards - Gambler
Ray Hemphill - Tom
Gene Redfern - Gambler
Bill Catching - Stomp
Daniel M. White - Attendant
Chuck Hayward - Cowhand

The race is on from Dodge City to Cheyenne to prove who has the better horse stock—Fitch (John Fiedler) or Wohaw (Chubby Johnson).

Production #1615-0408

356. **DOUBLE ENTRY**

Original air date: January 2, 1965
Written by Les Crutchfield
Directed by Joseph Sargent
Starring:
Special Guest Forrest Tucker - Brad McClain
Mel Gallagher - Yuma Joe
Roy Roberts - Mr. Botkin
Nora Marlowe - Passenger

Lew Brown - Pete Elder
Glenn Strange - Sam
Fred Coby - Wagoneer
Rudy Sooter - Fiddler
Cyril Delevanti - Jake Bookly

Matt's old friend Brad McClain (Forrest Tucker) arrives in Dodge with an interest in buying the stage line and a bigger interest in the scheduled gold shipments.
Production #1615-0419

357. RUN SHEEP RUN
Original air date: January 9, 1965
Written by John Meston
Directed by Harry Harris, Jr.
Starring:
Special guest Burt Brinckerhoff - Tom Stocker
James Nusser - Louie Pheeters
Tom Fadden - Lem Hubley
Ted Knight - Bill Miller
Ann Barton - Beth Miller
Arthur Malet - Cox
George Keymas - Harry Crane
Davey Davison - Mary Stocker
Peter Whitney - Dan Braden

Tom and Mary Stocker (Burt Brinckerhoff and Davey Davison) sell their ranch to Dan Braden (Peter Whitney) and a misunderstanding regarding payment leads to a killing.
Production #1615-0420

358. DEPUTY FESTUS
Original air date: January 16, 1965

CHICKEN December 5, 1964. James Arness and Glenn Corbett.

Written by Calvin Clements
Directed by Harry Harris, Jr.
Starring:
Don Beddoe - Halligan
Shug Fisher - Emery

Bill Zuckert - Mr. Jacobsen
Michael Petit - Glen
Royal Dano - Lambert
Carl Reindel - Dave Carson
Denver Pyle - Claudius
Ken Mayer - Tiplett
Glenn Strange - Sam
Harold Ensley - Waiter

Matt locks up three ruffians and then has to leave town. He deputizes Festus to care for the jailbirds, who turn out to be his cousins.

Production #1615-0422

359. ONE KILLER ON ICE

Original air date: January 23, 1965
Written by Richard Carr
Directed by Joseph H. Lewis
Starring:
Special Guest John Drew Barrymore - Anderson
Richard Carlyle - Carl
Glenn Strange - Sam
Eddie Hice - Frank
Dennis Hopper - Billy Kimbo
Anne Helm - Helena Dales
Philip Coolidge - Owney Dales

Bounty Hunter Anderson (John Drew Barrymore) enlists aid from Matt to protect him from an ambush when he sets out to bring a prisoner into custody.

Production #1615-0421

360. CHIEF JOSEPH

Original air date: January 30, 1965
Story by Thomas Warner
Teleplay by Clyde Ware
Directed by Mark Rydell
Starring:
Victor Jory - Chief Joseph
Robert Loggia - Lt. Cal Tripp
Michael Keep - Yellow Bear
Dennis Cross - Three Hand
Leonard Stone - Mr. Wiley
Howard Culver - Clerk
Joe Maross - Charlie Britton
Willard Sage - Corly Watts

Tensions reach a boiling point as Chief Joseph (Victor Jory) becomes seriously ill and must stay at the Dodge House before traveling on to a peace summit with President Grant.

Production #1615-0424

361. CIRCUS TRICK

Original air date: February 6, 1965
Written by Les Crutchfield
Directed by William F. Claxton
Starring:
Walter Burke - Elko
Elizabeth MacRae - April
Warren Oates - Speeler
Isabel Jewel - Madame Ahr
Ken Scott - Eddie
Roy Roberts - Mr. Botkin
Roy Barcroft - Roy
Glenn Strange - Sam

AUNT THEDE December 19, 1964. Ken Curtis and Jeanette Nolan.

HAMMERHEAD December 26, 1964. Linda Foster and Ken Curtis.

DOUBLE ENTRY January 2, 1965. James Arness and Forrest Tucker.

A traveling circus spells trouble for Matt, Festus and his girlfriend April (Elizabeth MacRae)—especially after she joins the show.
Production #1615-0407

362. SONG FOR DYING
Original air date: February 13, 1965
Written by Harry Kronman
Directed by Allen Reisner
Starring:
Special Guest Theodore Bikel - Martin
Roger Ewing - Ben Lukens
Lee Majors - Dave Lukens
Russell Thorson - Mace
Sheldon Allman - Cory Lukens
Glenn Strange - Sam
Robert F. Simon - Will Lukens
Ford Rainey - Hode Embry

A wandering minstrel (Theodore Bikel) remains a mystery to all—except for Doc and the vengeful Will Lukens (Robert F. Simon) and his family.
Production #1615-0425

363. WINNER TAKE ALL
Original air date: February 20, 1965

Written by Les Crutchfield
Directed by Vincent McEveety
Starring:
Tom Simcox - Curly
John Milford - Pinto
Margaret Bly - Karen
H. M. Wynant - Relko
Allen Jaffe - Gunman

ONE KILLER ON ICE January 23, 1965. John Barrymore, Jr., Anne Helm and James Arness.

Ralph J. Rowe - Stableman
Nestor Paiva - Barman

Curly (Tom Simcox) and Pinto (John Milford) are two brothers who share hot tempers and the affection for the same woman (Margaret Bly).
Production #1615-0415

364. ELIAB'S ALM

Original air date: February 27, 1965
Written by Will Corry
Directed by Richard C. Sarafian
Starring:
Jim Hampton - Eliab Haggen
Donald O'Kelly - Dealer
Gregg Palmer - Jake Craig
Glenn Strange - Sam
Hank Patterson - Hank
Larry Barton - Citizen
Dee J. Thompson - Widow Pearl Winton

    Eliab Haggen (Jim Hampton) arrives in Dodge City to settle a longtime score with his favorite uncle, Festus.
    Production #1615-0423

365. THURSDAY'S CHILD

Original air date: March 6, 1965
Written by Robert Lewin
Directed by Joseph H. Lewis
Starring:
Special Guest Jean Arthur - Julie Blane
Joe Raciti - Vardis
Roy Barcroft - Roy
Hank Patterson - Hank
Suzanne Benoit - Amy Blane
Glenn Strange - Sam
Fred Coby - Clint Marston
Scott Marlowe - Lon Blane

    Mystery surrounds an old friend of Kitty's, Julie Blane (Jean Arthur), who stops in Dodge to visit while en route to Wichita to see her son and help during the upcoming birth of her grandchild.
    Production #1615-0426

366. BRECKINRIDGE

Original air date: March 13, 1965
Written by Les Crutchfield
Directed by Vincent McEveety
Starring:
John Warburton - Judge Danby
Elisha Cook - Jocko Beal
Glenn Strange - Sam
Hank Patterson - Hank
Harry Harvey, Sr. - Old Man
Dorothy Neumann - Woman
Howard Culver - Hotel Clerk
Jack Perkins - Bully
Ben Cooper -Breck Taylor
Robert Sorrells - Sled Grady

    A young Eastern attorney (Ben Cooper) quickly discovers that the law of the West differs slightly than what he is used to normally.
    Production #1615-0427

367. BANK BABY

Original air date: March 20, 1965
Written by John Meston
Directed by Andrew V. McLaglen
Starring:
Jacques Aubuchon - Bert
Gail Kobe - Grace
Virginia Christine - Bess
Hampton Fancher - Milton

THURSDAY'S CHILD March 6, 1965. Milburn Stone and Jean Arthur.

Roy Roberts - Mr. Botkin
Harry Carey, Jr. - Fisher
William Boyett - Harry
Cliff Ketchum - Teller

Bert (Jacques Aubuchon) kidnaps a baby from a camp of pilgrims as part of his master plan to rob the bank in Dodge City.
Production #1615-0405

368. **THE LADY**
Original air date: March 27, 1965
Written by John Mantley
Directed by Mark Rydell
Starring:
Special Guest Eileen Heckart - Hattie Silks
Walter Sande - Charlie
Hank Patterson - Hank
Glenn Strange - Sam
James Nusser - Louie Pheeters
Clifton James - Sam Hare
Michael Forest - Ray Pate
R. G. Armstrong - Jud Briar
Katharine Ross - Liz Beaumont

Hattie Silks (Eileen Heckart) runs out of money on her way to San Francisco and must accept a temporary job at the Long Branch. She meets Jud Briar (R. G. Armstrong) and romance blossoms, much to the chagrin of her selfish niece Liz (Katharine Ross).
Production #1615-0430

369. **DRY ROAD TO NOWHERE**
Original air date: April 3, 1965
Written by Harry Kronman
Directed by Vincent McEveety
Starring:
Special Guest James Whitmore - Amos Campbell
Reed Morgan - Pete Moreland
James Nusser - Louie Pheeters
Glenn Strange - Sam
Howard Culver - Howie
John Saxon - Dingo

Julie Sommars - Bess Campbell
L. Q. Jones - Wally

Temperance preacher Amos Campbell (James Whitmore) arrives to dry out Dodge, meeting opposition from the citizens, Miss Kitty and a gunfighter (John Saxon).
Production #1615-0429

370. TWENTY MILES FROM DODGE
Original air date: April 10, 1965
Written by Clyde Ware
Directed by Mark Rydell
Starring:
Special Guest Darren McGavin - Will Helmick
Everett Sloane - Follansbee
Aneta Corsaut - Eleanor Starkey
Tony Haig - Johnny Hutton
Stafford Repp - Otie Schaffer
William Fawcett - Bert Fraley
Noam Pitlik - Dobbs
Gerald S. O'Loughlin - Grant Shay
Val Avery - Donner

A band of ruthless outlaws kidnap passengers from a stagecoach, including gambler Will Helmick (Darren McGavin) and Miss Kitty.
Production #1615-0428

371. THE PARIAH
Original air date: April 17, 1965
Written by Calvin Clements
Directed by Harry Harris, Jr.
Starring:

Special Guest John Dehner - Paolo Scanzano
Steve Ihnat - Ben Hooker
Tom Reese - Wayne Hooker
Lee Van Cleef - John Hooker
Don Keefer - Newspaper Editor
Glenn Strange - Sam
and Donald Losby - Thomas Scanzano
Ilka Windish - Rosita Scanzano

While protecting his family, poor farmer Paolo Scanzano (John Dehner) kills outlaw John Hooker (Lee Van Cleef). The reward is nice, but the price he has to pay for what happened, becomes steep.
Production #1615-0432

BRECKENRIDGE March 13, 1965. Amanda Blake and Ben Cooper. (photo courtesy of Ben Cooper)

372. GILT GUILT

Original air date: April 24, 1965
Written by Kathleen Hite
Directed by Harry Harris, Jr.
Starring:
Jan Clayton - Mary
Andrew Duggan - Crail
Peter Brooks - Sully
William Phipps - Drifter
William Boyett - Jake
James Nusser - Louie Pheeters
Roy Barcroft - Roy

Drought ruins the farm of Mary (Jan Clayton) and she and her son develop scurvy—Doc must act quickly to save them both.
Production #1615-0402

373. BAD LADY FROM BROOKLINE

Original air date: May 1, 1965
Written by Gustave Field
Directed by Michael O'Herlihy
Starring:
Special Guest Betty Hutton - Molly McConnell
John Hubbard - LaFarge
Jonathan Kidd - Harper
Billy Bowles - Willie McConnell
Ollie O'Toole - Herb
Jan Peters - Curley
Glenn Strange - Sam
Eddie Hice - Cowboy
Tom McCauley - Ben
Claude Akins - Sy Sherne

BAD LADY FROM BROOKLINE May 1, 1965. Betty Hutton, Ken Curtis and James Arness.

Molly McConnell (Betty Hutton) and her son Willie (Billy Bowles) arrive in Dodge City only to be informed that Matt has killed her husband.
Production #1615-0431

HONEY POT May 15, 1965. Rory Calhoun and Joanna Moore.

374. **TWO TALL MEN**
Original air date: May 8, 1965
Written by Frank Q. Dobbs and Robert C. Stewart, Jr.

Directed by Vincent McEveety
Starring:
Special Guest Harry Townes - Abihu Howell
Jay Ripley - Ned
Maurice McEndree - Newspaperman
Preston Pierce - Tommy
Glenn Strange - Sam
Ben Cooper - Breck
George Lindsey - Billy

With Matt out of town, Festus and Breck (Ben Cooper) trail those responsible for the savage and senseless beating that happened to Doc.
Production #1615-0435

375. **HONEY POT**
Original air date: May 15, 1965
Written by John Meston
Directed by Harry Harris, Jr.
Starring:
Special Guest Rory Calhoun - Ben Stack
Dick Wessel - Sol Durham
John Crawford - Hal Biggs
Harry Bartell - Jems Riley
Harry Lauter - Gregory Bellow
Hank Patterson - Hank
Roy Barcroft - Roy
Charles Maxwell - Hy Evers
Glenn Strange - Sam
Joanna Moore - Honey Dare

Ben Stack (Rory Calhoun) is an old friend of Matt's and while visiting Dodge, meets and falls in love with Honey Dare

(Joanna Moore), then kills her jealous husband.
Production #1615-0434

376. THE NEW SOCIETY

Original air date: May 22, 1965
Written by Calvin Clements
Directed by Joseph Sargent
Starring:
Special Guest James Gregory - Scanlon, Sr.
Richard X. Slattery - Coor
Sandy Kenyon - Bennings
Lew Brown - Eli Wall
Ian Wolfe - Old Man Wall
Elizabeth Perry -Vera Scanlon
Dennis Cross - Aaron
Garry Walberg - Roy
Victor Izay - Depositor
Fred Coby - Sy
Linda James - Sue Ann
Jeremy Slate - Tom Scanlon
Jack Weston - Wesley

When Matt arrives in a small town to investigate an unsolved murder, he is met with fear, hostility and the ire of John Scanlon (James Gregory).
Production #1615-0436

377. HE WHO STEALS

Original air date: May 29, 1965
Written by John Meston
Directed by Harry Harris, Jr.
Starring:
Special Guest Russ Tamblyn - Billy Waters

Roger Torrey - Steve Hays
Lane Bradford - Dan O'Hare
Will J. White - Beckett
James Nusser - Louie Pheeters
Glenn Strange - Sam
Harold J. Stone - Jeff Sutro
Len Wayland - Jim Donner
Larry Ward - Sid Perce
Stanley Adams - Charlie Rath

Idolization leads to lying when Billy Walters (Russ Tamblyn) covers up for buffalo hunter turned thief Jeff Sutro (Harold J. Stone).
Production #1615-0451

SEASON ELEVEN

Produced by Philip Leacock
Associate Producer - John Mantley

378. SEVEN HOURS TO DAWN

Original air date: September 18, 1965
Directed by Vincent McEveety
Written by Clyde Ware
Starring:
Special Guest John Drew Barrymore - Mace Gore
Michael Vandever - Raider
Al Lettier (later Lettieri) - Smitty
Allen Jaffe - Jack Dawn
Glenn Strange - Sam

Charles Seel - Barney
Morgan Woodward - Deeks
Jerry Douglas - Clark
Johnny Seven - Barens

Mace Gore (John Drew Barrymore) leads a ruthless gang of vermin into Dodge, disarms Matt, and takes over—completely ransacking the town and terrifying the townspeople.
Production #1615-0433

379. THE STORM

Original air date: September 25, 1965
Directed by Joseph Sargent
Written by Paul Savage
Starring:
Special Guest Forrest Tucker - Adam Benteen
Willard Sage - Cantwell
Mary Lou Taylor - Hope Woodley
Lincoln Demyan - Cowboy
Charles Seel - Barney
Glenn Strange - Sam
Stevan Darrell - Judge
Stuart Margolin - Sheriff
Victor Izay - Bartender
Shug Fisher - Hank Cooters
Rudy Sooter - Rudy
Tim McIntire - Claude Benteen
Richard Evans - Ab Benteen
Ruth Warrick - Clara Benteen
Kelly Thordsen - Mel Woodley

Friendship is tested as the sons of Adam and Clara Benteen (Forrest Tucker and Ruth Warrick) allow a buffalo hunter take the blame for a murder they accidentally committed.
Production #1615-0456

380. CLAYTON THADDEUS GREENWOOD

Original air date: October 2, 1965
Directed by Joseph Sargent
Written by Calvin Clements
Starring:
Special Guest Jack Elam - Sam Band
Allen Jaffe - Webster
Glenn Strange - Sam
William Henry - Waiter
Paul Fix - Greenwood, Sr.
Sherwood Price - Frank Band
Robert Sorrells - Zachary
Introducing Roger Ewing - Clayton Thaddeus Greenwood

Thad (Roger Ewing) swears revenge on those who bullied his father (Paul Fix) into a fatal heart attack. He trails the men into Dodge City.
Production #1615-0454

381. TEN LITTLE INDIANS

Original air date: October 9, 1965
Directed by Mark Rydell
Written by George Eckstein
Starring:
Special Guest Nehemiah Persoff - Jack Pinto
Rafael Campos - Miguel Samando
Zalman King - Billy Coe
Nina Roman - Nancy
Stanja Lowe - Neddie Cannon
Don Ross - Lafe Cannon

THE BOUNTY HUNTER October 30, 1965. Amanda Blake, Milburn Stone and Robert Lansing.

THE STORM September 25, 1965. Ruth Warrick And Forrest Tucker.

Glenn Strange - Sam
Warren Oates - Al Tresh
John Marley - Ben Pringle
Bruce Dern - Doyle Phleger

A group of gunfighters arrive in Dodge believing a $25,000 bounty has been put on Matt's head. An old friend of the marshal (Nehemiah Persoff) enters the fray and the gunmen begin killing one another.
    Production #1615-0452

382. TAPS FOR OLD JEB

Original air date: October 16, 1965
Directed by James Sheldon
Written by Les Crutchfield
Starring:
Special Guest Ed Begley - Jeb Carter
Glenn Strange - Sam
Rudy Sooter - Rudy
Wayne Rogers - Stretch Morgan
Morgan Woodward - Sholo
Arthur Batanides - Feeter Kreb
Don Keefer - Milty Sims

Rugged old prospector Jeb (Ed Begley) brags he has struck it rich—news that invites robbery attempts.
    Production #1615-0463

383. KIOGA

Original air date: October 23, 1965
Directed by Harry Harris, Jr.
Written by Robert Lewin
Starring:
Special Guest Neville Brand - Jayce McCaw
Roy Roberts - Bodkin
John Hubbard - Storekeeper
Hank Patterson - Hank
Ken Renard - Father Kioga
Howard Culver - Howie
John War Eagle - Katawa
Nina Roman - Nancy

Glenn Strange - Sam
Catherine Wyles - Sister Kioga
Teno Pollick - Kioga

Kioga (Teno Pollick) tracks Jayce McCaw (Neville Brand) on foot after his father (Ken Renard) is murdered and his family robbed.
Production #1615-0453

384. THE BOUNTY HUNTER
Original air date: October 30, 1965
Directed by Harry Harris, Jr.
Written by Paul Savage
Starring:
Special Guest Robert Lansing - Luke Frazer
James Anderson - Hal
Hal Lynch - Ken
Gregg Palmer - Doak
Amber Flower - Amy Jensen
Glenn Strange - Sam
Charles Seel - Barney Danches
Victor Izay - Bartender
Jon Kowal - Rancher
Jason Johnson - Homesteader
Wright King - Lon Jensen
Bert Freed - Chris Thornton
Lisabeth Hush - Mal Jensen

Retired bounty hunter Luke Frazer (Robert Lansing) returns to work—causing suspicion and bewilderment when he begins tracking a suspected murderer who happens to be a respected farmer (Wright King).
Production #1615-0457

THE BOUNTY HUNTER October 30, 1965. Robert Lansing and Ken Curtis.

385. THE REWARD
Original air date: November 6, 1965
Directed by Marc Daniels
Written by Gilbert Ralston, Scott Hunt and Beth Keele
Starring:
Special Guest James Whitmore - Jim Forbes
Berkeley Harris - Farmer
Julio Medina - Pedro

Norman Burton - Ed
Sue Collier - Bar Girl
Roy Roberts - Botkin
Glenn Strange - Sam
James Nusser - Louie Pheeters
Gil Rankin - Hank Purvis
David Ladd - Brian Forbes
Peter Whitney - Jason Holt
Fred J. Scollay - Clint Fisher

Jim Forbes (James Whitmore) is a convicted swindler. After serving his time, he returns to Dodge bent on proving his innocence and squashing his cowardly image.
Production #1615-0462

386. **MALACHI**
Original air date: November 13, 1965
Directed by Gary Nelson
Written by William Putman
Starring:
Special Guest Harry Townes - Malachi Harper
Robert Sorrells - Bar Cowboy
Rex Holman - Shobin
Woodrow Chambliss - Knowles
Joey Wilcox - Boy
Glenn Strange - Sam
Hank Patterson - Hank
James Nusser - Louie Pheeters
Jack Elam - Del Ordman
Edward Andrews - Ethan Harper

Malachi Harper (Harry Townes) is a drunken bum who poses

as a marshal to impress his rich brother Ethan (Edward Andrews).
Production #1615-0461

387. **THE PRETENDER**
Original air date: November 20, 1965
Directed by Vincent McEveety
Written by Calvin Clements

THE REWARD November 6, 1965. David Ladd, Ken Curtis, James Whitmore, James Arness.

MALACHI November 13, 1965. Harry Townes guest stars as Malachi Harper.

THE AVENGERS December 18, 1965. James Gregory, John Saxon, Les Brown, Jr., Amanda Blake, Ken Curtis and Milburn Stone.

GOLD MINE December 25, 1965. Tom Nardini, Roger Ewing and Amanda Blake.

Starring:
Special Guests Tom Simcox - Frank Dano
Tom Skerritt - Edmund Dano
Athena Lorde - Mrs. Dano
Harry Davis - Daniels
Gregg Palmer - Sheriff Jackson
Sam Edwards - Stage Driver
Glenn Strange - Sam
Rudy Sooter - Rudy
Julie Sommars - Elsie Howell
Nehemiah Persoff - Mr. Dano

Returning from prison, brothers Frank and Edmund Dano (Tom Simcox and Tom Skerritt) must face their embittered father (Nehemiah Persoff).
Production #1615-0465

388. SOUTH WIND
Original air date: November 27, 1965
Directed by Allen Reisner
Written by Jack Bartlett
Starring:
Michael Whitney - Cavalry Captain
Ryan Hayes - Wade Bonney
Gregg Palmer - Blacksmith
Bruce Dern - Judd Print
Pat Cardi - Homer Bonney
Bob Random - Verlyn Print
Michael Davis - Coy Print

Homer Bonney (Pat Cardi) witnesses his father's murder and is left for dead on the prairie. Rescued by Doc, the boy is filled with hatred and swears revenge.
Production #1615-0460

389. THE HOSTAGE
Original air date: December 4, 1965
Directed by Vincent McEveety
Teleplay by Clyde Ware
Story by Joe Ann Johnson
Starring:
Special Guest Darren McGavin - Lon Gorman
Vito Scotti - Torreon
Willis Bouchey - Sheriff Hockley
Charles Seel - Barney
I. Stanford Jolley - Sheriff Foley
Glenn Strange - Sam
Tom Reese - Wade Keys
Simon Oakland - Carl Mandee

Festus and Thad trail four convicts who are fleeing to Mexico with a prisoner—Marshal Dillon.
Production # 1615-0455

390. OUTLAW'S WOMAN
Original air date: December 11, 1965
Directed by Mark Rydell
Written by Clyde Ware
Starring:
Special Guest Lane Bradbury - Allie Sommers
Gene Tyburn - Eddie
Ted Jordan - Hank Wheeler
Peggy Rea - Dress Shop Owner
Roy Barcroft - Jonas

Glenn Strange - Sam
Lou Antonio - Harve Kane
Lonny Chapman - Dove Bailey
Vincent Beck - Coley Martin

THE RAID January 22 & 29, 1966. Ken Curtis and James Arness.

Allie Sommers (Lane Bradbury) is drawn back into an outlaw gang when she is told Matt killed her brother. With revenge as her guide, she leads Matt into an ambush.
Production #1615-0468

391. THE AVENGERS
Original air date: December 18, 1965
Directed by Vincent McEveety
Written by Don Mullally
Starring:
Special Guest James Gregory -
    Judge Calvin Strom
Glenn Strange - Sam
Olan Soule - Barber
Ed McCready - Freight Agent
John Saxon - Cal Strom, Jr.
Les Brown, Jr. - Mark Strom

Festus kills the son of a twisted Judge (James Gregory) during an attack on Miss Kitty. His honor feels that Festus and Kitty conspired to kill his son and seeks to punish them "legally" in his court.
Production #1615-0467

392. GOLD MINE
Original air date: December 25, 1965
Directed by Abner Biberman
Written by Scott Hunt and Beth Keele
Starring:
Argentina Brunetti - Louise Danby
Dort Clark - Claims Clerk
John Harmon - Hotel Clerk
Glenn Strange - Sam
Russ Bender - Sheriff
John Anderson - Pa Gibbijoh
Paul Carr - Jud Gibbijohn

Michael Vandever - Ed Gibbijohn
Tom Nardini - Richard Danby

Kitty inherits a gold mine and Thad is asked to accompany here to her property. Their journey is fraught with outlaws, a dysfunctional family, even quicksand.
Production #1615-0464

393. DEATH WATCH
Original air date: January 8, 1966
Directed by Mark Rydell
Written by Calvin Clements
Starring:
Special Guest Albert Salmi - Holly
Ariane Quinn - Amy Boyle
Charles Wagenheim - Halligan
Robert Foulk - Fields
Karl Lukas - Williams
Steve Gravers - Wales
Glenn Strange - Sam
Howard Culver - Hotel CLerk
Sam Flint - Jake
Rudy Sooter - Bartender
Frank Silvera - John Drago
Richard Evans - Austin Boyle
Willard Sage - Walker
Alfred Ryder - Flint

Outlaw John Drago (Frank Silvera) is wounded by two bounty hunters who bring the man into Dodge to collect a $30,000 dollar reward from Mexico.
Production #1615-0466

THE RAID January 22 and 29, 1966. Richard Jaeckel and John Anderson.

394. SWEET BILLY, SINGER OF SONGS
Original air date: January 15, 1966
Directed by Alvin Ganzer
Written by Gustave Field
Starring:
Special Guest Bob Random - Sweet Billy
Diane Ladd - Lulu
Judy Carne - Pearl
Woodrow Chambliss - Waiter

Shug Fisher - Emery
Glenn Strange - Sam
Alice Backes - Widow Folsome
Brooke Bundy - Orabelle
Royal Dano - Lambert
Slim Pickens - Pony Beal

Another member of the Haggen family tree, Sweet Billy (Bob Random) comes into Dodge City looking for a woman to walk down the aisle with.
Production #1615-0469

395. **THE RAID - PART I**
Original air date: January 22, 1966
Directed by Vincent McEveety
Written by Clyde Ware
Starring:
Special Guest Gary Lockwood - Jim Stark
John Kellogg - T. R. Stark
Percy Helton - Mr. Early
Preston Pierce - Jeff Fraley
Ted Jordan - Shiloh
Glenn Strange - Sam
Edmund Hashim - Johnny Barnes
Dee Pollock - Tom Carlyle
Roy Engel - Sheriff
Tony Haig - Billy
Olan Soule - Barber
Charles Seel - Barney
Michael Fox - Hotel Clerk
Arthur Peterson - Banker
Gregg Palmer - Bartender
Jeremy Slate - Web Fraley
Jim Davis - Clell Williams

KILLER AT LARGE February 5, 1966. Geraldine Brooks and Ken Curtis.

Richard Jaeckel - Pence Fraley
Michael Conrad - Cash McLean
John Anderson - Les McConnell

All hell breaks loose when Jim Stark (Gary Lockwood) leads a ruthless band of outlaws on a bank robbing spree and into Dodge City.
Production #1615-0458

396. THE RAID - PART II
Original air date: January 29, 1966
Directed by Vincent McEveety
Written by Clyde Ware
Starring:
Special Guest Gary Lockwood - Jim Stark
John Kellogg - T. R. Stark
Percy Helton - Mr. Early
Preston Pierce - Jeff Fraley
Ted Jordan - Shiloh
Glenn Strange - Sam
William Fawcett - 1st Stage Man
James Nusser - Louie Pheeters
Leonard Greer - 1st Posse Man
Phil Chambers - 2nd Stage Man
Fred Coby - 3rd Stage Man
Jeremy Slate - Web Fraley
Jim Davis - Clell Williams
Richard Jaeckel - Pence Fraley
Michael Conrad - Cash McLean
John Anderson - Les McConnell

Death and destruction hits Dodge as Jim Stark (Gary Lockwood) and his gang rob the bank, set fire to the town and kidnap Doc.
Production #1615-0459

397. KILLER AT LARGE
Original air date: February 5, 1966
Directed by Marc Daniels
Written by Calvin Clements
Starring:
Special Guest Geraldine Brooks - Esther Harris
Stuart Erwin - Doc Brown
Tim O'Kelly - Sandy
Glenn Strange - Sam
Hardie Albright - Storekeeper
Gilman Rankin - Horse Trader
Cyril Delevanti - Grandpa Harris
Craig Hundley - James
John Pickard - Gabin
Jim Beggs - Jace
Robert Ballew - Grange
Jonathan Lippe - Ira
Morgan Jones - Coor

Festus leaves town after a killing a drunken medicine-show sharpshooter. Widow Esther Harris (Geraldine Brooks) helps him regain his confidence and face his problems.
Production #1615-0471

398. MY FATHER'S GUITAR
Original air date: February 12, 1966
Directed by Robert Totten
Written by Hal Sitowitz
Starring:
Special Guest Beau Bridges - Jason
Glenn Strange - Sam
Robin Blake - Mattie
Louis Massad - Cowboy
Steve Ihnat - Jack
Charles Dierkop - Dan
Dub Taylor - Sonny Starr
William Bramley - Jed Woodard

Young Jason (Beau Bridges) treasures the guitar that once belonged to his father more than anything else in the world.
Production #1615-0474

399. WISHBONE
Original air date: February 19, 1966
Directed by Marc Daniels
Written by Paul Savage
Starring:
Billy Beck - Tonkins
Michael Fox - Buffalo Hunter
Glenn Strange - Sam
Natalie Masters - First Gossip
Joan Granville - Second Gossip
Lew Gallo - Spellman
Victor French - Travers
Lyle Waggoner - Aikens

Matt is hot on the trail of the three murderers who robbed a stagecoach while Festus is hot on Doc's trail. Doc is bitten by a rattlesnake and Festus struggles to save his cantankerous friend's life.
Production #1615-0473

400. SANCTUARY
Original air date: February 26, 1966
Directed by Harry Harris, Jr.
Written by Calvin Clements
Starring:
Special Guest Sean Garrison - Reverend John Porter
Jack Grinnage - Gorman
Martin Priest - Baker
Charles Wagenheim - Halligan

Marcia Blakesley - Mrs. Ayers
Glenn Strange - Sam
Howard Culver - Howie
Woodrow Chambliss - Hotel Porter
Joan Blackman - Phyllis Bowmen
Virginia Gregg - Miss Howell
Larry Ward - Ayers
Richard Bradford - Paul Wiley

Doc is summoned to a church to treat a wounded bank robber, who is holding three people hostage, including Reverend Porter (Sean Garrison).
Production #1615-0472

401. HONOR BEFORE JUSTICE
Original air date: March 5, 1966
Directed by Harry Harris, Jr.
Teleplay by Frank Q. Dobbs
Story by Frank Q. Dobbs and Robert Stewart, Jr.
Starring:
Special Guest France Nuyen - Sarah
Ralph Moody - Joseph Walks In Darkness
George Keymas - Thunder Man
Ken Renard - Indian Blacksmith
Richard Gilden - Little Walker
James Almanzar - Barking Dog
Ted Jordan - Indian Policeman
Michael Ansara - Grey Horse
Barton MacLane - Herkimer Crawford
Harry Bartell - Elias Franklin
Noah Beery - John Two Bears

Thad tries to save pretty Indian Sarah's (France Nuyen) father who has just been sentenced to die for a crime he did not commit.

Production #1615-0475

402. THE BROTHERS

Original air date: March 12, 1966
Directed by Tay Garnett

HONOR BEFORE JUSTICE March 5, 1966. France Nuyen.

Written by Tom Hanley
Starring:
Special Guests Scott Marlowe - Ed
Bobby Crawford - Billy
Eddie Firestone - Carl Wilkins

Kathryn Harrow - Ellen Crandall
Roy Roberts - Mr. Botkin
James Nusser - Louie Pheeters
William Sailor Vincent - Peter Sommars
Tom Reese - Okie
   Warren Vanders - Wat
   Edmund Hashim - Durgen
   Joseph Hoover - Dave Crandall
   Mark Sturges - Will Taylor

An outlaw waits for his older brother to set him free and Matt's friends become targets of threatened violence.

Production #1615-0470

403. WHICH DR.

Original air date: March 19, 1966
Directed by Peter Graves
Written by Les Crutchfield
Starring:
Special Guest R. G. Armstrong - Argonaut
Gregg Palmer - Herk
Glenn Strange - Sam
Shelley Morrison - Addie
George Lindsey - Skeeter
Elisabeth Fraser - Daisy Lou
Claire Wilcox - Piney

Rest and relaxation is the last thing Doc and Festus enjoy while on a fishing trip—they are kidnapped by a group of buffalo hunters.

Production #1615-0476

PARSON COMES TO TOWN April 30, 1966. Sam Wanamaker.

404. **HARVEST**
Original air date: March 26, 1966
Directed by Harry Harris, Jr.

Written by Les Crutchfield
Starring:
Special Guest James MacArthur - David McGovern
Alma Platt - Gran McGovern
Ted Jordan - Leemer
Fred Coby - Marty
George Kennedy - Ben Payson
Karl Swenson - Ian McGovern
Lesley Ann Warren - Betsy Payson

Two fathers already in a dispute regarding land rights, now
have to deal with a romance between their children Betsy Payson
(Lesley Ann Warren) and David McGovern (James MacArthur).
Production #1615-0477

405. **BY LINE**
Original air date: April 9, 1966
Directed by Allen Reisner
Written by Les Crutchfield
Starring:
Special Guest Chips Rafferty - Angus McTabbott
Glenn Strange - Sam
Gertrude Flynn - Essie Benlan
Dorothy Neumann - Customer
Adrienne Marden - Townswoman
Johnny Francis - Store Clerk
Fletcher Fist - Cowboy
Denver Pyle - Clab Chummer
Dabbs Greer - Jonas
Ted DeCorsia - Merl Benlan
Maudie Prickett - Mrs. Preeker
Stefan Arngrim - Jock

He cannot read or write, so who better than Festus to work for the Dodge City newspaper?
Production #1615-0479

406. **TREASURE OF JOHN WALKING FOX**

Original air date: April 16, 1966
Directed by Marc Daniels
Teleplay by Clyde Ware
Story by Leo Bagby
Starring:
Special Guest Leonard Nimoy - John Walking Fox
Ted Gehring - Holtz
Tom McCauley - Banjo
Glenn Strange - Sam
Kelton Garwood - Percy Crump
Howard Culver - Howie
Richard Webb - Aaron Tigue
Lloyd Gough - Jacob Beamus
Jim Davis - Gainer

Old gold coins from a long lost treasure spark a fever in Dodge with mystery and bigotry surrounding the bearer, John Walking Fox (Leonard Nimoy).
Production #1615-0480

407. **MY FATHER, MY SON**

Original air date: April 23, 1966
Directed by Robert Totten
Written by Hal Sitowitz
Starring:
Special Guest Jack Elam - Jim Barrett
John McLiam - Doherty
Glenn Strange - Sam

Billy Halop - Bartender
Scott Hale - Gunsmith
James Nusser - Louie Pheeters
Teno Pollick - David Barrett
Lee Van Cleef - Ike Jeffords
Charles Kuenstle - Bernie Jeffords
Del Monroe - Will Jeffords
James Gammon - Arnie Jeffords
Zalman King - Joey Jeffords

Gunfighter Jim Barrett (Jack Elam) kills again and his victim's family, as well as his own son David Barrett (Teno Pollick), swear revenge.
Production #1615-0478

408. **PARSON COMES TO TOWN**

Original air date: April 30, 1966
Directed by Marc Daniels
Written by Verne Jay
Starring:
Special Guest Sam Wanamaker - Asa Longworth
Glenn Strange - Sam
Howard Culver - Howie
Hank Patterson - Hank
Kelton Garwood - Percy Crump
Ted Jordan - Burke
Woodrow Chambliss - Lathrop
Charles Wagenheim - Halligan
Elizabeth Rogers - Hostage
Joan Granville - Mother
Kevin Burchett - Boy
Lonny Chapman - Sipes
John McLiam - Dougherty

Asa Longworth (Sam Wanamaker) comes to Dodge City wearing the coat of a dead man. His purpose while in town? To watch a man die.

Production #1615-0482

409. PRIME OF LIFE

Original air date: May 7, 1966
Directed by Robert Totten
Written by Dan Ullman
Starring:
Special Guest Douglas Kennedy - John Stoner
Lyn Edgington - Wilma
Cal Naylor - Brad
Barbara Wilkin - Woman
Glenn Strange - Sam
James Nusser - Louie Pheeters
Ted French - Barkeep
Jonathan Lippe - Kyle Stoner
Joe Don Baker - Woody Stoner
Martin West - Jack Brown
Victor French - Joe Smith

Former lawman John Stoner (Douglas Kennedy) refuses to believe that his sons Woody and Kyle (Joe Don Baker and Jonathan Lippe) are murderous hold up men.

Production #1615-0481

SEASON TWELVE

Now produced and broadcast in color.

Produced by Philip Leacock

Associate Producer - John Mantley
Story Consultant - Paul Savage

410. SNAP DECISION

Original air date: September 17, 1966
Directed by Mark Rydell
Written by Dick Carr
Starring:
Sam Gilman - Gilcher
Glenn Strange - Sam
Hank Patterson - Hank
Howard Culver - Howie
Orville Sherman - Preacher
Claude Akins - Marshal Clint Tucker
Michael Strong - Shaver
Michael Cole - Kipp

Clint Tucker (Claude Akins) now wears the badge in Dodge when Matt resigns after being forced to kill a man who was once a friend.

Production #1615-0203

411. THE GOLDTAKERS

Original air date: September 24, 1966
Directed by Vincent McEveety
Written by Clyde Ware
Starring:
Special Guest Martin Landau - Britton
William Bramley - John Struck
Glenn Strange - Sam
John Boyer - Warner
Woodrow Chambliss - Garvey
Charles Wagenheim - Halligan

THE GOLDTAKERS September 24, 1966. Roger Ewing, Ken Curtis and Glenn Strange.

Ted Jordan - Burke
Roy Jenson - Troy
Brad Weston - Jenkins
Charles Francisco - Kale
Michael Greene - Holcroft
and Denver Pyle re-creating the role of Caleb Nash

Britton (Martin Landau) and his gang impersonate cavalry soldiers and arrive in Dodge to melt down a stolen gold shipment.
Production #1615-0204

412. THE JAILER
Original air date: October 1, 1966
Directed by Vincent McEveety
Written by Hal Sitowitz
Starring:
Special Guest Miss Bette Davis - Etta Stone
Bruce Dern - Lou Stone
Robert Sorrells - Mike Stone
Zalman King - Jack Stone
Glenn Strange - Sam
Tom Skerritt - Ben Stone
Julie Sommars - Sara Stone

Six years after the hanging of her husband, widow Etta Stone (Bette Davis) seeks revenge on Matt. When her sons are released from prison they kidnap Kitty, and their murderous plans are set in motion.
Production #1615-0206

413. THE MISSION
Original air date: October 8, 1966
Directed by Mark Rydell

Written by Richard Carr
Starring:
Rafael Campos - Young Soldier
Robert Tafur - Colonel Romero
Ruben Moreno - Captain
Mike Abelar - Soldier
Bert Madrid - Blacksmith

THE JAILER October 1, 1966. James Arness, Amanda Blake and Bette Davis.

Bob Random - Reb Jessup
Robert F. Simon - Colonel Amos Jessup
Steve Ihnat - Ashe
Warren Oates - Lafe
Arch Johnson - Sgt. Macklin
Jim Davis - Jim Basset

THE JAILER October 1, 1966. Amanda Blake and James Arness.

Three saddle bums confront Matt in Mexico and the marshal battles to regain his badge, horse and prisoner. Matt is wounded and falls under the care of Colonel Amos Jessup (Robert F. Simon).

Production #1615-0205

414. THE GOOD PEOPLE

Original air date: October 15, 1966
Directed by Robert Totten
Written by James Landis
Starring:
Steve Gravers - Jed Bailey
Glenn Strange - Sam
Charles Wagenheim - Halligan
Kelton Garwood - Percy Krump
Ted Jordan - Burke
Woodrow Chambliss - Lathrop
Clyde Howdy - Henry Biggs
Frederic Downs - Judge Evers
James O'Hara - Sutton
Allen Case - Gabe Rucker
Tom Simcox - Seth Rucker
Shug Fisher - Silas Shute
Morgan Woodward - Ben Rucker

Ben Rucker (Morgan Woodward) defiantly hangs an innocent man and lays the blame on a bounty hunter.

Production #1615-0210

415. GUNFIGHTER, R.I.P.

Original air date: October 22, 1966
Directed by Mark Rydell
Teleplay by Hal Sitowitz
Story by Michael Fisher
Starring:
Special Guests Darren McGavin - Joe Bascome

France Nuyen - Ching Lee
Don Hammer - Barber
H. T. Tsiang - Chung Fa
Glenn Strange - Sam
Allen Emerson - Burt
Stefan Gierasch - Mark Douglas
Michael Conrad - Paul Douglas

While Ching Lee (France Nuyen) nurses wounded Joe Bascome (Darren McGavin) back to health, the gunfighter begins

MAD DOG January 14, 1967. George Lindsey and Ken Curtis.

to have second thoughts regarding his latest assignment—killing Matt Dillon.

Production #1615-0215

416. THE WRONG MAN
Original air date: October 29, 1966
Directed by Robert Totten
Teleplay by Clyde Ware
Story by Robert Lewin
Starring:

Special Guest Carroll O'Connor - Hootie Kyle
Glenn Strange - Sam
James Almanzar - Morell
Mel Gaines - Squeak
Gilman Rankin - Purvis
Victor Izay - Dutch
Terry Frost - Stage Driver
Kevin O'Neal - James Kyle
Charles Kuenstle - Wilton Kyle
Clifton James - Tenner Jackson
James Anderson - Harmon

Farmer Hootie Kyle (Carroll O'Connor) loses his money in a poker game. When the game winner is later found robbed and murdered, the evidence points to Hootie.

Production #1615-0208

417. THE WHISPERING TREE
Original air date: November 12, 1966
Directed by Vincent McEveety
Written by Calvin Clements

Starring:
Special Guest John Saxon - Virgil Stanley
Donald Losby - Bryant
Christopher Pate - Curtis
Rex Holman - Garr
Allen Jaffe - Ryan
Roy Barcroft - Roy
Ted Jordan - Burke
Fred Coby - Station Attendant
Kathleen O'Malley - Mother
Stephen McEveety - Boy
Lane Chandler - Guard
Jacqueline Scott - Ada Stanley
Edward Asner - Redmond
Morgan Woodward - Earl Miller

After serving several years in prison, Virgil Stanley (John Saxon) returns home to his wife Ada (Jacqueline Scott) and family. Virgil begins searching for stolen money he had hidden on his property.
Production #1615-0201

418. THE WELL
Original air date: November 19, 1966
Directed by Marc Daniels
Written by Francis Cockrell
Starring:
Elizabeth Rogers - Mrs. Davis
Glenn Strange - Sam
Woodrow Chambliss - Lathrop
Charles Wagenheim - Halligan
Ted Jordan - Burke
Ted Gehring - Boyd

MAD DOG January 14, 1967. Ken Curtis.

Karl Lukas - Lake
Pete Kellett - Monk
Robert Ballew - Tim Grady
Madgel Dean - Mother
Guy Raymond - Dr. Tobias
Joan Payne - Janie
Lawrence Casey - Jim Libby

421

Dodge City is hit hard with a drought and Matt permits a rainmaker to try and work his magic, much to the relief of of the townspeople.

Production #1615-0209

419. STAGE STOP

Original air date: November 26, 1966
Directed by Irving J. Moore
Written by Hal Sitowitz
Starring:
Special Guest John Ireland - Jed Coombs
Michael Vandever - Lingo
Sid Haig - Wade Hansen
Glenn Strange - Sam
Andy Albin - Charlie Woodson
Anne Whitfield - Lori Coombs
Joseph Ruskin - Curt Hansen
Steve Raines - Driver
Jack Ging - Simon Dobbs

Doc is armed and dangerous during attempted robberies on a stagecoach and later at a waystation. The station master (John Ireland) is in on the bandits' plans.

Production #1615-0212

420. THE NEWCOMERS

Original air date: December 3, 1966
Directed by Robert Totten
Written by Calvin Clements
Starring:
Daniel Addis - Vasquez
Glenn Strange - Sam
Laurence Aten - Joey

John Pickard - Vigilante
Karl Swenson - Lars Karlgren
Jon Voight - Petter Karlgren
Robert Sorrells - Handley
Ben Wright - Birger Engdahl
James Murdock - Pony
Charles Dierkop - Silvee

Immigrant Lars Karlgren (Karl Swenson) is confronted by a blackmailer who states he saw his son Petter (Jon Voight) commit a murder.

Production #1615-0218

421. QUAKER GIRL

Original air date: December 10, 1966
Directed by Bernard L. Kowalski
Written by Preston Wood
Starring:
Special Guest William Shatner - Fred Bateman
William Bryant - Kester
Glenn Strange - Sam
Joseph Breen - George
Anna Karen - 1st Woman
Nancy Marshal - 2nd Woman
Ariane Quinn - Cora Ellis
Liam Sullivan - Benjamin Ellis
Warren Vanders - John Thenly
Ben Johnson - Vern Morland
Timothy Carey - Charles "Buster" Rilla
Tom Reese - Dave Westerfeldt

After a brutal fight, Thad is mistaken for outlaw Fred Bateman (William Shatner) while the two recover at a

Quaker settlement.
Production #1615-0202

422. THE MOONSTONE
Original air date: December 17, 1966

OLD FRIEND February 4, 1967. Fritz Weaver and Amanda Blake.

Directed by Dick Colla
Written by Paul Savage
Starring:
Special Guest Mike Kellin - Chad Timpson
Glenn Strange - Sam
Ted Jordan - Burke
Fred Coby - Rankin

Jeff Palmer - Todd
Tom Skerritt - Orv Timpson
Gail Kobe - Madge
Warren Kemmerling - Del Phillips

The past catches up with Chad Timpson (Mike Kellin) when his former partner in crime Del Phillips (Warren Kemmerling) is released from prison.
Production #1615-0216

423. CHAMPION OF THE WORLD
Original air date: December 24, 1966
Directed by Marc Daniels
Written by Les Crutchfield
Starring:
Special Guest Alan Hale - Bull Bannock
Don Keefer - Wally
Glenn Strange - Sam
Ted Jordan - Burke
Charles Wagenheim - Halligan
Jane Dulo - Cora Argyle
Arthur Peterson - Drunk
Ralph Rose - Gopher Freely
Pete Kellett - Mac
Troy Melton - Zac
Dan Tobin - Professor
John McLiam - Dougherty
Gale Robbins - Maude

THE FAVOR March 11, 1967. James Daly and Amanda Blake.

Former heavyweight boxing champ Bull Bannock (Alan Hale, Jr.) tries to woo Miss Kitty into selling him the Long Branch saloon.
Production #1615-0214

424. THE HANGING

Original air date: December 31, 1966

Directed by Bernard L. Kowalski
Teleplay by Calvin Clements
Story by Calvin Clements, Jr.
Starring:
Edmund Hashim - Saline
Glenn Strange - Sam
Hank Patterson - Hank
Charles Wagenheim - Halligan
Ted Jordan - Burke
Byron Foulger - Ollie
Tom Stern - Billy Boles
Kit Smythe - Ivy
Robert Knapp - Warren
Henry Darrow - Oro
Anna Navarro - Maria
Larry Ward - Preston
Morgan Woodward - Beaumont
Richard Bakalyan - Teems

Gallows are being built in Dodge as the accused vows never to swing from a rope.
Production #1615-0207

425. SATURDAY NIGHT

Original air date: January 7, 1967
Directed by Robert Totten
Written by Clyde Ware
Starring:
Special Guest Leif Erickson - Virgil Powell
Louis Massad - Bert
John Garwood - Shep
Al Dunlap - Herrick
Link Harget - Lucky
Glenn Strange - Sam

Clyde Howdy - Ed Underwood
Frederic Downs - Mr. Titus
Rudy Sooter - Rudy
Victor French - C. K. Ross
Dub Taylor - Cook
James Almanzar - Houndog
Lawrence Mann - Chick
William Watson - Carl Craddock

Trail boss Virgil Powell (Leif Erickson) saves Matt and his prisoner Carl Craddock (William Watson) after they drink poisoned water from a well.
Production #1615-0220

426. **MAD DOG**

Original air date: January 14, 1967
Directed by Charles R. Rondeau
Written by Jay Simms
Starring:
George Murdock - Jim Travers
Butch Patrick - Tom John
Glenn Strange - Sam
Bert Madrid - Townsman
George Lindsey - Pinto Watson
Sammy Reese - Buff Watson
Hoke Howell - Roan Watson
Iggie Wolfington - Mayor Juke Wheeler
Dub Taylor - Bartender
Denver Pyle - Dr. Henry S. Rand

The three Watson brothers (George Lindsey, Sammy Reese and Hoke Howell) think Festus is a notorious hired gunfighter.
Production #1615-0217

427. **MULEY**

Original air date: January 21, 1967
Directed by Allen Reisner
Written by Les Crutchfield
Starring:
Special Guest Lane Bradbury - Lucky
Glenn Strange - Sam
Ted Jordan - Burke
Howard Culver - Howie
Zalman King - Muley
Anthony Call - Pell
Marc Cavell - Arky
Ross Hagen - Kay Cee

Muley (Zalman King) wants to kill Matt and rob the bank, but his thoughts of a pretty girl named Lucky (Lane Bradbury) cloud his mind.
Production #1615-0213

428. **MAIL DROP**

Original air date: January 28, 1967
Directed by Robert Totten
Written by Calvin Clements
Starring:
Special Guests Eddie Hodges - Billy Johnson
John Anderson - Roberts
Glenn Strange - Sam
Woodrow Chambliss - Lathrop
Sarah Selby - Ma Smalley
James Nusser - Louie Pheeters
Steve Raines - Steve
Ted French - Jeb
Bing Russell - Walsh

A young runaway named Billy Johnson (Eddie Hodges) befriends Festus until he sees his father's image on a wanted poster in Matt's office.

Production #1615-0222

429. OLD FRIEND

Original air date: February 4, 1967
Directed by Allen Reisner
Written by Clyde Ware
Starring:
Special Guest Fritz Weaver - Marshal Burl Masters
James Chandler - Vern
Robert B. Williams - Charley
William Benedict - Gus
Glenn Strange - Sam
Joe Haworth - Drover
Kelton Garwood - Percy Crump
Pete Dunn - Willie
Delphi Lawrence - Willa
Valentino DeVargas - Cheeno
Carlos Rivas - Trail
David Renard - Boley
Lew Brown - Fret Smith

Marshal Burl Masters (Fritz Weaver) is a "shoot first ask questions later" lawman who arrives in Dodge counting on his friendship with Matt to round up an outlaw gang.

Production #1615-0211

430. FANDANGO

Original air date: February 11, 1967
Directed by James Landis
Written by Don Ingalls

Starring:
Joe Higgins - Smithy
Walter Baldwin - Old Man
Fletcher Bryant - Ben Tyson
Mario Alcalde - Lorca
Diana Muldaur - Laurel Tyson
Paul Fix - Doc Lacey
Shug Fisher - Chengra
Torin Thatcher - John Tyson

Matt and his prisoner Lorca (Mario Alcade) are being pursued by John Tyson (Torin Thatcher), bent on avenging his brother's death.

Production #1615-0219

431. THE RETURNING

Original air date: February 18, 1967
Directed by Marc Daniels
Written by James Landis
Starring:
Special Guest Lois Nettleton - Amy Todd
Kenneth Mars - Clyde Hayes
Glenn Strange - Sam
Roy Barcroft - Jonas
Ted Jordan - Burke
Roy Roberts - Mr. Bodkin
Billy Halop - Barney
Troy Melton - Barton
Michael Ansara - Luke Todd
Steve Sanders - Ethan Todd
Johnnie Whitaker - Shem Todd
Jonathan Lippe - Billy Judd
Richard Webb - Will Hayes

Amy Todd (Lois Nettleton) is an honest but struggling woman faced with the temptation of spending $20,000 stolen by her husband (Michael Ansara) and his buddies.

Production #1615-0221

432. THE LURE

Original air date: February 25, 1967
Directed by Marc Daniels
Written by Clyde Ware
Starring:
Special Guests Stephen McNally - Dal Neely
Kim Darby - Carrie Neely
Woodrow Chambliss - Swiger
Len Wayland - Station Master
Fred Coby - Stage Driver
Ted Jordan - Burke
Troy Melton - Hennington
Mike Jeffers - Bank Manager
Martin Brooks - Young
Val Avery - Trent
Warren Vanders - Boles
Paul Picerni - McGee
John Pickard - Vanner

Kitty is in the eye of the storm when she is put between outlaw Dal Neely (Stephen McNally) and his estranged daughter Carrie (Kim Darby).

Production #1615-0224

433. NOOSE OF GOLD

Original air date: March 4, 1967
Directed by Irving J. Moore
Written by Preston Wood

Starring:
Special Guest Steve Ihnat - John Farron
Barton MacLane - Willard Kerner
Glenn Strange - Sam
Ted Jordan - Burke
Charles Wagenheim - Halligan
Jack Bailey - Ben Leary
Harry Basch - Milt Agnew
Robert B. Williams - Sheriff Porter
Michael Preece - Harry Barnes
Sam Gilman - Jim Gunther
Vincent Gardenia - Charles Shepherd
Jan Shepard - Edna Farron

Assistant attorney-general Charles Shepherd (Vincent Gardenia) uses his friendship to capture fugitive John Farron (Steve Ihnat).

Production #1615-0226

434. THE FAVOR

Original air date: March 11, 1967

Directed by Marc Daniels
Written by Don Ingalls
Starring:
Special Guest James Daly - John Crowley
Glenn Strange - Sam
Troy Melton - Stage Driver
Shirley Wilson - Townswoman
Fred J. Scollay - Morgan Haley
William Bramley - Adam Haley
Lew Gallo - Kelly Bates
Diane Ladd - Bonnie Mae Haley

Kitty has to make a tough decision—turn in wanted John Crowley (James Daly) who once saved her life—or ignore the law and worst of all, Matt.

Production #1615-0223

435. MISTAKEN IDENTITY

Original air date: March 18, 1967
Directed by Robert Totten
Written by Paul Savage and
    Les Crutchfield
Starring:
Special Guest Albert Salmi -
    Ed Carstairs
Hal Lynch - Mel Gates
Ken Mayer - Timmons
Sam Melville - Dunster
Ted Jordan - Nathan Burke

Matt and Thad bring ailing cowboy Mel Gates (Hal Lynch) to Dodge only to discover a fugitive (Albert Salmi) has been posing as the man for some time.

Production #1615-0277

436. LADIES FROM ST. LOUIS

Original air date: March 25, 1967
Directed by Irving J. Moore
Written by Clyde Ware
Starring:
Special Guest Claude Akins -
    Worth Sweeney
Henry Darrow - Segurra

John Carter - Doyle
Vic Tayback - Gaines
Ralph Roberts - Williams
Lew Brown - Outlaw
Lois Roberts - Sister Louise
Venita Wolf - Sister Margaret

LADIES FROM ST. LOUIS March 25, 1967. Aneta Corsaut, Lois Roberts, Venita Wolf, Kelly Jean Peters, Josephine Hutchinson and Ken Curtis.

Glenn Strange - Sam
Ted Jordan - Burke
Josephine Hutchinson - Sister Ellen
Aneta Corsaut - Sister Ruth
Kelly Jean Peters - Sister John

Believing wounded outlaw Worth Sweeney (Claude Akins) saved their lives, a group of traveling nuns bring the man into Dodge but are reluctant to turn their hero over to the law.
Production #1615-0228

437. NITRO! - PART I
Original air date: April 8, 1967
Directed by Robert Totten
Written by Preston Wood
Starring:
Robert Rothwell - Joe Keller
Dub Taylor - Farnum
Glenn Strange - Sam
Gene O'Donnell - Express Manager
Pete Kellett - Cowboy
Carl Pitti - Gambler
John Breen - Waiter
David Canary - George McClaney
Bonnie Beecher - Anne Gilchrist
Tom Reese - Ben Stearman
Eddie Firestone - Red Bailey

To court Bonnie Beecher (Anne Gilchrist), young drifter George McClaney (David Canary) earns money by extracting nitroglycerine from sticks of dynamite for a gang of bank robbers.
Production #1615-0225

438. NITRO! - PART II
Original air date: April 15, 1967
Directed by Robert Totten
Written by Preston Wood
Starring:
Dub Taylor - Farnum
Robert Rothwell - Joe Keller
Scott Hale - Dying Man
Glenn Strange - Sam
Howard Culver - Hotel Clerk
David Canary - George McClaney
Bonnie Beecher - Anne Gilchrist
Tom Reese - Ben Stearman
Eddie Firestone - Red Bailey

George McClaney (David Canary) agrees to make one last batch of nitroglycerin for outlaw Ben Stearman (Tom Reese) and his gang.
Production #1615-0230

SEASON THIRTEEN

Now on Monday evenings from 7:30 to 8:30.

Produced by John Mantley
Associate Producer - Joseph Dackow
Story Consultant - Paul Savage

439. THE WRECKERS
Original air date: September 11, 1967
Directed by Robert Totten

THE WRECKERS September 11, 1967. Amanda Blake and James Arness.

Written by Hal Sitowitz
Starring:
Warren Oates - Tate Crocker
Charles Seel - Eli
Warren Vanders - Reb
Trevor Bardette - Clete Walker
Rex Holman - Frankie
James Almanzar - Indio
Gene Rutherford - Jud
Charles Kuenstle - Luke
Edmund Hashim - Monk Wiley
James Nusser - Louie Pheeters
Glenn Strange - Sam
Ted Jordan - Burke
Lew Brown - Ben Paisley
Charles Wagenheim - Halligan
Joe Haworth - Townsman
Bobby E. Clark - Stage Attendant
Jerry Brown - Shotgun Rider
Joe Yrigoyen, Sr. - Stage Driver
Bob Duggan - Man

After bandits cause their stage to wreck, Kitty makes a desperate attempt to conceal Matt's identity by pinning his badge on unconscious convict Monk Wiley (Edmund Hashim).
Production #1615-0251

440. CATTLE BARONS
Original air date: September 18, 1967
Directed by Gunnar Hellstrom
Written by Clyde Ware
Starring:
Special Guests Forrest Tucker - John Charron

Robert Wilke - Luke Cumberledge
John Milford - Blair Smith
Lew Brown - Frank Holtz
Robert Sampson - McKenny
Brad Johnson - Laskin
Fred Coby - Tooley
Woodrow Chambliss - Lathrop
James Nusser - Louie Pheeters
Charles Wagenheim - Halligan
Steven Liss - Boy
Mike Howden - Drover
Clyde Howdy - Cowboy
Hank Wise - Townsman

Matt is in the middle of two feuding cattle barons (Forrest Tucker and Robert Wilke) during a massive cattle drive.
Production #1615-0261

441. THE PRODIGAL
Original air date: September 25, 1967
Directed by Bernard McEveety
Written by Calvin Clements
Starring:
Special Guest Lew Ayres - Jonathan Cole
Charles Robinson - Amos Cole
Richard Evans - William Cole
Lee Krieger - Eli
Lamont Johnson - Stoner
Kelly Thordsen - Regal
Ted Gehring - Lemuel
Glenn Strange - Sam
Charles Wagenheim - Halligan
James Nusser - Louie Pheeters

A slick journalist convinces a family and Matt to reopen a twelve-year old case and everyone in town seems to cover up for the prime suspect—the marshal himself.

Production #1615-0229

442. **VENGEANCE! - PART I**

Original air date: October 2, 1967
Directed by Richard Sarafian
Written by Calvin Clements
Starring:
James Stacy - Bob Johnson
Special Guest John Ireland - Parker
Kim Darby - Angel
Buck Taylor - Leonard Parker
Paul Fix - Sloan
James Anderson - Hiller
Royal Dano - Rory Luken
Victor French - Eben Luken
Sandy Kelvin - Floyd Binnes
Glenn Strange - Sam
James Nusser - Louie Pheeters
Ted Jordan - Burke
Rudy Sooter - Rudy
Morgan Woodward - Zack Johnson

Matt tries to help drifter Bob Johnson (James Stacy) after Parker (John Ireland) and his men rough him up and kill two of his friends.

Production #1615-0252

443. **VENGEANCE! - PART II**

Original air date: October 9, 1967
Directed by Richard Sarafian
Written by Calvin Clements
Starring:
James Stacy - Bob Johnson
Special Guest John Ireland - Parker
Kim Darby - Angel
Buck Taylor - Leonard Parker
Paul Fix - Sloan
James Anderson - Hiller
Royal Dano - Rory Luken
Victor French - Eben Luken
Morgan Woodward - Zack Johnson

Johnson (James Stacy) is ordered out of Dodge after he kills Parker's (John Ireland) son Leonard (Buck Taylor). He plans on finishing the job and rides straight into Parker's town.

Production #1615-0253

444. **A HAT**

Original air date: October 16, 1967
Directed by Robert Totten
Written by Ron Bishop
Starring:
Special Guest Chill Wills - Red Conniston
Tom Simcox - Jed and Ben Conniston
Robert Sorrells - Louieville
Glenn Strange - Sam
Ted Jordan - Burke
Hank Patterson - Hank
Scott Hale - Clem
Gene O'Donnell - Waiter
Bill Erwin - Townsman
Ed McCready - Villager
Lee DeBroux - Cowpuncher

THE PRODIGAL September 25, 1967. James Arness, Charles Robinson and Ken Curtis.

Don Happy - Storekeeper
Shirley Wilson - Wife
Gene Evans - Clint Sorils
H. M. Wynant - Martin Brewer

Clint Sorils (Gene Evans) and Red Conniston (Chill Wills) are caught up in a life or death struggle—over a hat.
Production #1615-0254

445. **HARD LUCK HENRY**
Original air date: October 23, 1967
Directed by John Rich
Written by Warren Douglas
Starring:
Special Guest John Astin - Hard-Luck Henry Haggen
Royal Dano - Jefferson Dooley
Ken Drake - Sheriff
Michael Fox - Jed Walsh
Mary Lou Taylor - Martha Walsh
Bobby Riha - Charlie Walsh
Glenn Strange - Sam
Ted Jordan - Burke
Anthony James - Reb Dooley
John Shank - Truly Dooley
and "The Haggens"
    Charles Kuenstle - Homer
    Bo Hopkins - Harper
    Mayf Nutter - Heathcliffe

Festus and a chest filled with gold help fuel an already hot mix-up with the Haggen bunch, including Hard Luck Henry Haggen (John Astin).
Production #1615-0262

446. MAJOR GLORY

Original air date: October 30, 1967

Directed by Robert Totten

Teleplay by Dick Carr

Story by Dick Carr and Clyde Ware

Special Guest Carroll O'Connor - Major Vanscoy

Lawrence Mann - Lanny

Russ Siler - Guard

William L. Sumper - Soldier

Victor French - Sgt. Spear

Robert F. Lyons - Maxwell

Link Wyler - Doak

Two army deserters are planning to kill the sergeant (Victor French) who is trailing them. Festus is framed for the attack on the sergeant and Matt and Major Vanscoy (Carroll O'Connor) square off over the charges.

Production #1615-0257

447. THE PILLAGERS

Original air date: November 6, 1967

Directed by Vincent McEveety

Written by Calvin Clements

Starring:

Special Guest John Saxon - Pedro Manez

Vito Scotti - Savrin

Paul Picerni - Ganns

William Bramley - Turner

Buck Taylor - Newly O'Brian (became O'Brien later)

Allen Jaffe - Johns

Glenn Strange - Sam

Harry Harvey, Sr. - Eli

Ted Jordan - Burke

Joseph Schneider - Juan

THE PRODIGAL September 25, 1967. Lew Ayres and Milburn Stone.

Don G. Ross - Cobb

Cal Naylor - Corporal

Chris Stephens - Corporal Of Guard

Young gunsmith Newly (Buck Taylor) and Miss Kitty are abducted by Pedro Manez (John Saxon) and his gang. By threat of death, Newly is forced to doctor Manez' wounded brother Juan

(Joseph Schneider).
Production #1615-0259

448. PRAIRIE WOLFER
Original air date: November 13, 1967
Directed by Robert Butler
Written by Calvin Clements
Starring:
Special Guest Jon Voight - Cory
Lou Antonio - Rich
Kelly Jean Peters - Adele
Charles McGraw - Dolen
I. Stanford Jolley - Grandpa
Glenn Strange - Sam
Ted Jordan - Burke
Matt Emery - Trail Boss

When Festus is left in charge, misinformation leads two trappers (Jon Voight and Lou Antonio) to steal $20,000 in place of the money due them for their pelts.
Production #1615-0255

449. STRANGER IN TOWN
Original air date: November 20, 1967
Directed by Darrell Hallenbeck
Teleplay by John Dunkel
Story by John Dunkel and Emily Mosher
Starring:
Special Guests Pernell Roberts - Dave Reeves
Jacqueline Scott - Anne Madison
R. G. Armstrong - Carl Anderson
Henry Jones - Harvey Cagle
Eric Shea - Billy Madison

A HAT October 16, 1967. Ken Curtis and Chill Wills.

Billy Halop - Bartender
Jon Kowal - Shamrock Casey
Jerry Catron - Victim
James Nusser - Louie Pheeters
Glenn Strange - Sam
Kerry MacLane - Spud

Hired gun Dave Reeves (Pernell Roberts) arrives in Dodge to kill Carl Anderson (R. G. Armstrong). His job takes a strange

twist when he discovers that Anderson has been courting his estranged wife Anne (Jacqueline Scott).
Production #1615-0263

450. **DEATH TRAIN**

Original air date: November 27, 1967
Directed by Gunnar Hellstrom
Written by Ken Trevey
Starring:
Special Guests Dana Wynter - Isabel Townsend
Morgan Woodward - Harl Townsend
Norman Alden - Purlie Loftus
Buck Taylor - Newly
Mort Mills - Jack Marple
Ed Bakey - Reverend Bright
Zalman King - Willy Groom
Sam Melville - Zack Hodges
Trevor Bardette - Conductor

Matt must quarantine a private train owned by Harl and Isabel Townsend (Morgan Woodward and Dana Wynter) due to a threat of spotted fever. Doc puts his own life on the line to treat the ill passengers.
Production # 1615-0264

451. **ROPE FEVER**

Original air date: December 4, 1967
Directed by David Alexander
Written by Chris Rellas
Starring:
Special Guest Ralph Bellamy - Sheriff Bassett
Anna Lee - Amy Bassett
George Murdock - Bret Gruber

STRANGER IN TOWN November 20, 1967. Pernell Roberts and Amanda Blake.

Sam Gilman - Bates
Buck Taylor - Newly
Ken Mayer - Shad
Hal Baylor - Luke Summers
Dennis Cross - Zeb Butler
Ted Gehring - Keno
Glenn Strange - Sam
Hank Patterson - Hank

DEATH TRAIN November 27, 1967. Norman Alden and Dana Wynter.

Gertrude Flynn - Townswoman

Sheriff Bassett (Ralph Bellamy) feels important again after killing a bank robber and arresting Festus on a trumped-up charge.
Production #1615-0260

452. **WONDER**
Original air date: December 18, 1967

Directed by Irving J. Moore
Teleplay by William Blinn
Story by Mary Worrell and William Blinn
Starring:
Richard Mulligan - Jud Pryor
Norman Alden - Deke Franklin
Warren Berlinger - Ed Franklin
Jackie Russell - Annie Franklin
Fay Spain - Willy
Ken Swofford - Bo Warrick
Tony Davis - Wonder

Matt assists an Indian boy named Wonder (Tony Davis) and his drifter friend Jud Pryor (Richard Mulligan) when they are threatened by cowboys with a score to settle.
Production #1615-0258

453. **BAKER'S DOZEN**
Original air date: December 25, 1967
Directed by Irving J. Moore
Written by Charles Joseph Stone
Starring:
Peggy Rea - Mrs. Roniger
Harry Carey - Will Roniger
Harry Lauter - Henry Rucker
Mitzi Hoag - Clara Remick
Ed McCready - Fred Remick
Buck Taylor - Newly
Sam Greene - Robber
James Nusser - Louie Pheeters
Denver Pyle - Judge Blent
Ted Jordan - Burke
Phyllis Coghlan - Old Lady

DEATH TRAIN November 27, 1967. Milburn Stone and Dana Wynter.

Charles Wagenheim - Halligan
Tyler MacDuff - Bailiff
William Murphy - Monk
Dana Dillaway - Mary
Keith Schultz - Timothy

Gary Grimes - Bede

After delivering triplets, Doc must take care of the little ones after their mother dies. Matt, Kitty and Festus pitch in and lend a much needed hand.
Production #1615-0265

454. THE VICTIM

Original air date: January1, 1968
Directed by Vincent McEveety
Teleplay by Arthur Rowe
Story by Hal Sitowitz
Starring:
Special Guests James Gregory - Wes Martin
Beverly Garland - Lee Stark
Cliff Osmond - Bo Remick
John Kellogg - Sheriff Joe Wood
Kevin Hagen - Judge Josh Pike
Warren Vanders - Lefty
Edmund Hashim - Brock
Roy Jenson - Crow
Willis Bouchey - Jim Stark
Gregg Palmer - Deputy Reed
Tim O'Kelly - Billy Martin

Bo Remick (Cliff Osmond) is a big but simple minded man who cares deeply for Lee Stark (Beverly Garland). When he defends her honor and kills Billy Martin (Tim O'Kelly), his maniacal father (James Gregory) swears revenge.
Production #1615-0268

455. DEADMAN'S LAW

Original air date: January 7, 1968

Directed by John Rich
Written by Calvin Clements, Jr.
Starring:
Special Guests John Dehner - Sam Wall
Gunnar Hellstrom - Eriksson
Buck Taylor - Newly
Eddie Little Sky - The Indian
Craig Curtis - Sonny
Ralph Manza - Marco
Gregg Palmer - Fry
Robert Brubaker - Head Wrangler
Steve Raines - Trail Boss
Baynes Barron - Newt
Alex Sharp - Rustler
Glenn Strange - Sam
Ted Jordan - Burke
Woodrow Chambliss - Lathrop
James Nusser - Louie
Hank Patterson - Hank
Jonathan Harper -Percy Crump

Matt is presumed dead but Kitty, Doc and Festus refuse to believe this. To make matters worse, members of a cattleman's association want to take over the law in Dodge.
Production #1615-0269

456. NOWHERE TO RUN
Original air date: January 15, 1968
Directed by Vincent McEveety
Teleplay by Ron Honthaner
Story by Robert Totten
Starring:
Mark Lenard - Ira Stonecipher

ROPE FEVER December 4, 1967. Ken Curtis and Ralph Bellamy.

Ilka Windish - Vera Stonecipher
Bob Random - Bishop
J. Robert Porter - Mark Stonecipher
Buck Taylor - Newly
Dan Ferrone - Honker

Tom Brown - Ed O'Connor
Michael Burns - Dale Stonecipher
Glenn Strange - Sam
Harry Harvey, Sr. - Storekeeper
William Tannen - John Hirschbeck
Ted Jordan - Burke
Woodrow Chambliss - Lathrop
James Nusser - Louie Pheeters
Charles Wagenheim - Halligan

Young Mark Stonecipher (J. Robert Porter) runs with wrong crowd (Bob Random and Dan Ferrone) that results in a deadly robbery.
Production #1615-0270

457. **BLOOD MONEY**
Original air date: January 22, 1968
Directed by Robert Totten
Written by Hal Sitowitz
Starring:
Special Guest Nehemiah Persoff - Alex Skouras
Anthony Zerbe - Nick Skouras
Donna Baccala - Elenya Skouras
Buck Taylor - Newly
James Anderson - Jesse Hill
Hank Brandt - Hank
Mills Watson - Brent
Jonathan Harper - Percy Crump
Howard Culver - Howie
Michelle Breeze - Saloon Girl
Glenn Strange - Sam
James Nusser - Louie Pheeters
Troy Melton - Jake Walker
Lee De Broux - Stu Radford

Gunfighter Nick Skouras (Anthony Zerbe) has his gun hand shot by his father (Nehemiah Persoff), in a drastic attempt to change his ways.
Production #1615-0267

458. **HILL GIRL**
Original air date: January 29, 1968
Directed by Robert Totten
Written by Calvin Clements

BAKER'S DOZEN December 25, 1967. James Arness, Milburn Stone, Amanda Blake and Ken Curtis.

Starring:
Special Guest Lane Bradbury - Merry Florene
Victor French - Roland
Anthony James - Elbert
Buck Taylor - Newly
Dabbs Greer - Jonas
Glenn Strange - Sam
Ted Jordan - Burke

Newly is involved with Merry Florene (Lane Bradbury), a pretty hill girl, but her brothers (Victor French and Anthony James) have other plans.
Production #1615-0273

459. THE GUNRUNNERS
Original air date: February 5, 1968
Directed by Irving J. Moore
Written by Hal Sitowitz
Starring:
Special Guest Michael Constantine - Noah Meek
Jim Davis - Jubal Gray
Dick Peabody - Patch
James Griffith - Wade Lester
John McLiam - Bender
Dan Ferrone - Tahrohon
Lane Bradford - Reese
X Brands - Singleton
Glenn Strange - Sam

Aged trapper Noah Meek (Michael Constantine) seeks those who severely wounded his Indian companion Tahrohon (Dan Ferrone).
Production #1615-0272

460. THE JACKALS
Original air date: February 12, 1968
Directed by Alvin Ganzer
Written by Calvin Clements, Jr.
Starring:
Special Guest Paul Richards - Mel Deevers
Tige Andrews - Santillo
Felice Orlandi - Emilio
Ward Wood - Bates
Michael Vandever - Poorly
Alex Montoya - Bandito
David Renard - Policeman
Martin Garralaga - Older Padre
Rico Alaniz - Young Padre
Jorge Moreno - Perino
Ruben Moreno - 2nd Bandito
Ellen Davalos - Wife
Olga Velez - Juanita
Glenn Strange - Sam
Carmen Austin - Mexican Girl
Joe De Santis - Sheriff Mark Handlin

Sheriff Mark Handlin (Joe De Santis) is murdered by four ruthless saddle tramps who flee to Mexico with Matt hot on their trail.
Production #1615-0256

461. THE FIRST PEOPLE
Original air date: February 19, 1968
Directed by Robert Totten
Written by Calvin Clements
Starring:
Special Guests Gene Evans - Thomas Evans

Todd Armstrong - John Eagle Wing
James Almanzar - Mako
James Lydon - Baines
Jack Elam - William Pringe
Glenn Strange - Sam
Richard Hale - White Buffalo
Eddie Little Sky - Indian Policeman
Bill Erwin - Captain

Matt is in the middle of the struggle between John Eagle Wing (Todd Armstrong) and Thomas Evans (Gene Evans), an unscrupulous Indian agent.
Production #1615-0271

462. MR. SAM'L
Original air date: February 26, 1968
Directed by Gunnar Hellstrom
Written by Harry Kronman
Starring:
Special Guests Ed Begley - Mr. Sam'l
Larry Pennell - Ben Akins
Sandra Smith - Marcie
Duke Hobbie - Dave Akins
Buck Taylor - Newly
Mark Richman - Norm Trainer
Tom Brown - Ed O'Connor
Woodrow Chambliss - Lathrop
James Nusser - Louie Pheeters
Ted Jordan - Burke

Can mysterious Mr. Sam'l (Ed Begley) end the drought that has hit Dodge City? There are many who questions his gifts, including his resentful daughter Marcie (Sandra Smith).
Production #1615-0274

463. A NOOSE FOR DOBIE PRICE
Original air date: March 4, 1968
Directed by Richard C. Sarafian
Written by Antony Ellis
Starring:
Special Guest Chill Wills - Elihu Gorman
Shug Fisher - Dobie Price
Sheldon Allman - Skeets Walden
Robert Donner - Gil Boylan
E. J. Andre - Joe Karcher
Rose Hobart - Melanie Katcher
Hank Patterson - Hank
Glenn Strange - Sam
Owen Bush - Jackson Narramore
Michael Greene - Corny Tate
Ted Jordan - Burke
Raymond Mayo - Harry Walden
John (Bear) Hudkins - Mick Smith
Bob Herron - Jabez

Matt is forced into an uneasy alliance with Elihu Gorman (Chill Wills) while in pursuit of two men who escaped from jail in Dodge City.
Production #1615-0266

SEASON FOURTEEN

Produced by John Mantley
Associate Producer Joseph Dackow
Executive Story Consultant - Paul Savage

HILL GIRL January 29, 1967. Lane Bradbury and Victor French. (photo courtesy of Lane Bradbury)

464. LYLE'S KID
Original air date: September 23, 1968

Directed by Bernard McEveety
Written by Calvin Clements
Starring:
Special Guest Morgan Woodward - Grant Lyle
Robert Pine - Jeffery Lyle
Charlotte Considine - Iris
Buck Taylor - Newly
Sam Melville - Jack Garvin
Ken Mayer - Tuttle
Joe De Santis - Hoxy
James Nusser - Louie Pheeters
Glenn Strange - Sam
Lew Palter - Hillman
Mills Watson - Drover
I. Stanford Jolley - Attendant
Jonathan Harper - Percy Crump

Seeking vengeance, former sheriff Grant Lyle (Morgan Woodward) plans to confront the man who caused his retirement and to use his son Jeffrey Lyle (Robert Pine) as his weapon.
Production #1615-0302

465. THE HIDE CUTTERS
Original air date: September 30, 1968
Directed by Bernard McEveety
Written by Jack Turley
Starring:
Special Guests Cliff Osmond - Chunk
Michael Burns - Arlie Joe
Conlan Carter - Bodiddly
Ken Swofford - Sugar John
Eddie Firestone - Weevil
Joseph Campanella - Amos McKee

THE HIDE CUTTERS September 30, 1968. Ken Curtis and Joseph Campanella.

Gregg Palmer - Clete Davis
Steve Raines - Lawson
Mike Howden - Colton

A group of hide cutters led by Chunk (Cliff Osmond) stalk hardened cattleman Amos McKee (Joseph Campanella) and his drovers. Injured, Festus, along with Matt, join the drive.
Production #1615-0305

466. **ZAVALA**
Original air date: October 7, 1968
Directed by Vincent McEveety
Written by Paul Savage
Starring:
Special Guests Miriam Colon - Amelita Avila
Jim Davis - Ben Rawlins
Jose Chavez - Jurato
Rico Alaniz - Blacksmith
Jonathan Lippe - Alex Rawlins
Rex Holman - Smitty
Robert Sorrells - Oakes
Warren Vanders - Densen
Manuel Padilla, Jr. - Paco Avila
Larry D. Mann - Bakman
David Renard - Mexican Policeman
Nacho Galindo - Masseur
Elizabeth Germaine - Dorita

While tracking outlaws in Mexico, Matt befriends little Paco Avila (Manuel Padilla, Jr.) and his mother Amelita (Miriam Colon).
Production #1615-0301

467. **UNCLE FINNEY**
Original air date: October 14, 1968

Directed by Bernard McEveety
Written by Calvin Clements
Starring:
Special Guests Victor French - Roland Daniel
Anthony James - Elbert Moses
Buck Taylor - Newly
Burt Mustin - Uncle Finney
Lane Bradbury recreating the role of Merry Florene
Roy Roberts - Mr. Bodkin
Steve Raines - Wagon Driver
James Nusser - Louie Pheeters
John Dolan - Frank
Monte Hale - Bank Teller
Glenn Strange - Sam
Ted Jordan - Burke
Pete Kellett - Joe
Margaret Bacon - Woman In Bank

103 year-old horse thief, Finney (Burt Mustin) is brought in for the bounty on his head by nephews Roland (Victor French) and Elbert (Anthony James).
Production #1615-0311

468. **SLOCUM**
Original air date: October 21, 1968
Directed by Leo Penn
Written by Ron Bishop
Starring:
Special Guest Will Geer - Slocum
Dub Taylor - Noah Riker
Ross Hagen - Luke Riker
James Wainwright - Mark Riker

Lee Lambert - Paul Riker
Mills Watson - Peter Riker
Steve Sandor - John Riker
James Nusser - Louie Pheeters
Lew Brown - 1st Cowboy
Charles Kuenstle - 2nd Cowboy
Glenn Strange - Sam
Bill Erwin - Judge

Frontiersman Slocum (Will Geer) is in a heated battle with Noah Riker (Dub Taylor) and his ruthless sons.
Production #1615-0396

469. **O'QUILLIAN**
Original air date: October 28, 1968
Directed by John Rich
Written by Ron Bishop
Starring:
Special Guests John McLiam - O'Quillian
Victor French - Clay Tynan
Anthony James - Chickenfoot
Buck Taylor - Newly
James Nusser - Louie Pheeters
Vaughn Taylor - Judge Fletcher Anderson
Glenn Strange - Sam
Ken Drake - Parker
Steve Raines - Briggs
Roy Barcroft - Roy
Peggy Rea - Rosey
Woodrow Chambliss - Lathrop
Ted Jordan - Burke
Iron Eyes Cody - Indian

ZAVALA October 7, 1968. Manuel Padilla, Jr. and Jose Chavez.

Trouble follows and erupts everywhere likeable Irishman O'Quillian (John McLiam) goes, especially in the Long Branch Saloon, much to Kitty's dismay.
Production #1615-0304

470. **9:12 TO DODGE**
Original air date: November 11, 1968

Directed by Marvin Chomsky
Written by Preston Wood
Starring:
Special Guests Joanne Linville - Elizabeth Devon

ZAVALA October 7, 1968. James Arness and Miriam Colon.

Todd Armstrong - Johnny August
Robert Emhardt - Conductor
Frank Marth - Leitner
Johnny Haymer - Ned Stallcup
Harry Lauter - Michael Drennan
Fred Coby - Mokey
Lee De Broux - Tim
Tom Waters - Fox
Link Wyler - Peter Frye
Harry Harvey, Sr. - Dispatcher
Bobby E. Clark - Barstow
Troy Melton - Miles
William Murphy - Hugh
Rush Williams - Williams
Dan Terranova -Devlin
Ed Long - Karns
Pete Kellett - Joe

Prisoner Johnny August (Todd Armstrong) is escorted to Dodge by Matt and Doc on a train. The trip turns dangerous when a gang decides to free August.
Production #1615-0308

471. **ABELIA**
Original air date: November 18, 1968
Directed by Vincent McEveety
Written by Calvin Clements
Starring:
Special Guests Jacqueline Scott - Abelia
Jeremy Slate - Judd Ward
Tom Stern - Tom Cole
Buck Taylor - Newly
Jack Lambert - Gar

Gregg Palmer - Wales
Mike Durkin - Jonathan
Susan Olsen - Marianne
Jack Chaplain - Deeter Ward

Judd Ward (Jeremy Slate) and his gang take over the home of Abelia (Jacqueline Scott) in a desperate attempt to stave off Matt and his posse.
Production #1615-0312

472. **RAILROAD**

Original air date: November 25, 1968
Directed by Marvin Chomsky
Written by Arthur Rowe
Starring:
Special Guest Jim Davis - Wes Cameron
Ramon Bieri - Forbes
Roy Jenson - Larnen
Buck Taylor - Newly
James Nusser - Louie Pheeters
Buck Holland - O'Shay
Shug Fisher - Jim Graham
Don Hanmer - Lindsey
James McCallion - Amos Billings
Glenn Strange - Sam
Ted Jordan - Burke
Charles Wagenheim - Halligan

Homesteader Jim Graham (Shug Fisher) is asked to sell his land to the railroad. Trouble erupts when he refuses and Matt agrees with his decision.
Production #1615-0314

473. **THE MIRACLE MAN**

Original air date: December 2, 1968
Directed by Bernard McEveety
Written by Calvin Clements
Starring:
Special Guests Don Chastain - Bob Sullivan
Sandra Smith - Lorna Wright
William Bramley - Miller
Buck Taylor - Newly
Joseph Walsh - Gerard
Bruce Watson - Howard
Lisa Gerritsen - Nettie
Margie DeMeyer - Prudence
Kevin Cooper - Jacob
John Crawford - Drunk
Christopher Knight - Boy

Lorna Wright (Sandra Smith) rescues slick talker Don Chastain (Bob Sullivan) from the townspeople he has angered.
Production #1615-0313

474. **WACO**

Original air date: December 9, 1968
Directed by Robert Totten
Written by Ron Bishop
Starring:
Special Guests Victor French - Waco Thompson
Louise Latham - Polly Cade
Harry Carey, Jr. - Nathan Cade
Tom Reese - Slick Regan
Joy Fielding - Ann Cade
Mills Watson - Hood
Lee DeBroux - Fuller

UNCLE FINNEY October 14, 1968. Anthony
James, Burt Mustin and Victor French.
(photo courtesy of Anthony James)

SLOCUM October 21, 1968. James Arness and Ross Hagen.

ABELIA November 18, 1968.
Jacqueline Scott and Ken Curtis.
(photo courtesy of Jacqueline Scott)

THE MONEY STORE December 30,
1968. Pamelyn Ferdin and Eric Shea.

MANNON January 20, 1969. Ken Curtis.

THE TWISTED HERITAGE January 6, 1969. Amanda Blake and Virginia Gregg.

GOLD TOWN January 27, 1969. Lane Bradbury, Ken Curtis and Eve Plumb. (photo courtesy of Lane Bradbury)

Pat Thompson - One Moon
Liz Marshall - Lillie
Lawrence Mann - Gamble

Matt has his hands full while attempting to take prisoner Waco Thompson (Victor French) back to Dodge. Waco's gang is hot on their trail, and to make matters worse, Matt encounters a pregnant Indian woman who is need of immediate medical care.
Production #1615-0316

475. LOBO
Original air date: December 16, 1968
Directed by Bernard McEveety
Written by Jim Byrnes
Starring:
Special Guest Morgan Woodward - Luke Brazo
Sheldon Allman - Badger
Sandy Kenyon - Catlin
Buck Taylor - Newly
Ken Swofford - Guffy
Eddie Firestone - Riney
David Brian - Branch Nelson
Fred Coby - Wes Flood
Glenn Strange - Sam
James Nusser - Louie Pheeters
William Murphy - Ethen

Matt and mountain man Luke Brazo (Morgan Woodward) join forces to hunt an elusive wolf that has been threatening local livestock.
Production #1615-0315

476. JOHNNY CROSS
Original air date: December 23, 1968
Directed by Herschel Daugherty
Written by Calvin Clements
Starring:
Jeff Pomerantz - Johnny Cross
Kelly Jean Peters - Vera
Buck Taylor - Newly
Dean Stanton - Hodge
John Crawford - Yates
Shug Fisher - Franks
Charles Thompson - Mr. Cross
Glenn Strange - Sam
Ted Jordan - Burke

Newly comes to the aid of wanted man Johnny Cross (Jeff Pomerantz), fighting off bounty hunters while trying to clear his name.
Production #1615-0309

477. THE MONEY STORE
Original air date: December 30, 1968
Directed by Vincent McEveety
Written by William Blinn
Special Guests Charles Aidman - Ray Jarvis
William Schallert - Ezra Thorpe
Virginia Vincent - Louise Thorpe
Pamelyn Ferdin - Annie Jarvis
Eric Shea - Mike Jarvis
Buck Taylor - Newly
Roy Roberts - Mr. Bodkin
Glenn Strange - Sam
Ted Jordan - Burke

Children Annie and Mike Jarvis (Pamelyn Ferdin and Eric Shea) inadvertently "rob" the bank in an attempt to help their poor father (Charles Aidman).

Production #1615-0303

478. THE TWISTED HERITAGE
Original air date: January 6, 1969
Directed by Bernard McEveety
Teleplay by Arthur Rowe and Paul Savage
Story by Robert Heverly and Jack Turley
Starring:
Special Guest John Ericson - Blaine Copperton
Virginia Gregg - Jessie Copperton
David McLean - Webb
Nora Marlowe - Ma Dagget
Lisa Gerritsen - Tracey Copperton
Conlan Carter - Logan Dagget
Charles Kuenstle - Elan Dagget
Richard O'Brien - Simpson
Joshua Bryant - Young
Steve Raines - Driver #1
James Nusser - Louie Pheeters
Robert Luster - Cookie
Robert Karnes - Driver #2

Kitty manages to save the life of fellow stage passenger Blaine Copperton (John Ericson) but then has to deal with his twisted tyrant of a mother (Virginia Gregg).

Production #1615-0317

(Blooper Alert) Huge mistake—Virginia Gregg leaves a room in a blue polka dot dress and enters another room immediately dressed in grey.

THE INTRUDER March 3, 1969. Eric Shea.

479. TIME OF THE JACKALS
Original air date: January 13, 1969
Directed by Vincent McEveety
Teleplay by Richard Fielder
Adaptation by Paul Savage
Story by Richard Fielder

Starring:
Special Guests Leslie Nielsen - Jess Trevor
Beverly Garland - Leona
Edmund Hashim - Tim Jackson
Buck Taylor - Newly
Kip Whitman - Daggett
Charles Maxwell - Del Rainey
Jonathan Lippe - Lucas Brant
Robert Knapp - Dan Foley
Sid Haig - Cawkins
James Nusser - Louie Pheeters
Glenn Strange - Sam
Ted Jordan - Burke
Art Stewart - Trail Hand

Woodrow Chambliss - Lathrop
Tom Brown - Ed O'Connor
Charles Wagenheim - Halligan
Howard Culver - Howie
Michelle Breeze - Chris
Fred Dale - Townsman

Leona (Beverly Garland) is wounded in a gunfight between Matt and gang members. She is a former girlfriend of Matt's and now he is tracking her current beau, Jess Travor (Leslie Nielsen).
Production #1615-0310

480. **MANNON**
Original air date: January 20, 1969
Directed by Robert Butler
Written by Ron Bishop
Starring:
Special Guest Steve Forrest - Mannon
Buck Taylor - Newly
Glenn Strange - Sam
James Nusser - Louie Pheeters
Roy Barcroft - Roy
Charles Seel - Barney
Ted Jordan - Burke

THE INTRUDER March 3, 1969. Eric Shea and Ken Curtis.

Former Quantrill rider Will Mannon first guns down Festus then takes over Dodge during Matt's absence. He is feared by everyone except for Kitty, then vows to kill her man upon his return.
Production #1615-0319

THE GOOD SAMARITANS March 10, 1969. Brock Peters and James Arness on the set.

481. **GOLD TOWN**

Original air date: January 27, 1969
Directed by Gunnar Hellstrom
Written by Calvin Clements

Starring:
Special guests Lou Antonio - Smiley
Lane Bradbury - Merry Florene
Anthony James - Elbert Moses
Harry Davis - Shorty
Chubby Johnson - Oldtimer
Buck Taylor - Newly
Paul Wexler - Stone
Jack Searl - Hale
Kathryn Minner - Grandmother
James Nusser - Louie Pheeters
Pete Kellett - Spectator
Glenn Strange - Sam
Ted Jordan - Burke
Eve Plumb - Sue

    Smiley and Elbert (Lou Antonio and Anthony James) are once again run out of Dodge and now scheme to swindle folks with an abandoned gold mine.
    Production #1615-0318

482. **THE MARK OF CAIN**

Original air date: February 3, 1969
Directed by Vincent McEveety
Written by Ron Bishop
Starring:
Special Guest Nehemiah Persoff
Louise Latham - Louise
Robert DoQui - Sadler
Buck Taylor - Newly
Kevin Coughlin - Tom
Stanley Clements - McInnerny
Robert Totten - Corley

Glenn Strange - Sam
Ted Jordan - Burke
James Nusser - Louie Pheeters
Roy Barcroft - Roy
Olan Soule - Waiter

Respected Dodge City rancher Driscoll (Nehemiah Persoff) is revealed to have been a cold-blooded prison commandant during the Civil War.
Production #1615-0322

483. THE REPRISAL
Original air date: February 10, 1969
Directed by Bernard McEveety
Teleplay by Paul Savage and Jack Hawn
Story by Jack Hawn
Starring:
Special Guest Joe Don Baker - Tom Butler
Eunice Christopher - Sara Butler
Buck Taylor - Newly
John Pickard - Forbes
James Nusser - Louie Pheeters
Jack Lambert - Garth
Dennis Cross - Jinks
I. Stanford Jolley - Jeb
Glenn Strange - Sam
Ted Jordan - Burke
Charles Wagenheim - Halligan
Woodrow Chambliss - Lathrop

Doc's decision to save an outlaw's life before delivering a baby has disastrous results, with the father-to-be (Joe Don Baker) swearing revenge.
Production #1615-0321

484. THE LONG NIGHT
Original air date: February 17, 1969
Directed by John Rich
Teleplay by Paul Savage
Story by Dick Carr
Starring:
Bruce Dern - Guerin
Lou Antonio - Mace
Susan Silo - Rita Lane
Robert Totten - Ben Miller
Buck Taylor - Newly
Robert Brubaker - Henry Wade
James Nusser - Louie Pheeters
Russell Johnson - Diggs
Rex Holman - Broker
Glenn Strange - Sam
Ted Jordan - Burke
Victor Tayback - Rawlins
Matt Emery - Keever

Kitty, Doc, Sam and Louie are held hostage at the Long Branch by a crazed bunch of bounty men led by Guerin (Bruce Dern). They want Ben Miller (Robert Totten) and the $10,000 reward posted for the man, who has surrendered to Matt.
Production #1615-0275

485. THE NIGHT RIDERS
Original air date: February 24, 1969
Directed by Irving J. Moore
Written by Calvin Clements
Starring:
Special Guests Jeff Corey - Judge Proctor
Robert Pine - Eliot Proctor

Bob Random - Jay Proctor
Warren Vanders - Williams
Robert Karnes - Ross
Norman Alden - Berber
Ed Bakey - Farmer
Scott Hale - Bernaby
James Nusser - Louie Pheeters
Glenn Strange - Sam
Ted Jordan - Burke

Judge Proctor (Jeff Corey) leads a group of fanatical looters out to reclaim what was lost during the Civil War. When they arrive in Dodge, they get more than they bargained for—acting deputy Festus Haggen.

Production #1615-0323

486. THE INTRUDER

Original air date: March 3, 1969
Directed by Vincent McEveety
Written by Jim Byrnes
Starring:
Special Guests Charles Aidman - Riley Sharp
John Kellogg - Henry Decker
Gail Kobe - Ellie Decker
Eric Shea - Timmy
Ralph James - Hall
Ted Jordan - Burke
Robert Gravage - Ennis

Festus and wounded prisoner Riley Sharp (Charles Aidman) arrive at the Decker ranch, and a strange marital situation slowly unravels.

Production #1615-0325

487. THE GOOD SAMARITANS

Original air date: March 10, 1969
Directed by Bernard McEveety
Written by Paul Savage
Starring:
Special Guests Brock Peters - Cato
Rex Ingram - Juba
Robert DoQui - Benji
Paulene Myers - Mama Olabelle
Hazel Medina - Erlene
Lynn Hamilton - Reba
Sam Melville - Croyden
Davis Roberts - Ike
L. Q. Jones - Kittridge
Pepe Brown - Heck
Alycia Gardner - Willa
Dan Ferrone - Jeb
John Brandon - Timmons

Cato and Juba (Brock Peters and Rex Ingram) are ex-slaves who offer much needed shelter to a severely wounded Marshal Dillon.

Production #1615-0324

488. THE PRISONER

Original air date: March 17, 1969
Directed by Leo Penn
Written by Calvin Clements
Starring:
Special Guest Jon Voight - Steven Downing
Ramon Bieri - Jarvis
Ned Glass - Pink Simmons

THE GOOD SAMARITANS March 10, 1969. Rex Ingram.

Buck Taylor - Newly
Paul Bryar - Sheriff
Kenneth Tobey - Bob Mathison
James Nusser - Louie Pheeters
Glenn Strange - Sam

Tom Brown - Ed O'Connor
Ted Jordan - Burke
David Fresco - Barber
Jan Peters - Cardplayer

Bounty hunter Jarvis (Ramon Bieri) brings prisoner Steven Downing (Jon Voight) into Dodge. Downing manages to save Miss Kitty from a load of freight that falls off a wagon, who then "wins" the prisoner in a card game from the heartless Jarvis.
Production #1615-0320

489. EXODUS 21:22
Original air date: March 24, 1969
Directed by Herschel Daugherty
Written by Arthur Rowe
Starring:
Special Guest Steve Ihnat - Frank Reardon
William Bramley - Cane
Kaz Garas - Keith
Buck Taylor - Newly
Brandon Carroll - Lloyd
Lane Bradford - Bradford
James Nusser - Louie Pheeters
Glenn Strange - Sam
Ted Jordan - Burke
Sarah Hardy - Farm Girl

Frank Reardon (Steve Ihnat) has already killed four of the seven men responsible for the death of his wife and unborn child, and he hopes to find the final three in Dodge.
Production #1615-0307

SEASON FIFTEEN

Executive Producer - John Mantley
Producer - Joseph Dackow
Executive Story Consultant - Calvin Clements

490. THE DEVIL'S OUTPOST

Original air date: September 22, 1969
Directed by Philip Leacock
Teleplay by Jim Byrnes and Robert Barbash
Story by Robert Barbash
Starring:
Special Guests Robert Lansing - Yancy Tyce
Jonathan Lippe - Cody Tyce
Karl Swenson - McGruder
Sheila Larkin - Abby Tilman
Ken Swofford - Loomis
Warren Vanders - Bo Harper
Val de Vargas - Pacos
Charles Kuenstle - Kelly
I. Stanford Jolley - Tilman
Sabrina Scharf - Lora
Troy Melton - Mike Lennox
Joe Higgins - George Miller
Sam Edwards -Telegrapher
William Tannen - Townsman
Joe Haworth - Cowboy
Ed Long - Farley

Cody Tyce (Jonathan Lippe) is captured by Matt after an attempted stage holdup. His older brother Yancy (Robert Lansing) is relentless in his pursuit to free his brother.
Production #1615-0356

491. STRYKER

Original air date: September 29, 1969
Directed by Robert Totten
Written by Herman Groves
Starring:
Special Guest Morgan Woodward - Josh Stryker
Joan Van Ark - Sarah Jean Stryker
Royal Dano - Jessup
Mills Watson - Reager
James Nusser - Louie Pheeters
Andy Devine - Jed Whitlow
Walter Sande - Cal Hoskins
Glenn Strange - Sam
Ted French - Dish
Don Happy - Cowboy #1

Josh Stryker (Morgan Woodward) is a former Dodge City lawman who returns after a fifteen year stretch in prison with nothing else on his mind but killing his successor, Matt Dillon.
Production #1615-0352

492. COREYVILLE

Original air date: October 6, 1969
Directed by Bernard McEveety
Written by Herman Groves
Starring:
Special Guest Nina Foch - Agatha Corey
Kevin Coughlin - Billy Joe Corey
Thomas Hunter - Frank Corey
Bruce Glover - Titus Wylie
Jo Ann Harris - Ellie
John Shuck - Amos Blake

STRYKER September 29, 1969. Andy Devine and Amanda Blake.

James Almanzar - Hankin
Special Guest Appearance Ruth Roman - Flo Watson
Bill Erwin - Juror
Charles Fredericks - Clel Wilson
Pete Kellett - Guard #1
Bill Catching - Guard #2
Gary Combs - Guard #3

In the bizarre town of Coreyville, Matt becomes embroiled in a revenge plot between Agatha Corey (Nina Foch), Flo Watson (Ruth Roman) and accused murderer Titus Wylie (Bruce Glover).
Production #1615-0361

493. DANNY
Original air date: October 13, 1969
Directed by Bernard McEveety
Written by Preston Wood
Starring:
Special Guest Jack Albertson - Danny Wilson
Vito Scotti - Indiana
Frank Marth - Ed Wickes
Rayford Barnes - Carl Dahlman
Jonathan Harper - Percy Crump
Scott Brady - Heenan
Glenn Strange - Sam
Tom Brown - Ed O'Connor
Woodrow Chambliss - Lathrop
Steve Raines - Stage Driver

Fearing his life is coming to an end, aging con man Danny Wilson (Jack Albertson) begins to plan his extravagant funeral and wake.
Production #1615-0354

COREYVILLE October 6, 1969. Nina Foch and Ruth Roman.

494. HAWK
Original air date: October 20, 1969
Directed by Gunnar Hellstrom
Written by Kay Lenard and Jess Carneol
Starring:
Special Guests Louise Latham - Phoebe Clifford
Brendon Boone - Hawk

Hilarie Thompson - Rachel Clifford
Michael-James Wixted - Amos Clifford
Robert Brubaker - Dave Clifford
X Brands - Renegade Indian
Bill Hart - Renegade #2
Hal Needham - Renegade #3
Glen Randall, Jr. - Renegade #4

Former Apache captive Phoebe Clifford (Louise Latham) refuses to acknowledge her half-Indian son Hawk (Brendon Boone).
Production #1615-0360

495. A MAN CALLED SMITH
Original air date: October 27, 1969
Directed by Vincent McEveety
Written by Calvin Clements
Starring:
Special Guest Jacqueline Scott - Abelia
Val Avery - Bull
Susan Olsen - Marianne
Michael Durkin - Jonathan
Special Guest Appearance
    Earl Holliman - Will
Roy Roberts - Mr. Bodkin
Sid Haig - Buffalo Hunter
William Fawcett - Old Prospector
Ted Jordan - Burke
Margarita Cordova - Saloon Girl

Will (Earl Holliman) returns to the home of the wife, Abelia (Jacqueline Scott)

he abandoned many years ago. He gets her involved in a stolen gold scheme in return for his promise to once again leave her and the children alone.
Production #1615-0351

496. CHARLIE NOON
Original air date: November 3, 1969
Directed by Vincent McEveety
Written by Jim Byrnes
Starring:
Special Guests James Best - Charlie Noon

DANNY October 13, 1969. Amanda Blake and Jack Albertson.

Miriam Colon - The Woman
Ronny Howard - Jamie
Edmund Hashim - Lone Wolf
Kip Whitman - Takawa

Matt is confronted by Indians while travelling with an Indian widow and her white stepson (Miriam Colon and Ronny Howard) and condemned prisoner Charlie Noon (James Best).
Production #1615-0363

497. THE STILL

Original air date: November 10, 1969
Directed by Gunnar Hellstrom
Written by Calvin Clements
Starring:
Special Guests Lane Bradbury - Merry Florene

DANNY October 13, 1969. James Arness and Jack Albertson.

Anthony James - Elbert Moses
Shug Fisher - Uncle Titus
James Westerfield - Franks
J. Edward McKinley - Mr. Bishop
Ted Jordan - Burke
Trent Lehman - Chester
Glenn Strange - Sam

They're back, and this time Elbert (Anthony James) and Uncle Titus (Shug Fisher) hide a prize bull and a moonshining still in the cellar of the school where Merry Florene (Lane Bradbury) is teaching.
Production #1615-0362

498. A MATTER OF HONOR

Original air date: November 17, 1969
Directed by Robert Totten
Written by Joy Dexter
Starring:
Special Guests John Anderson - Jess Fletcher
Katherine Justice - Lydia Fletcher
Tom Simcox - C. V. Fletcher
Dan Ferrone - Otis Fletcher
Richard Bakalyan - Billy Holland
Walter Sande - Cal Haines
James Nusser - Louie Pheeters
Jack Bailey - Judge Brooker
Glenn Strange - Sam
Lawrence Mann - Prosecutor
Bob Burrows - Ranch Hand

Town drunk Louie Pheeters (James Nusser) is a loveable man who is accused of a murder he witnesses in the stable after

sleeping off his latest celebration.
Production #1615-0355

499. **THE INNOCENT**
Original air date: November 24, 1969
Directed by Marvin Chomsky
Written by Walter Black
Starring:
Special Guest Eileen Heckart -
	Athena Partridge Royce
Barry Atwater - Yewker
Anthony James - Loyal Yewker
Lee de Broux - Zeal Yewker
Tom Nolan - Sonny
Eddie Little Sky - Indian Chief
Manuel Padilla, Jr. - Indian Boy
Robert B. Williams - Phelps
Rush Williams - Stage Driver

Athena Partridge Royce (Eileen Heckart) and travelling companion Festus are targets for crazed Yewker (Barry Atwater) and his equally crazed sons.
Production #1615-0353

500. **RING OF DARKNESS**
Original air date: December 1, 1969
Directed by Bernard McEveety
Written by Arthur Dales
Starring:
Special Guest Tom Drake - Ben Hurley
John Crawford - Pinto
Rex Holman - Carr

A MAN CALLED SMITH October 27, 1969. Jacqueline Scott and Earl Holliman. (photo courtesy of Jacqueline Scott)

Anthony Caruso - Gulley
Pamela Dunlap - Susan Hurley

Ben Hurley (Tom Drake) is blackmailed by a gang to steal horses and in order to protect his blind daughter Susan (Pamela Dunlap) he blames the crime on Newly.
Production #1615-0359

501. **MACGRAW**

Original air date: December 8, 1969
Directed by Philip Leacock
Written by Kay Lenard and Jess Carneol
Starring:
Special Guests J. D. Cannon - Jake MacGraw
Michael Larrain - Dave Wilson
Diana Ewing - Ella Horton
Sam Melville - Garvey
Charles Kuenstle - Wilkes
Ned Wertimer - Jud Douglas
Ted Jordan - Burke
Glenn Strange - Sam
Tom Brown - Ed O'Connor
Sid Haig - Eli Crawford
Allen Jaffe - Ed Crawford
Bobby Hall - Hamilton
Sam Edwards - Barfly

Jake MacGraw (J. D. Cannon) returns to Dodge after serving twenty years in prison. The former gunfighter claims rehabilitation and takes a job playing piano in the Long Branch.
Production #1615-0364

502. **ROOTS OF FEAR**

Original air date: December 15, 1969
Directed by Philip Leacock
Written by Arthur Browne, Jr.
Starring:
Special Guests John Anderson - Amos Sadler
Louise Latham - Emilie Sadler
Cliff Osmond - Daniel Sadler
Warren Vanders - Ridge Sadler

THE INNOCENT November 24, 1969. Ken Curtis and Eileen Heckart.

Walter Burke - George Acton
Jody Foster (later Jodie) - Susan Sadler
Roy Roberts - Mr. Bodkin
Ted Jordan - Burke
Arthur Peterson - Judge Brooker
Tom Brown - Ed O'Connor
Robert Karnes - Charlie
Paul Micale - Assistant Teller
Hank Wise - Townsman

When a panic closes the bank in Dodge, dirt farmer Amos Sadler (John Anderson) plans to break in and only take what he feels is rightfully his.
Production #1615-0366

503. THE SISTERS
Original air date: December 29, 1969
Directed by Philip Leacock
Written by William Kelley
Starring:
Special Guest Jack Elam - Pack Landers
Lynn Hamilton - Mother Tabitha
Gloria Calomee - Sister Charles
Susan Batson - Sister Blanche
CeCe Whitney - Ivy Landers
Chris Hundley - Toby
Erica Petal - Gail

RING OF DARKNESS December 1, 1969. Pamela Dunlap and Buck Taylor.

Pack Landers (Jack Elam) is a drunken wanderer who plots his latest scheme involving three black nuns (Lynn Hamilton, Gloria Calomee and Susan Batson).
Production #1615-0348

504. THE WAR PRIEST
Original air date: January 5, 1970
Directed by Bernard McEveety
Written by William Kelley
Starring:
Special Guests Forrest Tucker - Sergeant Holly
Richard Anderson - Gregorio
John Crawford - Amos Strange
Sam Melville - Lt. Snell
Richard Hale - El Cuerno
Glenn Strange - Sam
Link Wyler - 1st Sentry
Tom Sutton - 2nd Sentry
Pete Kellett - Shotgun
Vincent Deadrick - 1st Trooper

Kitty is kidnapped by wounded Apache war priest Gregorio (Richard Anderson) and is trailed by cork-puller Sergeant Holly (Forrest Tucker).
Production #1615-0367

505. THE PACK RAT
Original air date: January 12, 1970
Directed by Philip Leacock
Written by Jim Byrnes and Arthur Browne, Jr.
Starring:
Special Guests William C. Watson - Sam Danton
Manuel Padilla, Jr. - Sancho

THE SISTERS December 29, 1969. Jack Elam, Lynn Hamilton, Susan Batson and Gloria Calomee. (photo courtesy of Jack Elam)

THE WAR PRIEST January 5, 1970. Forrest Tucker.

Heidi Vaughn - Martha Mason
Loretta Swit - Belle Clark
Glenn Strange - Sam
Woodrow Chambliss - Lathrop
Robert Brubaker - Jake Hawkins
Robert Rithwell - Shotgun
Tom Sutton - Shockley
Bill Catching - Trapp

A simple retrieval of prisoner Sam Danton (William C. Watson) gets complicated for Matt when his travels include a multitude of people, including a little thief named Sancho (Manuel Padilla, Jr.).

Production #1615-0369

506. **THE JUDAS GUN**

Original air date: January 19, 1970
Directed by Vincent McEveety
Written by Harry Kronman
Starring:
Special Guests Ron Hayes - Boyd Avery
Peter Jason - Cully Haimes
Richard X. Slattery - Noah Haimes
Laurie Mock - Janie Bolden
Sean McClory - Clete Bolden
Glenn Strange - Sam
Tom Brown - Ed O'Connor
Margarita Cordova - Bar Girl
William Fawcett - Liveryman

Brad David - Teddy
Ralph Neff - Town Bum

Ranchers Haimes (Richard X. Slattery) and Bolden (Sean McClory) fight again when their children (Peter Jason and Laurie Mock) fall in love. Things worsen when Boyd Avery (Ron Hayes), a gunfighter, enters the picture.

Production #1615-0365

507. DOCTOR HERMAN SCHULTZ, M. D.

Original air date: January 26, 1970
Directed by Bernard McEveety
Teleplay by Calvin Clements
Story by Benny Rubin
Starring:
Special Guest Benny Rubin - Dr. Herman Schultz
Ted Jordan - Burke
Glenn Strange - Sam
Howard Culver - Howie
Pete Kellett - Stoney

Doc's old friend Dr. Schultz (Benny Rubin) arrives in Dodge and practices his hypnotic powers on a hapless Festus. When money is stolen, Doc begins to suspect his colleague.

Production #1615-0370

508. THE BADGE

Original air date: February 2, 1970
Directed by Vincent McEveety
Written by Jim Byrnes
Starring:
Special Guest Henry Jones - Papa Steiffer

Beverly Garland - Claire Hollis
John Milford - John Dawson
Jack Lambert - Locke
Roy Jenson - Keller
James Nusser - Louie Pheeters
Glenn Strange - Sam
Mary Angela - Bea
John Flinn - Wordon
William O'Connell - Jackson
Ted Jordan - Burke
Fred Coby - Sloan

Matt is again wounded doing his job and Kitty decides she has had enough. She joins her friend Claire Hollis (Beverly Garland) away from Dodge, but her plans of a new life are interrupted by corrupt Papa Steiffer (Henry Jones).

Production #1615-0374

509. ALBERT

Original air date: February 9, 1970
Directed by Vincent McEveety
Written by Jim Byrnes
Starring:
Special Guests Patricia Barry - Kate Schiller
Milton Selzer - Albert Schiller
L. Q. Jones - Nix
Bob Random - Tom Clark
William Schallert - Jake Spence
Roy Roberts - Mr. Bodkin
Glenn Strange - Sam
Dorothy Neumann - Emily Cushing
Natalie Masters - Mrs. Bodkin

Cold blooded Jake Spence (William Schallert) and his men are foiled in their latest robbery attempt by meek bank clerk Albert Schiller (Milton Selzer).

Production #1615-0368

510. KIOWA

Original air date: February 16, 1970
Directed by Bernard McEveety
Written by Ron Bishop
Starring:
Special Guests Victor French - Ed Vail
Dub Taylor - Rev. Finney Cox
John Beck - Albert Vail
Lucas White - Russ Vail
Jean Allison - Martha Vail
Joyce Ames - Melissa Vail
Richard Angarola - Quichero
Richard Lapp - Tomani
Angela Carroll - Indian Woman
Glenn Strange - Sam
Ted Jordan - Burke

Ed Vail (Victor French) and his sons reluctantly team with Matt and Reverend Finney Cox (Dub Taylor) as they pursue the Indians who abducted Ed's daughter Melissa (Joyce Ames).

Production #1615-0372

511. CELIA

Original air date: February 23, 1970
Directed by Philip Leacock
Written by Harry Kronman
Starring:
Special Guests Cliff Osmond - Ben Sommars

DOCTOR HERMAN SCHULTZ, MD January 26, 1970. Benny Rubin and Milburn Stone.

Melissa Murphy - Celia Madden
Frank Marth - Martin Blake
Roy Roberts - Mr. Bodkin
George Petrie - Carl
Charles Seel - Barney
Steve Raines - 1st Driver
Glenn Strange - Sam
Troy Melton - 2nd Driver
Vincent Deadrick - Cowboy #1
Ace Hudkins - Cowboy #2

Blacksmith Ben Sommars (Cliff Osmond) is expecting the arrival of his mail-order bride Celia Madden (Melissa Murphy). The pretty girl is soon suspected to be a swindler,

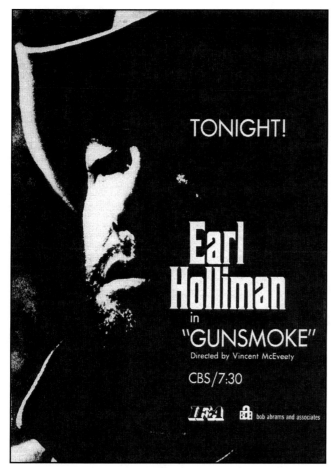

HACKETT March 16, 1970. Trade ad featuring Earl Holliman in the title role.

especially by Newly.
Production #1615-0373

512. MORGAN

Original air date: March 2, 1970
Directed by Bernard McEveety
Written by Kay Lenard and Jess Carneol
Starring:
Special Guest Steve Forrest - Morgan
Carlotte Stewart - Jenny
Hank Brandt - Clint
Jonathan Lippe - Carter
Mills Watson - Greer
Ed Long - Trent
James Nusser - Louie Pheeters
Charles Seel - Barney
Read Morgan - Lieutenant
Jack Garner - Telegrapher
I. Stanford Jolley - Zack
Fletcher Bryant - Hawkins

Vain outlaw Morgan (Steve Forrest) is shot in the face by Kitty when he and his men take over Dodge. While awaiting the arrival of Matt and a shipment of gold, he orders Doc to fix his wounds and Newly and Festus to fix a gattling gun they plan on using to cut the transport soldiers and Matt down with.
Production #1615-0375

513. THE THIEVES

Original air date: March 9, 1970
Directed by Philip Leacock
Written by Thomas Thompson
Starring:
Special Guests Michael Burns - Eric Tabray
Royal Dano - Gideon Hale
John Schuck - Burt Tilden

Timothy Burns - Billy Clarke
Bill Callaway - Shuffles
Glenn Strange - Sam
James Nusser - Louie Pheeters
Daphne Field - Mrs. Hale

While on probation, three boys (Michael Burns, Bill Callaway and Timothy Burns) are given odd jobs, and one in particular, Eric (Burns) falls under the guiding hand of Sam the bartender.
Production #1615-0371

514. HACKETT
Original air date: March 16, 1970
Directed by Vincent McEveety
Written by William Kelley
Starring:
Special Guests Earl Holliman - Hackett
Morgan Woodward - Quentin Sargent
Jennifer West - Geneva Sargent
Robert Totten - Tully
Ken Swofford - Bronk
Glenn Strange - Sam
Woodrow Chambliss - Lathrop

Quentin Sargent (Morgan Woodward) is the target of revenge by former partner Hackett (Earl Holliman). Hackett served prison time because Quentin turned coward prior to their planned train holdup.
Production #1615-0376

515. THE CAGE
Original air date: March 23, 1970
Directed by Bernard McEveety

Written by Calvin Clements
Starring:
Special Guests Steve Carlson - Roy Stewart
Paul Stewart - Sanders
Gregg Palmer - Benson
Ken Mayer - Blake
Robert Swan - Weden
Hank Brandt - Luke Stewart
Allen Jaffe - Gresley
Jorge Moreno - Alfonso
Introducing Laura Figueroa - Maria
Joaquin Martinez - Pepe
Renata Vanni - Mrs. Ramos
Ted Jordan - Burke
Pedro Regas - Elderly Mexican
Arageli Rey - Elderly Mexican Woman

Matt and Festus rescue Roy Stewart (Steve Carlson) from a prison transport wagon when it is attacked by his former gang of gold thieves.
Production #1615-0357

SEASON SIXTEEN

Executive Producer - John Mantley
Produced by Joseph Dackow (13 episodes)
Produced by Leonard Katzman (remainder)
Executive Story Consultant - Calvin Clements

516. CHATO
Original air date: September 14, 1970

Directed by Vincent McEveety
Written by Paul F. Edwards
Starring:
Special Guests Ricardo Montalban - Chato
Miriam Colon - Mora
Peggy McCay - Mrs. Cooter
William Bryant - Marshal Cooter
Rodolfo Hoyos - Juanito
Robert Knapp - Surgeon
Pedro Regas - Old Man
Jim Sheppard - Case

Matt combines personal reasons with his professional duty as he tracks an elusive killer known as Chato (Ricardo Montalban). In a deadly game of cat and mouse, the marshal uses Chato's woman, Mora (Miriam Colon) as bait.
Production #1615-0409

517. THE NOOSE
Original air date: September 21, 1970
Directed by Vincent McEveety
Written by Arthur Browne, Jr.
Starring:
Special Guest Tom Skerritt - Fred Garth
William Fawcett - Nebs
Glenn Strange - Sam
Ted Jordan - Burke
Woodrow Chambliss - Lathrop
Hank Patterson - Hank

Fifteen years ago a boy witnessed the hanging of his father. Now a man, Fred Garth (Tom Skerritt) returns to Dodge and plans to settle the score by hanging Doc, and forcing Kitty, Festus and Matt to watch.
Production #1615-0401

518. STARK
Original air date: September 28, 1970
Directed by Robert Totten
Written by Donald S. Sanford
Starring:
Special Guests Richard Kiley - Lewis Stark
Shelly Novack - Adam Bramley
Henry Wilcoxon - John Bramley
Suzanne Pleshette - Glory Bramley
Rusty Lane - Bo
Bob Burrows - Charlie

Clever bounty hunter Lewis Stark (Richard Kiley) is not above the law, especially after he arrests the brother of wealthy Glory Bramley (Suzanne Pleshette).
Production #1615-0403

519. SAM McTAVISH, M. D.
Original air date: October 5, 1970
Directed by Bernard McEveety
Written by Gerry Day and Bethel Leslie
Starring:
Special Guests Vera Miles - Dr. Sam
Arch Johnson - Barn Bascomb
Lisa Gerritsen - Christina
Dee Carroll - Ellen Bascomb
Amzie Strickland - Minnie Carver
Tom Fadden - Harley
Kathleen O'Malley - Bridget O'Reilly
Glenn Strange - Sam

CHATO September 14, 1970. Ricardo Montalban is superb in the title role.

Harry Harvey, Sr. - Johnson
Read Morgan - Dan Slade
Robert Rothwell - Joe Slade
Lance Thomas - Tom Slade
Glenn Redding - Frank O'Reilly

Not knowing Sam is short for Samantha, Doc hires Dr. Sam McTavish (Vera Miles) to fill in for him while he is on vacation. Ever the chauvinist, Doc is at first upset, then charmed, by his lovely colleague.
Production #1615-0410

520. GENTRY'S LAW
Original air date: October 12, 1970
Directed by Vincent McEveety
Written by Jack Miller
Starring:
Special Guests John Payne - Amos Gentry
Louise Latham - Claire Gentry
Peter Jason - Colt Gentry
Robert Pine - Ben Gentry
Shug Fisher - Orly Grimes
Don Keefer - Floyd Babcock
Darlene Conley - Leelah Case
John Flinn - Buel
Robert Totten - Abner

Powerful land baron Amos Gentry (John Payne) is above the law when it comes to his sons (Peter Jason and Robert Pine), regardless of the crime they committed or the circumstances surrounding the act.
Production # 1615-0404

521. SNOW TRAIN - PART I
Original air date: October 19, 1970
Directed by Gunnar Hellstrom
Written by Preston Wood
Starring:
Special Guests In Alphabetical Order
Eddie Applegate - Al
Tim Considine - Scott Coleman
Pamela Dunlap - Ada Coleman
Dana Elcar - Pennigrath
Roy Engel - Tibbett
Gene Evans - Billy
Eddie Firestone - Hap
Ron Hayes - Floyd Coleman
Clifton James - Sam Wickes
Richard D. Kelton - Bud
Doreen Lang - Mae
Ken Lynch - Lucas
John Milford - Clay Foreman
Anne Seymour - Sarah
Loretta Swit - Donna
Richard Lapp - Running Fox
X Brands - Red Willow
Ronald A. One Feather, Lemoyne L. LaPointe and
    LeMoyne W. Millard as The Hunters

Chief Red Willow (X Brands) stops the train and demands that the two men who sold his braves poisoned whiskey be turned over to his tribe for punishment.
Production #1615-0406

522. SNOW TRAIN - PART II
Original air date: October 26, 1970

Directed by Gunnar Hellstrom
Written by Preston Wood
Starring:
Ron Hayes - Floyd
Tim Considine - Scott
Pamela Dunlap - Ada
Roy Engel - Tibbett
Eddie Firestone - Hap
Bill Erwin - Telegrapher
Ken Lynch - Lucas

John Milford - Clay
Loretta Swit - Donna
Dana Elcar - Pennigrath
Eddie Applegate - Al
Richard D. Kelton - Bud
Anne Seymour - Sarah
Doreen Lang - Mae
Gene Evans - Billy
Clifton James - Wickes
X Brands - Red Willow

Richard Lapp - Running Fox
LeMoyne W. Millard, Ronald A. One Feather,
    and Lemoyne L. LaPointe as The
    Hunters

Matt must fight three braves after he slips off the train to find help for the trapped and wounded passengers, who begin to panic in his absence and rush Festus.
    Production #1615-0407

523. **LUKE**
Original air date: April 3, 1972
Directed by Bernard McEveety
Written by Jack Miller
Starring:
Special Guests Morgan Woodward -
    Luke Dangerfield
Katherine Justice - Doris Prebble
and Anthony Costello - Austin Keep
Rex Holman - Moses Reedy
Glenn Strange - Sam
Howard Culver - Howie

THE NOOSE September 21, 1970. Milburn Stone and Tom Skerritt.

Victor Izay - Bull

Wounded and dying outlaw Luke Dangerfield wants to see the daughter he abandoned several years ago.
Production #1615-0412

524. THE GUN
Original air date: November 9, 1970
Directed by Bernard McEveety
Written by Donald S. Sanford
Starring:
Special Guests Kevin Coughlin - Randy Gogan
L. Q. Jones - Sumner Pendleton
Patricia Morrow - Stella Felton
Sam Melville - Wade Pasco
Ken Mayer - Greenwood
Stanley Clements - Ed Jacobi
Robert Phillips - Vance Jessop
Ted Jordan - Burke
Jack Garner - Kemble
Eric Chase - Joseph
Jon Jason Mantley - Tom
Marie Mantley - Anne
Glenn Strange - Sam
Foster Brooks - Sporting Gentleman #1
Frank Biro - Sporting Gentleman #2
Henry Wise - Townsman #1
Bert Madrid - Townsman #2

In a fluke incident, young Randy (Kevin Coughlin) kills a notorious gunman. A shady newsman (L. Q. Jones) exploits the young man and his act of heroism.
Production #1615-0408

STARK September 28, 1970. Richard Kiley stars in the titular role.

525. THE SCAVENGERS

Original air date: November 16, 1970
Directed by Robert Totten
Written by Jim Byrnes
Starring:
Special Guests Yaphet Kotto - Piney Biggs
Cicely Tyson - Rachel
Slim Pickens - Colley
Roy Jenson - Rath
Link Wyler - Logan
Victor Holchak - Lieutenant
James Almanzar - Ogana
Eddie Little Sky - Scarface
Victor Izay - Barkeep
Glenn Strange - Sam
Ted Jordan - Burke
Jerelyn Fields - Merrilee Biggs
Henry Wise - Livery Man
Steve Raines - Driver

Barry Brown - Jared Sprague
June Dayton - Martha Sprague
Annette O'Toole - Edda Sprague
Dack Rambo - Ira Pickett
I. Stanford Jolley - Beecher
Ray Young - Joseph
Herb Vigran - Judge Brooker
Ted Jordan - Burke
Robert Swan - Texan
Glenn Strange - Sam

Piney Biggs (Yaphet Kotto) stabs himself and claims to be the sole survivor of an Indian massacre. Feted as a hero, his tale soon turns sour and his wife (Cicely Tyson) and child may be in danger, innocent people may be executed, or he could be killed himself.
Production #1615-0411

526. THE WITNESS

Original air date: November 23, 1970
Directed by Philip Leacock
Written by Shimon Wincelberg
Starring:
Special Guests Harry Morgan - Osgood Pickett
Tim O'Connor - Arnie Sprague

GENTRY'S LAW October 12, 1970. John Payne.

SNOW TRAIN October 19 and 26, 1970. James Arness.

Cold blooded without a heart killer Osgood Pickett (Harry Morgan) will stop at nothing to see that his murderous son Ira (Dack Rambo) is set free.

Production #1615-0405

527. McCABE

Original air date: November 30, 1970
Directed by Bernard McEveety
Written by Jim Byrnes
Starring:
Special Guests Dan Kemp - McCabe
Jim Davis - Sheriff Shackwood
David Brian - Clay White

Mitch Vogel - Dobie
Jon Lormer - Judge Clairborne
Robert Sorrells - J. W. Hicks
Mills Watson - Kipp
Lew Brown - Weaver
Tani Phelps - Ami
Marie Cheatham - Abigail Hartly
Trevor Bardette - Conductor
Tom Sutton - Lennie
Pete Kellett - Bartender

After a disappointing visit with his family, prisoner McCabe (Dan Kemp) escapes from Matt, only to face the threat of a lynch mob and a biased magistrate.

Production #1615-0402

528. THE NOON DAY DEVIL

Original air date: December 7, 1970
Directed by Philip Leacock
Written by William Kelley
Starring:
Special Guest Anthony Zerbe - Heraclio Cantrell and
    Father Hernando Cantrell
Warren Vanders - Bones Cunningham
Ernest Sarracino - Quito Vega
Anthony Cordova - Brother Antonio
Pepe Callahan - John Hike
Natividad Vacio - Diego
Annette Cardona - Rita
Fred Coby - Doctor
Tony Davis - Indian Boy
Julio Medina - Rodriguez
Bert Madrid - Carlos

Hernando and Heraclio Cantrell (Anthony Zerbe) are identical twins—one is a priest, the other a wanted robber and killer.

Production #1615-0413

529. SERGEANT HOLLY

Original air date: December 14, 1970
Directed by Bernard McEveety
Written by William Kelley
Starring:
Special Guests Forrest Tucker - Sgt. Holly
Albert Salmi - Willis Jeeter
Victor Eberg - Luke Pinero
Gregg Palmer - Bodine
David Kenard - Chico Fuentes
Vito Scotti - The Indian
Med Flory - Corp. Steckey
Glenn Strange - Sam
Read Morgan - Roy Gast
Bob Morgan - Lomax
Frank Hotchkiss - Corp. Tuttle

Kitty reluctantly helps Sergeant Holly (Forrest Tucker) clear his name after the whiskey soaked cavalry man is accused of robbing the payroll.

Production #1615-0414

530. JENNY

Original air date: December 28, 1970
Directed by Robert Totten
Written by Jack Miller
Starring:
Special Guests Steve Ihnat - Lucas Pritchard
Lisa Gerritsen - Jenny
Rance Howard - Judge Franklin

Glenn Strange - Sam
Ted Jordan - Burke
Steve Raines - Ed Reilly
Bob Burrows - Driver

Newly arrests Lucas Pritchard (Steve Ihnat) just as his daughter Jenny (Lisa Gerritsen) arrives in Dodge looking for him because her mother has passed away.

Production #1615-0415

531. CAPTAIN SLIGO

Original air date: January 4, 1971
Directed by William Conrad
Written by William Kelley
Starring:
Special Guests Richard Basehart - Captain Aron Sligo
Salome Jens - Josephine Burney
Royal Dano - Watney
Stacy Harris - Leonard
Robert Totten - Blacksmith
Bobby Eilbacher - Tim Burney
Geri Reischl - Anne Burney
Larry Finley - Bartender
Matt Emery - Trail Boss
Brian Foley - Cowboy
Boyd "Red" Morgan - Tanner
Glenn Strange - Sam
Fred Stromsoe - Tobin
Troy Melton - Rackley
Bob Herron - Vern

Widow Josephine Burney (Salome Jens) is courted by sea captain Aron Sligo, who decides to rest his sails near Dodge.

Production #1615-0416

THE SCAVENGERS November 16, 1970. Yaphet Kotto and Cicely Tyson.

WITNESS November 23, 1970. James Arness and Harry Morgan on the set.

THE GUN November 9, 1970. Ken Curtis as Festus in a pie-eating contest.

THE NOON DAY DEVIL December 7, 1970. Anthony Zerbe plays the dual roles of two brothers—one an outlaw, the other a priest.

SERGEANT HOLLY December 14, 1970. Forrest Tucker and Albert Salmi.

JENNY (1970) December 28, 1970. Lisa Gerritsen guest-stars in the titular role.

THE TYCOON January 25, 1971. Shug Fisher.

532. MIRAGE

Original air date: January 11, 1971
Directed by Vincent McEveety
Written by Jack Miller
Starring:
Special Guest John Anderson - Lemuel
Gary Wood - Tom
Mary Rings - Elsie
Bill Zuckert - Hotel Clerk
Harry Raybould - Maddox
Robert Knapp - Deputy
Dan White - Stocker
Kevin Burchett - Adam

After chasing and killing outlaw Maddox (Harry Raybould) far into the desert, Festus returns to Dodge near death with a clouded memory and fuzzy story regarding what had happened.
Production #1615-0417

533. THE TYCOON

Original air date: January 25, 1971
Directed by Bernard McEveety
Written by Robert Vincent Wright
Starring:
Special Guests Shug Fisher - Titus
Nora Marlowe - Ma Fowler
Gwynne Gilford - Dora Lou
John Beck - Moody Fowler
James Minotto - Amos Fowler
Herman Poppe - Clarence Carver
Glenn Strange - Sam

THE TYCOON January 25, 1971. Ken Curtis.

Ted Jordan - Burke
Walter Edmiston - Henry Folsom
Charles Wagenheim - Parson Mueller

Festus inherits $500 and with the help of his good friend Titus (Shug Fisher) becomes quite the man about town.

Production #1615-0418

534. JAEKEL

Original air date: February 1, 1971
Directed by Bernard McEveety
Teleplay by Calvin Clements
Story by Thelma and True Boardman
Starring:
Special Guests Eric Braeden - Carl Jaekel
Julie Gregg - Beth Wilson
John Crawford - Norman Wilson
Mia Bendixsen - Penny Wilson
Victor Tayback - Dirks
Glenn Strange - Sam
James Chandler - Warden
Scott Edmonds - Doctor
Bob Golden - Guard
Ted Jordan - Burke

Carl Jaekel (Eric Braeden) is released from prison and returns to Dodge for the woman he once planned to marry. Beth Wilson (Julie Gregg) has since married and has a little daughter (Mia Bendixsen).

Production #1615-0420

535. MURDOCK

Original air date: February 8, 1971
Directed by Robert Totten
Written by Jack Miller
Starring:
Special Guests Jack Elam - Lucas Murdock

JAEKEL February 1, 1971. Julie Gregg and Mia Bendixsen.

Bob Random - Scott
Anthony Caruso - Townsend
Jim Davis - Amos Carver
Clint Howard - Lonny
Tom Waters - Morris
Tim Burns - Braly
Liz Marshall - Ruth
Glenn Strange - Sam
Ted Jordan - Burke
Bobby Clark - Gatlin
Gary Combs - Fairchild

Lawman Lucas Murdock (Jack Elam) trails a murderous gang into Dodge, and with Matt's assistance plans to arrest them all. His plans change drastically when he realizes that his son (Bob

Random) is a member of the gang.
Production #1615-0419

536. **CLEAVUS**
Original air date: February 15, 1971
Directed by Vincent McEveety
Written by Donald Z. Koplowitz and Richard Davids Scott
Starring:
Special Guest Robert Totten - Cleavus Lukens
Arthur Hunnicutt - Uriah Spessard
William Challee - Baylock
Robert Cornthwaite - Clerk
Glenn Strange - Sam
Robert B. Williams - Woody
Henry Wise - Waiter

Down on his luck Cleavus Lukens (Robert Totten) accidentally kills a prospector and is suddenly prosperous—and in love with a disinterested Kitty.
Production #1615-0424

537. **LAVERY**
Original air date: February 22, 1971
Directed by Vincent McEveety
Written by Donald S. Sanford
Starring:
Special Guests Anthony Costello - Keith Lavery
Judi West - April
Karl Swenson - Mr. Hubert
Ken Swofford - Harry
David Huddleston - Arno
David Carradine - Clint
Glenn Strange - Sam

Chanin Hale - Verna
Jack Perkins - Trapper
Hank Patterson - Hank

On probation, Keith Lavery (Anthony Costello) has a hard enough time staying out of trouble—the last thing he needs is a reunion with his old partners in crime.
Production #1615-0421

538. **DIRTY SALLY - PART I**
(also referred to as PIKE)
Original air date: March 1, 1971
Directed by Bernard McEveety
Written by Jack Miller

DIRTY SALLY March 1 & 8, 1971. Jeanette Nolan and Dack Rambo.

Starring:
Special Guests Jeanette Nolan - Sally Fergus
Dack Rambo - Cyrus Pike
Cliff Osmond - Macomb
William Mims - Hawkins
Jim Boles - Sutro
Ross Hagen - Hicks
Glenn Strange - Sam
Ted Jordan - Burke
Woodrow Chambliss - Lathrop
William Murphy - Loomis
Jon Jason Mantley - Billy
Maria Mantley - Girl #1
John Puglia - Boy #1
Susan Newmark - Girl #2
Billy McMickle - Boy #2

Crusty drunk Dirty Sally (Jeanette Nolan) finds a young wounded outlaw named Pike (Dack Rambo) and nurses him back to health.
Production #1615-0422

539. DIRTY SALLY - PART II
Original air date: March 8, 1971
Directed by Bernard McEveety
Written by Jack Miller
Starring:
Special Guests Jeanette Nolan - Sally Fergus
Dack Rambo - Cyrus Pike
Cliff Osmond - Macomb
Ross Hagen - Hicks
Glenn Strange - Sam
Ted Jordan - Burke

William Murphy - Loomis

As Pike (Dack Rambo) begins to mend, he leaves the care of old Sally, who soon faces death threats from his outlaw pals who are interested in his current status and location.
Production #1615-0423

SEASON SEVENTEEN

Now broadcast at 8pm on Monday nights.

Executive Producer - John Mantley
Producer - Leonard Katzman
Associate Producer - Ron Honthaner
Executive Story Consultant - Jack Miller

540. THE LOST
Original air date: September 13, 1971
Directed by Robert Totten
Teleplay by Jack Miller
Story by Warren Vanders
Starring:
Special Guests Mercedes McCambridge - Mrs. Mather
Royal Dano - Henry Mather
Laurie Prange - Wild Child
Link Wyler - Lamond Mather
Charles Kuenstle - Valjean Mather
Dee Carroll - Mrs. Grayson
Jerry Brown - Abel Grayson
Peggy Rea - Mrs. Roniger
Maria Mantley - Maria
Jon Jason Mantley - Jon

Terry Lynn Wood - Elsie

Kitty is the sole survivor of a stagecoach accident and finds herself stranded, but not alone. A wild child (Laurie Prange) slowly joins her and they later encounter crazed Mrs. Mather (Mercedes McCambridge) and her trashy kinfolk.
Production #1615-0512

541. PHOENIX
Original air date: September 20, 1971
Directed by Paul Stanley
Written by Anthony Lawrence
Starring:
Special Guests Glenn Corbett - Phoenix
Mariette Hartley - Kate Hume
Gene Evans - Jess Hume
Ramon Bieri - John Sontag
Frank Corsentino- Frake
Ted Jordan - Burke

Phoenix (Glenn Corbett) is released from prison and immediately hires out to kill retired lawman Jess Hume (Gene Evans). When he meets up with Hume and his wife Kate (Mariette Hartley), a friendship develops and his ability to do his "job" becomes vexed.
Production #1615-0503

542. WASTE - PART I
Original air date: September 27, 1971
Directed by Vincent McEveety
Written by Jim Byrnes
Starring:
Special Guests Jeremy Slate - Ben Rodman

Ellen Burstyn - Amy Waters
Johnnie Whitaker - Willie Hubbard
David Sheiner - Preacher
Rex Holman - Oakley
Ken Swofford - Speer
Don Megowan - Lucas
Shug Fisher - Jed Rascoe

THE LOST September 9, 1971. Amanda Blake in the episode that ultimately changed her career.

WASTE September 27 & October 4, 1971. Ruth Roman and Johnnie Whitaker.

Special Guest Appearance Ruth Roman - Maggie Blaisedell
George Chandler - Silas Hubbard
Don Keefer - Drunk
Emory Parnell - 1st Prospector
Lloyd Nelson - 2nd Prospector
Lieux Dressler - Victoria
Merry Anders - Shirley
Claire Brennen - Lisa
Lee Pulford - Orphan Girl

    While Matt is tracking outlaw Ben Rodman (Jeremy Slate) he encounters a homeless boy (Johnnie Whitaker) and a wagon full of saloon girls squired by Maggie Blaisedell (Ruth Roman).
    Production #1615-0511

543. **WASTE - PART II**
Original air date: October 4, 1971
Directed by Vincent McEveety
Written by Jim Byrnes
Starring:
Special Guests Jeremy Slate - Ben Rodman
Ellen Burstyn - Amy Waters
Johnnie Whitaker - Willie Hubbard
David Sheiner - Preacher
Rex Holman - Oakley
Ken Swofford - Speer
Don Megowan - Lucas
Shug Fisher - Jed Rascoe
Special Guest Appearance Ruth Roman - Maggie Blaisedell
George Chandler - Silas Hubbard
Claire Brennen - Lisa
Emory Parnell - 1st Prospector

Lloyd Nelson - 2nd Prospector
Lieux Dressler - Victoria
Merry Anders - Shirley

    Ben Rodman (Jeremy Slate) and his gang corner Matt and his motley group of companions in an old deserted fort, where they struggle to survive without water and food.
    Production #1615-0511

544. **NEW DOCTOR IN TOWN**
Original air date: October 11, 1971
Directed by Philip Leacock
Written by Jack Miller
Starring:
Special Guest Pat Hingle - Dr. Chapman
Glenn Strange - Sam
Ted Jordan - Burke
Woodrow Chambliss - Lathrop
Lane Bradford - Dump Hart
Sarah Selby - Ma Smalley
Jon Lormer - Cody Sims
Charles Wagenheim - Halligan

    Doc leaves town hastily after a young patient passes away. Dr. Chapman (Pat Hingle) fills in for Doc and finds his welcome less than cordial. Newly is severely injured and the new doctor in town is put to the test.
    Production #1615-0505

545. **THE LEGEND**
Original air date: October 18, 1971
Directed by Philip Leacock

Written by Calvin Clements, Jr.
Starring:
Special Guests Kim Hunter - Bea Colter
Jan-Michael Vincent - Travis Colter
Greg Mullavey - Virgil Colter
Richard D. Kelton - Clayt Colter
Pat Hingle - Dr. Chapman
Ted Jordan - Burke
Glenn Strange - Sam
Michael Greene - Slim
Lloyd Nelson - Slater
Read Morgan - Eddie
Bryan O'Byrne - Mr. Palmer
Ken Mayer - Farmer
Victor Izay - Bull
Patrick Dennis Leigh - Prairie Scavenger
Red Currie - Carrot
Dick Cangey - Workman

Much to her discouragement, Bea Colter (Kim Hunter) fears her youngest son Travis (Jan-Michael Vincent) will follow in the footsteps of his deceased father and his outlaw brothers (Richard D. Kelton and Greg Mullavey).
Production #1615-0507

546. TRAFTON
Original air date: October 25, 1971
Directed by Bernard McEveety
Written by Ron Bishop
Starring:
Special Guests Victor French - Trafton
Sharon Acker - Tereese Farrell
Paul Stevens - Reverend English

Philip Carey - Bannion
Marie Windsor - Mary K.
Mike Mazurki - Whale
Patti Cohoon - Maria Farrell
Manuel Padilla, Jr. - Manuel
Glenn Strange - Sam
Ted Jordan - Burke
Clay Tanner - Capps
Fred Stromsoe - Prew
Bill Catching - Brant

Trafton (Victor French) is a ruthless cold blooded killer but three words may end his murderous ways—"I forgive you"—stated by a dying priest the outlaw has just shot.
Production #1615-0504

547. LYNOTT
Original air date: November 1, 1971
Directed by Gunnar Hellstrom
Written by Ron Bishop
Starring:
Special Guests Richard Kiley - Tom Lynott
Peggy McCay - Pene Lynott
Jonathan Lippe - Wallace
William Bramley - Anderson
Gregg Palmer - Nicols
Anthony Caruso - Talley
Pat Hingle - Dr. Chapman
Ken Lynch - Rolling
Claudia Bryar - Manda Weaver
Eddie Quillan - Barkeep
Tom Brown - Ed O'Connor
Glenn Strange - Sam

John Quade - Shaw
Ted Jordan - Burke
Al Wyatt - Heavy #1
Bobby Clark - Heavy #2

NEW DOCTOR IN TOWN October 11, 1971. Amanda Blake and Pat Hingle.

Former lawman Tom Lynott (Richard Kiley) saves Matt's life and fills in for the recuperating marshal. His somnolent approach to peace keeping forces Matt back into action before he is one-hundred percent.

Production #1615-0509

548. **LIJAH**

Original air date: November 8, 1971
Directed by Irving J. Moore
Written by William Blinn

Starring:

Special Guests Denny Miller - Lijah
Harry Townes - Hale Parker
Erin Moran - Rachel
William Wintersole - Will Standish
Tom Brown - Ed O'Connor
Woodrow Chambliss - Lathrop
Pat Hingle - Dr. Chapman
Lane Bradford - Dump Hart
Howard Culver - Howie
Herb Vigran - Judge Brooker
Pete Kellett - Frank
Glenn Strange - Sam
Charles Wagenheim - Halligan
Ted Jordan - Burke
Dan Flynn, Jr. - Tack
Henry Wise - Hank

A mysteriously silent mountain man, Lijah (Denny Miller) is accused of not one, but three murders and a puzzled Dr. Chapman (Pat Hingle) may be his only saving grace.

Production #1615-0506

549. **MY BROTHER'S KEEPER**

Original air date: November 15, 1971
Directed by Paul Stanley
Written by Arthur Dales

Starring:
Special Guests John Dierkes - Indian
Pippa Scott - Sarah Mather
Malcolm Atterbury - Cob
Charles McGraw - Squawman
Pat Hingle - Dr. Chapman
Dana Laurita - Mandy
Ray Reinhardt - Preacher
Sarah Selby - Ma Smalley
Glenn Strange - Sam
Charles Wagenheim - Halligan
Red Morgan - Kroll
Donna DeLacey - Woman

Reactions differ greatly when Festus brings an elderly Indian (John Dierkes) wishing to die in peace into Dodge for medical treatment.
Production #1615-0508

550. **DRAGO**
Original air date: November 22, 1971
Directed by Paul Stanley
Written by Jim Byrnes
Starring:
Special Guests Buddy Ebsen - Drago
Ben Johnson - Hannon
Edward Faulkner - Trask
Del Monroe - Flagg
Rick Gates - Gillis
Pat Hingle - Dr. Chapman
Tani Phelps Guthrie - Clara
Jim Skaggs - Sheepherder

Larry Randles - Larry
Mitchell Silberman - Ruben

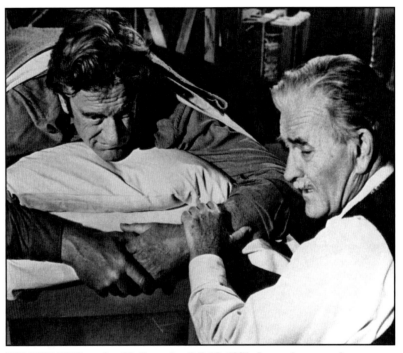

THE BULLET *November 29, December 6 & 13, 1971. James Arness and Milburn Stone.*

When a gang of killers led by Hannon (Ben Johnson) take the life of his boss Miss Clara (Tani Phelps Guthrie), former mountain man Drago (Buddy Ebsen) is merciless in his pursuit.
Production #1615-0510

551. **THE BULLET - PART I**
Also known as GOLD TRAIN: THE BULLET.

Original air date: November 29, 1971
Directed by Bernard McEveety
Written by Jim Byrnes
Starring:
Special Guests Eric Braeden - Jack Sinclair
Katherine Justice - Beth Tilton
Robert Hogan - Capt. Darnell
Warren Kemmerling - Conductor
Sam Melville - Nebo
John Crawford - Blanchard
Harry Carey, Jr. - Kelliher
Jonathan Lippe - Roper
Pepe Callahan - Secos
Walter Sande - Caldwell
Mills Watson - Pony
Robert Sorrells - Concho
Eddie Firestone - Orely
Dan Ferrone - Private
Sian Barbara Allen - Allie Dawson
Special Guest Appearance Alejandro Rey - Father Sanchez
Norman Alden - Amos Potter
Harry Harvey, Sr. - Drummer
Pete Kellett - Sergeant
Jon Kowal - Dunn
Glenn Strange - Sam
Ted Jordan - Burke
Denny Arnold - Fireman

Doc returns to Dodge just as Matt is shot in the back. The wound is too close to his spine and Doc suggests a colleague in Denver is the only person to remove the bullet.
Production #1615-0514

552. THE BULLET - PART II

Original air date: December 6, 1971
Directed by Bernard McEveety
Written by Jim Byrnes
Starring:
Special Guests Eric Braeden - Jack Sinclair
Katherine Justice - Beth Tilton
Robert Hogan - Capt. Darnell
Warren Kemmerling - Conductor
Sam Melville - Nebo
John Crawford - Blanchard
Harry Carey, Jr. - Kelliher
Jonathan Lippe - Roper
Pepe Callahan - Secos
Walter Sande - Caldwell
Mills Watson - Pony
Robert Sorrells - Concho
Eddie Firestone - Orely
Dan Ferrone - Private
Sian Barbara Allen - Allie Dawson
Special Guest Appearance Alejandro Ray - Father Sanchez
Norman Alden - Amos Potter
Harry Harvey, Sr. - Drummer
Pete Kellett - Sergeant
Jon Kowal - Dunn
Glenn Strange - Sam
Ted Jordan - Burke

Jack Sinclair (Eric Braeden) and his gang interrupt the train that is transporting Matt and a large gold shipment to Denver, Colorado.
Production #1615-0515

553. THE BULLET - PART III

Original air date: December 13, 1971
Directed by Bernard McEveety
Written by Jim Byrnes
Starring:
Special Guest Eric Braeden - Jack Sinclair
Katherine Justice - Beth Tilton
Robert Hogan - Capt. Darnell
Warren Kemmerling - Conductor
Sam Melville - Nebo
John Crawford - Blanchard
Harry Carey, Jr. - Kelliher
Jonathan Lippe - Roper
Pepe Callahan - Secos
Walter Sande - Caldwell
Mills Watson - Pony
Robert Sorrells - Concho
Eddie Firestone - Orely
Dan Ferrone - Private
Sian Barbara Allen - Allie Dawson
Special Guest Appearance by Alejandro Rey - Father Sanchez
Pete Kellett - Sergeant
Harry Harvey, Sr. - Drummer
Jon Kowal - Dunn
Glenn Strange - Sam
Ted Jordan - Burke

Doc, with assistance from Kitty, must operate on Matt immediately as the outlaws decide to return to the train, intent on killing the seriously injured lawman.
Production #1615-0516

554. P. S. MURRY CHRISTMAS

Original air date: December 27, 1971
Directed by Herb Wallerstein
Written by William Kelley
Starring:
Special Guests Jeanette Nolan - Emma Grundy
Patti Cohoon - Mary
Jodie Foster - Patricia
Erin Moran - Jenny
Josh Albee - Michael
Brian Morrison - Owen
Willie Aames - Tom
Todd Lookinland - Jake
Special Guest Appearance Jack Elam - Titus Spangler
Glenn Strange - Sam
Jack Collins - J. Stedman Edgecomb
Ted Jordan - Burke
Herb Vigran - Judge Brooker
Sarah Selby - Ma Smalley
Maudie Pickett - Mrs. Pretch

Seven runaway children and child at heart Titus Spangler (Jack Elam) team up to soften the soul of Emma Grundy (Jeanette Nolan), the orphanage headmistress.
Production #1615-0513

555. NO TOMORROW

Original air date: January 3, 1972
Directed by Irving J. Moore
Written by Richard Fielder
Starring:
Special Guests Sam Groom - Ben Justin
Pamela McMyler - Elizabeth Justin

H. M. Wynant - Morris Cragin
Steve Brodie - Garth Brantley
Henry Jones - J. Luther Gross
Richard Hale - Old Luke
Herb Vigran - Judge Brooker
Liam Dunn - Eli Bruder
Robert Nichols - Warden
Joe Haworth - Rider
Leo Gordon - Hargis
Glenn Strange - Sam
Ted Jordan - Burke
Dan Flynn - Kyle Brantley
Allan Fudge - Bailiff

Framed for horse stealing, honest Ben Justin (Sam Groom) makes a rash decision to elude the law and punishment to provide for his expectant wife (Pamela McMyler).
Production #1615-0517

556. **HIDALGO**
Original air date: January 10, 1972
Directed by Paul Stanley
Written by Colley Cibber
Starring:
Special Guests Thomas Gomez - Agustin
Linda Marsh - Lucero
Fabian Gregory - Lucho
David Renard - Gorio
Edward Colmans - Cuero
Stella Garcia - Chona
Julio Medina - Fermin
Alfonso Arau - Mando

P.S. MURRY CHRISTMAS December 27, 1971. Jack Elam and Ken Curtis.

Tracking outlaw Mando into Mexico, Matt is seriously wounded by his cutthroat gang. He is found by Lucho (Fabian Gregory) and tended to by his sister (Linda Marsh), who happens to be Mando's woman.
Production #1615-0501

557. **TARA**
Original air date: January 17, 1972
Directed by Bernard McEveety

ONE FOR THE ROAD January 24, 1972. Jeanette Nolan returns as Dirty Sally.

Written by William Kelley
Starring:
Special Guests Michele Carey - Tara Hutson
and L. Q. Jones - Gecko Ridley
Laurence Delaney - Roy Hutson
Ken Swofford - Dirk
James McCallion - Mr. Fletcher
Ken Mayer - Pudge
Harry Hickox - Bank Officer
John Dullaghan - Bank Teller
Glenn Strange - Sam
Ted Jordan - Burke
Sarah Selby - Ma Smalley
Natalie Masters - Woman
Charles Seel - Barney
Howard Culver - Howie
Gene Tyburn - Shotgun
Don Pulford - Young Man
Denny Arnold - Messenger

     Newly has fallen for beautiful Tara Hutson (Michelle Carey) but her shady past and checkered future may be his ultimate undoing.
     Production #1615-0522

558. ONE FOR THE ROAD
Original air date: January 24, 1972
Directed by Bernard McEveety
Written by Jack Miller
Starring:
Special Guest Jack Albertson - Lucius Prince
Special Guest Appearance Jeanette Nolan - Sally Fergus
Melissa Murphy - Miss Elsie
Victor Holchak - Tom Rickaby

Herb Vigran - Judge Brooker
Glenn Strange - Sam
Ted Jordan - Burke
Dorothy Neumann - Old Woman
Jack Perkins - Bouncer

Dirty Sally is back (Jeanette Nolan) and she wants Lucius Prince (Jack Albertson) a fellow imbiber. Lucius is rich and his daughter's current beau comes gunning for him.
Production #1615-0520

559. THE PREDATORS
Original air date: January 31, 1972
Directed by Bernard McEveety
Written by Calvin Clements
Starring:
Special Guests Claude Akins - Howard Kane
Jacqueline Scott - Abelia
Jodie Foster - Marianne
Brian Morrison - Jonathan
George Murdock - Cole Matson
Tom Brown - Ed O'Connor
Mills Watson - Currie
Lew Brown - Smith
Read Morgan - Brown
Glenn Strange - Sam
Ted Jordan - Burke

Two predators descend on Abelia's (Jacqueline Scott) ranch—a vicious dog and a vicious man (Claude Akins)—both proven to be killers.
Production #1615-0518

560. YANKTON
Original air date: February 7, 1972
Directed by Vincent McEveety
Written by Jim Byrnes
Starring:
Special Guests Forrest Tucker - Will Donavan
Nancy Olson - Henrietta Donavan
Pamela Payton-Wright - Emma Donavan
Special Guest Appearance James Stacy - Yankton
Woodrow Chambliss - Lathrop
Ted Jordan - Burke
Hank Patterson - Hank
Margaret Bacon - Dressmaker
Glenn Strange - Sam
Tom Sutton - Pete
Bill Hart - Cowboy #1
Bennie Dobbins - Cowboy #2

Revenge gone awry in a tale involving a wealthy rancher (Forrest Tucker), his daughter (Pamela Payton-Wright) and a saddle tramp named Yankton (James Stacy).
Production #1615-0521

561. BLIND MAN'S BLUFF
(The episode erroneously is called BLIND MAN'S BUFF in the credits)
Original air date: February 21, 1972
Directed by Herb Wallerstein
Written by Ron Honthaner
Starring:
Special Guests Anne Jackson - Phoebe Preston
Victor French - Jed Frazer
George Lindsey - Charlie Clavin

Charles Kuenstle - Hank McCall
Woodrow Chambliss - Lathrop

Phoebe Preston (Anne Jackson) comes to the aid of Jed Frazer (Victor French) after he was ambushed by two men and left to die.
Production #1615-0519

562. **ALIAS FESTUS HAGGEN**
Original air date: March 6, 1972
Directed by Vincent McEveety
Written by Calvin Clements
Starring:
Special Guests Ramon Bieri - Doyle
Lieux Dressler - Susie
Robert Totten - Walker
Booth Coman (should be Colman, misspelled in credits) - Rand
Gregg Palmer - Guthrie
William Bryant - Bennett
Rayford Barnes - Grebbs
Herb Vigran - Judge Brooker
Jon Lormer - Judge Clayborne
Glenn Strange - Sam
Ted Jordan - Burke
Bill Erwin - Bailiff
Tom McFadden - Luke
Rusty Lane - Sheriff Buckley
Ed McCready - Scotty
Louie Elias - Cowboy
Lloyd Nelson - Shorty

Festus is mistaken for a murderer and arrested by Doyle (Ramon Bieri). Matt does his best to clear his friend, but things begin to look hopeless when the killer's wife identifies Festus as her husband.
Production #1615-0523

563. **THE WEDDING**
Original air date: March 13, 1972
Directed by Bernard McEveety
Written by Harry Kronman
Starring:
Special Guests Morgan Woodward - Walt Clayton
Sam Elliott - Cory Soames
Melissa Newman - Donna Clayton
Lane Bradford - Joe Eggers
Fran Ryan - Mrs. Keller
James Chandler - Reverend Keller
Larry Barton - Townsman
George Wallace - Sheriff Henning
Ted Jordan - Burke
Byron Mabe - Sandy Carr
Troy Melton - Pete Calder
Jason Wingreen - Dr. Cleery

Cory Soames (Sam Elliott) and Donna Clayton (Melissa Newman) want to marry but their union is steadfastly opposed by her father (Morgan Woodward) who will stop at nothing to ruin their plans.
Production #1615-0502

SEASON EIGHTEEN

Executive Producer - John Mantley
Producer - Leonard Katzman

Associate Producer - Ron Honthaner
Executive Story Consultant - Jack Miller

564. THE RIVER - PART I

Original air date: September 11, 1972
Directed by Herb Wallerstein
Written by Jack Miller
Starring:
Special Guests Jack Elam - Pierre
Miriam Colon - Paullette Duvalier
Slim Pickens - Charlie Utter
Patti Cohoon and Clay O'Brien - the runaways
Roger Torrey - Finn MacCool
Jerry Gatlin - Lapin
Red Morgan - Suggs
Pete Kellett - Hodad
Jack Perkins - Drunk
Lloyd Nelson - Cardsharp
Don Megowan - Lolo Grimes
Gene Tyburn - Poe
Chanin Hale -Apple Pie Lady
Pete Logan - Addis
Ronald Manning - Stinson
Daniel J. Flynn - Store Clerk

Matt has recovered money stolen by Charlie Utter (Slim Pickens) and his gang. To escape, Matt must make a perilous dive into a river, where he is saved by two runaways (Patti Cohoon and Clay O'Brien) on a raft.
Production #1615-0560

565. THE RIVER - PART II

Original air date: September 18, 1972
Directed by Herb Wallerstein
Written by Jack Miller
Starring:
Special Guests Jack Elam - Pierre
Miriam Colon - Paullette
Slim Pickens - Charlie Utter
Patti Cohoon and Clay O'Brien - the runaways
Roger Torrey - Finn MacCool
Jerry Gatlin - Lapin
Red Morgan - Suggs
Pete Kellett - Hodad
Maudie Prickett - Aunt Ida
Gene Tyburn - Poe
Don Megowan - Lolo Grimes
Ronald Manning - Stinson

Pierre and Paullette (Jack Elam and Miriam Colon) join Matt and the children as the Utter gang still pursues them and the money.
Production 1615-0561

566. BOHANNAN

Original air date: September 25, 1972
Directed by Alf Kjellin
Written by William Kelley
Starring:
Special Guests Richard Kiley - Bohannan
Linda Marsh - Lydia Walden
Vincent Van Patten - Heck Walden
Ed Bakey - Goody Stackpole
Helen Kleeb - Dorcas Wentzel
Rege Cordic - Reverend
Ted Jordan - Burke
Glenn Strange - Sam

Woodrow Chambliss - Lathrop

Bohannan (Richard Kiley) is a traveling faith healer who arrives in Dodge and faces his toughest cure yet, a young boy named Heck (Vincent Van Patten).
Production #1615-0555

567. **THE JUDGEMENT**
Original air date: October 2, 1972
Directed by Philip Leacock
Written by Shimon Wincelberg
Starring:
Special Guests Ramon Bieri - Musgrove
Tim O'Connor - Gideon
Mariette Hartley - Fiona Gideon
Katherine Helmond - Ena Spratt
Richard Kelton - Ab Craddock
Special Guest Appearance William Windom - Ira Spratt
Jon Locke - Orval
Glenn Strange - Sam
Ted Jordan - Burke
Charles Wagenheim - Halligan
Melissa Gilbert - Spratt's Child

Revenge-seeking Musgrove (Ramon Bieri) has already killed and will kill again as he searches for Ira Spratt (William Windom), the man responsible for his prison term.
Production #1615-0553

568. **THE DRUMMER**
Original air date: October 9, 1972
Directed by Bernard McEveety
Written by Richard Fielder

Starring:
Special Guests Victor French - Daniel Shay
Fionnuala Flanagan - Sarah Morgan
Bruce Glover - Enoch Brandt
Kiel Martin - Ike Daggett
Special Guest Appearance Brandon Cruz - Jimmy Morgan
Glenn Strange - Sam
Ted Jordan - Burke
Woodrow Chambliss - Lathrop
Herb Armstrong - Sayers
Hank Patterson - Livery Man
Paul Sorensen - Trent

A traveling salesman (Victor French) arrives in Dodge and gets much more than he had hoped for—grim reminders of his sordid past.
Production #1615-0554

569. **SARAH**
Original air date: October 16, 1972
Directed by Gunnar Hellstrom
Written by Calvin Clements
Starring:
Special Guests Anne Francis - Sarah
Anthony Caruso - Pappy Quinn
Jonathan Lippe - Sonny
Michael Lane - Digby
Rex Holman - Ed
George Keymas - Deering
John Orchard - Taylor
Kay E. Kuter - Warren
Larry Duran - Vesco
Ronald Manning - Engels

THE RIVER September 11 and 18, 1972. James Arness.

Alberto Pina - Liveryman

Matt meets up with former girlfriend Sarah (Anne Francis) at a robbers roost, and then poses as her husband when Pappy Quinn (Anthony Caruso) and his gang arrive for shelter.
Production #1615-0558

570. THE FUGITIVES
Original air date: October 23, 1972
Directed by Irving J. Moore
Written by Charles Joseph Stone
Starring:
Special Guests James Olson - Bede Stalcup
Victor Tayback - Bill Hankins
Russell Johnson - Link Parrin
Troy Melton - Curly Danzig
Darrell Larson - Danny Stalcup
Glenn Strange - Sam
Ted Jordan - Burke

Bede Stalcup (James Olson) and his gang kidnap Doc and Festus and force Doc to tend to his injured brother Danny (Darrell Larson). Festus escapes and returns with Matt to save Doc. In the effort, Festus is gravely wounded.
Production #1615-0551

571. ELEVEN DOLLARS
Original air date: October 30, 1972
Directed by Irving J. Moore
Written by Paul Savage
Starring:
Special Guests Susan Oliver - Sarah Elkins
Diane Shalet - Charity Spencer

THE RIVER September 11 & 18, 1972. Patti Cohoon, Clay O'Brien and James Arness.

500

Josh Albee - Chad
Ike Eisenmann - Clay
E. J. Andre - Jeb Spencer
Ted Jordan - Burke
Roy Engel - Sandor
Phil Chambers - Beckwith
Charles Wagenheim - Halligan
Sam Edwards - 1st Wolfer
A. G. Vitanza - 2nd Wolfer
Owen Bush - Hotel Clerk
Gloria LeRoy - Claire
Tom Waters - Bartender

Festus sets out a long journey to deliver an inheritance to the daughter of a late friend. Among the obstacles along the way, a group of thieving hide hunters.
Production #1615-0559

572. **MILLIGAN**
Original air date: November 6, 1972
Directed by Bernard McEveety
Written by Ron Bishop
Starring:
Special Guests Harry Morgan - John Milligan
Lynn Carlin - Janet Milligan
Sorrell Booke - Gerald Pandy
Patti Cohoon - Wendy Milligan
Scott Walker - Mattis
Special Guest Appearance Joseph Campanella - Jack Norcross
John Pickard - Bob Power
Lew Brown - Reeves
Read Morgan - Potter
Gene Tyburn - Logan

Robert Swan - Looter
Charles Macaulay - Dofeny
Glenn Strange - Sam
Ted Jordan - Burke
Todd Bass - Tom
Sammee Lee Jones - Girl

In a sad twist, mild farmer John Milligan (Harry Morgan) shoots a wanted man with a Robin Hood image and the townspeople side with the outlaw instead of making Milligan a hero.
Production #1615-0552

573. **TATUM**
Original air date: November 13, 1972
Directed by Gunnar Hellstrom
Written by Jim Byrnes
Starring:
Special Guests Gene Evans - Tatum
Sandra Smith - Maddy
Sheila Larken - Marion
Jay MacIntosh - Gwenn
Jeff Pomerantz - Dirk Mitchell
Ana Korita - Kata
Ken Tobey - Ed Terrall
Lloyd Nelson - Clergyman
Neil Summers - Joe Beel
Robert Tindall - Man #1
Duncan Inches - Man #2

Former outlaw Tatum (Gene Evans) is mauled by a bear while protecting his Indian wife and small son. Dying, he wishes to be reunited with his estranged daughters.
Production #1615-0556

574. THE SODBUSTERS

Original air date: November 20, 1972

Directed by Robert Butler

Written by Ron Bishop

Starring:

Special Guests Alex Cord - Pete Brown

Katherine Justice - Clarabelle

Dawn Lyn - Maria

Leif Garrett - John

Robert Viharo - Dick Shaw

Special Guest Appearance Morgan Woodward -
    Lamoor Underwood

Richard Bull - Deems

Joe di Reda - Navin

Colin Male - Gene Hill

Jim Boles - Kesting

Harrison Ford - Print

Paul Prokop - Dan

Norman Bartold - Darga

Evans Thornton - Murphy

A range war erupts between Pete Brown (Alex Cord) and Lamoor Underwood (Morgan Woodward) with Matt in the middle.
    Production #1615-0557

575. THE BROTHERS

Original air date: November 27, 1972

Directed by Gunnar Hellstrom

Written by Calvin Clements

Starring:

Special Guests Steve Forrest - Cord Wrecken

Joe Silver - Beal Brown

Richard O'Brien - Carter

Angus Duncan - Jay Wrecken

Regis J. Cordic - Sheriff Crane

Eddie Ryder - The Undertaker

Edward Faulkner - Drummer

Reid Cruickshanks - Mr. Denton

Terry Wilson - Liveryman

Danil Torpe - Alf

Glenn Strange - Sam

Ted Jordan - Burke

Howard Culver - Howie

John Harper - Percy Crump

Nancy Fisher - Flo

Jon Kowal - Barfly Joe

Al Berry - Barfly Bob

Daniel M. White - Oldtimer

Phil Chambers - Shotgun

Kitty shoots wanted killer Jay Wrecken (Angus Duncan) and his brother, Cord (Steve Forrest), travels to Dodge to seek revenge.
    Production #1615-0564

576. HOSTAGE!

Original air date: December 11, 1972

Directed by Gunnar Hellstrom

Written by Paul F. Edwards

Starring:

Special Guests William Smith - Jude Bonner

Geoffrey Lewis - Lafitte

Marco St. John - Virgil Bonner

Nina Roman - Amy Lee

Glenn Strange - Sam

Ted Jordan - Burke

502

Woodrow Chambliss - Lathrop
James Chandler - Governor
Hal Baylor - Toke
Sandra Kent - Martha
Stafford Repp - Sheriff Tanner

ARIZONA MIDNIGHT January 1, 1973. Ken Curtis and friend.

Jude Bonner (William Smith) and his dog soldiers ride into to Dodge seeking revenge against Matt, who arrested his brother Virgil (Marco St. John), and is executed for his crimes. In retribution, Bonner kidnaps Kitty, who is viciously abused and then gunned down in front of the Long Branch. The badge comes off and Matt ferociously tracks Bonner down.

Production #1615-0566

577. JUBILEE

Original air date: December 18, 1972

Directed by Herb Wallerstein
Teleplay by Paul Savage
Story by Jack Freeman
Starring:
Special Guests Tom Skerritt - Tuck Frye
Collin Wilcox-Horne - Bess Frye
Alan Hale - Dave Chaney
Scott Brady - Ed Wells
Glenn Strange - Sam
Ted Jordan - Burke
Woodrow Chambliss - Lathrop
Lori Rutherford - Annie Frye
Todd Cameron - Caleb Frye
Whitey Hughes - Billy Banner

A prized quarter horse named Jubilee leads owner Tuck Frye (Tom Skerritt) to dream big and ultimately neglect his farm and family.

Production #1615-0565

578. ARIZONA MIDNIGHT

Original air date: January 1, 1873
Directed by Irving J. Moore
Written by Dudley Bromley
Starring:
Special Guests Billy Curtis - Arizona
Mills Watson - Fred

THIS GOLDEN LAND March 5, 1973. Ken Curtis, Paul Stevens and James Arness.

Ken Mayer - Ed
Stanley Clements - Red
Glenn Strange - Sam
Ted Jordan - Burke
Sandy Powell - Beatrice

   Midget Arizona (Billy Curtis) arrives in Dodge claiming he

will turn into an elephant at midnight. 'Nuff said.
   Production #1615-0563

579. HOMECOMING
Original air date: January 8, 1973
Directed by Gunnar Hellstrom
Written by Calvin Clements
Starring:
Special Guests Richard Kelton -
   Rick Wilson
Robert Pratt - Raymond Wilson
Lynn Marta - Prudence
Lurene Tuttle - Anna Wilson
Stuart Margolin - John Mophet
Claudia Bryar - Mrs. Bronson
Ted Jordan - Burke
Ivy Jones - Martha Beal

   Rick and Raymond Wilson
(Richard Kelton and Robert Pratt)
are outlaws on the run to Mexico.
Their mother is dying and they take
time for a last visit, but didn't count
on Doc treating her at home.
   Production #1615-0568

580. SHADLER
Original air date: January 15, 1973
Directed by Arnold Laven
Written by Jim Byrnes
Starring:
Special Guests Earl Holliman - Boone Shadler

Diana Hyland - Dallas Fair
Denver Pyle - Cyrus Himes
Linda Watkins - Abby Shadler
Pat Conway - Varnum
Ken Lynch - McKee
John Davis Chandler - Rogers
Donald Barry - Dobson
James Jeeter - Creech
John Carter - Father Walsh
Bill Erwin - Mr. Jonas
Meg Wyllie - Mrs. Evans
Alex Sharp - Reno
Tom Pittman - Elmer
Barry Cahill - Walters
Wallace Earl - Farina

Posing as a priest, convict Boone Shadler (Earl Holliman) escapes prison and, while attempting to retrieve stolen money, he is forced to help Newly in the aid of a stricken town.
Production #1615-0567

581. **PATRICIA**
Original air date: January 22, 1973
Directed by Alf Kjellin
Written by Calvin Clements
Starring:
Special Guests Jess Walton - Patricia
Ike Eisenmann - Johnny
John Baer - Johnny's father
Glenn Strange - Sam
Ted Jordan - Burke
Gail Bonney - Mrs. Peary
Donald Elson - Brown
Richard Lundin - Stage Driver

Newly and Patricia (Jess Walton) survive a tornado together. Romance blossoms and the loving couple marry. Sadly, their happiness does not last long as Doc delivers tragic news regarding the new bride and her health.
Production #1615-0569

582. **QUIET DAY IN DODGE**
Original air date: January 29, 1973
Directed by Alf Kjellin
Written by Jack Miller
Starring:
Special Guests Margaret Hamilton - Edsel Pry
Leo Gordon - Job Spelling
Shug Fisher - Dobie Crimps
Douglas V. Fowley - Buck Doolin
John Fiedler - Mr. Ballou
Helen Page Camp - Mrs. Ballou
J. Pat O'Malley - Drummer
Walker Edmiston - Ludlow
Herb Vigran - Judge Brooker
Willie Ames - Andy
Glenn Strange - Sam
Ted Jordan - Burke
Woodrow Chambliss - Lathrop
Charles Wagenheim - Halligan
Henry Wise - Hank
Michelle Breeze - Sadie

Sleep deprived Matt must deal with a brutal prisoner (Leo Gordon), a saloon brawl, cranky Edsel Pry (Margaret Hamilton), a young troublemaker and worst of all, a scorned Kitty.
Production #1615-0571

583. WHELAN'S MEN

Original air date: February 5, 1973
Directed by Paul F. Edwards
Written by Ron Bishop
Starring:
Special Guests Robert Burr - Dan Whelan
William Bramley - Loomis
Noble Willingham - Tuck
Harrison Ford - Hobey
Frank Ramirez - Breed
Gerald McRaney - Gentry
Bobby Hall - Musgrove
Seamon Glass - Acker
Ed Craig - Partridge
Richard Hale - Miner
Glenn Strange - Sam
Ted Jordan - Burke
Roy Roberts - Mr. Bodkin
Tom Brown - Ed O'Connor

After robbing everything in sight, Dan Whelan (Robert Burr) and his men wait in the Long Branch for Matt to return. Kitty joins their poker game and the stakes are high—Matt's life.
Production #1615-0562

584. KIMBRO

Original air date: February 12, 1973
Directed by Gunnar Hellstrom
Written by Jim Byrnes
Starring:
Special Guests John Anderson - Adam Kimbro
Michael Strong - Peak Stratton
William Devane - Moss Stratton
Tom Falk - Billy Stratton
Rick Weaver (Dennis Weaver's son) - Turkey Stratton
Doreen Lang - Mary Bentley
Ted Jordan - Burke
Lisa Eilbacher - Melody
Wendell Baker - John

Once a mentor to Matt, Adam Kimbro (John Anderson) is now forced to clean stables just for drinking money. Knowing how he handled the badge before, Matt deputizes his friend in hopes of restoring his self-esteem.
Production #1615-0570

585. JESSE

Original air date: February 19, 1973
Directed by Bernard McEveety
Written by Jim Byrnes
Starring:
Special Guests Brock Peters - Jesse Dillard
Don Stroud - Pete Murphy
Regis J. Cordic - Marshal Halstead
Robert Pine - Link
Leonard Stone - Abel Glass
Jim Davis - Dave Carpenter
Ted Gehring - Sheriff Bradley
Norman Bartold - Sheriff
Larry Finley - Barkeep
Lloyd Nelson - Dr. Miller
Pete Kellett - Drucker
Karen Welch - Agnes

Festus risks everything to defend his old friend Jesse Dillard (Brock Peters). Newly and Festus must decide between duty and friendship when the law and a group of drovers try to decide Jesse's fate.

Production #1615-0572

586. **TALBOT**
Original air date: February 26, 1973

THIS GOLDEN LAND March 5, 1983. Paul Stevens.

Directed by Vincent McEveety
Written by Jim Byrnes
Starring:
Special Guests Anthony Zerbe - Talbot
Salome Jens - Katherine

Peter Jason - Pope
Bill Williams - Red
Ken Swofford - Harkey
Robert Donner - Brown
Robert Totten - Eli
Glenn Strange - Sam
Ted Jordan - Burke
Charles Wagenheim - Halligan
Howard Culver - Howie
Charles Macauley - Mr. Dofeny
Chanin Hale - Sally
Link Wyler - Dealer
Henry Wise - Hank
Ed McCready - Man
Victor Izay - Bull
Jack Perkins - Charlie
Gloria Dixon - Shirley
Tom Sutton - Tom
Jennifer Yelland - Alice

Love and jealousy make bank robbery plans go awry as outlaw Talbot (Anthony Zerbe) falls for Katherine (Salome Jens), then kills her abusive husband. Meanwhile, Talbot's colleagues try to force him to follow the original plans.

Production #1615-0574

587. **THIS GOLDEN LAND**
Original air date: March 5, 1973
Directed by Gunnar Hellstrom
Written by Hal Sitowitz
Starring:
Special Guests Paul Stevens - Moshe Gorofsky

Victor French - Ruxton
Richard Dreyfuss - Gearshon
Kevin Coughlin - Calvin
Joseph Hindy - Laibel
Bettye Ackerman - Zisha
Wayne McLaren - Homer
Scott Seles - Semel
Robert Nichols - Barkeep

Moshe Gorofsky (Paul Stevens) and his family move to Kansas, but their dreams are shattered when his youngest son is roughed up and dies at the hand of Ruxton (Victor French) and his men.

Production #1615-0573

SEASON NINETEEN

Executive Producer - John Mantley
Producer - Leonard Katzman
Associate Producer - Ron Honthaner
Executive Story Consultant - Jack Miller

588. WOMEN FOR SALE - PART I
Original air date: September 10, 1973
Directed by Vincent McEveety
Written by Jim Byrnes
Starring:
Special Guests James Whitmore - Timothy Fitzpatrick
Kathleen Cody - Cynthia
Dawn Lyn - Marcy
Nicholas Hammond - Britt

Sally Kemp - Rachel
Lieux Dressler - Liz
Gregory Sierra - Blue Jacket
Dan Ferrone - Dan Ross
Larry D. Mann - Pritchard
Charles Seel - Josiah
Special Guest Appearance Shani Wallis - Stella
Gilbert Escandon - Ten Bears
Ronald Manning - Hoxie
Francesca Jarvis - Mother

Blue Jacket (Gregory Sierra) and his band of Comanche renegades kidnap women and children, including Stella and Marcy (Shani Wallis and Dawn Lyn), for white slave trader Timothy Fitzpatrick (James Whitmore), who in turn plans to sell them in Mexico.

Production #1615-0607

589. WOMEN FOR SALE - PART II
Original air date: September 17, 1973
Directed by Vincent McEveety
Written by Jim Byrnes
Starring:
Special Guests James Whitmore - Timothy Fitzpatrick
Kathleen Cody - Cynthia
Dawn Lyn - Marcy
Nicholas Hammond - Britt
Lieux Dressler - Liz
Dan Ferrone - Dan Ross
Charles Seel - Josiah
Special Guest Appearance Shani Wallis - Stella
Gregory Sierra - Blue Jacket
Sally Kemp - Rachel

Edgar Monetathchi - Comanche Chief
Gilbert Escandon - Ten Bears
Ronald Manning - Hoxie

With Matt in pursuit, things begin to fall apart for the white slave traders. To make matters worse, one outlaw named Britt (Nicholas Hammond) begins to fall for a pretty captor—Cynthia (Kathleen Cody).
Production #1615-0607

590. MATT'S LOVE STORY

Original air date: September 24, 1973
Directed by Gunnar Hellstrom
Written by Ron Bishop
Starring:
Special Guests Michael Learned - Mike Yardner
Keith Andes - Starcourt
Jonathan Lippe - Monte Rupert
William Schallert - Cordelius
Special Guest Appearance Victor French - Les Dean
Glenn Strange - Sam
Richard Lundin - Canoot
S. Michael De France - Mio
Neil Summers - Man

Les Dean (Victor French) shoots Matt, who is hot on his trail. The injury causes Matt to suffer from amnesia, and he is found left for dead by Mike Yardner (Michael Learned). As Matt mends, the two fall in love, but their happiness is short-lived—Dean returns to the scene.
Production #1615-0609

591. THE BOY AND THE SINNER

Original air date: October 1, 1973
Directed by Bernard McEveety
Written by Hal Sitowitz
Starring:
Special Guest Ron Moody - Noah Beal
Vincent Van Patten - Colby Eaton
Warren Vanders - Otis Miller
John Crawford - Hugh Eaton
Ken Lynch - Jess Bradman
Read Morgan - Jack Beaver
Florida Friebus - Mrs. Travis
Hal Baylor - Boomer
Victor Izay - Bull

Noah Beal (Ron Moody) is a drunken beggar who constantly exchanges his pride for the bottle, until he meets young Colby Eaton (Vincent Van Patten), who wants to change the man's ways.
Production #1615-0604

592. THE WIDOW MAKER

Original air date: October 8, 1973
Directed by Bernard McEveety
Written by Paul F. Edwards
Starring:
Special Guests Steve Forrest - Scott Coltrane
David Huddleston - Dad Goodpastor
Randolph Roberts - Kid Chama
Barra Grant - Teresa
Glenn Strange - Sam
Ted Jordan - Burke
Hank Patterson - Hank
Jerry Gatlin - Buck Lennart

WOMEN FOR SALE September 10 & 17, 1973. Kathleen Cody.

James Chandler - Preacher
Don Carter - Boy
Rand Bridges - Deak Towler
J. R. Clark - Sundog Wheeler

Ken Konopka - Station Master
Phil Chambers - Stage Driver
Louis Elias - R. J.
Jeff Parks - Zeke

Former shootist Scott Coltrane (Steve Forrest) tries to live down his reputation and begin a new life with the woman he loves, Teresa (Barra Grant).
Production #1615-0610

593. KITTY'S LOVE AFFAIR
Original air date: October 22, 1973
Directed by Vincent McEveety
Teleplay by Paul Savage
Story by S. L. Kotar, J. E. Gessler and Paul Savage
Starring:
Special Guests Richard Kiley - Will Stambridge
Leonard Stone - Corley Deems
Christopher Connelly - Sheb Deems
Paul Picerni - Grimes
Don Keefer - Turner
Jack Perkins - Drummer
Gerald McRaney - Lonnie Colby
Del Monroe - Coots
Virginia Baker - Mrs. Colby
Ted Jordan - Burke
Woodrow Chambliss - Lathrop
Charles Wagenheim - Halligan
Richard D. Hurst - Mayhew
Ed Long - Morg
Rayford Barnes - Dowel
James Almanzar - Clel
Pete Kellett - Curt

Another broken date leads Kitty to continue her journey to

WOMEN FOR SALE September 10 & 17, 1973. James Arness and Shani Wallis.

511

St. Louis without Matt. Her stage is attacked by outlaws and ex-gunfighter Will Stambridge (Richard Kiley) rescues her. When the dust settles, Will decides to relocate to Dodge City, and the gossip begins.

Production #1615-0611

594. THE WIDOW AND THE ROGUE
Original air date: October 29, 1973
Directed by Bernard McEveety
Teleplay by Paul Savage
Story by Harvey Marlowe and Paul Savage
Starring:
Special Guests James Stacy - J. J. Honegger
Beth Brickell - Martha Cunningham
Clay O'Brien - Caleb Cunningham
Helen Page Camp - Woman
Monika Svensson - Daughter
Walker Edmiston - Station Master
Paul Sorenson - Farmer
Richard Lundin - Stage Driver

Festus has his hands full as he attempts to bring in charming rogue J. J. Honegger (James Stacy), who is facing two years in jail.

Production #1615-0606

595. A GAME OF DEATH...AN ACT OF LOVE...PART I
Original air date: November 5, 1973
Directed by Gunnar Hellstrom
Written by Paul F. Edwards
Starring:
Special Guests Morgan Woodward - Bear Sanderson
Paul Stevens - Cicero Wolfe
Whitney Blake - Lavinia Sanderson

MATT'S LOVE STORY September 24, 1973. Michael Learned and James Arness.

John Pickard - Captain Sykes
Geoffrey Horne - Lieutenant Briggs
X Brands - Renegade #1
Ivan Naranjo - Renegade #2
Peter Canon - Red
Clay Tanner - Joe Bob
Special Guest Appearance Donna Mills - Cora Sanderson

Glenn Strange - Sam
Ted Jordan - Burke
Howard Culver - Howie
Victor Leono - Renegade Leader
Richard Lundin - Brewer

After Indians kill his wife and destroy his home, Bear Sanderson (Morgan Woodward) swears revenge. Matt is unsuccessful in finding legal representation for the Indian suspects, including mysterious visiting lawyer Cicero Wolfe (Paul Stevens).
Production #1615-0602

596. A GAME OF DEATH...AN ACT OF LOVE...PART II
Original air date: November 12, 1973
Directed by Gunnar Hellstrom
Written by Paul F. Edwards
Starring:
Special Guests Morgan Woodward - Bear Sanderson
Paul Stevens - Cicero Wolfe
Michael Learned - May Lassiter
Garry Walberg - Dekker
John Pickard - Captain Sykes
Geoffrey Horne - Lieutenant Briggs
X Brands - Renegade #1
Ivan Naranjo - Renegade #2
Herb Vigran - Judge Brooker
Special Guest Appearance Donna Mills - Cora Sanderson
Whitney Blake - Lavinia Sanderson
Glenn Strange - Sam
Ted Jordan - Burke
Hank Patterson - Hank
Owen Bush - Bailiff
Robert Karnes - Mr. Lauter

Victor Leono - Renegade Leader
Richard Lundin - Brewer

Cicero Wolfe (Paul Stevens) agrees to represent the Indians and is revealed to be half-Indian himself. This further enrages Bear Sanderson (Morgan Woodward) and his daughter Cora (Donna Mills).
Production #1615-0602

597. LYNCH TOWN
Original air date: November 19, 1973
Directed by Bernard McEveety
Teleplay by Calvin Clements
Story by Joann Carlino and Ann Snyder and Calvin Clements
Starring:
Special Guests David Wayne - Judge Warfield
Mitch Vogel - Rob Fielder
Warren Kemmerling - Sheriff Ridder
Ken Swofford - Jake Fielder
Norman Alden - Tom Hart
Julie Cobb - Minnie Nolen
Nancy Jeris - Kate Geer
Scott Brady - John King

Drunken judge Warfield (David Wayne) is under the thumb of town boss John King (Scott Brady), and Matt has little hope for a fair trial for murder suspect Jake Fielder (Ken Swofford).
Production #1615-0601

598. THE HANGING OF NEWLY O'BRIEN
Original air date: November 26, 1973
Directed by Alf Kjellin
Written by Calvin Clements

Starring:
Special Guest Billy Green Bush - Kermit
Jimmy Van Patten - Tim
Jessamine Milner - Grandma
Rusty Lane - Grandpa

Donald Elson - Farmer Buey
Billie Bird - Old Woman
Arthur Malet - Oldtimer
Erica Hunton - Little Girl

THE BOY AND THE SINNER October 1, 1973. James Arness and Ron Moody.

Jan Burrell - Anna
Glenn Strange - Sam
Ted Jordan - Burke
Deborah Dozier - Ronda
Walter Scott - John
Bobby Hall - Adrian

Newly's medical skills are put to the test as he is sent to treat families in a backwoods community. When a patient dies, Kermit (Billy Green Bush) and others threaten his life.

Production #1615-0605

599. SUSAN WAS EVIL
Original air date: December 3, 1973
Directed by Bernard McEveety
Written by William Keys
Starring:
Special Guests Art Lund - Boswell
Kathy Cannon - Susan
George Di'Cenzo - Newt
Henry Olek - Sam
Special Guest Appearance Kathleen Nolan - Nellie
Jim Gammon - Dudley
Robert Brubaker - Murphy

A severely wounded outlaw is brought to a remote relay station, where the operator (Kathleen Nolan) and her niece Susan (Kathy Cannon) argue bitterly over the man's treatment.

Production #1615-0613

600. THE DEADLY INNOCENT
Original air date: December 17, 1973

Directed by Bernard McEveety
Written by Calvin Clements
Starring:
Special Guests Russell Wiggins - Billy
Charles Dierkop - Barnett
Herb Vigran - Judge Brooker
Ted Jordan - Burke
Jack Garner - Pete
William Shriver - Crooms
Erica Hunton - Annie
Denny Arnold - Slim

At the sight of any violence to anyone or anything, young and simple Billy (Russell Wiggins) reacts with uncontrollable power and anger.
Production #1615-0617

601. THE CHILD BETWEEN
Original air date: December 24, 1973
Directed by Irving Moore
Written by Harry Kronman
Starring:
Special Guests Sam Groom - Lew Harrod
Alexandra Morgan - Makesha
John Dierkes - Dahoma
Eddie Little Sky - Goriko
Pete Kellett - 1st Hidecutter
Bill Hart - 2nd Hidecutter
Alex Sharp - 3rd Hidecutter

Lew Harrod and his Indian wife Makesha (Sam Groom and Alexandra Morgan) seek medical advice from Newly for their infant child, then block his treatment attempts.
Production #1615-0612

THE BOY AND THE SINNER October 1, 1973. Ron Moody.

602. A FAMILY OF KILLERS
Original air date: January 14, 1974
Directed by Gunnar Hellstrom
Written by William Keys

Starring:
Special Guests Glenn Corbett - Hargraves
Anthony Caruso - Elton Sutterfield
Mills Watson - Crazy Charley
Morgan Paull - Ham
Zina Bethune - Jonnalee
George Keymas - Tobin
Frank Corsentino - Jacob
Stuart Margolin - Brownie

A lawman named Hargraves (Glenn Corbett) is wounded and his deputy killed by Elton Sutterfield (Anthony Caruso) and family. Matts wants to bring them back alive—Hargraves wants to kill every one of them.
Production #1615-0616

603. **LIKE OLD TIMES**
Original air date: January 21, 1974
Directed by Irving J. Moore
Written by Richard Fielder
Starring:
Special Guests Nehemiah Persoff - Ben Rando
Dan Travanty (later known as Daniel J. Travanti) - Barker
Charles Haid - Hargis
Gloria DeHaven - Carrie
Ted Jordan - Burke
Roy Roberts - Mr. Bodkin
Tom Brown - O'Connor
Charles Wagenheim - Halligan
Victor Izay - Bull
Robert Brubaker - Bartender
Rhodie Cogan - Mrs. Hopewell
Hal Bokar - Clay
Richard Lundin - Stage Driver

Renowned safe cracker Ben Rando (Nehemiah Persoff) is released after a lengthy stay in prison and he hopes to rekindle a romance with Carrie (Gloria DeHaven).
Production #1615-0619

604. **THE TOWN TAMERS**
Original air date: January 28, 1974
Directed by Gunnar Hellstrom
Written by Paul Savage
Starring:
Special Guests Jim Davis - Luke Rumbaugh
Jean Allison - Martha
Ike Eisenmann - Caleb
Rex Holman - Aikens
Leo Gordon - Badger
Sean McClory - Sham
James Jeter - Barker
Kay Kuter - McCurdy
James Chandler - Preacher
Julie Bennett - Kate
Don Megowan - Michael
Clay Tanner - Texan Leader
Ed Call - Farmer
Mary Betten - Farmer's Wife
Larry Randles - Texan Rider

Marshal Luke Rumbaugh (Jim Davis) and Matt team up to clean up the lawless town of Hilt. Things go well until Luke's relationship with Martha (Jean Allison) and her son Caleb (Ike Eisenmann) cloud his judgement and Badger (Leo Gordon) and his men plan to take advantage.
Production #1615-0614

THE WIDOW MAKER October 8, 1973. Steve Forrest and Barra Grant.

THE WIDOW MAKER October 8, 1973. James Arness and Steve Forrest.

KITTY'S LOVE AFFAIR October 22, 1973. Richard Kiley and Amanda Blake.

A GAME OF DEATH...AN ACT OF LOVE
November 5 & 12, 1973. Buck Taylor, James
Arness and X Brands.

THE IRON BLOOD OF COURAGE February 18,
1974. Mariette Hartley.

THE FOUNDLING February 11, 1974. Kay Lenz.

THE IRON BLOOD OF COURAGE February 18,
1974. Gene Evans and James Arness.

605. THE FOUNDLING
Original air date: February 11, 1974
Directed by Bernard McEveety
Written by Jim Byrnes
Starring:
Special Guests Kay Lenz - Lettie
Bonnie Bartlett - Maylee
Donald Moffat - Joseph Graham
Dran Hamilton - Agnes Graham
Don Collier - Eli Baines
Jerry Hardin - Bob Ranger
Ted Jordan - Burke
Woodrow Chambliss - Lathrop
Robert Brubaker - Bartender

Matt tries to find a home for a baby when the child's grand-parents reject the infant based on illegitimacy, leaving the mother, Lettie (Kay Lenz), distraught.
Production #1615-0621

606. THE IRON BLOOD OF COURAGE
Original air date: February 18, 1974
Directed by Gunnar Hellstrom
Written by Ron Bishop
Starring:
Special Guests In Alphabetical Order
Lloyd Bochner - Burdette
Eric Braeden - Talley
Patti Cohoon - Ronilou
Miriam Colon - Mignon
Gene Evans - Shaw Anderson
Mariette Hartley - Ellie Talley
John Milford - Hutchinson

THE SCHOOLMARM February 25, 1974. Charlotte Stewart.

Bing Russell - Rolfing
Robert Karnes - Chandler
John Baer - Nichols
Lloyd Nelson - Morris
Jerry Gatlin - Toey
Elizabeth Harrower - Mrs. O'Roarke
Nick Ramus - Lynit

Ranchers fight Shaw Anderson (Gene Evans) over water rights with a lawyer named Burdette (Lloyd Bochner), hiring a gunfighter (Eric Braeden) to ensure victory over Shaw.

Production #1615-0622

607. **THE SCHOOLMARM**

Original air date: February 25, 1974
Directed by Bernard McEveety
Written by Dick Nelson
Starring:
Special Guests Charlotte Stewart - Sarah Merkle
Lin McCarthy - Carl Pruitt
Scott Walker - Stokes
Todd Lookinland - Lester
Howard Culver - Howie
Laura Nichols - Eliza
Janet Nichols - Mary Beth
Kevin C. McEveety - Thomas

Raped, school teacher Sarah Merkle (Charlotte Stewart) fears she will lose her job if her resulting pregnancy is discovered by the townspeople of Dodge.

Production #1615-0623

608. **TRAIL OF BLOODSHED**

Original air date: March 4, 1974
Directed by Bernard McEveety
Written by Earl W. Wallace
Starring:
Special Guests Kurt Russell - Buck Henry
Tom Simcox - Rance Woolfe
Harry Carey, Jr. - Amos Brodie
Janit Baldwin - Joanie

THE SCHOOLMARM February 25, 1974. Todd Lookinland and Ken Curtis.

Larry Pennell - John Woolfe
Special Guest Appearance Craig Stevens - The Gambler
Woodrow Chambliss - Lathrop
Nina Roman - Rita
Read Morgan - Bartender
Gloria Dixon - Lady Card Dealer

Mr. Lathrop (Woodrow Chambliss) is savagely beaten by

COWTOWN HUSTLER March 11, 1974. Jack Albertson.

DISCIPLE April 1, 1974. Dennis Redfield.

COWTOWN HUSTLER March 11, 1974. Jack Albertson and James Arness.

DISCIPLE April 1, 1974. Dennis Redfield and James Arness.

Rance Woolfe (Tom Simcox), who then kills his brother (Larry Pennell) and wounds his nephew (Kurt Russell).

Production #1615-0615

609. COWTOWN HUSTLER
Original air date: March 11, 1974
Directed by Gunnar Hellstrom
Written by Jim Byrnes
Starring:
Special Guests Jack Albertson - Moses
Jonathan Goldsmith Lippe - Dave Rope
Nellie Bellflower - Sally
Dabbs Greer - Joe Bean
Henry Beckman - Thaddius McKay
John Davis Chandler - Willie Tomsen
Richard O'Brien - Adam Kearney
Lew Brown - Beeton
Robert Swan - Cox
Chuck Hicks - Turner

Pool player Moses (Jack Albertson) teams up with sly Dave Rope (Jonathan Goldsmith Lippe) and his girlfriend Sally (Nellie Bellflower), hoping for one last high stakes win.

Production #1615-0618

610. TO RIDE A YELLER HORSE
Original air date: March 18,1974
Directed by Vincent McEveety
Written by Calvin Clements
Starring:
Special Guests Louise Latham - Mrs. Shepherd
Kathleen Cody - Anna May
Thomas Leopold - Chester
John Reilly - Orlo
Parker Stevenson - Steven
Simon Scott - Mr. Rogers
Herb Vigran - Judge Brooker
Elizabeth Harrower - Mrs. O'Roarke

Neither Newly or Orlo (John Reilly) are considered good enough for lovely Anna May (Kathleen Cody). Her mother (Louise Latham) would prefer her daughter to court Steven (Parker Stevenson), the son of a wealthy rancher.

Production #1615-0624

611. DISCIPLE
Original air date: April 1, 1974
Directed by Gunnar Hellstrom
Written by Shimon Wincelberg
Starring:
Special Guests Dennis Redfield - Lem
Frank Marth - Loveday
Marco St. John - Darcy
Paul Picerni - The New Marshal
Robert Phillips - Bill Jim
R. L. Armstrong - Ransom
David Huddleston - Asa
Claire Brennen - Sissy
Ted Jordan - Burke
Robert Brubaker - Bartender
Woodrow Chambliss - Lathrop
Charles Wagenheim - Halligan
Charles Seel - Barney
Bobby E. Clark - Junior

Doc removes another bullet from Matt, who is shot during a

robbery attempt. The shooting maims the lawman, rendering his gun arm useless. Matt meets Lem (Dennis Redfield), an army deserter, who has an aversion to violence and the two must band together to fight off an outlaw gang.

Production #1615-0620

SEASON TWENTY

Executive Producer - John Mantley
Producer - Leonard Katzman
Associate Producer - Ron Honthaner
Executive Story Consultant - Jack Miller

612. MATT DILLON MUST DIE!
Original air date: September 9, 1974
Directed by Victor French
Written by Ray Goldrup
Starring:
Special Guests Morgan Woodward - Abraham Wakefield
Joseph Hindy - Jacob
Bill Lucking - Esau
Henry Olek - Issaac
Douglas Dirkson - Abel
Frederick Herrick - Laban
Elaine Fulkerson - Annabel

Matt must kill Laban Wakefield (Frederick Herrick) which arouses the wrath of his crazed widowed father Abraham (Morgan Woodward). With the help of his four surviving sons, they go after Matt, and with an hour head start, hunt him down.

Production #1615-0661

613. A TOWN IN CHAINS
Original air date: September 16, 1974
Directed by Bernard McEveety
Written by Ron Bishop
Starring:
Special Guests In Alphabetical Order
Ramon Bieri - Big Thicket
Gretchen Corbett - Arlene
Lance LeGault - Oregon
Ron Soble - Clatch
Don Stroud - Foss
Russell Wiggins - Pryor
Med Flory - Sheriff Van Werkle
John Crawford - Muller
Thad Hall - Shields
Lloyd Nelson - Welch
Neil Summers - Townsman
Paul C. Thomas - Mr. Burry
Francesca Jarvis - Martha
Bernice Smith - Helen
Mari Martin - Dorothy
Margaret L. Kingman - Mary

Big Thicket (Ramon Bieri) and his gang pose as Union officers and decide to hit one more town for a last heist, with Matt trailing closely behind.

Production #1615-0656

614. THE GUNS OF CIBOLA BLANCA - PART I
Original air date: September 23, 1974
Directed by Gunnar Hellstrom
Written by Paul Savage

Starring:
Special Guests Harold Gould - Lucius Shindrow
Dorothy Tristan - Lyla
Richard Anderson - Coltraine
James Luisi - Ivers
Henry Beckman - Dr. Rhodes
Gloria Le Roy - Mady

MATT DILLON MUST DIE! September 9, 1974. Morgan Woodward and James Arness.

Jackie Coogan - Stoudenaire
Shug Fisher - Mule Skinner
Michael Cristofer - Ben
Kurt Grayson - Evans
Rex Holman - Badger
Lloyd Nelson - Dundee
Gilbert Escandon - Hatajo
Walter Roy Smith II - Freight Clerk

Richard Lundin - Stagecoach Driver

Doc and Lyla (Dorothy Tristan) are taken prisoner after surviving an attack on their stage. The attack was orchestrated by comanchero leader Lucius Shindrow (Harold Gould).
Production #1615-0654

615. THE GUNS OF CIBOLA BLANCA - PART II
Original air date: September 30, 1974
Directed by Gunnar Hellstrom
Written by Paul Savage
Starring:
Special Guests Harold Gould - Lucius Shindrow
Dorothy Tristan - Lyla
Richard Anderson - Coltraine
James Luisi - Ivers
Henry Beckman - Dr. Rhodes
Gloria LeRoy - Mady
Michael Cristofer - Ben
Rex Holman - Badger
Shug Fisher - Mule Skinner
Kurt Grayson - Evans
Richard Lundin - Stagecoach Driver
Gilbert Escandon - Hatajo

With Doc long overdue, Matt and company set out to find him. They pose as gun runners to gain entrance into the Shindrow stronghold, which is under the suspicious eye of right hand man Coltraine (Richard Anderson).
Production #1615-0654

616. THIRTY A MONTH AND FOUND
Original air date: October 7, 1974

MATT DILLON MUST DIE! September 9, 1974. James Arness and Bill Lucking.

Directed by Bernard McEveety
Written by Jim Byrnes
Starring:
Special Guests Gene Evans - Will Parmalee
Nicholas Hammond - Doak
Van Williams - Quincy
Ford Rainey - Storekeeper
Kim O'Brien - Katherine
Special Guest Appearance David Brian - Tait Cavanaugh
Victor Izay - Bull
Hal Baylor - Railroader
Bonnie Jedell - Delilah
Hank Kendrick - Sheriff

With their way of life coming to an unwanted end, three cowboys, including Will Parmalee (Gene Evans), refuse to accept change, which slowly leads to their doom.
Production #1615-0653

617. **THE WIVING**
Original air date: October 14, 1974
Directed by Victor French
Written by Earl W. Wallace
Starring:
Special Guests Harry Morgan - Jed Hockett
Karen Grassle - Fran
John Reilly - Ike
Linda Sublette - Emily
Herman Poppe - Luke
Michele Marsh - Sarah
Dennis Redfield - Shep
Fran Ryan - Hannah
Robert Brubaker - Floyd

A TOWN IN CHAINS September 16, 1974. James Arness and Gretchen Corbett.

Rod McGaughy - Cowboy #1
Bobby E. Clark - Cowboy #2

Insipid tale about farmer Jed Hockett (Harry Morgan) and the edict he issues his three sons—go to town and come back with brides.
Production #1615-0652

618. **THE IRON MEN**
Original air date: October 21, 1974
Directed by Gunnar Hellstrom
Written by John Mantley
Starring:
Special Guests Cameron Mitchell - Chauncey Demon

Barbara Colby - Kathy Carter
Eric Olson - Johnny Carter
George Murdock - Luke
William Bryant - Sheriff
Marc Alaimo - Kane
Paul Gehrman - Dubbins
Alec Murdock - Mace
Special Guest Appearance John Russell - Carl Ryker

He used to battle outlaws, but now Chauncey Demon battles the bottle. With Matt's help, the former badge rehabilitates to fight Carl Ryker (John Russell) and his men.
Production #1615-0660

619. THE FOURTH VICTIM
Original air date: November 4, 1974

A TOWN IN CHAINS September 16, 1974. James Arness and Russell Wiggins.

Directed by Bernard McEveety
Written by Jim Byrnes
Starring:
Special Guests Biff McGuire - Potter
Leonard Stone - Ray Price
Ted Jordan - Burke
Paul Sorensen - Bill Saxbe
Howard Culver - Howie
Woodrow Chambliss - Lathrop
Victor Killian - Homer Jones
Lloyd Perryman - Henry Meeker
Frank K. Janson - Jeb Nelson
Al Wyatt - Earl Haines
Ben Bates - Second Man
Alex Sharp - Third Man

A mysterious killer is loose in Dodge and Doc appears to be the next victim. Doc refuses Matt's suggestion to hide and instead uses himself as bait to flush out the murderer.
Production #1615-0659

620. THE TARNISHED BADGE
Original air date: November 11, 1974
Directed by Michael O'Herlihy
Written by Robert Vincent Wright
Starring:
Special Guest Victor French - Sheriff Bo Harker
Pamela McMyler - Jenny Blair
Nick Nolte - Barney Austin
Gary Walberg - Toby
James Lydon - Charlie Boggs
Eddie Firestone - Hotel Clerk
Ross Elliott - Conway

THE GUNS OF CIBOLA BLANCA September 23 & 30, 1974. Harold Gould.

THE WIVING October 14, 1974. Herman Poppe, Linda Sublette and Michelle Marsh.

THE GUNS OF CIBOLA BLANCA September 23 & 30, 1974. James Luisi, Dorothy Tristan and Milburn Stone.

THIRTY A MONTH AND FOUND October 7, 1974. Ken Curtis and Van Williams.

Special Guest Appearance Ruth McDevitt - Gramma Boggs
Sam Edwards - Travis
William Katt - Lonnie Weeks
Hank Worden - Claude
Eddie Quillan - Telegrapher
Steve Raines - Pete
Jon Locke - Abe
Robert Swan - Slim
Jimmy McNichol - Willie

Matt runs afoul of old friend Sheriff Bo Harker (Victor French) who is more town tamer than lawman. Matt is asked to fire Harker, which sets off a chain of events including the killing of Barney Austin (Nick Nolte).
Production #1615-0657

621. IN PERFORMANCE OF DUTY
Original air date: November 18, 1974
Directed by Gunnar Hellstrom
Written by William Keys
Starring:
Special Guests Eduard Franz - Judge Kendall
Paul Koslo - Cory
Bonnie Bartlett - Agnes Benton
Rance Howard - Frank Benton
Martin Kove - Gutherie
Michael MacRae - Alf
David Huddleston - Emmett
Ted Jordan - Burke
Robert Brubaker - Floyd
Bill Erwin - Snood
Ted Lehman - Jury Foreman

Emmett (David Huddleston) and his gang senselessly kill Frank Benton (Rance Howard) and seriously wound his wife Agnes (Bonnie Bartlett). Matt arrests the bunch, but with lack of evidence, they may be freed.
Production #1615-0658

622. ISLAND IN THE DESERT - PART I
Original air date: December 2, 1974
Directed by Gunnar Hellstrom
Written by Jim Byrnes
Starring:
Special Guests Strother Martin - Ben Snow
William C. Watson - Gard Dixon
Regis Cordic - Sheriff Grimes
Hank Brandt - John Lipon
Ted Jordan - Burke

Festus is wounded by outlaw Gard Dixon (William C. Watson) and left in the desert to die. He is rescued by crazed desert rat Ben Snow (Strother Martin).
Production #1615-0662

623. ISLAND IN THE DESERT - PART II
Original air date: December 9, 1974
Directed by Gunnar Hellstrom
Written by Jim Byrnes
Starring:
Special Guests Strother Martin - Ben Snow
William C. Watson - Gard Dixon
Regis Cordic - Sheriff Grimes
Hank Brandt - John Lipon

Snow (Strother Martin) and Festus trek through the desert with the injured deputy packing gold for the crazy man. They soon

meet up with the one (William C. Watson) who wounded Festus.
Production #1615-0662

624. THE COLONEL

Original air date: December 16, 1974
Directed by Bernard McEveety
Written by Arthur Dales
Starring:
Special Guests Lee J. Cobb - Josiah
Julie Cobb - Anne
Richard Ely - Bill Higgins
Todd Lookinland - Corporal
Randolph Roberts - Obie
Roy Jenson - Jeff Higgins
Robert Brubaker - Floyd
Pete Kellett - Biggs
Dan Travanty - Carl

Former military officer turned drunk Josiah (Lee J. Cobb) is
confronted with a sudden uneasy reunion with his daughter Anne
(Julie Cobb), who is planning to wed Carl (Dan Travanty).
Production #1615-0651

625. THE SQUAW

Original air date: January 6, 1975
Directed by Gunnar Hellstrom
Written by Jim Byrnes
Starring:
Special Guests John Saxon - Gristy Calhoun
Arlene Martel - Quanah
Tom Reese - Charlie Dent
Morgan Paull - Brinker
William Campbell - Striker

THE IRON MEN October 21, 1974. James Arness and John Russell.

Harry Middlebrooks - Dobie
X Brands - Chief

Outlaw Gristy Calhoun (John Saxon) is pursued by Matt and
the gang of men he double-crossed. Quanah (Arlene Martel), an
Indian woman, soon figures in his flight and eventual capture.
Production #1615-0665

THE IRON MEN October 21, 1974. Cameron Mitchell.

626. **THE HIDERS**
Original air date: January 13, 1975

Directed by Victor French
Written by Paul Savage
Starring:
Special Guests Ned Beatty - Karp
Mitch Vogel - Dink
Lee De Broux - Quincannon
Robert Donner - Belnap
Damon Douglas - Billy
Sierra Brandt - Martha
Ellen Blake - Mrs. Belnap
Ted Jordan - Burke
Woodrow Chambliss - Lathrop

Karp (Ned Beatty) is the shady leader of hide cutters who takes a strong dislike to Festus, who would like to see his men, particularly Dink (Mitch Vogel), lead better lives.
Production #1615-0666

627. **LARKIN**
Original air date: January 20, 1975
Directed by Gunnar Hellstrom
Written by Jim Byrnes
Starring:
Special Guests Richard Jaeckel - Larkin
Anthony Caruso - Lon
Robert Gentry - Tucker
Robert Sorrells - Hickory
Maggie Malooly - Woman
Michael Le Clair - Jess
Jack Rader - Angus
Kathleen Cody - Melissa
Elliott Lindsay - Farmer
Gilman W. Rankin - Waiter

THE TARNISHED BADGE November 11, 1974. Pamela McMyler and James Arness.

Newly and his prisoner Larkin (Richard Jaeckel) face seemingly insurmountable odds as crazed bounty hunters trail both

men. Newly is wounded in his race to reach Dodge City.

Production #1615-0667

628. THE FIRES OF IGNORANCE

Original air date: January 27, 1975
Directed by Victor French
Written by Jim Byrnes
Starring:
Special Guests Allen Garfield - Henry Decory
John Vernon - Oliver Harker
Lance Kerwin - Tommy Harker
Diane Shalet - Ami Harker
George DiCenzo - Mr. Bruce
Karen Oberdiear - Sallie
Herb Vigran - Judge Brooker
John Pickard - Bud
Ted Jordan - Burke
Charles Wagenheim - Halligan
Robert Brubaker - Floyd
Janet Nichols - Lucy

Farmer Oliver Harker (John Vernon) takes his son Tommy (Lance Kerwin) out of school to help with chores on the farm—much to the disappointment of his teacher (Allen Garfield).

Production #1615-0668

629. THE ANGRY LAND

Original air date: February 3, 1975
Directed by Bernard McEveety
Teleplay by Jim Byrnes
Story by Herman Groves
Starring:
Special Guest Carol Vogel - Rachel

IN PERFORMANCE OF DUTY November 18, 1974. Eduard Franz, Ken Curtis.

IN PERFORMANCE OF DUTY Martin Kove, Michael MacRae and David Huddleston.

IN PERFORMANCE OF DUTY Paul Koslo and James Arness.

IN PERFORMANCE OF DUTY David Huddleston and Ken Curtis.

Eileen McDonough - Bessie
Bruce M. Fischer - The Man
Dayton Lummis - Mr. Holmby
Phil Chambers - Farmer

Young Bessie (Eileen McDonough) is orphaned and forced to live with her aunt Rachel (Carol Vogel). Rachel recently lost her own son and husband and fears accepting her niece will result in another loss.
Production #1615-0669

630. BRIDES AND GROOMS
Original air date: February 10, 1975
Directed by Victor French
Written by Earl W. Wallace
Starring:
Special Guests Harry Morgan - Jed Hockett
David Soul - Ike
Amanda McBroom - Fran
Linda Sublette - Emily
Herman Poppe - Luke
Michele Marsh - Sarah
Dennis Redfield - Shep
Spencer Milligan - Jinx Tobin
Ray Girardin - Cluff Tobin
Fran Ryan - Hannah
Special Guest Appearance Jim Backus - Reverend Sims
Jerry Hoffman - Dub
Bobby E. Clark - Farmboy

Insipid sequel to an insipid episode, *The Wiving*. Jed Hockett (Harry Morgan) now want his sons to marry their brides

ISLAND IN THE DESERT December 2 & 9, 1974. Strother Martin and Ken Curtis.

and get back to work.
Production #1615-0673

631. HARD LABOR
(This was the last episode to be filmed).
Original air date: February 24, 1975
Directed by Bernard McEveety
Teleplay by Earl W. Wallace
Story by Hal Sitowitz

THE COLONEL December 16, 1974.
James Arness, Julie Cobb and Lee J. Cobb.

THE COLONEL December 16, 1974.
Julie Cobb.

THE HIDERS January 13, 1975.
Ken Curtis and Ned Beatty.

THE COLONEL December 16, 1974.
Lee J. Cobb.

THE FIRES OF IGNORANCE January 27, 1975.
Lance Kerwin and John Vernon.

THE SQUAW January 6, 1975.
John Saxon.

THE FIRES OF IGNORANCE January 27, 1975. Allen Garfield.

Starring:
Special Guests John Colicos - Judge Flood
Hal Williams - Widge
William Smith - Latch
Kevin Coughlin - Elton
Ben Piazza - Fifer

Gregory Sierra - Osuna
Gerald McRaney - Pete Murphy
Don Megowan - Mike
Jackie Russell - Bar Girl
Lloyd Nelson - Jury Foreman
Fred Lerner - Guard

Maniacal Judge Flood (John Colicos) illegally convicts Matt to life at hard labor, where he joins Elton and Latch (Kevin Coughlin and William Smith) digging for silver in the judge's mine.
Production #1615-0674

632. **I HAVE PROMISES TO KEEP**
Original air date: March 3, 1975
Directed by Vincent McEveety
Teleplay by William Putman and Earl W. Wallace
Story by William Putman
Starring:
Special Guests David Wayne - Reverend Byrne
Tom Lacy - Reverend Atkins
Ken Swofford - Dunbar
Fran Ryan - Hannah
Ted Jordan - Burke
Ken Renard - Tonkowa
Trini Telez - Meala
John Wheeler - Waiter
Ed McCready - Freight Agent

Prejudice reigns when ailing preacher Reverend Byrne (David Wayne) wants to open a house of God meant for both Indians and whites.
Production #1615-0671

633. THE BUSTERS

Original air date: March 10, 1975
Directed by Bernard McEveety
Written by Jim Byrnes
Starring:
Special Guests Gary Busey - Harve Daley
John Beck - Mitch Hansen
Lynn Benesch - Zoe
Gregg Palmer - Simeon Reed
Randy Boone - Hub Miller
Fran Ryan - Hannah

Harve and Mitch (Gary Busey and John Beck) are bronc busters who dream big trying to win enough money for a ranch in Montana. A woman (Lynn Benesch) and an injury to Harve, shatter those dreams.
Production #1615-0672

634. MANOLO

Original air date: March 17, 1975
Directed by Gunnar Hellstrom
Teleplay by Earl W. Wallace
Story by Harriet Charles and Earl W. Wallace
Starring:
Special Guests Nehemiah Persoff - Alejo Etchahoun
Robert Urich - Manolo Etchahoun
Mark Shera - Joachim Etchahoun
Alma Leonor Beltran - Engrace
Fran Ryan - Hannah
Jess Walton - Kattalin Larralde
Brion James - Joe Barnes
Michael Gregory - Sebation
Claudio Martinez - Vitorio
James Almanzar - Artola Larralde

BRIDES AND GROOMS February 10, 1975. Jim Backus.

I HAVE PROMISES TO KEEP March 3, 1975. David Wayne.

I HAVE PROMISES TO KEEP March 3, 1975. David Wayne, Ken Curtis and Ken Renard.

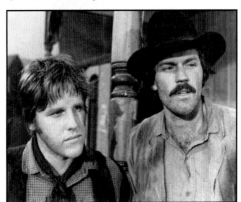

THE BUSTERS March 10, 1975. Gary Busey and John Beck.

THE SHARECROPPERS March 31, 1975. Terry Williams.

Ted Jordan - Burke
Mike Howden - Tom

Basque traditions are rocked by a son (Robert Urich) and his stubborn, hard-headed father Alejo Etchahoun (Nehemiah Persoff).
Production #1615-0670

635. THE SHARECROPPERS
Original air date: March 31, 1975
Directed by Leonard Katzman
Written by Earl W. Wallace
Starring:
Special Guests Susanne Benton - Av Marie
Victor French - Dibble Pugh
Terry Williams - Abel
Jacques Aubuchon - Linder Hogue
Bruce Boxleitner - Toby Hogue
Lisa Eilbacher - Lailee
Graham Jarvis - Rupert
Ted Jordan - Burke
Robert Brubaker - Floyd
Danil Torpe - Hargis
Chanin Hale - Woman

Av Marie (Susanne Benton) pushes her lazy family, including her father Dibble (Victor French) into planting crops before they lose their land.
Production #1615-0663

THE SHARECROPPERS March 31, 1975. Terry Williams and Graham Jarvis.

GUNSMOKE: RETURN TO DODGE The reunion of Matt Dillon and Kitty Russell, September 26, 1987.

THE MOVIES

For years following the 1975 cancellation, rumors abounded about a TV movie project for Matt and the gang, and for ten years, it remained just that, rumors. When asked in the early eighties if she would consider reviving her role as Miss Kitty, Amanda Blake quickly replied, "I'd bustle up in a heartbeat, Honey!"

The first reunion attempt did not involve producer John Mantley or CBS, it appears. Writer Paul Savage was hired by an independent producer to pen a *Gunsmoke* project. Savage recalled, "It evolves that Kitty has a niece, a beautiful girl, working in a hotel, and it turns out that it is hers and Matt's daughter. The daughter is kidnapped... typical *Gunsmoke* story."

The project did not reach fruition with the producer only securing the rights to the original theme song. Savage was paid handsomely for his script, which included a touching scene with Festus at Boot Hill where Doc is buried. James Arness liked the treatment so much he felt it should be filmed regardless, if even under different circumstances. According to Savage, "Jim Arness got into it to the extent of saying he liked the script enough; he said

TWO PROS Earl Holliman as Jake Flagg and James Arness in a scene from RETURN TO DODGE. Holliman practically stole the film.

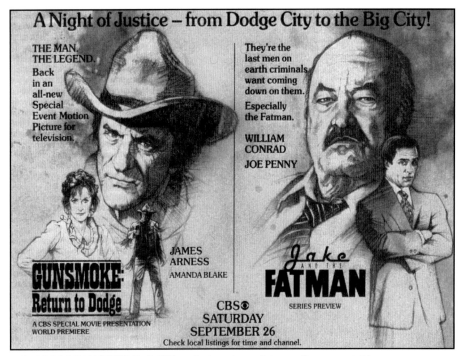

A Night of Justice – from Dodge City to the Big City!

**THE MAN.
THE LEGEND.**

Back in an all-new Special Event Motion Picture for television.

**GUNSMOKE:
Return to Dodge**

A CBS SPECIAL MOVIE PRESENTATION
WORLD PREMIERE

JAMES ARNESS
AMANDA BLAKE

They're the last men on earth criminals want coming down on them.
Especially the Fatman.

WILLIAM CONRAD
JOE PENNY

Jake AND THE **FATMAN**
SERIES PREVIEW

CBS⬤
SATURDAY
SEPTEMBER 26
Check local listings for time and channel.

IRONIC PROGRAMMING Both Dillons had projects airing on the same night.

'Hell, let's just change the name and change everything around and we'll make it.' Well, it never happened."

In 1986, CBS formally announced that the Long Branch Saloon would again open for business. With Mantley producing, former *Gunsmoke* alum from behind the camera included writer Jim Byrnes, casting director Pam Polifroni and director Vincent McEveety. "It was fun, I loved working with Jim again. I liked the show, very melodramatic," offered McEveety. *Gunsmoke:*

Return to Dodge would air on September 26, 1987.

As a producer, Mantley always had the reputation, as far as money was concerned, of being "tighter than the paper on the wall." This perception was substantiated further when two very unpopular decisions were made even before the cameras started to roll. First, it was announced that the entire film would be shot in Canada, which led to ugly letters and phone calls received by the network, and many fans and Western enthusiasts began to cry foul.

Second and much worse, was the news that Ken Curtis and Festus would not be back. Mantley insulted Curtis with an offensive and paltry salary offer, of which the actor resoundingly refused. When interviewed in 2001, Mantley was asked why Festus wasn't in *Return to Dodge,* and initially he would not discuss the decision or even Curtis, stating, "I will not talk about him." Later in the conversation, he offered what happened when he made the offer to Curtis and what his reaction was..."I received a cussing over the phone like I've never experienced before."

According to longtime Curtis family friend, artist/actor Jimmy Don Cox, Curtis read the first script and liked it. "He was looking forward to it. He was excited about it because he loved playing Festus," Cox recalled. Mantley then made drastic changes to the script regarding the Festus character and adding insult to injury, offered the actor next to nothing financially. Cox continued, "Ken told Mantley, 'I'm not taking that money and I'm not doing that script that you screwed up—don't you ever call me again.' He disliked Mantley ever since." Curtis vowed to never again speak to Mantley, and for that matter, CBS as well. This is a shame, for his presence in the film would have been welcome, and the final product would have been better overall. However, Curtis, along with Milburn Stone and Glenn Strange, were seen in flashback sequences culled from the episodes *Mannon* and *The Badge*, originally airing in 1969 and 1970, respectively.

With one professional relationship destroyed, another was revived temporarily. Amanda Blake and Mantley arrived at a truce, and Blake would again portray Kitty Russell. Joining Blake and Arness were series veterans Buck Taylor as Newly and Fran Ryan as Hannah.

Former and frequent guest-stars Earl Holliman and Steve Forrest were on hand also. Forrest reprised his role as the villainous shootist Will Mannon, one of the program's most memorable heavies. Holliman, as Jake Flagg, turns in a bravura scene-stealing performance, that combined the best of Jim Byrnes' writing, and the actors' ability to enhance and improve upon his characterization.

"I thought Earl Holliman was terrific in *Return to Dodge*," admitted McEveety. In a September 1987 *TV Guide* article, Mantley explained a feeling Arness had with the original script, "...one of the supporting roles, for a character Jake Flagg, was better than Dillon's. Jim called me and said, 'If you really want me to do this, all right, but I'll have to play Jake Flagg.' "Whatever script changes occurred, the role of Flagg was not seriously affected and Holliman would ultimately steal the show.

"I owe all of that to Vince McEveety and John Mantley," recalled Holliman. CBS originally wanted Victor French for Jake Flagg, but the actor was unavailable during the scheduled shoot. "They called me over and wanted to see how gruff I could look. I grew a full beard, which to my surprise was white. They had to brush dye through it to match my hair." Holliman improvised his voice to fit his perception of Flagg, with idea and character blending perfectly. "I was a little concerned, I have a youthful voice. I worked on that hoarse kind of whiskey voice I did. I remember I took a tape recorder with me and I'd practice at night with my lines," recalled Holliman. "CBS saw the first couple days of rushes, they called Vince and they complained. They said, 'What's Earl Holliman doing? It doesn't even sound like Earl Holliman.' I liked doing something strange, a little different. Vince liked it and John liked it, but the rest of the powers that be did not like it at the time."

Upon reflection, Holliman clearly enjoyed his time on the film. "It was fun for me, it was a fun part. And to work opposite Tantoo Cardinal, who was a marvelous, wonderful Canadian Indian actress...lovely, lovely lady." Cameraman Charles Correll paid the actor a nice compliment on his first day filming, as Holliman related, "The first scene I did, I was hiding behind something yelling back and forth, and he came up to me immediately and was very complimentary on how he thought I had the character...it was very nice." His final scene proved memorable also. "The death scene was fun, that whole sequence was fun to do. That shootout and dying in ol' Matt's arms," chuckled Holliman.

The veterans involved in the production, and to a lesser extent, the subsequent outings, found that many things had changed since the days of the original series. The network rarely involved themselves in the day to day production of *Gunsmoke*, trusting completely the production staff. By the seventies, the networks regarded the show so well-tuned that it could practically produce itself. Pam Polifroni recalled working on these films, "They were difficult...by this time the network had changed completely...the powers that be were much more involved with what went on in the shows. They wanted to be involved in everything. They would send their eleven-year-old executives to tell us how to do this and that, (she laughs), and it was very tough sometimes."

The shoot was an emotional one for Blake. Recalling her first scenes, the actress related in the same *TV Guide* article, "When I came in this morning, I went straight to the Long Branch, alone, and sat down. I didn't know what

MANNON RETURNED TO DODGE ALSO Steve Forrest reprises the role of Will Mannon, perhaps the most memorable villain in the long history of the series.

to expect. But it was so right, so perfect. And then I began to cry..." Always closest to co-star Milburn Stone, Blake continued, "Doc...Milburn would just be in his glory here. He was not only Doc, but our technical adviser. He would

544

STILL OWNS THE LONG BRANCH Fran Ryan reprised her role from season twenty as Miss Hannah in RETURN TO DODGE.

straighten us out, even if we didn't need straightening out. I miss him so much."

Aside from not including Curtis, the production had other obstacles to overcome. Long since retired, Dillon was now a mountain man. When we first see the character in full buckskin regalia, it is more of a shock than the

relief of seeing an old friend. His hair is illogically dyed darker than it was during the twentieth season of the series, and at times the actor looked more like a member of the rock group Herman's Hermits than he did as a man of the West. Blake, on the other hand, looked wonderful, especially considering her recent cancer battle. Unfortunately, her speech at times was hard to understand because of the speech impediment she had incurred from the dreaded disease.

On the plus side, the script was pure Jim Byrnes, now one of the best Western writers working on television. An example of his snappy dialogue appeared early in the film when Dillon has the drop on a gunfighter named Logan...

DILLON: Drop the gun...(Logan does so)...now that hideout gun that's holding up your backbone.
LOGAN: (takes out and drops pistol from back of belt) You don't leave a man a lot, do ya marshal?
DILLON: Mister, you didn't bring a whole lot with you.

Both Arness and the writing are right on the money. His first scene with Blake is wonderful, and the two pros reflect a line that Kitty has, "Old habits die hard." This poignant scene, although brief, takes the viewer immediately back to the best the series had to offer. The film also benefits greatly from the beautiful job done by director of photography Charles Correll and a wonderful score by Jerrold Immel.

GUNSMOKE II: THE LAST APACHE James Arness returns to familiar togs in the second GUNSMOKE TV movie, which originally aired on March 18, 1990.

The project was received well, however, praise was not unanimous. Susan Paynter of the *Seattle Post-*

Intelligencer said, in part, "*Gunsmoke: Return to Dodge* proves that the TV Western is not dead, it's comatose...the pace of the movie is slightly slower than wind erosion...there are more wrinkles here than at a Fresno Raisin Festival." That said, most of the reviews were split and the ratings were solid enough to label the project a hit. CBS ordered another installment almost immediately.

Gunsmoke: Return to Dodge, CBS TV, September 26, 1987 Two hours.

Matt Dillon turned in his badge years before and has retired to the mountains. A vengeful ex-con, Logan, tracks the former lawman and unsuccessfully tries to gun him down. On the way to Dodge City with his attempted killer, Matt is attacked by a motley group of mountain trash, leaving him seriously wounded. Dillon awakens in familiar surroundings with a familiar face greeting him. Kitty Russell, hearing of his ordeal, has travelled from New Orleans to tend to her favorite "cowboy." At the same time, one of the worst outlaws that ever entered Dodge is released from prison. Will Mannon wants to kill Matt and exact his revenge on Kitty. Knowing this, another prisoner, Jake Flagg, escapes to find and warn his good friend Dillon.

James Arness, Matt Dillon; Amanda Blake, Kitty; Buck Taylor, Newly; Fran Ryan, Hannah; Earl Holliman, Jake Flagg; Ken Olandt, Lt. Dexter; W. Morgan Sheppard, Digger; Patrice Martinez, Bright Water; Tantoo Cardinal, Little Doe; Steve Forrest, Mannon; Mickey Jones, Oakum; Frank M. Totino, Logan; Robert Koons, Warden Brown;

KIDNAPPED Joe Lara plays an Apache warrior who abducts Matt's daughter Beth, played by Amy Stock-Poynton.

KNIFE FIGHT Geoffrey Lewis as Bodine roughs it up with Matt Dillon in THE LAST APACHE.

REUNITED Michael Learned and James Arness, together again after MATT'S LOVE STORY from 1973.

Walter Kaasa, Judge Collins; Georgie Collins, Mrs. Collins; Tony Epper, Farnum; Louie Elias, Bubba; Ken Kirzinger, Potts; Denny Arnold, Clyman; Alex Green, The Flogger; Paul Daniel Wood, Harry; Larry Muser, Wilber; Robert Clinton, Guard; Frank Huish, Watt; Jacob Rupp, Hutter; Mary Jane Wildman, Indian Woman

Flashback sequences featured: Ken Curtis, Ted Jordan, Tom Brown.

This picture is affectionately dedicated to the memory of...Milburn Stone, Glenn Strange, James Nusser, Woodrow Chambliss, Charles Waggenheim, Charles Seel, Roy Barcroft

Casting by Pam Polifroni C.S.A.; Produced by John Mantley; Written by Jim Byrnes; Directed by Vincent McEveety

With development beginning in 1988, the second *Gunsmoke* television movie would not see completion and premiere until March of 1990, with several factors involved. Viewer reaction to *Return to Dodge* was, for the most part, positive, with only two concerns voiced loud and clear from the public; no Canadian locations or filming and more screen time for a favored actress and character, Amanda Blake and Miss Kitty. Initially, producer Mantley agreed, stating that filming would take place in Texas and that Kitty would have a more prominent part in the story. After rejecting a rough draft of the first script in 1988, Mantley did an about face and, surprisingly to all involved, eliminated any storyline involving Kitty. Sadly, all of this would prove to be a moot point because at the

GUNSMOKE III: TO THE LAST MAN James Arness and the always reliable Morgan Woodward team up one more time on January 10, 1992.

time, Blake's health was beginning to deteriorate. Other delays were also health based; both Mantley and Arness had their share of minor medical problems during this time.

Writer Earl W. Wallace turned in the final script, *Gunsmoke: The Last Apache*, having written a handful of *Gunsmoke* episodes just over a decade earlier. Wallace cleverly combined elements from the 1956 John Ford

FATHER AND DAUGHTER James Arness as Matt Dillon shares a moment with Amy Stock-Poynton in a scene from TO THE LAST MAN.

classic *The Searchers* with the storyline and characters from a popular 1973 episode of the series, *Matt's Love Story*. Actress Michael Learned reprised her role of Mike

Yardner and turned in another competent, professional performance.

With Arness the only *Gunsmoke* regular in this story, (and remainder of the movies), casting was very important, once again falling into the capable hands of Pam Polifroni. She cast Richard Kiley in the key role of Chalk Brighton. Kiley already had four appearances on *Gunsmoke* on his resume, as well as his work on *How the West Was Won*. Originally, Polifroni had a hard time casting the multi-talented Kiley on the series. "I had the darnedest time convincing Mantley that Kiley was a good actor," recalled Polifroni. "I must have spent two or three seasons saying Richard Kiley's name and getting nowhere." Mantley often dismissed Kiley as "that singer" or "that man from La Mancha." Kiley was finally hired and, "...then Mantley wanted him for everything," continued Polifroni. *Star Search* winner and former *Dallas* cast member, Amy Stock-Poynton, would become the last *Gunsmoke* regular, appearing as Beth in this and all remaining entries in the series.

Clint Eastwood stock company member Geoffrey Lewis handles the villain chores and television Western icon, Hugh O'Brian would appear as General Miles.

The Last Apache returned to the "dusty" look that defined the original series. Star Arness looks much better and healthier than he did three years earlier. He and Learned worked well together again, picking up where they left off seventeen years earlier. "There were some sparks between the two of them; a real good chemistry. They related to one another very nicely," opined Polifroni.

Gunsmoke: The Last Apache,
CBS TV, March 18, 1990 Two hours.

Matt Dillon is unexpectedly called to the ranch of former lover Mike Yardner, only to find her property burnt and in ruins. Apaches raided the ranch, kidnapping her daughter Beth, who is the product of Matt and Mike's brief affair many years ago. Matt had no prior knowledge that he was a father, but upon discovering his daughter's plight, he and ranch foreman Chalk Brighton set out to rescue her from her renegade captors.

James Arness, Matt Dillon; Richard Kiley, Chalk Brighton; Amy Stock-Poynton, Beth Yardner; Geoffrey Lewis, Bodine; Joe Lara, Wolf; Joaquin Martinez, Geronimo; Sam Vlahas, Tomas; Hugh O'Brian, General Miles; Michael Learned, Mike Yardner; Peter Murnik, Lt. Davis; Robert Covarrubias, Bartender; Ned Bellamy, Capt. Harris; Dave Florek, Smiley; Kevin Sifuentes, Nachite; Robert Brian Wilson, Corporal; Blake Boyd, Fraley; James Milanesa, Sentry soldier.

This film is dedicated to the memory of our beloved friends and artists: Miss Amanda Blake, Stan Hough and writer emeritus, Mr. Ron Bishop

Produced by Stan Hough; Written by Earl W. Wallace; Directed by Charles Correll; Executive Producer, John Mantley; Consultant, James Arness; Casting by Pam Polifroni C.S.A., Robert Lagersen, Associate

Actors Pat Hingle and Morgan Woodward, both

> "THERE WERE SOME SPARKS BETWEEN THE TWO OF THEM; A REAL GOOD CHEMISTRY. THEY RELATED TO ONE ANOTHER VERY NICELY."

familiar to *Gunsmoke* fans, signed on for the third television movie installment in 1991. Hingle aptly replaced Milburn Stone while he recuperated from heart surgery, and Woodward portrayed a panoply of vivid characters, good and bad, during the series years. Amy Stock-Poynton returned as Beth, becoming a welcome addition to the *Gunsmoke* family. *Gunsmoke: To the Last Man*, began filming in Arizona in 1991, getting off to a rocky start. Writer Jim Byrnes received a phone call from producer John Mantley, not to write the script as one would suspect, but rather to take over the producing duties. Mantley had fallen seriously ill just prior to the commencement of shooting and felt that Byrnes was the only person who could handle the job. Reluctantly, Byrnes accepted, and by the time the last frame was shot, did an excellent job.

Hingle uncharacteristically plays a heavy and in a testament to his talent, does a very convincing job. Woodward, for most of his career, played some of the baddest men on celluloid. "Have you seen Morgan's license plate?" asked Pam Polifroni. "On one car it says 'BAD GUY.' People always come up to him and say 'Aren't you a bad guy?'" On this project, Woodward was a good guy, and he found the experience a rewarding one. "I enjoyed it very much," the actor recalled.

"It's a violent movie; Jim and I kill just about everything in sight except the cows," laughed Woodward. The final shootout was especially violent but well executed, save for a few continuity lapses. "It was good wasn't it? It was shown at the Directors Guild and the writer came up to me and said, 'I just want to offer

GUNSMOKE: THE LONG RIDE Ali MacGraw (Uncle Jane), James Arness (Matt Dillon) and James Brolin (John Parsley). CBS TV, May 8, 1993.

552

ARMED AND READY Matt Dillon is ready for a fight in THE LONG RIDE.

my profound thanks for your changing the dialogue.' I've got into hot water with writers before, but I've studied hard, worked hard and some of the dialogue just didn't fit. I'd always take it to the director, always got permission," Woodward continued. "In the final shootout, I've been wounded, already shot three of them, and I stand up and

Matt says, 'Well, how do you feel?' The writer had written 'Like hell.' Arness says, 'Let's get out of here.' Now, here's this old run-down lawman chicken-shit drunk, and Arness says, 'How do you feel?' And I straighten up and said, 'Like a lawman.' He just thought that was perfect, God Almighty." The scene was reminiscent of the final gunfight in Sam Peckinpah's classic *Ride the High Country*, with Woodward and Arness standing in for Randolph Scott and Joel McCrea; the Tucker brothers replacing the Hammond brothers.

Many on the project were concerned about Arness' health and physical condition. Woodward elaborated, "When I first worked with Jim he was 6' 7", I was 6' 3"; now I'm not short, but I lost three inches because some discs in my back are gone, but Jim was really stooped."

Gunsmoke: To the Last Man kept the legend alive and offered another entertaining chapter in the life of Matt Dillon.

Gunsmoke: To the Last Man, CBS TV, January 10, 1992 Two hours.

When his cattle are stolen by a ruthless gang, former lawman Matt Dillon saddles up and hits the trail alone to recover his herd. His daughter Beth decides not to return to boarding school, and along with a green ranch hand, Will, find and ride with Dillon in his quest to restore peace and administer justice. Joined by lawman Abel Rose, they soon find themselves up against Colonel Tucker and his sons—right in the middle of a territorial blood feud.

James Arness, Matt Dillon; Pat Hingle, Colonel Tucker; Amy Stock-Poynton, Beth; Matt Mulhern, Will McCall; Jason Lively, Rusty Dover; Joseph Bottoms, Tommy Graham; Morgan Woodward, Abel Rose; Mills Watson, Horse Trader; James Booth, Preacher; Amanda Wyss, Lizzie Tewksbury; Jim Beaver, Deputy Rudd; Herman Poppe, John Tewksbury; Ken Swofford, Charlie

"HE HAD HIMSELF A GREAT TIME AND THAT HE WANTED TO "DO IT AGAIN, SOON."

Tewksbury; Don Collier, Sheriff; Ed Adams, Billy Wilson; Kathleen Todd Erickson, Mrs. Oliver; Loy W. Burns, Kirby Tewksbury; Andy Sherman, Virgil Tucker; Clark A. Ray, Rowe Blevin; Michael F. Woodson, Bartender; Erol Landis, Cole Tucker; William J. Fisher, Undertaker; Stephen C. Foster, Luther; Ric San Nicholas, Tink; Jimmy Don Cox, Onlooker; Richard Glover, David Henry

This film is dedicated to the memory of John Meston Supervising Producer, Jim Byrnes; Producer, Ken Swor; Written by Earl W. Wallace; Directed by Jerry Jameson; Casting by Pam Polifroni C.S.A., Jan Powell, Associate; Consultant, James Arness

On his last day of filming *To the Last Man* in early 1991, James Arness announced to a surprised cast and crew that he had himself a great time and that he wanted to "do it again, soon." Almost immediately, plans were set into motion for *Gunsmoke: The Long Ride*. Jim Byrnes and Jimmy Don Cox engaged in small talk when Arness left the set and began tossing story ideas back and forth. With John Mantley unlikely to return to producing because of health concerns, Cox told Byrnes, "Why don't you call Kenny and bring back Festus? With ol' John out, I know Kenny could be talked back." Byrnes agreed with Cox, and the thought of Curtis returning made sense to all involved and was long overdue. It was not to be. Curtis died shortly after this latest *Gunsmoke* offering was in the can.

Gunsmoke: The Long Ride would air on CBS May 8, 1993. Despite multiple concerns from everybody from the network on down, Arness happily reprised Matt Dillon and jumped right into this latest production. Much like the original series, these films did not center on or rely on "star" characters. Always the anthology, the reunion movies were no different.

Pam Polifroni cast two Hollywood heavyweights, James Brolin as a shady preacher and Ali MacGraw as a feisty ex-prostitute, with both performers turning in stellar performances. As the years went by, fewer and fewer *Gunsmoke* alumni were involved in these productions. This time out, only Arness and Polifroni remained. "We were the only two people left from the series," lamented Polifroni.

Again, against all odds, Arness and company turned out another movie and another entertaining Western, during a time when the genre, save for endless reruns, was virtually non-existent on the nation's television screens. Now more than ever, *Gunsmoke* truly was the granddaddy of them all.

GUNSMOKE: ONE MAN'S JUSTICE James Arness and Bruce Boxleitner as Healy, February 10, 1994.

Gunsmoke: The Long Ride,
CBS TV, May 8, 1993 Two hours.

Bounty hunters interrupt the wedding ceremony of Matt Dillon's daughter Beth to Will McCall. They are deputies from New Mexico and arrive with a warrant for the arrest of Matt on a trumped up charge of murder. The former lawman, sure of his innocence, gives up peacefully. Upon arrival in New Mexico, Dillon learns that he has a high price on his head, dead or alive, and faces mob mentality. He escapes a lynching and begins to track the real killers, with the help of a former lady of the night and a boozing, down on his luck preacher.

James Arness, Matt Dillon; James Brolin, John Parsley; Amy Stock-Poynton, Beth; Christopher Bradley, Josh; Patrick Dollaghan, Deputy Monaghan; Don McManus, Braxton Junior; Marco Sanchez, Collie Whitebird; Ali MacGraw, Uncle Jane; Tim Choate, Merriwether; Michael Greene, Ike Barry; Stewart Moss, Doctor; Jim Beaver, Traveling Blacksmith; Sharon Mahoney, Miss Southwick; Richard Dano, Padgett; Ed Adams, Tebbel; John David Garfield, Skinner; Victor Izay, Pastor Zach; Doug Katenay, Two Hawk; Fred Lopez, Spinoza

Produced by Norman S. Powell; Written by Bill Stratton; Directed by Jerry Jameson; Executive Producer, James Arness; Casting by Pam Polifroni C.S.A. and Jan Powell

February 10, 1994. James Arness and CBS premiere the final *Gunsmoke* television movie. This was a tough

TOGETHER FOR THE LAST TIME James Arness and Amy Stock-Poynton starred together in the last GUNSMOKE television movie in 1994.

project for all concerned and probably the weakest of the reunion projects. Arness, always a commanding screen presence and a voice of authority, appears frail at times, even gaunt. He still gave his all, stoically portraying America's favorite marshal. By now, with the drastic changes in the business, coupled with the fact that since the release of *Gunsmoke: Return to Dodge* in 1987, the movies had less and less in common with the original series with each new installment. Change a name or two, and you could have had a *High Chapparal* or *Cimarron Strip* reunion project.

No longer given carte blanche by the studio, the series veterans found that the network executives began exercising more control and input. "They started getting more and more involved," explained Polifroni, "telling us who to cast and who we couldn't cast." On this final chapter in the televised *Gunsmoke* saga, studio interference was at an all-time high. "On this last one, poor Jim was beside himself. He would call me and say, 'Listen, you've got to help me here. I mean, I can't have any of these New York cowboys come in here...'" Polifroni continued. Arness wanted his former *How the West Was Won* cast mate Bruce Boxleitner to co-star and the studio disagreed. Polifroni agreed with Arness, and after a tough battle, the network relented. Aside from Polifroni and Boxleitner, Arness felt alone during this shoot. "Jim felt he didn't have anybody he knew or trusted...he didn't have Mantley, he didn't have Philip Leacock, he didn't have Jim Byrnes," reflected Polifroni.

A final ironic note...one day after the premiere of the last *Gunsmoke* television movie, the first actor to give a voice to Marshal Matt Dillon, radio's William Conrad, died on February 11, 1994.

Gunsmoke: One Man's Justice
CBS TV February 10, 1994 Two Hours

Following the brutal murder of his mother while traveling by stagecoach, a young teenage boy sets out to avenge her death. Matt Dillon offers his help to track the ruthless outlaw killers and is joined by a fellow stagecoach passenger, Davis Healy. Healy is a man of great mystery, but Dillon must trust him enough to bring the gang of killers to justice.

James Arness, Matt Dillon; Bruce Boxleitner, Healy; Amy Stock-Poynton, Beth; Alan Scarfe, Sean Devlin; Christopher Bradley, Josh; Mikey Lebeau, Martin; Kelly Morgan, Lucas Miller; Apesanahkwat, Six Eyes; Hallie Foote, Anna Miller; Clark Brolly, Man; Don Collier, Sheriff; Ed Adams, Waco; Wayne Anthony, Hotel Clerk; Bing Blenman, Hardcase; Tom Brinson, Potter; Dave Adams, Sam the Cook; Sandy Gibbons, Sheriff Clamber; Mike Kevil, Bobby; Richard Lundin, Stage Driver; Kyle Marsh, Cathy; Jonathan Mincks, Fred; Billy Joe Patton, Grady; Ric San Nicholas, Al; Forrie J. Smith, Donny; Robin Wayne, Henry

Executive Producer, James Arness; Written by Harry and Renee Longstreet; Directed by Jerry Jameson; Produced by Norman S. Powell, Jerry Jameson; Casting by Pam Polifroni, C.S.A. and Jan Powell.

CLOSE GROUP *Stone, Curtis, Blake and Burt Reynolds, on the set in 1965, enjoyed the company of one another away from the studio, often at dinner parties.*

GUNSMOKE - RECIPES FOR SUCCESS

I n what could be called an homage to Dodge City's favorite restaurant, Delmonico's, here is a sampling of tried and true recipes culled from the kitchens of the stars of *Gunsmoke*. As Festus might have said, "Hey, ya ol' scutter, let's git over to Delmonico's—I'm so hungry my belly thinks my throats done been cut." Look the menu over, surely one of these dishes will satisfy your appetite...

Amanda Blake's Fresh Lime Pie

1	cup sugar
3	tablespoons flour
1/4	teaspoon salt
1	cup boiling water
2	egg yolks (save whites for meringue), beaten
1/4	cup fresh lime juice
	Grated rind of 2 limes
1	tablespoon butter
4	tablespoons sugar

Mix together sugar, flour and salt; add boiling water and stir constantly. Add beaten egg yolks and cook until it

AMANDA BLAKE *Her pies were a hit with fellow cast members.*

CAMPFIRE COOKING Arness' chili recipe is great for outdoor get togethers.

thickens (not too long); then add lime juice, rind and butter. Cool and fill pre-baked pie shell. Add four tablespoons sugar to beaten egg whites to make meringue and spread over filling. Bake at 375 degrees until golden brown.

James Arness' Chili

4 to 5	pounds ground beef or venison
4 to 5	onions, chopped
4 to 5	tablespoons chili powder
1	4-ounce can chopped green chili peppers
1	15-ounce can chopped tomatoes
1 to 2	tablespoons cumin
1 to 2	tablespoons ground coriander
1 to 2	tablespoons red pepper flakes
2	fresh jalapeno peppers, chopped (optional)
2	15-ounce cans chili beans
1/4	cup Pace picante sauce
3	cups water
2	tablespoons lime juice
1/2	can beer (optional)

Brown the meat in a large Dutch oven. Add remaining ingredients. Cook, covered, for 4 hours, adding more water if needed. Makes 8 servings.

Dennis Weaver's Cheese Nut Loaf

1	cup dry bread crumbs
2	cups finely chopped walnuts
6	tablespoons minced onions
4	stalks of celery, finely chopped
	chopped olives to taste
4	eggs
2	cups half and half
1/2	teaspoon salt

560

2 teaspoons dry mustard
1 teaspoon paprika
1/8 teaspoon pepper
1/2 teaspoon marjoram
1 pound grated cheddar cheese
5 cups fresh whole-wheat bread crumbs

Preheat the oven to 350 degrees. In a bowl, mix the dry bread crumbs, walnuts, onion, celery and olives together. Stir in eggs and half and half. Add salt and spices to mix. In a separate bowl, mix cheese and fresh whole-wheat bread crumbs. Combine this bowl with first bowl. Place in a greased shallow loaf pan and bake for about 40 minutes. Makes 1 loaf.

Milburn Stone's Bean Soup

1 pound navy beans, washed
1 large smoked ham hock
3 potatoes, boiled and mashed
2 large onions, chopped
1 cup diced celery
2 garlic cloves, minced
5 quarts water
Salt, pepper and Accent to taste

In a large pot, cover beans with water and let soak overnight. Next morning, drain water and recover with 5 quarts fresh water. Add ham hock. Bring to boil. Lower heat and simmer beans until done. Add the rest of the

TIME FOR SUPPER? Milburn Stone checks to see if it is time for his bean soup.

ingredients with the exception of the salt and pepper. Let beans simmer for another hour or two. Remove hock bone and skin; chop meat and return to soup. Season to taste; serve.

Ken Curtis' Cucumber Salad

 1 package lime Jello
 1 cup boiling water
 1 cup Miracle Whip
 1 cup cottage cheese
 1 medium cucumber, diced
 1 small onion, chopped
 1 small can crushed pineapple, drained
 1 tablespoon lemon juice
 1½ cups chopped walnuts (optional)

Dissolve 1 package of lime Jell-O into 1 cup boiling water. Add remaining ingredients in order. Mix well and pour into Jell-O mold and refrigerate to chill.

Burt Reynolds' Beef Stew

 3 slices bacon cut into small pieces
 2 pounds lean beef cut into one-inch cubes
   Flour (enough to cover meat)
   Salt and pepper to taste.
 1 teaspoon sugar
   A few dashes of MSG
 1 onion, chopped
 1 clove garlic, minced
 ½ can beef broth or water
 1 bay leaf
   Pinch of thyme
 1 6-ounce can tomato sauce
 1 cup dry burgundy wine
 2 carrots, coarsely cut
 2 stalks celery, coarsely cut
 2 large potatoes, cut into quarters
 ½ cup fresh mushrooms

Cook bacon in large heavy pot. Salt and pepper beef and dredge in flour. Brown beef in bacon fat, turning often. Add a little oil if necessary. Sprinkle lightly with sugar. Add onion and garlic and brown lightly. Add tomato sauce, broth or water, wine, bay leaf and thyme. Cover and cook slowly for about 90 minutes. Add carrots, celery, potatoes and mushrooms. Uncover and cook until meat and vegetables are tender.

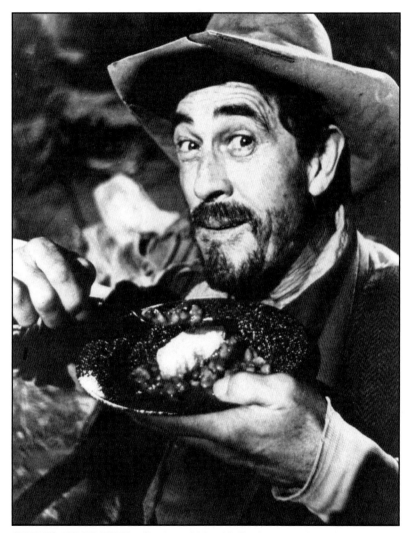

VITTLES ARE READY Ken Curtis and his wife Torrie were both good cooks and loved to entertain.

MATT AND KITTY THROUGH THE YEARS Circa 1955.

LEGACY

CIRCA 1961.

When *Gunsmoke* left the air on September 1, 1975, *The Washington Post* wrote a fitting epitaph for the granddaddy of all Westerns—"It went out the same way it came in—with high quality, honesty and uncommon honor." Field Historian at the University of Arizona, John D. Gilchriese, applauded the program's realism throughout the years, stating, "This program is so far ahead of its competition that there is no way to compare them. It has the subdued feeling of absolute, cold reality. Its pace, rhythm and devotion to the vernacular of those days stamp it as a classic in our times."

CBS had long ruled the airwaves, dominating the ratings for many years and earning the nickname the Tiffany Network. With shows such as *I Love Lucy, Perry Mason, The Jack Benny Show, The Ed Sullivan Show, Rawhide, The Beverly Hillbillies, The Twilight Zone, The Andy Griffith Show, Mannix* and *The Carol Burnett Show*, to name but a miniscule few, throw Walter Cronkite into the mix, and the network became the one that most American households turned to and tuned in. Many acknowledge that *Gunsmoke* was the centerpiece of the twenty-five year success story that was CBS—their reign of dominance

CIRCA 1973.

CIRCA 1987.

began to end once *Gunsmoke* was removed from their schedule. Certainly CBS would bounce back with programs such as *Magnum P.I.*, *Murder, She Wrote* , *Murphy Brown* and *Everybody Loves Raymond*, though never matching the monopolizing success it had once enjoyed.

The legend of *Gunsmoke* began, of course, with the radio version, and continues to grow today with countless television reruns daily worldwide. Comedian Tim Conway has provided voice-overs for TVLand for many years, including the following promo from 2001: "Second hand smoke is bad for you, but second hand *Gunsmoke* is good for you..." The show will flourish, certainly, for many years to come as the legacy of *Gunsmoke*, as well as its fan base, continues to expand. Here now, a few examples of the plaudits *Gunsmoke*, the best television Western series ever, has garnered throughout the years...

• Kansas Senator Frank Carlson, on the floor of the United States Senate once spoke of the legendary lawmen from Dodge City's historical past, including Wyatt Earp, Bat Masterson and Matt Dillon. Interrupting his speech, fellow Senators stated to Carlson that Earp and Masterson were indeed genuine legends from Dodge City's past but Dillon was nothing more than a fictional television character. Senator Carlson held his ground and shot back, "Does any man in this august body have the courage to state to his children and grandchildren that Matt Dillon never existed?"

• The Hollywood Walk of Fame was first envisioned in 1958 and was designated by the City of Los Angeles as a Cultural Landmark twenty years later. On both Hollywood Boulevard and Vine Street, celebrity names are centered in stars that feature a medallion representing their field (movies, television, music, etc.). Both James Arness and Dennis Weaver have stars for television. Burt Reynolds' star for film is located at 6838 Hollywood Boulevard and Milburn Stone has his star, also for television, at 6823 Hollywood Boulevard. There are no stars for Amanda Blake, Ken Curtis, Buck Taylor or Glenn Strange. Here's hoping that the Hollywood Chamber of Commerce will rectify these omissions one day.

• First published in 1985, the book *TV's Greatest Hits*, ranked the top 150 most popular TV shows of all-time using the following criteria: "The success, and rank,

MISS KITTY Amanda Blake proved popular with both male and female viewers—her character was far removed from most roles offered to women on television at the time.

of each show is based on its audience size and length of time on the air. The higher a program ranked during its run and the longer viewers kept it on, the higher it places

CONSISTENT DRAW James Arness and his portrayal of Marshal Matt Dillon is one of television's most enduring characters.

KICK IT UP Dennis Weaver's career flew into high gear during his time in Dodge City.

on the all-time list." With this in mind, authors Tim Brooks and Earle Marsh concluded, "The number-one program, interestingly, is first by a wide margin. The legendary Western *Gunsmoke* not only ran for twenty years—the longest run of any prime-time series with a continuing cast of characters—but also placed in the top ten for thirteen of those years!"

• In the early seventies, CBS was known as the "Country Broadcasting System." That image would soon change. "In 1971, CBS cancelled everything with a tree in it," remarked actor Ken Berry. Shows who got the axe that year included *Green Acres*, *The Beverly Hillbillies* and *Mayberry R.F.D. Gunsmoke* persevered.

• Many key ingredients blended together contributed to the success of *Gunsmoke. The New York Times* reported an important factor—decency—a factor significant more so today. "*Gunsmoke*—television's most ennobling and instructive weekly lesson," stated the *Times*. "Thanks to the influence of high-principled people who are never excitable, decency invariably prevails."

• The National Cowboy Hall of Fame and Western Heritage Center in Oklahoma City, Oklahoma, inducted *Gunsmoke* and stars James Arness, Ken Curtis, Milburn Stone and Dennis Weaver into their Hall of Great Western Performers. Stone was inducted posthumously, sadly passing away the previous year. Amanda Blake was inducted into the Hall previously in 1968, the first female performer so honored. Blake, Arness, Weaver, Curtis and Buck Taylor were present for the ceremony, along with

ETCHED IN STONE Milburn Stone brought realism to his role and the entire show as well. Whether performing before a camera or on a stage, he always gave one-hundred percent.

Stone's widow and family.

• In 1998, country music legends Johnny Cash and Willie Nelson appeared on *VH1 Storytellers* together. After singing *Don't Take Your Guns to Town*, they had this exchange between them:

CASH: You know the fast draw craze was going around

back in the late fifties, there was *Gunsmoke* and *Paladin*...

NELSON: I was selling encyclopedias in Fort Worth I think...

CASH: I used to stand in front of the TV and try to out-draw Jim Arness, (Nelson laughs), Grown man, yeah in my twenties...(he laughs).

NELSON: He's hard to beat.

CASH: He was hard to beat.

• In the April 2003 issue of *True West*, the magazine listed fifty moments that defined the West spanning the years 1804 to 1969. Leo Banks noted: "1955—*Gunsmoke* airs on CBS TV and becomes the most influential TV Western of all time, beating *The Life* and *Legend of Wyatt Earp*, *Bonanza*, *Lone Ranger*, *High Chaparral*, *Have Gun—Will Travel*, *The Virginian*, *Hopalong Cassidy* and many others. *Gunsmoke* made *True West's* top 50 list because of it's longevity, not its realism. The show ran 20 years and Matt and Kitty never...well, you know. Now that's myth-making."

• In 1998, *Entertainment Weekly* magazine ranked *Gunsmoke* number sixteen out of the 100 Greatest TV shows of all-time. In 1999, the magazine ranks the premiere of *Gunsmoke* number forty-seven of the 100 Greatest Moments in Television.

• *Law and Order* producer Dick Wolf, when asked how long his series would run, stated, "People can get tired of anything, but they didn't get tired of *Gunsmoke*

BADGES James Arness and Ken Curtis complemented each other perfectly.

570

HOLLYWOOD WALK OF FAME

for twenty years. I'm rather naked in my desire to get there." *Entertainment Weekly*, June 11, 2004.

• On October 6, 2004, Channel 4 NBC news from Los Angeles did a news story about computer voting. The spot featured background artwork showing a ballot—two prominent names on the ballot were Matt Dillon and Chester Goode.

• On the cover of the November 8, 2004 issue of the *National Examiner*, the masthead boasted, "The 50 Greatest TV Characters ever!" Inside, the magazine lists Marshal Matt Dillon as number thirty-one...no other Western character makes the list.

• During the 2004-2005 season, the BRAVO Channel hosted the marathon program *The 100 Greatest TV Characters*. Making the list were favorites ranging from Xena to Tony Soprano; Herman Munster to Mary Richards; and Archie Bunker, who ranked number one. Only two Western characters made the list, Bret Maverick at number thirty-three and Matt Dillon at forty-five. Forty-five, how apropos. The segment on Dillon went as follows:

HAL SPARKS, Actor/comedian: (deep voice) Matt Dillon—tall man, deep voice, big gun—any questions?
NARRATOR: *Gunsmoke* was TV's first adult Western. The story of the violence that moved West with young America and the story of a man who moved with it—Matt Dillon, the longest running character in prime-time dramatic history.
TOM SELLECK: I was a huge *Gunsmoke* fan.

TOM SHALES, *Washington Post* critic: How could you not like *Gunsmoke*—it's an American landmark.

JAMES GARNER: It was the model, you know, that everyone used. It had a little bit of humor, but mostly it was steely-eyed. And it was done well, Arness was really good and strong and big.

MELISSA GILBERT: He didn't stand up—he unfolded.

ED ASNER: He was massive, he was contained, he was wry—he was very wry.

TOM SELLECK: I think it's a classic because of the people. It is a character-driven show that takes place in a town, some people remember the name of the town, some don't. Some people remember a few of the plots, some don't. But what they do remember is Matt Dillon and Kitty and Chester.

TOM SHALES: James Arness was this towering figure at the center of the whole thing, and a real satisfactory representative of truth, justice and the American way.

• On the October 25, 2004 episode of the hit CBS comedy *Everybody Loves Raymond*, Robert (Brad Garrett) recalls a childhood quote from his father, Frank Barone (Peter Boyle) : "Stop brushing your teeth so loud, I'm trying to watch *Gunsmoke*!"

In honor of the fiftieth anniversary of the premiere episode, *Gunsmoke* celebrations were held all over the country. In Kanab, Utah, their annual *Legends of the West Roundup* was dedicated to the show. On September 10, 2005, Dodge City held a celebration honoring the fictional show set in their factual location. Fans the world over organized parties and tributes.

Television shows come and go. As tastes in entertainment change, *Gunsmoke* will stand as tall as its leading man and central character, regardless of the climate that surrounds a current viewing. Beyond CBS, TVLand and the channels Hallmark and Westerns, *Gunsmoke* will be enjoyed and continue to attract second, third and fourth generation fans. Thanks to Arness and Blake. Weaver, Stone, Taylor and Curtis. Thanks to Mantley, Byrnes, Savage, Harris, Warren, McLaglen and the brothers McEveety, etc. Paley and CBS. Thanks to the dedicated and professional crew members. And thanks most of all to Meston and Macdonnell for sharing their unique vision and gift of superb storytelling and characterizations.

NATIONAL COWBOY HALL OF FAME HONORS Ken Curtis, Amanda Blake, James Arness, Dennis Weaver and Buck Taylor join Milburn Stone's daughter Shirley Gleason, widow Jane Stone and his grandchildren in Oklahoma City, Oklahoma on April 25, 1981. (photo courtesy of Paul Savage)

THE END Title art used at the end of early episodes.

THE LAST WORD

At the end of most of the interviews, the subjects were asked to sum up the show *Gunsmoke* with one word. Some needed more than one word, but all gave their answers a lot of thought before responding.

Actor Morgan Woodward: **"Exceptional."**

Actor Anthony Caruso: **"Cowboy lore."**

Writer Jim Byrnes: **"Everlasting."**

Actor Paul Picerni: **"American classic."**

Actress Barbara Luna: **"Chemistry."**

Director Harry Harris, Jr.: **"Fulfilling creatively."**

Actress Katharine Ross: **"Moral."**

Casting director Pam Polifroni: **"Fantastic, wonderful, entertaining—how do you put that in one word?"** (long pause) **"Awesome."**

Actor Alex Cord: **"Classic."**

Actor William Smith: **"Fun."**

Fan Barbara D'Andrea: **"Lifesaving."**

Actor Paul Carr: **"Quality."**

Actress Beverly Garland: **"Professional."**

Actor Bob Donner: **"Classic."**

Actress Dawn Lyn: **"Integrity."**

Director Andrew V. McLaglen: **"Glorious Americana."**

Actor Robert Pine: **"Memorable."**

Actress Gwynne Gilford: **"History."**

Fan Laurie Savage: **"Institution."**

Actor Stuart Whitman: **"Wow."**

Actor Bo Hopkins: **"Classic."**

Actor Michael Forest: **"Integrity."**

Fan Eddie Costello: **"Cool."**

Actor Martin Kove: **"Americana."**

Director Bernard McEveety: **"Classic."**

Actor Lance Le Gault: **"Best Western ever made."**

Actor Jonathan Goldsmith Lippe: **"Wonderful."**

Actor Burt Reynolds: **"Class."**

INDEX

Aurness, Virginia. See Chapman, Virginia
Austin, Carmen, 441
Autry, Gene, 1, 68, 109, 225
Autry Museum of Western Heritage, *19*
The Avengers (Ep.391), 124, 406, 408
Avery, Val, 291, 397, 427, 461
Avonde, Richard, 281
Ayres, Lew, *205*, 431, *434*

B

Baccala, Donna, 440
Backes, Alice, 315, 410
Backus, Jim, 534, *537*
Bacon, Margaret, 445, 495
Bad Lady From Brookline (Ep.373), 398
The Bad One (Ep.287), 362
Bad Seed (Ep.216), 332-333
Bad Sheriff (Ep.212), 331
The Badge (Ep.204), 328
The Badge (Ep.508), *467*, 543, *Color 6*
Baer, Buddy, 288-*289*
Baer, John, 505, 519
Baer, Parley, 2, *xxviii*
Bagby, Leo, 415
Bagni, Gwen, 375
Bail, Chuck, 337
Bailey, Jack, 427, 462
Bailey, Raymond, 260, 298
Bakalyan, Richard, 424, 462
Baker, Joby, 353
Baker, Joe Don, 416, 455
Baker, Virginia, 299, 511
Baker, Wendell, 506
Baker's Dozen (Ep.453), 43, *81*, 83,

437-438, *440*
Bakey, Ed, 436, 456, 497
Bakke, Edla, 151
Baldwin, Janit, 520
Baldwin, Walter, 426
Balk, Martin, 300
Ballew, Robert, 411, 421
Bank Baby (Ep.367), 395-396
Banks, Leo, 570
Barbash, Robert, 458
Barcroft, Roy, 307, 327-328, 332, 362, 377, 388-389, 392, 395, 398-399, 407, 421, 426, 446, 453, 549
Bard, Katharine, 298
Bar-David, Shimon, 383
Bardette, Trevor, 314, 325, 431, 436, 477
Barnes, Rayford, 319, 332, 334, 350, 352, 373, 377, 386, 460, 496, 511
Barnes, Walter, 284, 299, 302
Barney Miller, 124
Barrey, Christopher, 380
Barrier, Michael, 352, 354
Barron, Baynes, 337, 351, 439
Barry, Donald, 361, 505
Barry, Gene, 72
Barry, Patricia, 295, 327, 467
Barrymore, John Drew, 161, 392, *394*, 400-401
Bartanides, Arthur, 386
Bartell, Harry, 266, 280, 324, 345, 365, 370, 383, 386, 399, 412
Bartell, Richard, 363
Bartlett, Bonnie, 519, 529
Bartlett, Jack, 407
Bartlett, Ronnie, 519
Bartold, Norman, 502, 506
Barton, Anne, *267*-268, 291, 305, 383,

387, 391
Barton, Larry, 395, 496
Basch, Harry, 427
Basehart, Richard, 478
Basic Instinct, 150
Bass, Todd, 501
Bassett, Joseph, 362
The Bassops (Ep.326), 377, 379
Batanides, Arthur, 386, 403
Bates, Ben, 527
Bates, Jeanne, 258
Batman, 125
Bat Masterson, 72
Batson, Susan, 465-466
Baucom, Billy, 361
Baxter, Alan, 340, 370
Baylor, Hal, *261*, 266, 283, 380, 436, 503, 509, 526
The Bear (Ep.142), 307
Beatty, Ned, 531, *535*
Beaver, Jim, 554, 556
Beck, Billy, 412
Beck, Jim, 308
Beck, John, 468, 481, 537-*538*
Beck, Vincent, 408
Becker, Ken, 293, 346
Becker, Terry, 265-266
Beckman, Henry, 354, 360, 522, 524
Beddoe, Don, 391
Beecher, Bonnie, 429
Beery, Jr., Noah, 376, 412
Beggs, Jim, 411
Begley, Ed, 403, 442
Bellamy, Ned, 551
Bellamy, Ralph, 166, 436-437, *439*
Belle's Back (Ep.191), 323
Bellflower, Nellie, 522

E

G

Gaines, Mel, 420
Galindo, Nacho, 445
Gallagher, Mel, 390
Gallo, Lew, 302, 316, 412, 427
The Gallows (Ep.255), 348
Galvin, Ray, 368
A Game of Death…an Act of Love…
Parts I and II (Ep.595 and Ep.596),
189, 512-513, *518*
Gammon, James, 415, 514
Ganzer, Alvin, 409, 441
Garas, Kaz, 457
Garcia, Stella, 493
Gardenia, Vincent, 427
Gardner, Alycia, 456
Gardner, Don, 261
Garfield, Allen, 174, 532, *536*
Garfield, John David, 556
Garland, Beverly, 76, 100, 203-204, *206*,
369, 438, 453, 467, 575
Garner, Jack, 469, 475, 515
Garner, James, 572
Garnett, Tay, 344, 347, 413
Garralaga, Martin, 441
Garrett, Brad, 572
Garrett, Leif, 193, 502
Garrison, Greg, 116
Garrison, Jane. See Stone, Jane
Garrison, Sean, 412
Garwood, John, 424
Garwood, Kelton, 337, 358, 415, 419, 426
Gates, Barbara. See Ford, Barbara
Gates, Curtis. See Curtis, Ken
Gates, Dan and Millie, 45

Gates, Nancy, 352
Gates, Rick, 490
Gatlin, Jerry, 497, 509, 519
Gator, 56
Gatteys, Bennye, 366
Gavin, James, 299
Gavin, John, 195
Gaynor, Steve, 380
Gebert, Gordon, 276
Greer, Will, 445-446
Gehring, Ted, 415, 421, 431, 436, 506
Gehrman, Paul, 527
General Parsley Smith (Ep.011), 260
Genest, Emile, 369, 383
Gentle Ben, 33, 159
The Gentleman (Ep.117), 299
Gentleman's Disagreement (Ep.189), 322
Gentry, Robert, 531
Gentry's Law (Ep.520), 128, 473, *476*
Gerard, Merwin, 365
Germaine, Elizabeth, 445
Geronimo Springs Museum, 214
Gerritsen, Lisa, 448, 452, 471, 478, *480*
Gessler, J. E., 511
The Getaway, 81
Gettysburg, 61
Ghostbusters, 151
The Giant Gila Monster, 47
The Giant Step, 158
Gibbons, Robert, 368
Gibbons, Sandy, 557
Gibson, Hoot, 64, 68, 185
Gibson, Mike, 308
Gielgud, Gwen Bagni, 362
Gierasch, Stefan, 420
Gifford, Alan, 299
Gilbert, Melissa, 498, 572

Gilchriese, John D., 565
Gilden, Richard, *2*, 258, 412
Gilford, Gwynne, 103, 193-195, 481, 575
Gilligan's Island, 152, 163, 165
Gilman, Sam, 416, 427, 436
Gilt Guilt (Ep.372), 398
Ging, Jack, 422
Girardin, Ray, 534
Gist, Robert, 258, 260, 295, 300
The Glass Menagerie, 29
Glass, Ned, 281, 284, 297, 321, 328, 376,
384-385, 456
Glass, Seamon, 506
Glaudi, Hap, 389
Gleason, Shirley, *573*
The Glory and the Mud (Ep.319), 375
Glover, Bruce, 458, 460, 498
Glover, Richard, 554
Gobel, George, 9
Goddard, Mark, 384
Gold Mine (Ep.392), *406*, 408-409
Gold Town (Ep.481), 136, 148, *450*, 454
Gold Train: The Bullet. See The Bullet
Golden, Bob, 482
Goldrup, Ray, 523
Goldsmith, Jerry, 150, 151
The Goldtakers (Ep.411), 416-418
Golm, Lisa, 265
Gomez, Thomas, 493
Gone Straight (Ep.059), 278
Gonzalez-Gonzalez, Pedro, 370
The Good People (Ep.414), 419
The Good Samaritans (Ep.487), *454*,
456-*457*
Goodwin, Harold, 317-318, 321
Goodwins, Bobby, 331
Gordon, Bruce, 293, 300, 328

K

P

S

Sanchez, Marco, 556
Sanctuary (Ep.400), 412
Sande, Walter, 337, 396, 458, 462, 491-492
Sanders, Hugh, 347
Sanders, Steve, 426
Sandor, Steve, 446
Sanford, Donald S., 471, 475, 483
San Nicholas, Ric, 554, 557
Santa Barbara, 153
Sarafian, Richard C., 395, 432, 442
Sarah (Ep.569), 124, 498, 500
Sargent, Dick, 347
Sargent, Joseph, 103, 278, 311, 352, 360, 367-368, 390, 400-401
Sarracino, Ernest, 477
Saturday Night (Ep.425), 424-425
Savage, Laurie, 43, 82, 85, 215, 217, 575
Savage, Paul, 4, 43, 49, 72, 74, 76, *80, 82*-85, 162-163, 165, 166, 169, 171-172, 187-188, 215, 369, 371, 374, 380, 401, 404, 412, 416, 423, 428-429, 442, 445, 452, 455-456, 500, 503, 511-512, 516, 523-524, 531, 541-542, 573
Saxon, Aaron, 298
Saxon, John, *140*, 166, 174, 396-397, *406*, 408, 421, 434, 530, 535
Say Uncle (Ep.199), 325, 327
Scarecrow and Mrs. King, 204
Scarfe, Alan, 557
The Scavengers (Ep.525), 476, *479*
Schallert, William, *125*-126, 213-214, *245, 291*, 293, 305, 309, 350, 368, 451, 467-468, 509
Scharf, Sabrina, 458
Schary, Dore, 12
Schiller, Norbert, 265

Schneider, Joseph, 434-435
Schoenbrun, Herman N., 151
The Schoolmarm (Ep.607), *519*-520
Schottelkotte, Al, 386
Schuck, John, 458, 469
Schultz, Keith, 438
Schuyler, Dorothy, 260, 265, 270, 281
Scollay, Fred J., 405, 427
Scot Free (Ep.337), 382-383
Scott, Brenda, 365
Scott, Evelyn, 265
Scott, Jacqueline, *49*, 123, 306, 354, *378*, 381, 421, 435-436, 447-449, 461, 463, 495
Scott, Ken, 392
Scott, Pippa, 341-*342*, 344, 490
Scott, Randolph, 553
Scott, Richard Davids, 483
Scott, Simon, 522
Scott, Walter, 514
Scotti, Vito, 407, 434, 460, 478
Scudero, Joe, 270
Seagram, Lisa, 373-374
The Search (Ep.268), 353, *355*
The Searchers, 47, *48*, 550
Seattle-Post Intelligencer, 546
Searl, Jack, 353, 454
Seay, James, 380
Seel, Charles, 335, 367, 373, 388, 401, 404, 407, 410, 431, 453, 468-469, 494, 508, 522, 549,Color 4
Selby, Sarah, 340, 346, 358, 362-363, 371, 377, 379, 425, 487, 490, 492, 494, Color 4
Seldes, Marian, 273
Seles, Scott, 508
Selfinger, Carol, 353

Selk, George, 258, 263, 267-268, 284-285, 287, 293, 295-296, 306, 309, 316, 319, 322, 325, 328-329, 331, 335-337, 339-340, 344, 349-350, 354, 358, 362-363, 365, 367, 369, 373
Selleck, Tom, 571-572
Selzer, Milton, 126, 318-319, 365, 374-375, 467-468
Selznick, David O., 12
Sentry, Frank, 336
Sergeant Holly (Ep.529), 478, *480*
Seven, Johnny, 344, 401
Seven Angry Men, 6, 8
Seven Hours to Dawn (Ep.378), 400-401
Seventh Heaven, 96
Seymour, Anne, 314, 329, 473-474
Sgt. Bilko, 251
Shadler (Ep.580), 504-505
Shahan, Rocky, 276, 388
Shales, Tom, 572
Shalet, Diane, 500, 532
Shane, 203
Shank, John, 433
Shannon, Harry, 332
Shannon, Richard, 348, 356-357
The Sharecroppers (Ep.635), *538*-539
Sharp, Alex, 284, 333, 335, 337, 365, 439, 505, 515, 527
Sharpe, Karen, 95-96, 190, *192*, 280, 375
Shatner, William, 100, 166, 422
Shaw, Elizabeth, 382
Shea, Eric, 435, *449*, 451-*453*, 456
Sheiner, David, 485, 487
Sheldon, James, 290, 403
Shelton, Al, 239
Shelton, Jacque, 373, 388-389
Shenandoah, 207

White, Jr., Bill, 267, 270
White, Lucas, 468
White, Robert S., 368
White, Will J., 256, 400
Whitehead, O. Z., 303
Whitfield, Anne, 327, 422
Whitman, Chris, 352
Whitman, Kip, 453, 462
Whitman, Stuart, 75, 195-197, 276, 575
Whitmore, James, 161, 396-397, 404-405, 508
Whitney, Cece, 351, 465
Whitney, Grace Lee, 348
Whitney, Michael, 407
Whitney, Peter, 198, 258, 277, 315, 339, 391, 405
Whittinghill, Dick, 361
Who Lives by the Sword (Ep.073), 283
Whorf, David, 295
Whorf, Richard B., 288, 290-291, 293, 295, 300, 302-305, 341
Wickwire, Nancy, 371, 373
The Widow and the Rogue (Ep.594), 512
The Widow (Ep.258), 343, 349
The Widow Maker (Ep.592), 204, 509, 511, 517
Widow's Mite (Ep.113), 298-299
Widrig, Clem R., 151
Wiensko, Bob, 321
Wiggins, Russell, 515, 523, 527
Wilcox, Claire, 413
Wilcox, Collin, 503
Wilcox, Joey, 405
Wilcoxon, Henry, 471
The Wild Bunch, 78, 81-82, 88, 191
Wilder, Billy, xxiii, 4
Wildman, Mary Jane, 549

Wild, Wild West, 66, 76
Wild Wild West (The Movie), 61
Wild West (Ep.101), 292, 295
Wilke, Robert, 300, 301, 315, 318, 322, 347, 379, 431
Wilkerson, Guy, 307, 353
Wilkin, Barbara, 416
Willard, Elen, 357-359
Williams, Adam, 345
Williams, Bill, 507
Williams, Grant, 307
Williams, Guinn, 185, 278
Williams, Guy, 107
Williams, Hal, 536
Williams, Robert B., 426-427, 463, 483
Williams, Rush, 447, 463
Williams, Terry, 538-539
Williams, Van, 194, 526, 528
Willingham, Noble, 506
Willock, Dave, 371, 388
Wills, Chill, 59, 253, 358, 359, 432-433, 435, 442
Wilson, Marie, 39
Wilson, Robert Brian, 551
Wilson, Shirley, 149, 427, 433
Wilson, Terry, 502
Wincelberg, Shimon, 476, 498, 522
Wind (Ep.145), 308, 310
Windish, Ilka, 397, 439
Windom, William, 125-126, 344, 360-361, 498
Windsor, Marie, 488
Wingreen, Jason, 496
Winner Take All (Ep.363), 394
Winslow, James, 294
Winters, Lee, 311
Winters, Shelley, 31, 116-117

Wintersole, William, 489
Wise, Hank, 431, 464
Wise, Henry, 475-476, 483, 489, 505, 507
Wise, Jr., James E., 17
Wishbone (Ep.399), 412
The Wistful Widow of Wagon Gap, 68
With a Smile (Ep.296), 366
Withers, Grant, 276-277
The Witness (Ep.526), 476-477, 479
The Wiving (Ep.617), 526, 528
Wixted, Michael-James, 461
Wolf, Dick, 570-571
Wolf, Venita, 428
Wolfe, Ian, 400
Wolfington, Iggie, 425
Women for Sale - Part I and Part II (Ep.588 and Ep.589), 192, 197, 508-511
Wonder (Ep.452), 437
Wood, Gary, 481
Wood, Paul Daniel, 549
Wood, Preston, 422, 427, 429, 447, 460, 473-474
Wood, Terry Lynn, 485
Wood, Ward, 278, 441
Woods, Harry, 283, 319
Woodson, Michael F., 554
Woodward, Morgan, 88, 122, 125, 147, 148, 162, 183, 187,198, 205, 287, 401, 403, 419, 421, 424, 432, 436, 443, 451, 458, 470, 474, 496, 502, 512-513, 523-524, 549, 551-554, 575
Woody, Sam, 330
Word of Honor (Ep.003), 256
Worden, Hank, 529
The Worm (Ep.203), 327-328
Worrell, Mary, 437

X

Y

Z

GOOD TIMES Were had by all as Amanda Blake, James Arness, Mariette Hartley and Dennis Weaver rehearse a scene from COTTER'S GIRL during season eight. (photo courtesy of Mariette Hartley)

ABOUT FIVE STAR PUBLICATIONS

Since 1985, Five Star Publications, Inc. has been setting the bar for publishing. An award-winning company, Five Star Publications is an industry leader in creativity, innovation, and customer service and is committed to helping authors reach new heights. Along with providing book production and marketing services in all genres, the Five Star Publications' team assist organizations with website redesign, logo design and corporate/product branding. Having received a multitude of prestigious awards for their books, Five Star authors shine brightly among their peers. Since 2005, more than 40 clients have received recognition for excellence. Five Star believes in contributing a portion of proceeds from book sales to various charitable organizations. It is a small way of making a difference, one book at a time.

At the helm is Linda F. Radke, President of Five Star Publications, Inc. Radke has 27 years of publishing experience and has earned countless international, national and state awards in publishing, marketing, and writing. Among her accolades, she authored *The Economical Guide to Self-Publishing* (2010 Paris Book Festival first-place winner and Writer's Digest Book Club selection) and *Promote Like a Pro: Small Budget, Big Show* (Doubleday Executive Program Book Club selection). She is also a founding member of the Arizona Book Publishing Association and was named "Book Marketer of the Year" by Book Publicists of Southern California. Radke resides in Chandler, Arizona. She can be reached at 480-940-8182, info@FiveStarPublications.com or www.FiveStarPublications.com.

ABOUT THE AUTHOR

Ben Costello is a self-confessed film and television buff. Starting at the age of five, he has appeared on stage in a variety of dramatic and comedic roles. He also enjoys writing and directing.

Along with fellow comedian John Babrowski, Costello has played in casinos and clubs from New York to Las Vegas, frequently portraying characters similar to Abbott and Costello (no, Ben and Lou Costello are not related). In fact, Costello and Babrowski performed the classic "Who's on First" routine at the Baseball Hall of Fame in Cooperstown, New York, to kick off the 2000 World Series. They were the first to do so since Abbott and Costello performed the skit there 44 years earlier.

Costello wrote, produced, and costarred in The Whitley & Costello Show in 1979. In 1987, he took the classic Laurel and Hardy movie Way Out West and adapted it for the stage, with the blessings of Lucille Hardy Price, widow of comedian Oliver Hardy.

In 1988, his play titled Company B debuted. The show, a slapstick musical tribute to World War II, was so popular that it spawned five stage sequels. For his work on this production, Costello won Best Actor, Writer, Director, and Production awards from various Southern California Theatre Leagues.

A divorced father of one, Costello makes his home in the desert community of Joshua Tree, California. He enjoys the company of family and friends, and when time permits, a good Maduro cigar.

RETURN TO DODGE...WITH YOUR FAVORITE GUNSMOKE CHARACTERS

GUNSMOKE
An American Institution

Celebrating 50 Years
of Television's Best Western

By Ben Costello

Foreword by Jim Byrnes • Preface by Jon Voight

Gunsmoke first aired on September 10, 1955, quickly becoming America's favorite television series. Author Ben Costello takes readers on a trip down memory lane in *GUNSMOKE: An American Institution – Celebrating 50 Years of Television's Best Western* - a remarkable testament to the on-screen characters and off-screen individuals who brought the show to life.

Author Beckey Burgoyne tells the story of one of those individuals. *Perfectly Amanda, Gunsmoke's Miss Kitty: To Dodge and Beyond* chronicles Amanda Blake's life and her tenacious journey to becoming the golden-hearted madam of the Long Branch Saloon - as well as her personal life beyond the soundstage.

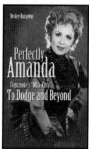

Item	Quantity	Unit price	Total Price
GUNSMOKE: An American Institution (Paperback) *ISBN: 978-1-58985-222-8*		$59.95 US / $61.95 CAN	
GUNSMOKE: An American Institution (Hardcover) – Limited supply available! *ISBN: 978-1-58985-014-9*		$75.00 US/ $77.00 CAN	
GUNSMOKE: An American Institution (eBook on CD-ROM) *ISBN: 978-1-58985-166-5*		$45.00 US / $46.00 CAN	
Perfectly Amanda, Gunsmoke's Miss Kitty *ISBN: 978-1-58985-163-4*		$29.95 US/ $31.95 CAN	
Add 8.8% sales tax on all orders originating in AZ			
Shipping–$10.00 for the first book and $2.50 for each additional book delivered to the same address. (US rates): Ground shipping only. Allow 1 to 2 weeks for delivery.			
		TOTAL	

Method of payment
❏ Visa ❏ MasterCard
❏ Discover Card ❏ American Express

Account Number: _____

Expiration Date: _____

Signature:_____

Note: credit cards will be charged only at time of shipment

Ship to:

Name: _____

Address: _____

City: _____

State: _____ Zip: _____

Daytime Phone: _____

E-Mail: _____

Send form to: Five Star Publications, Inc., P.O. Box 6698, Chandler, AZ 85246-6698 • **Fax orders:** 480-940-8787 • **Web orders:** www.fivestarpublications.com